Studies in the History of Medieval Religion

VOLUME XVIII

THE RELIGIOUS ORDERS IN
PRE-REFORMATION ENGLAND

Studies in the History of Medieval Religion

ISSN: 0955–2480

General Editor
Christopher Harper-Bill

Previously published volumes in the series
are listed at the back of this volume

THE RELIGIOUS ORDERS IN
PRE-REFORMATION ENGLAND

Edited by
JAMES G. CLARK

THE BOYDELL PRESS

First published 2002
The Boydell Press, Woodbridge

ISBN 0 85115 900 1

The Boydell Press is an imprint of Boydell & Brewer Ltd
PO Box 9, Woodbridge, Suffolk IP12 3DF, UK
and of Boydell & Brewer Inc.
PO Box 41026, Rochester, NY 14604–4126, USA
website: www.boydell.co.uk

A catalogue record of this publication is available
from the British Library

Library of Congress Cataloging-in-Publication data
The religious orders in pre-Reformation England/edited by James G. Clark
    p. cm. – (Studies in the history of medieval religion, ISSN
0955-2480; v. 18)
Includes bibliographical references and indexes.
    ISBN 0-85115-900-1 (alk. paper)
    1. Monasticism and religious orders – England – History – Middle Ages,
600–1500. I. Clark, James G. II. Series.
    BX2592.R45 2002
    271′.00942′09024–dc21   2002004411

This publication is printed on acid-free paper
Printed in Great Britain by
Antony Rowe Ltd, Chippenham, Wiltshire

Contents

Preface

The essays in this book originated as papers presented to a colloquium on the religious orders in later medieval and pre-Reformation England that was held at the University of York in September 1999. The colloquium drew together many of the established and younger scholars currently working in this field and presented an opportunity – perhaps for the first time – to reassess the character of monastic and mendicant life in England in the century before the Dissolution. Without exception the papers generated lively and wide-ranging discussion and it is hoped something of the flavour of these sessions, of new discoveries being aired and new interpretations being tested, is retained as they appear in print.

Both the colloquium and the book that follows it were made possible only through the assistance of many colleagues. Professor David Smith lent material and practical support in mounting the colloquium under the auspices of the Borthwick Institute of Historical Research and the *Monastic Research Bulletin*. Dr Phillipa Hoskin also gave up much of her time to the day-to-day management of the event through her office at the Borthwick. I am especially grateful to Dr Joan Greatrex who has proved a constant source of sound advice and unflagging encouragement from the earliest beginnings of the project. She assisted in planning the programme of speakers for the colloquium and has continued to offer her help in the preparation of this book. I would also like to thank Miss Barbara Harvey for her advice and encouragement (often over very congenial teas) during the later stages of the work. Finally, I am grateful to Caroline Palmer at Boydell & Brewer, for her interest in the book and for all her efforts in seeing it through to publication.

James G. Clark
King's Sutton
December 2001

Contributors

Jeremy Catto is Fellow, Tutor and University Lecturer in Medieval History at Oriel College, Oxford. He is the editor of the first two volumes in the *History of the University of Oxford*, published by Oxford University Press. His edition (with Linne Mooney) of the chronicle of the fourteenth-century Franciscan John Somner was published in *Chronology, Conquest and Conflict in Medieval England*, Camden Miscellany 34, Camden 5th Series 10 (1997). He is currently engaged in work on civil religion in the fifteenth century and on the historical aspects of late medieval language usage.

James G. Clark is a Lecturer in History at the University of Bristol. His research focuses on the English Benedictines, their life and learning in the later Middle Ages. He has published articles on monastic books, education, and chronicle writing, and on the process of the Dissolution itself. His book, *Monastic Learning in Late Medieval England*, is forthcoming with Oxford University Press.

Glyn Coppack is a senior Inspector of Ancient Monuments with English Heritage where he has been responsible for the research and conservation of some of the most important monastic sites in England. An archaeologist, he has directed major excavations at Thornholme Priory, Fountains Abbey, and Mount Grace Priory and has collaborated in a recent multi-disciplinary study of Rievaulx Abbey. His books include *The White Monks: The Cistercians in Britain, 1128–1540* (1998) and *Christ's Poor Men: The Carthusians in England* (2002).

Claire Cross is Emeritus Professor of History at the University of York, where she taught from 1965 to 2000, and is also a member of its Centre for Medieval Studies. Her recent publications include *The End of Medieval Monasticism in the East Riding of Yorkshire* (1993) and (with Noreen Vickers) *Monks, Nuns and Friars in Sixteenth-Century Yorkshire* (1995). She is currently working on the clergy of the diocese of York in the sixteenth century. She has published two volumes of ordination lists for the periods 1500–9 and 1561–1642 in the Borthwick List and Index series, and two further collections are forthcoming.

Peter Cunich is Lecturer in History at the University of Hong Kong. He has co-authored *A History of Magdalene College, Cambridge, 1428–1988* (1994) and is currently working on a financial history of the Court of Augmentations, 1536–1554.

Vincent Gillespie is Reader in English Language and Literature in the University of Oxford and a Fellow of St Anne's College. He has published on medieval devotional, mystical and para-mystical writing and on the history of the book in medieval England. He is co-editor of *The English Medieval Book* (2000), and his edition of the library *registrum* of Syon Abbey appeared as volume 9 of the Corpus of British Medieval Library Catalogues early in 2002.

Joan Greatrex was Associate Professor of History at Carleton University, Ottawa, until her retirement in 1984; she subsequently held the Bye Fellowship at Robinson College, Cambridge. Her publications include *A Biographical Register of the English Cathedral Priories* (1997). She is currently preparing a monograph on the English Cathedral priories in the later Middle Ages to be published by Oxford University Press.

Barbara Harvey was formerly Fellow and Tutor at Somerville College, Oxford where she taught medieval history, and is now an Emeritus Fellow of the college. Her publications include *Living and Dying in Medieval England: The Monastic Experience, 1100–1500* (1993) and, with Boydell & Brewer, *The Obedientiaries of Westminster Abbey and their Financial Records, c.1275 to 1540* (2002).

F. Donald Logan is Professor Emeritus of History at Emmanuel College, Boston. His field of research is late medieval ecclesiastical institutions. He is the author of *Runaway Religious in Medieval England, c.1240–1540* (1996) and *A History of the Church in the Middle Ages* (2002).

Marilyn Oliva is an Associate Professor of History at Fordham University, New York. Her interests are focused on medieval English religious women, and on aspects of prosopography. Her publications include *The Convent and the Community in Late Medieval England* (1998). She is currently editing a collection of the charters of East Anglian nunneries to be published in the Suffolk Charters series.

Michael Robson is Dean and Director of Studies in Theology and Religious Studies at St Edmund's College, Cambridge. His biography of Saint Francis of Assisi was published in 1997. His writings on the medieval Franciscans have appeared in a number of edited books and journals, and he is currently preparing a history of the order in the Middle Ages to be published by Boydell and Brewer.

Benjamin Thompson is Fellow, Tutor and University Lecturer in Medieval History at Somerville College, Oxford. His interests concern the church, its property and the aristocracy between the Conquest and the Reformation. He is the editor of *Monasteries and Society in Medieval Britain*, Harlaxton Medieval Studies 6 (1999).

R. N. *Swanson* is Professor of Medieval Ecclesiastical History at the University of Birmingham. His books include *Church and Society in Late Medieval England* (2nd edn., 1993), and *Religion and Devotion in Europe, c.1215–c.1515* (1995). His current work focuses on indulgences and confraternity in pre-Reformation England, the contribution to this volume being one of several articles around those general themes.

Abbreviations

BHL	*Bibliotheca Hagiographica Latina*, ed. A. Poncelet (6 vols., Brussels, 1898–1901)
BIHR	*Bulletin of the Institute of Historical Research*
BJRL	*Bulletin of the John Rylands Library*
BL	London, British Library
Borth. Inst.	Borthwick Institute of Historical Research, York
CCR	*Calendar of Close Rolls, AD 1227–1509*, ed. H. C. Maxwell Lyte *et al.* (61 vols., London, 1902–63)
CFR	*Calendar of Fine Rolls preserved in the Public Record Office*, ed. A. E. Bland, M. C. B. Dawes and H. C. Maxwell-Lyte (22 vols., London, 1911–62
Chapters, ed. Pantin	*Documents Illustrating the General and Provincial Chapters of the English Black Monks*, ed. W. A. Pantin, 3 vols., Camden Third Series, 45, 47, 54 (1931–7).
CIP	*Calendar of Inquisitions Post Mortem and other analogous documents preserved in the Public Record Office*, ed. J. E. G. Sharp, E. G. Atkinson, H. C. Maxwell-Lyte *et al.* (20 vols., London, 1904–)
Concilia, ed. Wilkins	*Concilia magnae Britanniae et Hiberniae*, ed. D. Wilkins (4 vols., London, 1731–7)
CPL	*Calendar of Entries in the Papal Registers relating to Great Britain and Ireland: Papal Letters, 1198–1513*, ed. W. H. Bliss, C. Johnston, J. A. Twemlow *et al.* (19 vols., London, 1893–1989)
CPR	*Calendar of Patent Rolls, AD 1216–1582*, ed. H. C. Maxwell Lyte *et al.* (74 vols., London 1901–)
CUL	Cambridge, University Library
Emden, *BRUC*	A. B. Emden, *A Biographical Register of the University of Cambridge* (Cambridge, 1963)
Emden, *BRUO*	*A Biographical Register of the University of Oxford to AD 1500*, ed. A. B. Emden (3 vols., Oxford, 1957–9).
Emden, *BRUO, 1501–40*	*A Biographical Register of the University of Oxford, 1501–40*, ed. A. B. Emden (Oxford, 1974)

EETS	Early English Text Society
EcHR	*Economic History Review*
EHR	*English Historical Review*
GL	London, Guildhall Library
Greatrex, BRECP	*A Biographical Register of the English Cathedral Priories*, ed. J. Greatrex (Oxford, 1997)
HJ	*Historical Journal*
ISTC	The Incunabula Short Title Catalogue, database compiled at the British Library (in progress)
JEH	*Journal of Ecclesiastical History*
Knowles, *Religious Orders*	D. Knowles, *The Religious Orders in England* (3 vols., Cambridge, 1948–59)
LP	*Letters and Papers Foreign and Domestic of the Reign of Henry VIII*, ed. J. S. Brewer *et al.* (22 vols. in 35, London, 1862–1932)
MRH	D. Knowles and R. N. Hadcock, *Medieval Religious Houses: England and Wales* (2nd edn., London, 1971)
NRO	Norwich, Norfolk Record Office
Oxford, Bodl.	Oxford, Bodleian Library
PBA	*Proceedings of the British Academy*
PL	*Patrologia Latina*, ed. J-P. Migne (217 vols., Paris, 1844–53)
PRO	London, Public Record Office
RCHME	Royal Commission on Historical Monuments: England
STC	*A Short-Title Catalogue of Books Printed in England, Scotland and Ireland, 1475–1640*, ed. A. W. Pollard and G. R. Redgrave, revs K. F. Pantzer and P. R. Rider (3 vols., London, 1991)
TCBS	*Transactions of the Cambridge Bibliographical Society*
TRHS	*Transactions of the Royal Historical Society*
VCH	*Victoria County History*
WAM	Westminster Abbey Muniments

INTRODUCTION

The Religious Orders in Pre-Reformation England

JAMES G. CLARK

> Ac now is religion a rydere, a rennere by stretes,
> a ledere of lovedays and a lond buggere,
> A prikere on a palfrey fro place to Manere,
> An heep of houndes at his ers as he a lord were.[1]

The religious orders at the end of the Middle Ages have always been disparaged. In the age of Langland himself, the decadence and deviance of monks, friars and nuns was already proverbial.[2] By the beginning of the sixteenth century the clamour of rumour and suspicion had intensified, fuelling a fundamental debate about their place in the church. There is no doubt that it was the conviction that monastic life had become corrupt and self-serving that drove those who brought about the Dissolution. From the reformers of the 1530s this passed directly into popular consciousness. For years after the Reformation, those who had no direct experience of the regular religious would recall how they had 'turned lazie, then, getting wealth, waxed wanton, and at last endowed with superfluity, became notoriously wicked'.[3] In many ways, these same assumptions continue to affect accounts of the period even today. It is still widely understood that England's monasteries and mendicant convents descended into a headlong decline more than a century before Henry VIII set about to destroy them. In their last years the lives of the religious were little more than a travesty of their early ideals and they drifted towards their end 'not in an heroic struggle . . . but with a foxhunt and a jolly dinner party under the greenwood tree'.[4]

In recent years many of the old assumptions about religious life in pre-Reformation England have been overturned. New research, much of it drawn from neglected sources in regional archives, has done much to

---

[1] *Piers Plowman*, Passus X, lines 311–14, quoted from *Piers Plowman: The B Version*, ed. G. Kane and E. T. Donaldson (London, 1975), p. 425.

[2] For the treatment of the religious orders in fourteenth-century literature see J. Mann, *Chaucer and Medieval Estates Satire: The Literature of the Social Classes and the General Prologue to the Canterbury Tales* (Cambridge, 1973), pp. 189–201; P. R. Szittya, *The Anti-Fraternal Tradition in Medieval Literature* (Princeton, 1986).

[3] Thomas Fuller, *The Church-History of Britaine: From the Birth of Jesus Christ until the Year MDCXLVIII* (London, 1655), p. 265.

[4] A. G. Dickens, *Late Monasticism and the Reformation* (London, 1992), p. 20.

challenge the traditional picture of a church on the brink of collapse. In fact it is now common to see pre-Reformation religion as far more adaptable, vigorous and popular at grass-roots level than either the politicians or the reformers of the 1530s had been prepared to accept.[5] But it seems there is no place in this revised picture for the older religious orders themselves. The vitality of pre-Reformation religion appears to have been founded almost exclusively on the parish and the public and private expressions of piety made by the laity. Apparently, the communities of monks, friars and nuns had long since been edged into the margins and their active contribution to social and spiritual life was minimal.[6] The only exception made is usually for the newer orders, notably the Carthusians and Brigittines, whose handful of houses appear to have been latterly fashionable amongst a spiritually self-conscious urban elite.[7] It is true that few historians today would accept the more extreme contemporary allegations; there were only 'a handful of individual failings',[8] and many were 'innocent (or not very guilty) victims'.[9] But most would nonetheless agree with the substance – if not the tone – of the reformers' message; monastic life was failing in fifteenth- and early sixteenth-century England, and the traditional image of a community of men and women serving God and the wider Christian community was, to a very great extent, a thing of the past.

The chapters in this book are intended to counter the recent neglect of the religious orders, to re-examine their place and performance in pre-Reformation society, and in doing so perhaps to challenge some of the assumptions that still prevail about them. They draw on the rich seam of research that has emerged in recent years both in Britain and America. There is no doubt that it is now possible to know far more about the monasteries and mendicant convents of fifteenth- and sixteenth-century England than it was when Dom David Knowles published his monumental study almost fifty years ago. The internal life and domestic economy of some of the most important and influential houses has been the subject of several

---

[5] For the most authoritative work see E. Duffy, *The Stripping of the Altars: Traditional Religion in England, 1400–1570* (New Haven and London, 1992) and C. Haigh, *English Reformations* (Oxford, 1993). In the same vein see also J. J. Scarisbrick, *The Reformation and the English People* (Oxford, 1984); C. Harper-Bill, *The Pre-Reformation Church in England* (London, 1989); R. N. Swanson, *Church and Society in Late Medieval England* (Oxford, 1989); R. Whiting, *The Blind Devotion of the People: Popular Religion and the English Reformation* (Cambridge, 1989); A. Brown, *Popular Piety in Late Medieval England: The Diocese of Salisbury, 1250–1550* (Oxford, 1995); B. Kümin, *The Shaping of a Community: The Rise and Reformation of the English Parish, c. 1400–1560* (Aldershot, 1996).

[6] See especially Whiting, *Blind Devotion of the People*, p. 113; Duffy, *Stripping of the Altars*, p. 5; Haigh, *English Reformations*, pp. 28–9.

[7] For the popularity of these orders see Knowles, *Religious Orders*, ii. 175–81; Swanson, *Church and Society*, pp. 269–70; Haigh, *English Reformations*, pp. 25–8.

[8] Whiting, *Blind Devotion of the People*, p. 119.

[9] Haigh, *English Reformations*, p. 337.

detailed studies.[10] The communities of women, given only cursory treatment by Knowles, have also found their own historians.[11] Through the work of Barbara Harvey on Westminster, we also know a great deal more about how the monks there (and elsewhere) fed, clothed and conducted themselves and cared for their dependents.[12] Even the process of dissolution itself has at last begun to attract some of the attention it deserves.[13]

One of the most significant developments in recent decades has been the variety of new, or newly discovered source materials to be made available to the historian. The century or so before 1540 has always been regarded as one of the least well documented in all monastic history. There are few of the chronicles, registers and other domestic papers that reveal so much about earlier medieval communities. The records of episcopal visitations, of course, are well preserved, but in general they offer only a selective and very stilted impression of internal life. Even for the Dissolution itself the evidence is patchy. In spite of its formidable reputation, the Court of Augmentations failed to leave the sort of paper trail that might have been expected. It has been the achievement of recent prosopographical studies to reveal how much about the lives of monks, friars and nuns can still be recovered from mundane compotus rolls, episcopal registers and even from the testamentary records of the laity.[14] Local archives have also been found to offer new

---

[10] B. F. Harvey, *Westminster Abbey and its Estates in the Later Middle Ages* (Oxford, 1977); J. H. Tillotson, *Monastery and Society in Late Medieval England: Selected Account Rolls from Selby Abbey, 1398–1537* (Woodbridge, 1988); *The Cartulary of the Augustinian Friars of Clare*, ed. C. Harper-Bill, Suffolk Charters 11 (Woodbridge, 1991); *The Bolton Priory Compotus, 1286–1325, together with an Account Roll for 1377–78*, ed. I. Kershaw and D. M. Smith, Yorkshire Archaeological Society, Record Series 154 (2000).

[11] J. H. Tillotson, *Marrick Priory: A Nunnery in Late Medieval Yorkshire*, Borthwick Papers 75 (York, 1989); R. Gilchrist, *Contemplation and Action: The Other Monasticism* (Leicester, 1995); M. Oliva, *The Convent and the Community in Late Medieval England: Female Monasteries in the Diocese of Norwich, 1350–1540* (Woodbridge, 1998); P. Lee, *Nunneries, Learning and Spirituality in Late Medieval English Society. The Dominican Priory of Dartford* (Woodbridge, 2001).

[12] B. F. Harvey, *Living and Dying in England, 1100–1500: The Monastic Experience* (Oxford, 1993).

[13] F. D. Logan, 'Thomas Cromwell and the Vicegerency in Spirituals: A Revisitation', *EHR* 103 (1988), pp. 658–67; R. W. Hoyle, 'The Origin of the Dissolution of the Monasteries', *HJ* 38/2 (1995), pp. 275–305; G. W. Bernard, 'The Making of Religious Policy, 1533–46: Henry VIII and the Search for the Middle Way', *HJ* 41/2 (1998), pp. 321–49; P. Cunich, 'The Dissolution of the Chantries', in *The Reformation and English Towns*, ed. P. Collinson and J. Craig (Basingstoke, 1995), pp. 159–74. See also the recent work of A. N. Shaw, 'The Northern Visitation of 1535–6: Some New Observations', *Downside Review* 116 (1998), p. 279; 'The Involvement of the Religious Orders in the Northern Risings of 1536/7: Compulsion Or Desire?', *Downside Review* 117 (1999), p. 89.

[14] J. Greatrex, 'Some Statistics of Religious Motivation', in *Religious Motivation: Biographical and Sociological Problems for the Church Historian*, ed. D. Baker, Studies in Church History 15 (1978), pp. 179–86; R. B. Dobson, 'The Prosopography of Late Medieval Cathedral Canons', *Medieval Prosopography* 15 (1995), pp. 67–92; M. Oliva,

insights into the suppressions.[15] At the same time, bibliographers have brought to light a large body of literary sources, many of them hitherto unstudied, which can be connected with the religious houses of the fifteenth and early sixteenth centuries.[16]

The chapters that follow build on this expanding body of evidence to make a wide-ranging reassessment of the regular religious before the Reformation. They consider not only their condition on the eve of the Dissolution but also the character of their lives across the later Middle Ages as a whole. It should be emphasized that the intention here is not to offer an *apologia* for pre-Reformation English monasticism. Certainly a number of the contributions do highlight some of the strengths of monastic and mendicant life in this period – most notably perhaps their intellectual activities and their continuing involvement in cultural and social life – that have not attracted due attention before. But they do also expose those points on which they were increasingly vulnerable. Indeed one contributor argues that to re-examine the monasteries in the light of recent revisionism is only to confirm the suspicions of contemporaries that they had served their purpose.[17] Whether or not the Dissolution was inevitable, however, is not the central issue here. Rather it is to suggest that only when we have restored the religious orders to their place in the social, cultural and confessional landscape of fifteenth- and sixteenth-century England can we come to a deeper understanding of the transformations of these turbulent years.

In spite of the tendency to place them at the margins, there is no doubt that the regular religious orders did remain a conspicuous presence in English society throughout the fifteenth and early sixteenth centuries. Few of those living in the north of the country, as well as in many central and southern parts, could have failed to notice the communities of religious men and women who lived alongside them. The great age of foundations had passed,

'Counting Nuns: A Prosopography of Late Medieval English Nuns in the Diocese of Norwich', *Medieval Prosopography* 16 (1995), pp. 66–7; Greatrex, *BRECP*.

[15] R. W. Dunning, 'Revival at Glastonbury, 1530–59', in *Renaissance and Renewal in Christian History*, ed. D. Baker, Studies in Church History 14 (1977), pp. 213–22; C. Cross, *The End of Medieval Monasticism in the East Riding of Yorkshire*, East Yorkshire Local History Series 47 (1993); J. G. Clark, 'Reformation and Reaction at St Albans Abbey, 1530–58', *EHR* 115 (2000), pp. 297–328.

[16] D. N. Bell, *What Nuns Read: Books and Libraries in Medieval English Nunneries*, Cistercian Studies Series 158 (Michigan, 1995); *The Libraries of the Cistercians, Gilbertines and Premonstratensians*, ed. D. N. Bell, Corpus of British Medieval Library Catalogues 3 (1992); *English Benedictine Libraries: The Shorter Catalogues*, ed. R. Sharpe, J. P. Carley, K. Friis-Jensen and R. M. Thomson, Corpus of British Medieval Library Catalogues 4 (1996); *The Libraries of the Augustinian Canons*, ed. T. Webber and A. G. Watson, Corpus of British Medieval Library Catalogues 6 (1998); A. Coates, *Medieval English Books: The Reading Abbey Collection from Foundation to Dispersal* (Oxford, 1999).

[17] See Benjamin Thompson's chapter below esp. pp. 199–5.

and with the Hundred Years War there had come a wave of suppressions not only of alien priories but also native foundations under royal jurisdiction.[18] But even so in 1500 there were still no fewer than 900 religious communities in England and Wales including 28 that had been established since 1350.[19] In purely numerical terms in fact, the regular religious were a more significant force in the reign of Henry VII than they had been ever before. By most estimates, there were probably about 6500 monks, friars and nuns living in England and Wales in 1400. By 1500 this number had swelled to more than 9000; an especially significant increase since the overall population level remained stagnant.[20]

Not only were they numerous, but even in their last years the regulars also retained a very public profile. From the second half of the fourteenth century they recovered something of their former prominence in the hierarchy of the church. Between 1340 and 1538 as many as sixty monastic and mendicant prelates were presented to sees in England, Ireland and Wales, including two who were elevated to the primacy of Canterbury. More than two thirds of these were friars and of their four main orders, the Dominicans were dominant.[21] As late as 1495 there were six regulars in the ranks of episcopacy and even during the 1530s there was still a handful of high profile monastic bishops. It was John Clerk, bishop of Bath and Wells and former monk of Bury St Edmunds, who extricated Henry VIII from the Cleves marriage in 1541.[22] For much of this period, it was also the older monastic orders that were the most active of all English clergy on an international stage. Two of the five Englishmen to receive the cardinal's hat in the two centuries before the Reformation were Benedictines: Adam Easton of Norwich and Simon Langham of Westminster.[23] Of the few sermons of English origin to circulate with the *acta* of Constance and Basle some of the best known were the work of monastic delegates, men such as Thomas Spofford, abbot of St Mary's York, and William Curteys, abbot of Bury St Edmunds.[24]

Nor was their role restricted to ecclesiastical affairs. The older monastic order in particular still proved to be a powerful and vocal presence within

---

[18] Knowles, *Religious Orders*, ii. 159–65. See also B. J. Thompson, 'Monasteries and their Patrons at Foundation and Dissolution', *TRHS*, 6th Series 4 (1994), pp. 103–23 at 112–15.

[19] For a comprehensive list of monastic and mendicant communities see *MRH*.

[20] The figures usually cited are from J. C. Russell, 'The Clerical Population of Medieval England', *Traditio* 2 (1944), pp. 177–212 at 184–212, and *MRH*, pp. 488–94. See also J. H. Tillotson, *Marrick Priory: A Nunnery in Late Medieval Yorkshire*, Borthwick Papers 75 (York, 1989), p. 1.

[21] Knowles, *Religious Orders*, ii. 154, 370–71; iii. 492–3.

[22] For Clerk's career see Emden, *BRUC*, p. 139.

[23] Knowles, *Religious Orders*, ii. 54–8. See also M. Harvey, *The English in Rome: Portrait of an Expatriate Community* (Cambridge, 1999), pp. 188–212.

[24] For the Benedictines' involvement in the councils see M. Harvey, *Solutions to the Schism: A Study of Some English Attitudes, 1378–1409* (St Ottilien, 1983). For a summary of Spofford's career see Emden, *BRUO*, iii. 1744.

the political establishment. No fewer than twenty-seven heads of religious houses were summoned to parliament regularly in the fifteenth century, a representation actually increased (by three) under Henry VIII.[25] Regulars can still be found as councillors or trusted courtiers for much of the period. The Lancastrians welcomed Carmelite friars into their court circle: Stephen Patrington was confessor to both Henry IV and his son before becoming bishop of Chichester, and Thomas Netter attended Henry V at his death in the Bois-de-Boulogne.[26] Even the early Tudors sought the society of leading Benedictines: Thomas Ramridge, the venerable abbot of St Albans, celebrated Christmas in the company of Henry VII, baptized his children and, eventually, conducted the King's own obsequies.[27]

It is important to recognize, of course, that as a constituency of the clergy the regular religious were never a homogeneous group. Certainly it was only ever a small number who enjoyed a prominence in public affairs, and there were many who lived out their lives in houses that were, as they always had been, far from the focus of events. There were also more fundamental differences in the experience of individual houses. Quite apart from the fact that each order followed its own rules and was dedicated to the pursuit of its own particular mission, there were also significant contextual and constitutional differences that could set houses – even those of the same order – on a different course. One fundamental distinction to be made is between the orders of the friars that operated in an urban context closely intertwined with secular society and the older monastic order that (generally speaking) did not. The friars' convents can also be distinguished by their cosmopolitan character: throughout the later Middle Ages the English congregations maintained close links with the continent and French, German, Italian and Spanish friars passed through their houses.[28]

Of all the regulars, it was amongst the Benedictines, the largest of the orders, that there was the greatest degree of stratification. Exceptionally, there were four abbeys (Bury St Edmunds, Evesham, St Albans) that enjoyed the status of an *exempt* house, which placed them beyond the reach of episcopal, seignorial and (usually) royal authority.[29] In practice these communities were entirely self-contained, conducting their own ordinations and elections without interference whilst remaining free from any episcopal visitation. Their independence also gave them greater self-confidence in their dealings with their patrons and it was often these houses that were most

---

[25] Knowles, *Religious Orders*, ii. 304.

[26] Knowles, *Religious Orders*, ii. 145–6. For full details of their careers see Emden, BRUO, ii. 1343–4; iii. 1435–6.

[27] LP, i/1. 20, 308.

[28] See R. B. Dobson, 'The Religious Orders, 1277–1540', in *The History of the University of Oxford II. Late Medieval Oxford*, ed. J. I. Catto and T. A. R. Evans (Oxford, 1992), p. 559. See also Michael Robson's essay below, p. 114.

[29] Several other houses, not all of them Benedictine, claimed exempt status, for which see Knowles, *Religious Orders*, i. 277–9; ii. 281; Swanson, *Church and Society*, p. 20.

closely involved in secular politics.[30] Though never actually 'exempt', there were also a dozen or more houses in this period that sought and (in most cases) secured 'mitred' status allowing their abbot to assume many of the privileges and some of the responsibilities of the diocesan.[31]

The eight Benedictine communities that served cathedral churches – at Canterbury (Christ Church), Coventry, Durham, Ely, Norwich, Rochester, Winchester and Worcester – can also be seen to represent a distinctive form of monastic community.[32] In numerical terms they were smaller than many independent abbeys, but generally their financial resources were far greater. Ostensibly under the authority of the bishop, in fact the prior of the monastery enjoyed more extensive powers than many of his counterparts and some were even known to assume the responsibilities of the diocesan. The spiritual and social life of these houses was also very different. Their liturgical and musical traditions were more directly affected by secular practice. It was common for the monks themselves to be closely involved with the laity and to engage in a wide range of preaching and other pastoral activities.[33]

The great majority of monasteries shared essentially the same constitutional position but there were still other factors that make it difficult to generalize about the manner of their lives. The disparities in wealth were very significant. The income of six Benedictine abbeys – Bury, Christ Church, Canterbury, Glastonbury, St Albans, Westminster, St Mary's, York – was greater than that of all the female houses taken together.[34] Even so it would be wrong to make a simple equation between the resources and size of a monastery and the kind of community life it was able to sustain. The networks of mutual support between houses were still sufficiently intact

---

[30] There is a need for a comprehensive study of the exempt abbeys. For the fortunes of one of them in the later Middle Ages see R. S. Gottfried, *Bury St Edmunds and the Urban Crisis: 1290–1539* (Princeton, 1982).

[31] Knowles, *Religious Orders*, i. 256; Swanson, *Church and Society*, pp. 18–24.

[32] To these could also be added the chapter of regular canons serving Carlisle Cathedral, although it was smaller and less lively than its Benedictine counterparts. See R. B. Dobson, 'Cathedral Chapters and Cathedral Cities: York, Durham, and Carlisle in the Fifteenth Century', *Northern History* 19 (1983), pp. 15–44.

[33] For recent studies of the cathedral priories see R. B. Dobson, 'The English Cathedral Priories in the Fifteenth Century', *TRHS*, 6th Series 1 (1991), pp. 151–72; id.,'The Monks of Canterbury in the Later Middle Ages, 1220–1540', in *A History of Canterbury Cathedral*, ed. P. Collinson, N. Ramsey and M. Sparks (Oxford, 1995), pp. 69–153; *Norwich Cathedral: Church, City and Diocese, 1096–1996*, ed. I. Atherton, E. Fernie, C. Harper-Bill and H. Smith (London and Rio Grande, 1995); A. Oakley, 'Rochester Priory, 1185–1540', in *Faith and Fabric: A History of Rochester Cathedral, 604–1994*, ed. N. Yates and P. Welsby (Cambridge, 1996), pp. 29–55; J. Greatrex, 'St Swithun's Priory in the Later Middle Ages', in *Winchester Cathedral: Nine Hundred Years, 1093–1993*, ed. J. Crook (Chichester, 1993), pp. 139–66.

[34] This is based on the assessment of monastic incomes made in 1535, for which see A. Savine, 'English Monasteries on the Eve of the Dissolution', in *Oxford Studies in Social and Legal History, I*, ed. P. Vinogradoff (Oxford, 1909), pp. 270–88.

to ensure many smaller houses could survive the frequent storms of the fifteenth and sixteenth centuries. So it was, for example, that under the wing of St Albans a tiny, poor, priory such as Tynemouth in Northumberland, continued to receive its own novices, send students to Oxford and expand its library well into the sixteenth century.[35] There is no doubt that the nature of monastic life was also determined to a degree by regional factors.[36] It is commonplace to highlight the special nature of the northern counties where religious houses were, of necessity, the focus of much commercial and social as well as spiritual activity.[37] But other regions could also claim to represent a distinctive monastic environment: the south west, where the religious houses remained a powerful economic and industrial presence, and where there were few friars; and East Anglia, where there was an unusually large number of small, impoverished foundations struggling to survive in an increasingly sophisticated confessional and cultural climate.[38]

Perhaps the one generalization that can safely be made about monastic (and to a lesser extent mendicant) life in the later Middle Ages is that it was in many respects markedly different from earlier centuries. It is a truism that the history of monasticism is one of constant reinvention and that historians must be wary of measuring the monks of one era by the standards of another, setting Lanfranc alongside Bede, or comparing John Lydgate to William of Malmesbury. But there are perhaps especially strong grounds for suggesting that the two centuries after 1350 represent a distinctive period in the history of the religious orders in England. To enter the monastic life in the fourteenth, fifteenth or early sixteenth centuries in spiritual terms may have meant the same as it had in the High Middle Ages or even earlier, but in many of its daily essentials it would have been a wholly different experience. Everything from the process of admission and training to the physical space of the monastery and even the notion of the common life itself had undergone fundamental change. This was not the consequence of a

---

[35] *Annales monasterii sancti Albani a Iohanne Amundsham conscripti*, ed. H. T. Riley, 2 vols., Rolls Series 28/5 (1870–71), ii. 309; *Registrum abbatiae Iohannis Whethamstede*, ed. H. T. Riley, 2 vols., Rolls Series 28/6 (1872–3), ii. 44, 68. For the library see N. R. Ker, *Medieval Libraries of Great Britain: A List of Surviving Books* (2nd edn., London, 1964), p. 191.

[36] Benjamin Thompson suggests that the circumstances surrounding the foundation of different houses and the fortunes of the founders' families also helped to shape these regional differences. See below pp. 171–8, esp. 175–8.

[37] For the northern religious houses see C. Haigh, *The Last Days of the Lancashire Monasteries and the Pilgrimage of Grace*, Chetham Society 17 (1967); Haigh, *Reformation and Resistance in Tudor Lancashire* (Cambridge, 1977), esp. pp. 125–7; C. Cross, *Monks, Friars and Nuns in Sixteenth-Century Yorkshire*, Yorkshire Archaeological Society, Record Series 150 (1995).

[38] For the religious houses of the south west see H. P. R. Finberg, *Tavistock Abbey: A Study in the Social and Economic History of Devon* (Cambridge, 1951). The religious culture of East Anglia has attracted considerable attention. In *Stripping of the Altars*, Duffy draws many examples from eastern England. See also Oliva, *Convent and the Community*, passim; Thompson, 'Monasteries and their Patrons', pp. 103–23.

natural decline in the rigour of conventual life but was rather the product of a conscious process of reform. Between 1277 and 1343 the English Benedictines conducted a wide-ranging overhaul of their customs in a series of reform statutes.[39] Their efforts were supported by the papacy, most notably in the canons *Summi magistri* issued by Benedict XII in 1336.[40] Benedict extended his message to the Cistercians and Regular Canons and by 1350 these orders had also adopted new statutes of their own.[41]

In many respects, the passing of this legislation marks a watershed in the history of the English monasteries. For the first time the Benedictines (and later the Regular Canons) found themselves under a centralized system of government headed by a single General Chapter empowered to enforce the customary legislation, to levy subsidies, and to subject each house to regular visitation. This did not remove all of the anomalies and exemptions from the congregation but it did ensure there was a far greater degree of uniformity in monastic life than ever before.[42] With its own structures and statutes, the General Chapter also served to formalize the separation of the Black Monks in England (and in their turn the Regular Canons) from the continental mainstream. This was reinforced further with the secession of the Cluniac and Premonstratensian houses from their respective parent communities during the Papal Schism.[43]

The legislation also made significant changes to conventual life. After generations of debate, the reformers recognized that much of the Rule of St Benedict could only be regarded as preceptive and their new statutes offered significant revisions to, and some relaxations from, observance *ad literam*. The regulations on diet, office holding, personal property and the mobility of the monks were modified. Liturgical duties were also revised, the length of offices reduced and some commemorations removed from the calendar altogether. At the same time, there was a conscious effort to give their devotions a more distinctively monastic character, and new commemorations for St Benedict were devised and others for local monastic saints and patrons were consciously encouraged. The communal nature of community life was also compromised: refectory meals, chapter meetings and even

---

[39] For the background to these reforms see Knowles, *Religious Orders*, i. 9–21; *Chapters*, ed. Pantin, i. 64–91; ii. 28–62.

[40] Knowles, *Religious Orders*, ii. 3–4. For the text of *Summi magistri* see *Concilia*, ed. Wilkins, ii. 585–613.

[41] Benedict XII addressed *Fulgens sicut stella* (12 July 1336) to the White Monks and *Ad decorum* (15 May 1339) to the Black Canons. For their impact on the latter see H. E. Salter, *Chapters of the Augustinian Canons*, Oxford Historical Society 74 (1920). See also P. F. McDonald, 'The Papacy and Monastic Observance in Late Medieval England', *Journal of Religious History* 14/2 (1986), pp. 117–32.

[42] For the working of the General Chapter see W. A. Pantin, 'General and Provincial Chapters of the English Black Monks, 1215–1540', *TRHS*, 4th Series 10 (1927), pp. 195–263 at 209–42.

[43] Knowles, *Religious Orders*, ii. 142–3, 160–61.

certain offices in the choir were no longer compulsory but minimum levels of attendance were recommended. It would be wrong to interpret this as a deliberate dilution of traditional monasticism. The aim of the capitular and papal legislators was to reform the regular life in such a way as to make it more realistic and more resilient in the contemporary world. Perhaps it is more aptly described as 'a bold attempt at modernization'.[44]

It was this impulse that informed the most important innovation of these years, a new programme for monastic education. The curriculum of studies in the cloister was reorganized to give greater emphasis to the fundamental academic disciplines of grammar, logic and philosophy, and it was required that a proportion of monks in every house was sent to university to pursue higher studies. Under the aegis of the General Chapter, a common house of studies was established at Oxford on the mendicant model.[45] It was expected that the students would return (as graduates) to their home communities to extend the work of teaching in the cloister and to undertake official duties on behalf of the house. This ambitious re-invention of monastic studies transformed the intellectual and social climate of English monasteries in the later Middle Ages. Monastic thought now became more closely aligned to contemporary secular trends. There was also a new hierarchy within communities, indeed within the congregation as a whole; the graduate monks emerged as the natural leaders of the order, and its spokesmen in their dealings with secular society.[46]

In some respects, these years also proved a turning point for women religious. Some of the enthusiasm for root and branch reform, especially in terms of education in the cloister, was transmitted from the monasteries to the nunneries under their jurisdiction. At the same time, the papacy aimed to bring a new rigour to female monasticism through the observance of strict enclosure imposed under Boniface VIII's bull *Periculoso* of 1298.[47] This had the potential to transform the lives of women religious in the later Middle Ages, separating them entirely from secular society and thus from their

---

[44] For the reform of community life see *Chapters*, ed. Pantin, i. 64–91; 28–62; *Concilia*, ed. Wilkins, ii. 585–613. The quotation comes from R. W. Southern, *Western Society and the Church in the Middle Ages* (London, 1970), p. 236.

[45] For the capitular statutes concerning monastic studies see *Chapters*, ed. Pantin, i. 75; ii. 55–8. The injunction to teach the liberal arts in the cloister was underpinned by Clement V's decretal *Ne in agro* issued in 1311.

[46] For the impact of this legislation on monastic studies see R. B. Dobson, *Durham Priory, 1404–46* (Cambridge, 1973), pp. 342–86; Dobson, 'The Religious Orders', in *Late Medieval Oxford*, ed. Catto and Evans, pp. 539–79; J. Greatrex, 'Monk Students From Norwich Cathedral Priory at Oxford and Cambridge, c.1300–1540', *EHR* 105 (1991), pp. 555–83; Greatrex, 'English Cathedral Priories and the Pursuit of Learning in the Late Middle Ages', *JEH* 45 (1994), pp. 396–411; *The Benedictines in Oxford*, ed. H. Wansborough and A. Marett-Crosby (London, 1997); J. G. Clark, 'University Monks in Late Medieval England', in *Medieval Monastic Education and Formation*, ed. C. Muessig and G. Ferzoco (London, 2001), pp. 56–70.

[47] For *Periculoso* and its impact see E. M. Makowski, *Canon Law and Cloistered Women: Periculoso and its Commentators* (Washington DC, 1997).

primary source of patronage. In fact there were frequent evasions. Famously, the nuns of Markyate Priory responded defiantly, throwing their copy of the bull back at the bishop of Lincoln when he arrived at their gates ready to enforce it.[48] Moreover, it seems a good many bishops were disinclined to enforce its terms strictly to the letter.[49] The evidence of wills and other parish records – as discussed by Marilyn Oliva in her chapter below – suggests that nuns did continue to interact closely with the outside world.[50]

There was no wide-ranging reform of the mendicant orders at the turn of the thirteenth century, but they too saw significant changes to their lives as a consequence of papal intervention. The bull *Super cathedram* published by Boniface VIII in 1300 not only restricted their right to acquire property but also placed their pastoral activities under new regulation, requiring all their activities, from hearing confessions to conducting funerals, to be licensed by the diocesan.[51]

The religious orders of the later Middle Ages did differ from their counterparts of earlier centuries but this difference should not in itself be taken as a sign of their incipient decline. Indeed there are many indications of their continued vitality in the century and half before the Dissolution. In terms of their financial condition the religious houses remained remarkably secure in spite of the difficult economic circumstances that prevailed after 1350. The Statute of Mortmain curtailed the further expansion of monastic estates and like many other landowners in the wake of the Black Death they were compelled to put a greater proportion of their property out to farm. But few of those houses of middle size or larger seem to have suffered long-term damage.[52] Recent studies have shown how some offset the worst of the situation by developing other sources of income. Several monasteries in south east England – Christ Church, Canterbury, St Albans, Rochester – increased their holdings of residential and commercial property in the city of London in the fifty years after 1349.[53] Those in the north and south west

[48] Lee, *Nunneries*, p. 90. See also Gilchrist, *Contemplation and Action*, pp. 106–56; N. B. Warren, *Spiritual Economies: Female Monasticism in Late Medieval England* (Philadelphia, 2001), pp. 5–6.

[49] See especially J. H. Tillotson, 'Visitation and Reform of the Yorkshire Nunneries in the Fourteenth Century', *Northern History* 30 (1994), pp. 1–21.

[50] See below pp. 159–61.

[51] For *Super cathedram* and its impact see Knowles, *Religious Orders*, i. 186–8; Swanson, *Church and Society*, p. 17; A. Williams, 'Relations between the Mendicant Friars and the Secular Clergy in the Later Fourteenth Century', *Annuale Medievale* 1 (1960), pp. 22–95.

[52] Knowles, *Religious Orders*, ii. 311–18. For individual studies see Dobson, *Durham Priory*, pp. 268–85; Harvey, *Westminster Abbey and its Estates*, pp. 66–7, 164–202; R. A. L. Smith, *Canterbury Cathedral Priory: A Study in Monastic Administration* (Cambridge, 1969), pp. 11–13, 90–104.

[53] Dobson, 'Monks of Canterbury', pp. 139–40; Oakley, 'Rochester Priory, 1185–1540', p. 39; *Annales monasterii sancti Albani*, ed. Riley, ii. 190; *Gesta abbatum monasterii sancti Albani*, ed. H. T. Riley, 3 vols., Rolls Series 28/4 (1867–8), iii. 376.

exploited the industrial potential of their lands; in the sixteenth century the monks of Tavistock were generating more than £900 per annum from their mines.[54] It is a measure of their continued prosperity that these larger houses committed themselves to new building projects in the second half of the fifteenth century. As Glyn Coppack discusses in detail below, the larger Cistercian houses, Forde, Fountains and Rievaulx, embarked on an ambitious programme of re-modeling.[55] Several Augustinian and Benedictine houses, such as Colchester, Evesham, Rochester and Waltham, also completed new churches during this period.[56]

Of course there remained enormous disparities in wealth between the largest and smallest houses, and in the harsh climate of the fifteenth century many of those with the most meagre endowments were brought to the brink of collapse. It is difficult to see how some survived on their diminishing returns. By 1535 the Augustinian priory of Burtle in Somerset supported a community of four or five on an income of £6 per annum, at a time when even an unskilled labourer could expect to earn £3 4s.[57] Some did descend into spiraling debt. The *Valor ecclesiasticus* records that Athelney Abbey owed more than £1000 in 1535 although its gross income was less then £300.[58] Generally speaking, the nunneries whose endowments had never matched those of male houses suffered most. More than 60% subsisted on an income lower than £100 per annum and as many as one third had less than £50. After 1500 the abbey of Nunburnholme, in North Yorkshire, supported six nuns with less than £10 per annum between them.[59]

It is likely that the mendicant convents faced growing financial pressures whatever their size and status. Lacking endowment as such, they became ever more dependent on the marketing of their spiritual services and the support of their benefactors. Henry VI came to the aid of the Oxford Greyfriars in 1453 with a renewal of the substantial royal grant.[60] Their counterparts at the York convent benefited from their close association with city authorities when, as Michael Robson recounts in his contribution here, they presented them with a pension in 1487.[61]

The comparative prosperity of many if not all of the monasteries in pre-Reformation England is borne out in their levels of recruitment. Amongst the Benedictines numbers remained stable right up to the decade before the Dissolution. For example, in 1438 there were seventy-three monks at

---

[54] Dobson, *Durham Priory*, pp. 278–9; Finberg, *Tavistock Abbey*, pp. 187–90; Savine, *English Monasteries*, p. 272.

[55] See below pp. 197–209.

[56] Scarisbrick, *Reformation and the English People*, p. 14.

[57] Savine, *English Monasteries*, p. 281. For a labourer's wages see C. Dyer, *Standards of Living in the Later Middle Ages: Social Change in England, c. 1200–1520* (rev. edn., Cambridge, 1998), pp. 222–33 at 227.

[58] Savine, *English Monasteries*, p. 212.

[59] Tillotson, *Marrick Priory*, pp. 2–3.

[60] Dobson, 'Religious Orders, 1370–1540', p. 559.

[61] See below p. 109.

Durham Cathedral Priory; a century later there were seventy-four.[62] There was equal stability even in the smaller communities: there were twenty-nine monks at Crowland Abbey in 1539, as there had been 200 years before; there were twenty-four at Selby at the Dissolution, only two less than in 1381.[63] It is striking that many houses seem to have recovered rapidly from the ravages of the Black Death. More than half the eighty monks at St Albans Abbey had died between 1349 and 1351 but by 1382 there were again more than sixty recorded in the community.[64] Christ Church, Canterbury, had more than doubled its pre-plague numbers as early as 1390.[65] Even some of the smaller houses experienced a recovery over the course of the fifteenth century. At Dunkeswell in Devon there were only eight monks in 1377, but by the beginning of the sixteenth century there were twenty.[66] Indeed in the second half of the fifteenth century England seems to have witnessed something of a surge in monastic vocations. The Premonstratensian community at Cockersand grew from seventeen in 1480 to more than twenty-five in 1536.[67] The Augustinian community at Missenden expanded from only five canons in 1518 to fourteen by 1530.[68] Even the chapter of canons at Carlisle, which had always been untypically small, grew from barely fifteen at the turn of the century to touch twenty-five by 1540.[69] Moreover, in the final decade before the Dissolution numbers seem to have remained stable. In his chapter below Donald Logan argues that amongst the Yorkshire houses there was no sudden rush to departure after the visitations of 1535.[70] A similar pattern emerges from the evidence elsewhere. There were forty-five monks at Winchester Cathedral Priory in 1536 and no fewer than fifty-seven nuns remained at Shaftesbury Abbey to make the surrender three years later.[71] It is worth noting, however, that there are few signs of a similar late surge in recruitment to the orders of the friars; the handful of new Observant houses were largely filled from existing Franciscan convents. When they arrived in 1534, with few exceptions, Cromwell's commissioners found communities on the point of extinction.[72]

---

[62] Dobson, 'Cathedral Chapters and Cathedral Cities', p. 23.

[63] *MRH*, pp. 63, 76.

[64] *Gesta abbatum*, ed. Riley, ii. 370; BL, Cotton MS Nero D VII, fol. 83r–v.

[65] *MRH*, p. 61; Dobson, 'Canterbury in the Later Middle Ages', pp. 69–153 at 116–17, although in her *BRECP* Joan Greatrex suggests numbers at the priory before 1349 were already very high.

[66] J. A. Sparks, *In the Shadow of the Black Downs: Life at the Cistercian Abbey of Dunkeswell and its Manors and Estates, 1201–1539* (Bradford-on-Avon, 1978), p. 103.

[67] Haigh, *Reformation and Resistance*, p. 73.

[68] Knowles, *Religious Orders*, iii. 70.

[69] Dobson, 'Cathedral Chapters and Cathedral Cities', p. 25.

[70] See below pp. 213–22 at 221–2.

[71] *MRH*, pp. 81, 265.

[72] The Dominican convent at Bristol had dwindled from an average of thirty to just five friars in 1528. The Franciscan convent in London had been reduced from seventy-two in 1315 to barely twenty in 1538. There were fewer than ten friars still living at the Augustinian houses at Leicester, Oxford and Stamford by 1535: *MRH*, pp. 215, 226,

The regular, even growing, recruitment of men and women to religious houses in the fifteenth and sixteenth centuries offers some clue as to the condition of life within their walls. It seems very likely that the customary patterns of monastic and mendicant observance did continue to a very great extent at least until the difficult days of the 1530s. Of course, there were now further opportunities for monks and friars to escape their conventual obligations. A university career could remove them from the cloister for more than a decade. For those with greater ambitions there was also preferment. Monastic leaders (rightly) regarded papal chaplaincies as the most insidious: between 1440 and 1464 some 200 were granted to English regulars alone.[73] But at the same time there were developments that succeeded in bringing communities closer together. The monastic orders were subject to an ever-expanding body of statutes and a regular cycle of capitular visitations (which continued down to the 1520s) perhaps ensuring rather stricter observance than in earlier periods.[74] As Barbara Harvey explains below, the reorganization of the noviciate and the extension of the period of custody meant that younger monks remained under the control of their superiors for upwards of a decade after their profession.[75] Even as seniors, most male religious would be bound to their own house with official responsibilities: in a typical community there may have been as many as two thirds of the monks holding office as an obedientiary or one of their deputies.[76]

It would be misleading, of course, to suggest that there were not serious lapses in observance on occasion. In the past much has been made of the record of episcopal visitations from the fifteenth and early sixteenth centuries, most notably the circuits conducted by bishops of Lincoln in the 1430s and 40s, and the bishops of Norwich and Lincoln (again) between 1490 and 1530.[77] The earlier records do bring to light a number of houses – Bardney and Eynsham amongst others – where minor infringements of the Rule, over diet, the instruction of novices and the custody of the cloister

242–4. See also A. B. Emden, A *Survey of Dominicans in England, based on the Ordination Lists in Episcopal Registers, 1268–1538* (Rome, 1967), pp. 27–30. For declining numbers at York see Michael Robson below p. 119.

[73] Knowles, *Religious Orders*, ii. 171–2. The Abbot of St Albans, Thomas de la Mare, was said to have condemned the practice at the time of the Papal Schism; *Gesta abbatum sancti Albani*, ed. Riley, ii. 204–5.

[74] For capitular visitations see *Chapters*, ed. Pantin, iii. 250–53.

[75] See below pp. 56–7.

[76] Knowles, *Religious Orders*, ii. 309–10; Harvey, *Living and Dying*, pp. 77, 100–2.

[77] These have all been printed: *Visitations of Religious Houses in the Diocese of Lincoln*, ed. A. H. Thompson, 3 vols., Canterbury and York Society 17, 24, 33 (1915–27); *Visitations in the Diocese of Lincoln*, ed. A. H. Thompson, 3 vols., Lincoln Record Society 35, 37 (1944–7); *Visitations of the Diocese of Norwich*, ed. A. Jessopp, Camden Society, New Series 43 (1888). For an overview of their contents see Knowles, *Religious Orders*, iii. 62–75. Joan Greatrex discusses the problems presented by these difficult – and it should not be forgotten, intimate – documents below p. 35.

were commonplace, and where the monastic community itself was deeply divided. But there is very little in this to suggest that these problems were any more endemic than they had been in earlier periods, for which no records survive. Indeed visitorial injunctions changed little in the two centuries before the Reformation, bishops employing the same formulaic questions as their thirteenth-century predecessors.[78] The latest records (dating from the second and third decades of the sixteenth century) do reveal more serious misdemeanors but even here there is no general pattern of problems. There were still houses in both dioceses for which their superior could report *omnia bene*. To this can also be added the favourable impression cast by the records of Bishop Richard Redman's visitations of Premonstratensian houses.[79]

In fact the genuine problems of this period seem to have involved individuals rather than institutions. Probably the most common offence was financial corruption. Cases of immorality were fewer than is often assumed. Between 1347 and 1540 there were only fifteen cases of immorality recorded amongst the numerous (and much visited) religious houses of Yorkshire.[80] Of course, there were some notorious scandals. Amongst the worst were the cases of Henry Arrowsmith, abbot of Vale Royal, who was convicted of rape in 1436, and the abbot of Dorchester, John Clifton, who was discovered with no fewer than five mistresses during a visitation in 1441.[81] It may be that for the majority the severity of the punishment was enough to deter them from following a similar course. After her conviction for immorality in 1530 Joan Hutton, a nun of Esholt, who was also pregnant, was imprisoned in a concealed chamber within the convent, from where she was brought out once a week to be formally scolded by her sisters in the chapter house.[82]

Perhaps the most common complaint made by episcopal visitors in this period was that many of the traditional rigours of the common life had been relaxed. In general it does appear that pre-Reformation religious did enjoy a greater degree of domestic comfort than their predecessors. By the beginning of the fifteenth century many of the older restrictions on monastic diet had been revised, a fact that Henry V was forced to acknowledge when he issued his constitutions for the Benedictine order in 1421.[83] Barbara Harvey's groundbreaking study of Westminster reveals that the Black Monks of the

---

[78] Knowles, *Religious Orders*, ii. 209–10.

[79] Knowles, *Religious Orders*, iii. 39–51. See also J. A. Gribben, *The Premonstratensian Order in Late Medieval England* (Woodbridge, 2001). For a different reading of these later visitation records see Benjamin Thompson's chapter below, pp. 184–8.

[80] Tillotson, 'Visitation and Reform', p. 19.

[81] T. Bostock and S. Hogg, *Vale Royal Abbey and the Cistercians, 1277–1538* (Northwich, 1999), p. 6; Knowles, *Religious Orders*, ii. 211.

[82] *VCH Yorks.*, iii. 162. See also Claire Cross's contribution below p. 149.

[83] *Chapters*, ed. Pantin, iii. 118; see also C. Harper-Bill, 'The Labourer is Worthy of his Hire', in *The Church in Pre-Reformation Society*, ed. C. M. Barron and Harper-Bill (Woodbridge, 1985), pp. 95–107 at 96.

fifteenth century could benefit from a diet that was high-energy and protein rich and was supplemented with a more-than-generous quantity of alchohol.[84] Indeed it appears that the opportunities for drinking increased in this period as monasteries made provision for brewing within their own precincts.[85] The standard of their accommodation was also much improved. It was now common for senior officials, graduates and other distinguished members of the community to occupy their own private chambers. Glyn Coppack describes here how the former infirmary hall at Fountains Abbey was remodelled in the fifteenth century to provide self-contained 'two-storey bed-sits' for senior monks.[86] Heads of the largest houses could now expect a suite of lodgings on the same scale as their secular counterparts, especially since many were rebuilt in the fifteenth and early sixteenth centuries. With the practice of paying religious an income becoming more widespread, it was also possible for them to ease their lives with the purchase of personal luxuries such as jewelry, furs and furnishings.[87] It is worth noting, however, that in the few personal inventories that survive there are as many scholarly books, personal relics and objects of devotion as there are luxury items. The personal possessions of Anne Clifford, a nun of Minster-in-Sheppey, included 'a table with a crucyfyx of wod payntyd and an image of our lady payntyd'.[88]

Indeed it would be wrong to conclude that every member of a religious community in pre-Reformation England resembled either Madame Eglantine or the well-upholstered Monk who was her travelling companion. It is hardly surprising that with an annual income in excess of £4500 the monks of Westminster enjoyed a lifestyle akin to that of the higher nobility.[89] But it is likely that even some members of their own order would have been as staggered as we are by such luxuries. Not every community was nearly so fortunate. It is true that their urban context meant that the mendicant convents were able to make the best of their straitened circumstances. But for the remote monasteries in rural locations it was more difficult. Probably the privations endured at Butley Priory in the 1530s were not wholly exceptional: there the monks were too poor to repair the holes in their roofs and so, as their visitor reported, they suffered from regular colds and chilblains.[90]

It is also worth remembering that there were many religious in this period who chose to separate themselves from the (growing) comfort of the convent buildings in search of a more eremitical existence. It is difficult to set a figure

---

[84] Harvey, *Living and Dying*, pp. 38–41.
[85] Harper-Bill, 'Labourer is Worthy of his Hire', p. 107.
[86] See below pp. 200–1.
[87] Harvey, *Living and Dying*, pp. 152–3; Lee, *Nunneries*, pp. 28–9; Tillotson, *Marrick Priory*, pp. 17–18.
[88] Gilchrist, *Contemplation and Action*, p. 130.
[89] For the income of Westminster Abbey see Savine, *English Monasteries*, p. 278.
[90] Harper-Bill, 'Labourer is Worthy of his Hire', p. 98.

on the number who adopted a reclusive life within their own precinct, but the impression is that the practice was widespread.[91] There were others who self-consciously cultivated an ascetic regime from within the community. The celebrated abbot of St Albans, Thomas de la Mare (died 1396), was said to have inspired many younger monks to adopt the same severe mortifications to which he subjected himself.[92]

Some houses were also open to wider currents of reform. Surviving books and library catalogues indicate that many English religious did engage with the new spirituality emerging from outside the clerical establishment. The Benedictines and the Regular Canons were enthusiastic readers of Rolle, Hilton and others.[93] In spite of their long-standing insularity, there is also a trace of continental influence in their libraries. One of the earliest English manuscripts of Thomas à Kempis's *Imitatio Christi* was compiled and copied by a monk of St Albans in about 1450.[94] The mendicants also showed some interest in these trends. The Observant movement had attracted more than two hundred recruits before 1530, many of them direct from existing Franciscan convents.[95] But the clearest commitment to on-going reform came from the small network of reformed communities, centered on the Charterhouses at London and Mount Grace and the Brigittine nunnery at Syon. From these houses emerged a succession of writers whose devotional and pastoral manuals enjoyed the widest readership in the century before 1540. Even as late as 1530 it was arguably their publications, such as the *Work for Householders* and the *Pomander of Prayer* that did most to shape the piety of the literate laity.[96]

Of course, this level of literary activity was exceptional, but there is no doubt that one of the distinguishing features of the religious orders as a whole was their continuing intellectual vitality. For the Benedictines in particular, the century after 1350 represents something of a cultural renaissance. To a great extent, the reforms of the General Chapter did succeed in reviving education and learning in the cloister. Novice and junior monks were now exposed to a wider range of studies and given the grounding

---

[91] Knowles, *Religious Orders*, ii. 219–22; Swanson, *Church and Society*, pp. 273–4. See also Oliva, *Convent and Community*, p. 155.

[92] *Gesta abbatum*, ed. Riley, iii. 404–5.

[93] *English Benedictine Libraries*, ed. Sharpe et al., B30. 33 (Evesham); B55. 24, 58 (Monk Bretton); B107. 14 (Westminster); B121. 11–14 (St Mary's, York); *The Libraries of the Augustinian Canons*, ed. Webber and Watson, A20. 907, 910–11 (Leicester); A36. 9, 21a, 421, 425 (Thurgarton). See also the extracts from Rolle made by the Durham monk Richard Segbroke in his commonplace book, BL, Arundel MS 507.

[94] The book is now Oxford, Bodl., Laud Misc. MS 215. Of course, these intellectual interests offer no indication that actual reform was likely. Benjamin Thompson argues below that the older monastic orders were too far integrated into the secular world to embrace a greater rigour in the manner of their lives. See p. 190.

[95] Knowles, *Religious Orders*, iii. 12–13.

[96] See Haigh, *English Reformations*, pp. 25–8; J. T. Rhodes, 'Syon Abbey and its Religious Publications in the Sixteenth Century', *JEH* 44 (1993), pp. 11–21.

in grammar, logic and philosophy envisaged by the reformers. In the cathedral priories and larger abbeys at least, graduates did give regular lectures and sermons to their brethren; several fifteenth-century examples survive from Gloucester, Norwich and Worcester.[97] Alongside these periods of formal instruction, many if not all of the monks also pursued independent studies of their own. Their books and book-lists bear witness to eclectic tastes embracing history, natural philosophy, astronomy, theology, and even classical literature and mythography.[98]

More significant than any of this, however, was their emergence as a major scholarly presence at the universities. From the foundation of their Oxford *studium* in 1277, they had expanded rapidly, occupying further colleges both there and at Cambridge before 1400. By the turn of the fifteenth century, the Black Monks undoubtedly formed the largest community, religious or secular, at either university.[99] Between 1500 and 1540 from Oxford alone there emerged no fewer than 324 monk graduates taken from as many as forty-two different houses.[100] Not only were they numerous, the monastic colleges at Oxford (in particular) could also claim a formidable reputation. It had been Benedictines there who were the first to dispute with John Wyclif and they had remained prominent amongst academic theologians and canon lawyers for much of the century that followed.[101] By 1500, the scholars at Canterbury and Gloucester Colleges were also showing more than a passing interest in humanism and the revival of the Classics.[102] In fact for a short moment it seemed as if humanism and monasticism were to be combined within a university setting. Both of Oxford's early sixteenth-century colleges, Brasenose (begun in 1509) and Corpus Christi (1516), were initially conceived of by their founders as monastic foundations.[103] Even at the end of 1520s, when William Wareham

---

[97] See Cambridge, Emmanuel College, MS II. 2. 7 (142) (Norwich); Oxford, Bodl., Bodley MS 649 (Gloucester); Laud Misc. MS 706 (Worcester); Worcester Cathedral Chapter Library MS F 10 (Worcester).

[98] See for example the following late medieval library catalogues: *English Benedictine Libraries*, ed. Sharpe *et al.*, B30 (Evesham); B43 (Glastonbury); B58 (Norwich); B68 (Ramsey).

[99] Dobson, 'Religious Orders, 1370–1540', pp. 547–52.

[100] P. Cunich, 'Benedictine Monks at the University of Oxford and the Dissolution of the Monasteries', in *The Benedictines in Oxford*, ed. Wansborough and Marrett Crosby, pp. 155–82 at 165.

[101] J. I. Catto, 'Wyclif and Wyclifism at Oxford, 1356–1430', in *A History of the University of Oxford II. Late Medieval Oxford*, ed. Catto and T. A. R. Evans (Oxford, 1992), pp. 175–261 at 204–7.

[102] W. A. Pantin, *Canterbury College, Oxford*, 3 vols., Oxford Historical Society, New Series 6–8 (1947–49), i. 81–2, 85–6; *The Letter Book of Robert Joseph, Monk of Evesham*, ed. H. Aveling and W. A. Pantin, Oxford Historical Society, New Series 19 (1967), pp. xxviii–xxxv.

[103] *A History of the University of Oxford III. The Collegiate University*, ed. J. McConica (Oxford, 1986), pp. 17–18. See also *Brasenose College Quatercentenary Monographs II*, ed. I. S. Leadam, R. W. Jeffrey *et al.*, Oxford Historical Society 53 (1909), p. 8.

scoured the universities for scholars to step up and repudiate Luther and his teaching, he included several monastic scholars in his final selection.[104] Of course, as Joan Greatrex observes below, the Benedictines' success in the academic arena was not without its costs. By the beginning of the sixteenth century at least it was becoming clear that in many cloisters traditional monastic studies had been cast aside in favour of more contemporary trends.[105]

Although they were subject to the same process of reform, there are few signs of similar intellectual life amongst the Cistercians and Regular Canons. It was not until 1437 that the White Monks founded their own *studium* at Oxford and there were never more than half a dozen scholars there before 1540.[106] The Regular Canons established a college only two years earlier and they also failed to foster a steady flow of graduates. Indeed, during its visitation, the Augustinian General Chapter discovered that only ten houses in the congregation had ever sent students to Oxford.[107] Even some of the more distinguished, such as Carlisle Cathedral Priory, had managed to evade their injunctions.[108] Ironically, it was the canons' earlier foundation at Oseney, the Augustinian abbey on the outskirts of Oxford, that produced the only really significant scholar of the later Middle Ages: John Walton, translator of Boethius's *Consolatio*.[109]

The level of learning in the nunneries is less clear. Probably far more of the women were literate (at least in the vernacular) than in earlier periods, a reflection of growing literacy amongst the gentry from whose ranks many of them were recruited, and the stricter entry requirements imposed increasingly by their bishops and monastic superiors.[110] There may also have been a sizeable minority who understood Latin, although it is significant that even at Syon Abbey the nuns made use of an English translation of the Divine Office.[111] Beyond their observance of the hours, it is difficult to say how many women actually involved themselves in independent reading or study. In contrast to male houses, very few books, book-lists or other forms of writing survive from this or any other period. There are only occasional glimpses of intellectual activity. The pages of a copy of Richard Fox's 1517 translation of the Rule of St Benedict were carefully corrected and glossed by Margaret Stanburne, prioress of St Mary's Stamford, who also signed her

---

[104] C. Cross, 'Oxford and the Tudor State', in *Collegiate University*, ed. McConica, pp. 117–50 at 123.

[105] See below p. 40.

[106] J. I. Catto, 'The Cistercians at Oxford, 1280–1539', in *The Benedictines in Oxford*, ed. Wansborough and Marett-Crosby, pp. 108–15.

[107] Salter, *Chapters of the Augustinian Canons*, pp. xxxvii, 99–100.

[108] Dobson, 'Cathedral Chapters and Cathedral Cities', p. 39.

[109] For Walton see Emden, *BRUO*, iii. 1975.

[110] For social origins of pre-Reformation nuns see Lee, *Nunneries*, p. 59; Oliva, *Convent and Community*, pp. 52–60.

[111] The translation was prepared for them by the Oxford theologian Thomas Gascoigne, see Lee, *Nunneries*, pp. 136–7.

name on the title page.[112] Bishop Fox had published his book to promote learning amongst the religious women in his diocese and there may have been other nuns who read their copies as carefully as Margaret.[113] At the turn of the fifteenth century, a manuscript anthology containing texts on the religious life was compiled by the nuns of Amesbury and used by successive generations of their sisters for their own 'goostly comforte and sum maner of instructyon'.[114] Lacking the formal structures that shaped the studies of the monks, much must have depended on the initiative of individual sisters. Undoubtedly there were many communities where books, other than those necessary for their priest to perform Divine Office, aroused little attention amongst the sisters. In her survey of Yorkshire nunneries below, Claire Cross has found only a handful of books being brought into the cloister and most of these are connected with the male priests who assisted them.[115]

In comparison to the standing they had enjoyed in the thirteenth and early fourteenth centuries, the pre-Reformation period was an undistinguished one for mendicant scholars. By 1400 their pre-eminence in the academic community had been challenged both by the expansion of the secular colleges and, undoubtedly, by the presence of the Benedictines. Their churches continued to dominate the Oxford skyline, book-hungry scholars still haunted the Franciscans' library, and the Augustinians hosted public disputations, but their own masters no longer attracted the following they had before 1350. Indeed it is a measure of their obscurity that between 1400 and 1500 not a single name of any Dominican or Franciscan regent master has been preserved.[116] Of course, the Oxford and Cambridge convents were only part of a network of mendicant schools and in many provincial centres learning did continue to flourish. Michael Robson describes below how in the fifteenth century the York Greyfriars still received students from across the continent.[117] The *studia* of the four main orders at London also remained important for much of the period: it was the London convent of the Franciscans that nurtured the talents of Henry Standish, one of the most prominent pre-Reformation mendicant scholars.[118] As Jeremy Catto argues below, it was in this context of practical education and evangelization that mendicant scholars made their most significant contribution in their last century. Indeed it is his contention that there is

---

[112] The book is now Oxford, Bodl. Arch. D. 15.

[113] See also M. Erler, 'Bishop Richard Fox's Manuscript Gifts to his Winchester Nuns: A Second Surviving Example', *JEH* 52 (2001), pp. 334–7.

[114] The book is now Oxford, Bodl., Add. MS A 42. See also Y. Parrey, 'Devoted Disciples of Christ: Early Sixteenth-Century Religious Life in the Nunnery of Amesbury', *Historical Research* 67 (1994), pp. 240–8 at 241. For similar patterns of reading see Lee, *Nunneries*, pp. 153–63.

[115] See below p. 151.

[116] Dobson, 'Religious Orders, 1370–1540', pp. 555–61. See also A. G. Little, *The Greyfriars in Oxford*, Oxford Historical Society 20 (1892).

[117] See below p. 114.

[118] For Standish see Knowles, *Religious Orders*, iii. 53–4.

still substantial scholarship to be found in the margins of the books they used for teaching and in sermon notebooks.[119]

Under scrutiny, it also appears that the reformed religious orders of the fifteenth and sixteenth centuries do not entirely deserve their reputation for learning that was upheld as much by contemporaries as it has been by modern historians. There were a number of important and influential writers to emerge from the Carthusian congregation in the century before the Reformation, most notably Nicholas Love, prior of Mount Grace and author of the *Mirrour of the Blessed Lyf of Jesu Christ*.[120] But as Vincent Gillespie reveals below, the claims that these communities were unrivalled power-houses of original scholarship have been overblown. His detailed analysis of the remains of the library at Syon Abbey suggests that the religious there were not such committed disciples of Christian humanism and other contemporary currents as has often been assumed.[121]

The revival of learning in the larger monasteries was matched by their return to some level of organized book-production. Indeed at the turn of the fourteenth century some of the older Benedictine houses – Christ Church, Canterbury, Bury St Edmunds, Durham, St Albans and Worcester – were almost self-sufficient in books.[122] The St Albans monks even erected a new, purpose-built *scriptorium*, employing copyists and illumina-tors to work there alongside them.[123] This was unusual, but even in smaller, poorer communities there were still some active scribes to be found. The wealthier houses also succeeded in attracting professional scribes and illuminators to work within their precincts. Even at the end of the fifteenth century foreign book craftsmen coming into England gravitated towards the larger religious houses.[124] Indeed it has been suggested that the beginnings of the insular tradition of tooled binding can be traced back to the monasteries of south east England in the second half of the fifteenth century.[125]

The fact that the older Benedictine houses also played an important role

---

[119] See below pp. 101–3.
[120] For Nicholas Love see *Nicholas Love's The Mirrour of the Blessed Lyf of Jesu Christ: A Critical Edition*, ed. M. G. Sargent (London and New York, 1992). See also E. M. Thomson, *The Carthusians in England* (London, 1930), pp. 339–40.
[121] See below pp. 75–95.
[122] Dobson, *Durham Priory*, pp. 376–8; A. Gransden, 'Some Manuscripts in Cambridge from Bury St Edmunds', in *Bury St Edmunds: Medieval Art, Architecture, Archaeology and Economy*, ed. Gransden (Leeds, 1998), pp. 228–85 at 239–44; R. M. Thomson, *A Descriptive Catalogue of the Medieval Manuscripts in Worcester Cathedral Library* (Cambridge, 2001), pp. xxv, xxxv–vii.
[123] *Gesta abbatum*, ed. Riley, iii. 393.
[124] Dobson, *Durham Priory*, p. 377; R. A. B. Mynors, 'A Fifteenth-Century Scribe: T. Werken', *TCBS* 1/2 (1950), pp. 97–104; M. Parkes, 'A Fifteenth-Century Scribe: Henry Mere', *Bodleian Library Record* 6 (1961), pp. 654–9.
[125] M. J. Foot, 'Bookbinding, 1400–1557', in *The Cambridge History of the Book III. 1400–1557*, ed. J. B. Trapp and L. Hellinga (Cambridge, 1999), pp. 109–27 at 116.

in the development of printing in the decades before the Dissolution has often been overlooked. Printing is usually seen as a tool of the reformers, a primary motor in the spread of Protestant religion. But in early Tudor England some of the earliest and most prolific presses operated under the patronage of monasteries. It is likely that the so-called 'Schoolmaster Printer' of St Albans – whose press, active from 1479, was only the second to be established outside Westminster – was associated with the monks of the abbey there. During the 1520s presses were established in the precincts of the monasteries at Abingdon and Tavistock and at the latter the printer was himself a monk.[126] At the beginning of the 1530s, the monks of St Augustine's Canterbury and St Albans also took to printing. Here the printers were professionals, but they worked in close collaboration with the monks, some of whose own compositions were amongst the works printed.[127] Their output was not confined to books for domestic use. Both monasteries used their presses to popularize their shrines: St Albans produced a revised edition of Lydgate's *Lives of St Alban and Amphibel* [STC 17025] in 1534, St Augustine's a version of the same poet's *Legend of St Augustine at Compton* in 1535.[128] Against the gathering storm, they also published polemics on the matter of religion, St Albans printing their second only months before their surrender.

As this indicates, the intellectual activities of pre-Reformation religious were not all inward looking. Indeed many of the older monasteries made new provisions for lay education in this period, establishing schools for local youths in their own precincts (usually attached to the almonry) and extending their educational patronage in the community beyond their walls. Since the demise of child oblation in the twelfth century, the monasteries had not taken a direct role in elementary education. These new schools presented an opportunity to recover something of their social and spiritual influence, as well as providing them with a ready source of recruits. By the early fifteenth century, at the cathedral priories and the other larger houses, the almonry schools had become a prominent and prestigious feature of the monastic precinct.[129] But even (and perhaps, especially) in the smaller and more remote houses, the school was also an important part of

---

[126] For the record of these presses see J. Ames, *Typographical Antiquities* (3 vols., London 1785–90), iii. 1439–40. For Tavistock see also Finberg, *Tavistock Abbey*, pp. 290–93.

[127] For these presses see Ames, *Typographical Antiquities*, iii. 1430–36, 1452–4. For St Albans see also Clark, 'Reformation and Reaction', pp. 304–5.

[128] No copy of the Canterbury book survives, but its title and colophon ('Canterberie at St Austen's') are recorded in a bookseller's inventory of 1595. See F. B. Williams, 'The Lost Books of Tudor England', *The Library*, 5th series, 33 (1978), pp. 1–14 at 10.

[129] For these developments see R. Bowers, 'The Almonry Schools of the English Monasteries, c. 1265–1540', in *Monastery and Society in Medieval Britain*, ed. B. J. Thompson (Stamford, 1999), pp. 176–222. See also N. Orme, *English Schools in the Middle Ages* (London, 1973), pp. 243–54; J. Greatrex, 'Norwich Cathedral Almonry School', in *The Church and Childhood*, ed. D. Wood, Studies in Church History 31 (1994), pp. 161–81.

their outreach.[130] Generally, precinct schools were filled with the children of their tenants, but many houses also took into their custody the offspring of their patrons. The practice remained popular right down to the Dissolution. In 1530 Lord Lisle entered his stepson into the household of the Abbot of Reading so that he might 'plythe hym to his learning both to Latin and Frenche'.[131] At St Mary's Winchester (Nunnaminster) in 1536 there were no fewer than twenty-six 'chyldren of lordys, knyghttes and gentylmen' amongst them the daughters of Sir Roger Copley, Sir Geoffrey Pole and also Lord Lisle.[132] In fact it appears that the education of the laity was one of the very last features of monastic life to founder at the end of the 1530s. Taking the surrenders of the smaller abbeys and priories in 1536, Cromwell's commissioners were surprised to find schoolchildren in their precincts.[133]

The larger monasteries and mendicant convents in this period were also prominent patrons of education. Many of them funded exhibitions for poor boys of within their liberty to study at university. As early as the 1330s, the monks of Worcester Priory had entered into a compact with the warden and fellows of Merton College, Oxford, jointly to support a dozen scholars from Worcester diocese.[134] Exceptionally, Selby Abbey offered to help a Dominican from the York convent to complete his studies at Oxford.[135] It is worth noting that the laity continued to look upon the religious houses as an appropriate channel for their own patronage of education. A widow of Winchcombe, Joan Huddlestone, gave monies to the Benedictine monks of the town to support the schooling of six local boys.[136] Similarly, William Martyn, a London merchant, bequeathed £5 to the London Greyfriars 'for the exhibicioun of a virtuous scoler'.[137]

Education was only one of many services religious houses still offered the local community. They continued to commit a part of their income to the charitable support of the sick and the poor. Critics complained that their giving represented only a fraction of their overall revenue, although reliable figures of their expenditure are difficult to come by. The impression is that it was often the houses of modest size and resources that remained the most committed to their traditional charitable activities.[138] The impoverished nuns of Marrick Priory devoted £9 4s. 7½d. to alms, as much as 14% of their

---

[130] See for example Haigh, *Reformation and Resistance*, p. 124; Tillotson, *Marrick Priory*, p. 20;
[131] *VCH Berks.*, ii. 68.
[132] *VCH Hants*, ii. 125.
[133] Cross, *End of Medieval Monasticism*, p. 15; Tillotson, *Marrick Priory*, p. 20; *VCH. Northants.*, ii. 120 (Pipewell); *VCH Wilts.*, ii. 272 (Staveley).
[134] *Liber ecclesiae Wigorniensis: A Letter Book of the Priors of Worcester*, ed. J. H. Bloom, Worcester Historical Society 27 (1912), pp. 39–40.
[135] Tillotson, *Monastery and Society*, p. 58.
[136] Savine, *English Monasteries*, p. 231.
[137] Dobson, 'Religious Orders, 1370–1540', p. 566.
[138] Harvey, *Living and Dying*, pp. 7–33; Haigh, *Reformation and Resistance*, pp. 120–21; Scarisbrick, *Reformation and the English People*, p. 51.

total annual income.[139] In contrast, the Benedictine monks of Tewkesbury, with an income in excess of £600 in the early sixteenth century, were said to have spent only £8 8s. 8d.[140] The greater, independent abbeys preferred to discharge their obligations through corrodies, which were often enjoyed by men of middle rank rather than genuine poor.[141] Probably it was in the north of England where there were few other charitable institutions that monastic almsgiving remained most active. It has been estimated that the Lancashire monasteries spent three times the national average on charitable activities.[142] Religious houses were also obliged to offer hospitality to all comers, which most continued to do, although as in their charitable efforts, they became ever more socially exclusive. There were some notably grand gestures towards potential guests: the monks of St Albans built a sumptuous royal suite alongside the conventual buildings; their counterparts at Selby also constructed a Royal Hall comprising some lavishly decorated chambers (complete with feather beds) and private gardens.[143] As Benjamin Thompson observes below, these efforts enabled a number of the larger, wealthier houses to re-establish their relationship with the traditional patrons on a new basis.[144]

Of course, even in the fifteenth and sixteenth centuries, religious houses interacted with the outside world on many other levels. They were major employers. There are few accurate figures for the numbers of servants supported by the monasteries and mendicant convents, but it may be that there were as many as two or three times the number of religious.[145] From the records of the 1535 Valor, it appears there were 144 servants at Tewkesbury Abbey, serving a monastic community of under forty.[146] The same source suggests that the servants outnumbered the monks at Winchcombe Abbey by almost ten-to-one.[147] A community's servants could include a wide variety of household attendants, craftsmen and unskilled labourers: the accounts of St Augustine's Abbey, Bristol even include a stipendiary mole-catcher.[148] Moreover, as Barbara Harvey has observed, the compotus rolls do not record the many other casual labourers and hangers-on who spent periods living and working in the precincts.[149] Probably, religious houses in less urbanized and more remote regions represented more in

---

[139] Tillotson, *Marrick Priory*, p. 21.
[140] Savine, *English Monasteries*, p. 235.
[141] Harvey, *Living and Dying*, pp. 179–90.
[142] Haigh, *Reformation and Resistance*, p. 120.
[143] For St Albans see *Gesta abbatum*, ed. Riley, ii. 282. For Selby see Tillotson, *Monastery and Society*, pp. 210, 250.
[144] See below pp. 180–3.
[145] Harvey, *Living and Dying*, p. 153.
[146] Savine, *English Monasteries*, p. 265.
[147] Savine, *English Monasteries*, p. 221.
[148] *The Compotus Rolls of St Augustine's Abbey, Bristol, for 1491–2 and 1511–12*, ed. G. Beachcraft and A. Sabin, Bristol Record Society 9 (1938), pp. 276–7.
[149] Harvey, *Living and Dying*, pp. 148–53.

commercial terms than merely a place of work. They must still have been magnets for tradesmen and a major market for consumer goods. Certainly they remained an important source of coinage: the Yorkshire monasteries were still offering banking facilities to their clients in the early sixteenth century.[150]

In fact it would be wrong to underestimate the extent to which monasteries and mendicant convents remained closely – and, in many cases, comfortably – integrated with the local lay community. In many urban areas the regulars managed to maintain remarkably good corporate relations. In his chapter Michael Robson describes how the Franciscans and the civic authorities of York co-operated with one another over matters of pastoral care and collaborated in the planning of public celebrations and processions. Their association is underlined with the example of Friar William Vavasour, who became a member of the city's Corpus Christi Guild and an executor of the wills of many prominent citizens. It was (perhaps increasingly) common for individual religious to form, like Vavasour, strong personal ties amongst the laity. In her study of bequests to women religious below, Marilyn Oliva has found that a growing number of nuns were named as beneficiaries, executors or supervisors of wills in the fifteenth and early sixteenth centuries.[151] John Tillotson has found a similar pattern in his study of Selby Abbey: the cellarer there even received legacies from the cloth merchants of York.[152]

Relations, of course, were not always harmonious. There were some conspicuous clashes. The abbot of Vale Royal was set upon and killed by a mob of local people in 1437.[153] In 1520 the abbey of Newnham in Devon was ransacked and the monks robbed of more than £600 by a crowd that included their own servants.[154] The older, independent abbeys, and especially the monastic boroughs, faced frequent (if less violent) challenges to their local power from tenants and townsmen with increasingly independent aspirations. Generally, the sources of dispute were the same as they ever had been, the title to land, the use of mills, the level of rents and tithes. There are comparatively few cases where these tensions brought an irrevocable breakdown in relations between the two communities. The townspeople of St Albans had rebelled repeatedly against the abbot and convent during the later Middle Ages, but when it came to the Dissolution they supported the monks and sought to restore the abbey.[155] Indeed in many places monastic and mendicant life still ran to the rhythm of the local community and religious and secular still came together for mutual support. During storms

[150] C. Cross, 'Monasticism and Society in the Diocese of York, 1520–40', *TRHS*, 5th Series 38 (1988), 131–45 at 137.
[151] See below p. 161.
[152] Tillotson, *Marrick Priory*, p. 54.
[153] Bostock and Hogg, *Vale Royal*, p. 6.
[154] Whiting, *Blind Devotion of the People*, p. 119.
[155] Clark, 'Reformation and Reaction', pp. 297–328.

the coastal houses of Cartmel, Cockersand and Coniston sounded their bells and lit fires to guide the fishing boats homeward.[156] Even as late as 1521 the parishioners of Reading rang the bells of their churches to join the monks in their mourning for their departed abbot.[157] Down to the Dissolution itself, the people of Redlingfield, Norfolk, relied on the bell of their priory church to mark the hours of their working day; there was no other timepiece.[158]

The key question is whether or not the monastic and mendicant orders also continued to occupy a place in the religious life of the laity. It should not be forgotten, of course, that the regulars were still directly involved in the ministry of the secular church. In the cathedral monasteries the priors regularly served as Vicar General, both in the bishop's absence and during a vacancy. In addition to those religious elevated to sees, there were many others who served as suffragans and some who held episcopal titles *in partibus infidelium* who conducted ordinations and other services.[159] It is difficult to say how many monks, regular canons and friars held benefices during the later Middle Ages but it does seem to have become common practice in some parts of the country. The Oxford theologian Thomas Gascoigne lamented in the 1440s that many people now only had access to baptism and other of the sacraments at the hands of the regulars.[160] Gascoigne himself was conscious of the number of parishes that had fallen into decline or even disappeared after the Black Death and there is no doubt that in more remote rural areas monastic and mendicant incumbents were not uncommon.[161] In pre-Reformation Lancashire no fewer than thirteen of the fifty-seven parishes were in the hands of the regulars.[162] Of course, it was a fundamental part of their mission for the friars to supplement the secular clergy in the parishes. But now the Black Canons and – to a lesser extent – the Black Monks also worked alongside them. Even where they did not provide an incumbent, these orders served as (generally) benevolent patrons of the churches under their jurisdiction, offering equipment (whether service books or vestments) and diverting their own resources towards the more substantial building repairs.

It is worth noting that the regulars' involvement in the life of the parish also extended to the plays, processions and other festival celebrations that punctuated the calendar. The drama cycles produced at fifteenth-century Bury St Edmunds were stage-managed – and, it has been suggested, were written – by the Benedictine monks of the abbey.[163] In the cathedral cities

[156] Haigh, *Reformation and Resistance*, p. 123.
[157] Brown, *Popular Piety*, p. 38.
[158] Oliva, *Convent and Community*, p. 149.
[159] Knowles, *Religious Orders*, ii. 369–75; Swanson, *Church and Society*, pp. 86–7.
[160] *Loci e libro veritatum*, ed. J. E. Thorold Rogers (Oxford, 1889), p. 171.
[161] It has been estimated that there was as many as 7% fewer parishes in England in 1530 than there had been around 1200.
[162] Haigh, *Reformation and Resistance*, p. 122.
[163] G. MacMurray Gibson, *Theater of Devotion: East Anglian Drama and Society in the Late Middle Ages* (Chicago and London, 1989), pp. 107–35; J. Griffiths, 'Thomas

and in other urban centres the regulars also joined with the secular clergy and the laity to mark the major feasts with processions and other public ceremonies. Some religious even involved themselves in their parishioners' own confraternities and guilds. The masters of the Luton confraternity were proud enough of the entrance of Robert Catton, abbot of St Albans, into their brotherhood that they depicted his admission on the opening leaf of their register.[164] Even in these activities, usually taken to be indicative of the growing independence of lay piety, the influence of the religious orders cannot be discounted.

Of course, the religious houses themselves, their churches, chapels, altars and shrines, also continued to occupy an important place in the devotional life of the laity. Even in 1500 the older monasteries could still claim a monopoly on popular relics. Canterbury (Benedictines) and Walsingham (Regular Canons) remained the most popular places of pilgrimage; the very last Jubilees of St Thomas at Canterbury in 1420 and 1470 were very successful.[165] The shrine of St Cuthbert tended by the monks of Durham Priory continued to command 'the hartes and prayers of alle the north'.[166] Their custody of powerful relics continued to bring supplicants even to the smallest communities. Even the lesser-known shrines still attracted a devoted following. The painted image of the Saviour Crucified in the possession of the nuns of Amesbury was still drawing pilgrims at the turn of the fifteenth century.[167] Such was the power of these places that some seem to have regarded the sanctity of martyrs and saints as a distinctly monastic phenomenon: it is interesting to note that the late medieval images in a Cambridgeshire church depict St Neot dressed in a Benedictine habit.

For some the monastic church was not simply a point of pilgrimage: it was the primary place of worship. For the permanent community of labourers, servants and other hangers-on, the precinct was their parish, and the nave of the conventual church, its side altars and adjoining chapels were the focal point of their devotions. For some people the absence of a functioning parish church left them no alternative but to make use of monastic facilities. In fifteenth-century Lancashire even some of the smallest priories were obliged to offer up their churches to the laity.[168] Co-habitation was also common in smaller towns where the historical ascendancy of the monastery had hindered the development of a parish structure. The monks of the priory at Dunster, in Somerset, not only shared their church with the laity, they

Hyngham, Monk of Bury, and the Macro Plays Manuscript', *English Manuscript Studies, 1100–1700*, 5 (1995), pp. 214–19.
[164] Bedford Record Office, Luton Fraternity Register, fols. 28r, 97r.
[165] See also Dobson, 'Canterbury in the Later Middle Ages', pp. 136, 140.
[166] Dobson, 'Cathedral Chapters and Cathedral Cities', p. 40.
[167] VCH Wilts., ii. 254.
[168] Such was the case for the priory churches at Cartmel and Holland in Lancashire. See Haigh, *Reformation and Resistance*, p. 122.

even allowed a dividing wall to be erected in the nave in 1498.[169] Of course, these arrangements were not always successful. Tensions between the monks and the townspeople of Sherborne in Dorset over the sharing of the abbey church became so great that in 1436 a mob burned the building to the ground. A similar dispute at Rochester required the arbitration of the archbishop of Canterbury, who ruled that each party should use a different entrance to the church to keep out of each other's way.[170]

The religious were conscious of the changing cultural and religious climate in which they lived and they made increasing efforts to make their precincts more palatable to lay worshippers. In his contribution below Glyn Coppack describes how the Cistercians at Fountains and Rievaulx adapted their churches to make them more accessible for and attuned to lay worshippers.[171] Their efforts are paralleled elsewhere. The Evesham monks even constructed a series of chapels for the use of the laity set into their perimeter walls. There was also much re-building (and re-launching) of monastic shrines. At Crowland the monks commissioned a new statue of their patron St Guthlac to be placed at the entrance to the abbey church. The Glastonbury monks preferred to entice the laity with miracle stories and other literature; they even mounted a series of boards bearing accounts of their foundation at the entrance to their church.[172]

Religious communities and their churches were not only the focus for occasional acts of conspicuous piety. They also continued to play a part – albeit, perhaps a diminishing one – in the everyday devotions of the laity. In spite of *Super cathedram*, the orders of the friars remained active in parish life as confessors and preachers as well as in other pastoral roles. Michael Robson has found that the York Franciscans still preached regularly in the city's churches and in the towns and villages in the vicinity. Even at the end of the fifteenth century, the townspeople of York still preferred to make their confession at one of the friars' churches, particularly during Lent.[173] The laity, especially in urban areas, also continued to look to the friars for assistance in their funeral rites. In fact testamentary evidence from the second half of the fifteenth century suggests they had become the single most popular choice for funeral-day prayers and for following the funeral procession. Friars – often several of them together – would lead the procession, suitably vested and carrying the cross. At York, they were

[169] K. L. French, *The People of the Parish: Community Life in a Late Medieval English Diocese* (Philadelphia, 2001), pp. 37–8.

[170] A. Oakley, 'Rochester Priory, 1185–1540', in *Faith and Fabric*, ed. Yates and Welby, pp. 30–55 at 35.

[171] See below pp. 200, 204, 206–7.

[172] For these efforts see J. G. Clark, 'Selling the Holy Places: Monastic Efforts to Win Back the People in Fifteenth-Century England', in *Social Attitudes and Political Structures in the Fifteenth Century*, ed. T. Thornton (Stroud, 2001), pp. 13–32 at 23–5.

[173] See below pp. 112–13.

sometimes even invited into the family house to keep a vigil by the body of the deceased.[174]

It seems there was less frequent recourse to the older monastic orders for services of this kind. The laity did continue to seek some spiritual assistance from the monasteries, but as Benjamin Thompson argues here, this was increasingly confined to immediate suffrages at the point of death rather than perpetual intercession or some other commemoration.[175] Moreover, many people now only turned to their nearby monastery for a one-off request of a token kind, often as part of a protective cordon of funeral-day prayers sought from a variety of religious institutions in the vicinity.[176] It was now only a minority who sought the spiritual support of their local monks all the way from the cradle to the grave.

Many of the spiritual services that the religious orders offered now merely duplicated those that were available in a parish context or elsewhere. But it would be wrong to suggest that there was now nothing in their religious observances that held a distinctive appeal to the devout layman. Many still sought a share in the spiritual benefits of a religious community through the privilege of confraternity. In his chapter below Robert Swanson shows how the promotion of confraternity became a crucial part of the friars' interaction with the laity in the later Middle Ages.[177] The larger monasteries also extended their provision for confrères in this period, turning it from an occasional honour conferred upon patrons into a living community of the faithful following the secular model. Also there were many who continued to value burial in the precincts of a religious community for its special spiritual rewards. In fifteenth-century York, the Grey Friars remained a popular burial-place for city notables.[178] Even in parts of East Anglia, where as Benjamin Thompson notes, many noble and gentry families now abandoned their original mausolea, the larger houses were still sought after for burials.[179]

Whether the promise of these and other services drew many people into a long-term – or even lifetime – benefaction of a religious house, however, must be doubted. It has been suggested that the traditional patrons of the monasteries – the noble and gentry families that for the most part had been their founders – had turned away from them by the beginning of the fifteenth century. Certainly there are signs of this in some regions where the rival attractions of a lively parish culture were considerable. Benjamin Thompson

---

[174] For York see Michael Robson's chapter below, p. 114. For similar trends elsewhere see J. Röhrkasten, 'London Mendicants in the Later Middle Ages', JEH 47 (1996), pp. 446–77 at 468–70.

[175] See below pp. 178–80.

[176] For examples of this in Warwickshire, Wiltshire and the south west see Scarisbrick, Reformation and the English People, pp. 42–8; Brown, Popular Piety, pp. 28–35; Whiting, Blind Devotion, pp. 55–7.

[177] See below pp. 121–54.

[178] See below pp. 115–16.

[179] Thompson gives the Cluniac priory at Thetford as an example, patronized down to the Dissolution by the dukes of Norfolk. See below p. 176.

has highlighted the number of Norfolk's smaller monasteries and priories that found themselves bereft of benefactors before 1500.[180] But this was not the trend everywhere. In the diocese of Salisbury the local elite remained conspicuous benefactors of the larger monasteries; the walls of the conventual church at Malmesbury were crowded with the blazons of great families including the Beauchamps, the Berkeleys, the Despensers and the Hungerfords.[181] There were even some noble families that continued to patronize monasteries to which they had no special connection other than the fact of their location within their own sphere of influence. Thus in the fifteenth century the Percies became energetic patrons and protectors of the Benedictine priory at Tynemouth.[182] Where traditional patrons did depart, it seems their place was often taken by benefactors of a lesser social position, such as urban men of business – the aldermen and burgesses – and even the more prosperous artisans and craftsmen. This may have been especially true of the great abbeys. The later pages of the St Albans Abbey *Liber benefactorum* (which continue down to 1512) are filled with the gifts of local landlords and merchants.[183] But there are also some signs of a similar trend in the benefaction of smaller houses. In her study of East Anglian nunneries, Marilyn Oliva has also found a marked rise in the number of benefactions received from the parochial gentry and yeoman families in the later fifteenth century.

When it came, the Dissolution removed religious communities that had continued for the most part to hold onto their traditions and retained in many respects an influential position in the local community. There is no doubt that in the two centuries before 1540 the communities of monks, friars, and nuns found themselves facing growing financial, political and social pressures. But these years were neither as dark nor as difficult for the religious orders as many earlier writers – beginning with the authors of the Reformation themselves – have led us to believe. The later Middle Ages was also a period of monastic reform, and it is likely that the efforts of the monastic General Chapters and the papacy proved successful in resolving some of the problems within the orders as well as restoring some degree of proper, uniform observance to many communities. In particular, the reforms of the late thirteenth and early fourteenth centuries ushered in a new age of monastic learning that amongst other achievements brought the Black Monks to the very forefront of academic life. There are also signs that for much of the period both monasteries and mendicant convents continued to enjoy a close relationship with the lay communities beyond their precinct walls. Their involvement in the devotions of the devout and increasingly

---

[180] Thompson, 'Monasteries and their Patrons', pp. 103–23.
[181] Brown, *Popular Piety*, p. 27.
[182] The extent of their benefactions is revealed in the *Liber benefactorum* of St Albans, the mother-house of Tynemouth.
[183] See BL, Cotton MS Nero D VII.

literate laymen may have diminished but they certainly did continue to play an important economic, educational and social role.

Given their place in pre-Reformation society, it is difficult to imagine how the men and women who served these communities came to be assimilated back into secular life after 1540. The fortunes of the ex-religious in sixteenth-century England still await a detailed study. In the final contribution here, Peter Cunich offers an original view of how some, if not all, may have struggled to come to terms with their loss.[184] Of course, one might also ask how English society as a whole adapted to the loss of nearly 900 religious houses so many of which remained active until the very end. There is no doubt that for many years the patterns of cultural, social and spiritual life in these places still bore the imprint of the communities that had themselves passed out of view.

[184] See below pp. 227–38.

After Knowles: Recent Perspectives in Monastic History

Joan Greatrex

In the last twenty years there has been an impressive increase of interest in the study of monastic history. Previously unexplored documentary sources have been yielding a wealth of information to a new generation of diligent students and scholars. We need only to glance at the works that have been published since the completion of Dom David Knowles's monumental four-volume history of the medieval English monastic and religious orders.[1] This remains a *sine qua non* for all students in the field because many of his conclusions still stand, even though they were by-and-large based on the printed sources then available to him. I have no doubt that he would gratefully acknowledge and welcome the fact that, while many sections of his narrative have been confirmed by later research, some can now be amplified and others qualified. He laid the foundations for subsequent studies which have, more recently, concentrated on individual orders, individual monasteries and specific aspects of the religious life.[2] Research and writing have advanced in the wake of the opening of new archives and of the continuing discoveries and identification of medieval manuscripts and muniments. Much original source material – charters, chronicles, episcopal *acta* and registers, and the works of medieval writers which were inaccessible to Knowles – has been edited and published. A monk himself, he was nonetheless objective in his approach to the history of his predecessors in whose tradition he stood. He could be highly critical of the monastic torpor that posed a recurring problem and deplored the decline of intellectual endeavour and the lack of saintly lives within the cloister during the last two centuries of English religious life. Forty years on the historian is perhaps more able to understand the late medieval monks and nuns who were increasingly affected by economic constraints, social unrest, and a new age in which material and secular interests were becoming dominant. With all of these the contemporary scene is familiar and stands in contrast to the more

[1] D. Knowles, *The Monastic Order in England: A History of its Development from the times of St Dunstan to the Fourth Lateran Council, 940–1216* (Cambridge, 1940); Knowles, *Religious Orders, passim.*

[2] For example, R. B. Dobson, *Durham Priory, 1400–1450* (Cambridge, 1973); B. Golding, *Gilbert of Sempringham and the Gilbertine Order, c.1130–c.1300* (Oxford, 1995); A. K. Warren, *Anchorites and their Patrons in Medieval England* (Berkeley, 1985).

confident and stable post-war era when Knowles was writing. He rightly castigates the falling away from strict obedience to the monastic rule and consequent de-spiritualization of monastic life but he seems to have failed to appreciate fully the impact of these external pressures on all aspects of daily life, both individual and collective, in the cloister.[3] Knowles wrote fluent and colourful prose, with an eloquence at times bordering on nostalgia, especially in his description of the highly charged events leading up to the Dissolution when, after several monks had been executed for refusal to surrender, the entire body of monks and nuns were turned out of their monasteries.[4]

The subtitle of Knowles's final volume of the trilogy, which appeared in 1959 was, surprisingly, 'The Tudor Age'. Its subject was the first half-century of monasticism under the early Tudor kings and Knowles was concerned to stress that these years should not be seen as the countdown to the Dissolution. The point he made in so doing continues to need emphasizing because much that was written before him, and that has been written since, has tended to assume, explicitly or implicitly, the inevitability of the final outcome. It is still easy to succumb to this false assumption that may unwittingly retain, hidden within it, a trace of unconscious personal prejudice from which none of us is entirely free. Knowles saw clearly that the Dissolution was not historically inevitable, that the years between 1485 and 1535 were not a period of 'decline and decay in an institution doomed to extinction through its own weaknesses and its failure to keep abreast of the times'.[5] Geoffrey Dickens thought otherwise; for him, with a few exceptions 'English monasticism was too old, too enfeebled, too forgotten to die violently amid dramatic passions'.[6] It must be admitted that the actual unfolding of events in the late 1530s seems to lend support to this view. Dickens was impressed by the 'decent individuals trying to operate a system which needed not merely organizational reform but a vast new influx of spiritual inspiration'.[7] Again, the apparent lack of any visible or active inspiration to bring about the revival of spiritual zeal would seem to confirm Dickens's conclusion.

However, more details of the mental and spiritual health of individual religious houses are gradually coming to light through recent research, and the complexity of the unfolding picture warns us to refrain from any hasty

---

[3] See Knowles, *Religious Orders*, ii. 354–64; iii. 456–68.

[4] Knowles's *Bare Ruined Choirs*, published posthumously in 1976, is an abridged, illustrated edition of the third volume of his *Religious Orders* series, aimed to appeal to a wider audience.

[5] H. O. Evenett, 'The Last Stages of Medieval Monasticism in England', *Studia Monastica* 2 (1960), pp. 387–419 at 388. This is a lengthy review article assessing Knowles's achievement on the completion of the four volumes.

[6] A. G. Dickens, 'The Register or Chronicle of Butley Priory, Suffolk, 1510–1535', in his *Late Monasticism and the Reformation* (London, 1994), pp. 1–84 at 23.

[7] Ibid., p. 12.

conclusions while the new evidence is still in the process of being gathered and collated. Nevertheless, it can be stated that what is beginning to emerge is a less negative appraisal than that provided by previous generations of historians and probably a somewhat more positive one than that of Knowles, at least with regard to the multitude of ordinary religious. What appears to me to be generally lacking from his impressive legacy to his successors in the field is the constant need to take into account that most monks and nuns have always been frail human beings, neither intellectually talented nor spiritually remarkable. This is not to be regretted since monastic communities living in accord with the Rule brook no distinction among their members: all are brothers and sisters in Christ; it is surely in this light that the historian must view them.

It should soon be possible to redress the balance of perspective, which until now has been unduly weighted against monks, nuns and canons, especially by the surviving episcopal visitation records of the fifteenth and sixteenth centuries. Although he resorted to them himself, Knowles was rightly sensitive in expressing regret that the historian should find it 'necessary to make any use at all of such intimate documents'.[8] The monks' depositions were given in private to the bishop or his deputy and there were severe penalties imposed on those who breached this confidentiality. It was a negative exercise for the sole purpose of detecting what was amiss within the community, many monks understandably seizing the opportunity to 'let off steam'. Irritation must often have been accentuated by the daily living in close proximity to one another, and some of the complaints to the ordinary were probably phrased in unnecessarily colourful terms. Moreover, it is not surprising that discrepancies appear among the deposition statements, as at Norwich in 1532 when two monks were described as university scholars while several other monks complained that none of their number were presently engaged in university studies.[9] Even an *omnia bene* on the part of deponents may be suspect in view of the possibility that, for one reason or another, some may have been reluctant to speak out. The reports of the monks are available for us to read and they cannot be ignored, but their interpretation is fraught with difficulty. One thing is fairly certain, however: anyone who immerses himself or herself in Hamilton Thompson's *Visitations of Religious Houses in the Diocese of Lincoln* for more than an hour at a stretch will become sorely depressed in being subjected to human beings revealing themselves as all too human for our comfort.[10]

[8] Knowles, *Religious Orders*, i. 84.
[9] *Visitations of the Diocese of Norwich, AD. 1492–1532*, ed. A. Jessopp, Camden Society, New Series 43 (1888), pp. 264, 266–7. It is true, of course, that contradictions relating to opinions are more frequent than those relating to fact, but the latter may be due to faulty copying or to misunderstanding about the period of time under inquiry.
[10] See A. H. Thompson's *Visitations of Religious Houses in the Diocese of Lincoln, I. AD. 1420–1436* (1915); *II. AD 1436–1449* (1919), *III. AD 1436–1449* (1927); *Visitations in*

It is true that any evidence to support continuing or renewed vitality in some sixteenth-century religious communities is offset by evidence of a decrease in discipline and fervour among the members of other communities, and this rules out the presence of any sustained, concerted attempts on the part of the orders themselves to initiate and implement programmes of reform. However, if even a noticeable number of young men and women were choosing to enter religious life at this time, when new possibilities were opening up to appeal to those who were considering secular careers, then, the attraction and the call were still recognizable forces in sixteenth-century society. Eamon Duffy has produced convincing evidence that the 'fifteenth and early sixteenth centuries in England witnessed a period of massive catechetical enterprise on the part not only of the bishops and parochial clergy, whose responsibility it mainly was, but also on the part of members of religious orders'.[11] Duffy's statement concerning the involvement of the religious orders might serve as an invitation to someone to take up this important theme which, apart from some recent research on Syon Abbey, has not received the attention it deserves.

It may be helpful to illustrate my point concerning the contrast in the conditions that prevailed in different houses. A few examples will be sufficient to show that only after much further study of the orders, and especially of individual monasteries, will it be possible to obtain a clearer, more accurate general assessment of the religious life of early Tudor England.

In his chapter on the monks of Christ Church, in the recently published volume on the history of Canterbury Cathedral, Barrie Dobson noted the gradual breakdown of community life which the growing apprehension and uncertainty, caused by the stepping up of state interference in the priory's internal affairs, only served to aggravate.[12] At York, on the other hand, among the four houses of friars, Dobson found a high level of performance in the preaching and writing activities to which their orders were dedicated. He also found evidence of the continuing respect and rapport enjoyed by the friars among York citizens as shown by the increase of bequests made to them in the 1530s.[13] The Christ Church monks derived similar benefits from good relations with their neighbours in the sixteenth century if we may judge by

the Diocese of Lincoln, 1517–1531 (3 vols., 1944–47). These are all publications of the Lincoln Record Society and the first three volumes are joint publications with the Canterbury and York Society.

[11] E. Duffy, The Stripping of the Altars: Traditional Religion in England, 1400–1580 (New Haven and London, 1992), 2–3.

[12] R. B. Dobson, 'The Monks of Canterbury in the Later Middle Ages', in A History of Canterbury Cathedral, ed. P. Collinson, N. Ramsay and M. Sparks (Oxford, 1995), pp. 69–153 at 150–53.

[13] R. B. Dobson, 'Mendicant Ideal and Practice in Late Medieval York', in Archaeological Papers from York presented to M. W. Barley, ed. P. V. Addyman and V. E. Black (York, 1984), pp. 109–22 at 116–20.

the frequent additions to the priory confraternity lists.[14] Conditions at St Mary's Worcester appear to have been more depressing than at Canterbury; the dissensions and divisions increased after the monks were directed to refer all their grievances to the secular authorities in accordance with the Act of Supremacy, and especially after they were forced to submit to the rigged election of the careerist monk of Crowland, Henry Holbech, as prior in 1536.[15] In contrast, Robert Dunning has detected signs of a late increase in the number of monks at Glastonbury, as I have at Ely in the mid-1530s.[16] It is also to be noted that Donald Logan has cautiously suggested that the lamentable state of Ramsey Abbey revealed in early sixteenth-century episcopal visitations may have shown some signs of improvement with the result that in 1530 a more regular, though still spiritually uninspired, community life appears to have been in place; the number of monks had risen and there were six novices.[17]

The enlargement of the monastic landscape between the eleventh and thirteenth centuries made it necessary for a series of adjustments as new and old orders, and their individual religious establishments scattered over the length and breadth of the land, learned to live on amicable terms and to co-operate with one another. Neither the tale of the extent to which this was achieved nor of how it was achieved, especially at the local level, has yet been fully investigated. There is indeed a growing body of evidence to suggest that there was more co-operation and less confrontation than has sometimes been imagined in the light of a few colourful instances, such as the ones recounted by Matthew Paris and the pulpit rivalry between Black Monks and Grey Friars about which the prior of Norwich complained in c.1360.[18] Franciscan lectors at Christ Church Canterbury in the late thirteenth and early fourteenth centuries are proof of the respect in which they were held by the monks who put them in charge of teaching their novices.[19] The loan and exchange of books furnish other examples of cordial relations as indicated by the gift of a fifteenth-century Norwich Carmelite

[14] BL, Arundel MS 68, fols. 1–9v.

[15] Greatrex, *BRECP*, p. 761 gives a brief summary of the election, and ibid., 824 some biographical details of Holbech.

[16] R. W. Dunning, 'Revival at Glastonbury 1530–39', in *Renaissance and Renewal in Christian History*, ed. D. Baker, Studies in Church History 14 (1977), pp. 213–22 at 219–22.

[17] F. D. Logan, 'Ramsey Abbey: The Last Days and After', in *The Salt of Common Life: Individuality and Choice in the Medieval Town, Countryside and Church. Essays Presented to J. Ambrose Raftis*, ed. E. de Windt, Studies in Medieval Culture 36 (Kalamazoo, 1995), pp. 513–45 at 535.

[18] For example, Matthew Paris's *Chronica Majora*, ed. H. R. Luard, 7 vols., Rolls Series 57 (1872–83), iv. 280, 660, 688, 695; also W. R. Thomson, 'The Image of the Mendicants in the Chronicles of Matthew Paris', *Archivum Franciscanum Historicum* 70 (1977), pp. 3–34. The Norwich complaint occurs in a letter printed in *Chapters*, ed. Pantin, iii. 28.

[19] W. A. Pantin, *Canterbury College, Oxford. IV*, Oxford Historical Society, New Series 30 (1985), p. 3.

author who dedicated his history of the Carmelite order to a *dilectissimo* monk friend in the cathedral priory of that city.[20]

All through the century and a half that preceded the Dissolution English men and women were entering monasteries and convents and living out their very ordinary, even humdrum lives, to a greater or lesser degree in accordance with the Rule to which they were subject. Ordinary people lack the colour, the drama and the magnetic attraction that surround the lives of the rare breed recognized as heroes and saints; but with all their faults they are the backbone of their communities, secular and religious. It is encouraging to know that now at last scholars have begun to investigate the latter *in situ* and to judge them on their own terms, as they were seen by their fellow monks and nuns, by their friends and other contemporaries. Take, for example, Thomas Wyking, monk of Christ Church Canterbury who, after his death in 1407, was remembered by his brethren as 'honest-issimus et purus tam in corpore quam in mente et habitu', a man who promoted peace and concord in the community and did not permit any grievance to linger without reconciliation.[21] There is also Thomas Chart I, another monk of Christ Church until his death in 1448: he was described as 'vir religiosus . . . pius, hillaris, largus, singulisque affabilis'.[22] And finally Richard Godmersham II, who died at Christ Church in 1468, where he too had been 'ab omnibus multum dilectus'.[23] Obituaries tend to present a rather more favourable view than might have been forthcoming, say, at a visitation; but they should not be underestimated in recording the community's collective appreciation of the special qualities of some of their brethren.

One of the problems that concerned the monastic orders in the fifteenth and early sixteenth centuries was the extent and effect of their involvement in university studies. The curriculum in theology, which had been built up on scholastic foundations, was directed toward the exercise of the intellect rather than to the deepening of the understanding, involving both mind and heart, that was at the centre of the monastic commitment. A Worcester monk student's notebook reveals that the tension was felt and the issue debated in the 1430s and 1440s when he jotted down the outline of a *disputatio*: the subject was whether or not it was right for a monk to leave the cloister for the purpose of achieving a doctorate in theology.[24] No such problem existed for the friars, all of whom accepted the importance of study; Grosseteste had early on warned the Franciscans that 'if they did not study they would quickly degenerate and become like the other orders who were

---

[20] This reference was kindly passed on to me by Richard Copsey, O.Carm. The Norwich monk was John Blakeneye, q.v. in Greatrex, *BRECP*, p. 484 and the manuscript is now Cambridge University Library, MS Ff.6.11.
[21] Greatrex, *BRECP*, pp. 328–9.
[22] Ibid., p. 112.
[23] Ibid., p. 171.
[24] Oxford, Bodl. MS 692, fol. 6; I owe this reference to Dr James Clark.

walking in darkness'.[25] Not until the early sixteenth century, among Benedictines, is there any indication of a revival of traditional monastic studies centred on the cloister. When Abbot Kidderminster of Winchcombe set up his 'altera nova universitas' within the abbey, was he setting a new trend that might have been followed by other communities if their demise had not come so soon?[26]

It is good news that the contents of monastic libraries, through their surviving manuscript volumes, early printed works and the medieval library catalogues, are currently being subjected to exhaustive scrutiny. Some of the catalogues contain extensive lists of the medieval holdings including many works that have since been lost. The medieval custom of binding together several, even many, often disparate and incomplete items means that each one must be identified and its relationship to other copies of the same work traced. This scholarly undertaking will at last make available details of the reference works for biblical and theological studies, handbooks for pastoral activity, devotional treatises, canon-law texts and commentaries, grammatical and literary works and volumes devoted to history. The presentation of this material will then permit those with the appropriate expertise to make realistic assessments of the breadth and depth of monastic studies possible within the cloister.[27]

A far reaching and constant concern, in which all late medieval religious orders were willingly or unwillingly involved, was that of their relations with the ecclesiastical establishment and the Crown. In the late fourteenth and, increasingly, in the fifteenth century, critics of the clerical and religious orders called for reform within the English church and, among the ecclesiastical hierarchy and literate laity, there was growing support for the Lancastrian and Tudor programme to extend the royal supremacy over the church.[28] In 1371 two Austin friars made a brief alliance with the lay lords who were calling on the church to share in the financial burden laid upon the laity by the renewal of the war with France.[29] Any further

[25] M. Sheehan, 'The Religious Orders, 1220–1370', in *The History of the University of Oxford I. The Early Oxford Schools*, ed. J. I. Catto (Oxford, 1992), pp. 193–221 at 197. For Grosseteste, of course, study meant biblical study and not the sophisticated subtleties of theological disputation.

[26] See the article by W. A. Pantin, 'Abbot Kidderminster and Monastic Studies', *Downside Review* 47 (New Series 28) (1929), pp. 198–211.

[27] I refer to the Corpus of British Medieval Library Catalogues (British Library and British Academy) now in progress which includes catalogues of all the major religious houses, and to the catalogues of surviving books, such as the one by Rodney Thomson of the manuscripts formerly in the library of Worcester Cathedral Priory; *A Descriptive Catalogue of the Medieval Manuscripts in Worcester Cathedral Library* (Cambridge, 2001).

[28] See J. Catto, 'Religious Change under Henry V', in *Henry V: The Practice of Kingship*, ed. G. L. Harriss (Oxford, 1985), pp. 97–115; also R. N. Swanson, *Church and Society in Late Medieval England*, rev edn. (Oxford, 1993), pp. 312–43.

[29] A. Gwynn, *The English Austin Friars in the Time of Wyclif* (Oxford, 1940), pp. 212–16.

indictment of the church's wealth on the part of the religious soon evaporated, however, when the subversive views of John Wyclif became public. His political writings gave a boost to the anti-clerical party but his radical theological opinions were unacceptable to all members of religious orders.[30] To my knowledge the political opinions of the English religious orders and their members, and their involvement in political affairs in the late fourteenth and fifteenth centuries, have not been singled out for prolonged examination; it would surely prove a fruitful subject for a doctoral thesis or a scholarly monograph.

While Knowles gave high marks to the St Albans Abbot Thomas de la Mare for his reforming zeal, exercised during his long presidency of the Benedictine Provincial Chapter and within his own community and its dependencies, he found no further evidence of reform coming from within the order before Henry V, on his victorious return from France, summoned the Black Monks to Westminster.[31] The King's motives in 1421 were undoubtedly mixed, a combination of personal piety and practical politics; and in the case of the Benedictines he considered himself and his royal forebears as founders and patrons of their ancient monasteries. To the assembly of more than 350 monks and prelates Henry expressed his deep concern that the monastic zeal of earlier days had become lukewarm and devotion had given way to negligence.[32]

Who were the King's advisers in this matter and whose influence was at work behind the scenes? Possibly his Carmelite confessors Thomas Netter and Stephen Patrington, and very probably Robert Layton, prior of the Carthusian house of Mount Grace and a former Benedictine.[33] This would help to explain Layton's presence at Westminster as one of three royal delegates appointed to discuss the King's articles of reform with a committee of six monks elected from among themselves.[34] The King's articles are similar in form and content to a series of episcopal injunctions following visitation, with the aim of raising the standard of regular life and discipline in practical matters such as those relating to private property, clothing, diet, blood-letting, sleeping arrangements and the like without reference to the instruction of novices, biblical study, lectio divina or interior dispositions commended by the Rule. In their response the monks succeeded in watering down many of the articles before agreeing to accept a much revised

---

[30] Ibid., p. 233.

[31] See Knowles, Religious Orders, ii. 41–8 for details of De la Mare's career.

[32] Ibid., ii. 182–4 and Chapters, ed. Pantin, ii. 98–9.

[33] For Netter and a summary of his teaching and preaching in defence of orthodoxy against Wyclif and the Lollards see Emden, BRUO, ii. 1343–4 and for Patrington, ibid., iii. 1435–6; the latter, however, died in 1417 and was succeeded by a Dominican, William Dyss, recommended by Archbishop Chichele: Original Letters, ed. H. Ellis (3 vols., London, 1824–46), i. 3–5. Layton is referred to by Knowles, Religious Orders, ii. 182 and Chapters, ed. Pantin, ii. 98.

[34] Chapters, ed. Pantin, ii. 99–100.

document.[35] This was an interesting and unusual precedent of which the outcome might have been more lasting had Henry survived. In the event it may well have had the effect of arousing an instinctive resistance to any further proposals of reform from any outside quarter.

There were more enduring and more fruitful results from another project of Henry V during his brief reign, namely that of the foundation of two new religious houses. One was the Carthusian house at Sheen, and the other the first Brigittine monastery in England, that of Syon.[36] Originating in Sweden the latter, like the Gilbertine monasteries, had been set up as a double order, for both men and women. The libraries at Syon housed an impressively large collection of both manuscripts and printed books; those of the brothers mainly in Latin, of the sisters in English. They were acquired through gift and purchase over the century and a quarter of the abbey's existence.[37] During this time Syon continued to attract university educated men and well born women, setting an example of strict observance and unflagging fervour within its enclosure. Despite the large size of the community, its influential connections and its royal foundation and patronage, it succumbed in 1539, although not without some spirited resistance.[38] Here there was neither decline nor reform; however, its vulnerability during its final crisis was possibly accentuated by its isolation as the only house of its order in the country. With regard to the present state of research on Syon I would venture to suggest that the time is ripe for a prosopographical study of the community. Individual members and some of their activities and writings have been the subject of scholarly articles; however, their place among their brothers and sisters within the context of their community life will not be adequately understood without a reconstruction of the monastic personnel. There is surely sufficient, if not abundant, evidence for such a study. To mention only one class of records that should prove informative, there are over 150 accounts of nun obedientiaries of which only a few of those of the sacrist and chambress, to my knowledge, have received notice.[39]

[35] The articles, the monks' response and the final modifications which they accepted are transcribed in *Chapters*, ed. Pantin, ii. 109–34.
[36] Knowles, *Religious Orders*, ii. 176–82.
[37] C. F. R. de Hamel, *Syon Abbey, The Library of the Bridgettine Nuns and their Peregrinations after the Reformation* (London, 1991), and J. T. Rhodes, 'Syon Abbey and its Religious Publications in the Sixteenth Century', *JEH* 44 (1993), pp. 11–25. See also Vincent Gillespie's contribution below, pp. 75–95.
[38] There were over seventy monks and nuns at the suppression; only Bury St Edmunds and Christ Church Canterbury were comparable in numbers. Knowles recounts the details leading up to its suppression in his *Religious Orders*, iii. 216–21.
[39] See M. C. Erler, 'Syon Abbey's Care for Books: Its Sacristan's Account Rolls, 1506/7–1535/6', *Scriptorium* 39 (1985), pp. 293–307. See also the lists in PRO, Ministers' Accounts (SC. 6) vol. 34 which also includes accounts of the abbess, treasuress, and cellaress temp. Henry VII and Henry VIII. It is possible that this particular source may not yield many names of nuns beyond those of the accounting officer. Attention should also be drawn to the more recent article by Ann Hutchison, 'What the Nuns Read: Literary Evidence from the English Bridgettine House, Syon Abbey', *Medieval*

The inner state of the Cistercian houses in England in the fifteenth century is not easily gauged. As exempt houses they were not obliged to undergo episcopal visitation but as subject to the central authority of the abbot of Cîteaux and the General Chapter they were visited at regular intervals by an appointed commissary or, more rarely, by the abbot himself. While few surviving records of visitation proceedings have been found to date there is hope of more being discovered in unexpected places, like the details in the so-called register of Hailes Abbey which Christopher Harper-Bill found and examined twenty years ago.[40] There is additional information in a collection of letters from the English abbots to the chapter at Cîteaux between 1442 and 1521, some of which provide colourful first-hand reports of the difficulties encountered in attempting to implement reform at the local level.[41] In the 1480s when the correction of abuses from within proved ineffective and the abbot of Cîteaux was distracted by the internal dissension between Cîteaux and Clairvaux, both the archbishops of Canterbury and York sought and obtained papal bulls authorizing them to carry out visitations of Cistercian and other exempt houses for purposes of much needed reform.[42] In the judgement of C. H. Talbot, the editor of the correspondence, the letters of the English abbots to their superiors at Cîteaux, when taken as a whole, show that 'the general level of monastic observance seems to have been pedestrian rather than bad or relaxed' because of 'a general inertia, itself due to a departure from the vital and fundamental principles of the Rule'.[43] Derek Baker's assessment is equally positive. He suggests that 'the English Cistercian community had within itself the possibilities and potential for decisive change and growth based upon a rediscovery and reapplication of past glories and standards, and a renewed expression of earlier spiritual values and teaching again in vogue'.[44]

In reviving and strengthening royal control over all sections of the church including the religious orders the first two Tudor monarchs, like their Lancastrian predecessor, were aware that they required not only the prayers of its members but active support as well. To this end they considered it their responsibility to ensure that standards of devotion and regular observance

Studies 57 (1995), pp. 205–22. A list of nuns present at the election of an abbess in 1518 has been preserved and would provide a useful base on which to construct a prosopographical study; see ibid., p. 214, n. 44.

[40] C. Harper-Bill, 'Cistercian Visitation in the Late Middle Ages: The Case of Hailes Abbey', BIHR 53 (1980), pp. 103–14.

[41] C. H. Talbot, Letters from the English Abbots to the Chapter at Cîteaux, 1442–1521, Camden Society, 4th Series 4 (1967).

[42] Talbot, Letters, pp. 7–9. See also A. Goodman, 'Henry VII and Christian Renewal', in Religion and Humanism, ed. K. Robbins, Studies in Church History 17 (1981), pp. 115–25 at 117.

[43] Talbot, Letters, p. 15.

[44] D. Baker, 'Old Wine in New Bottles: Attitudes to Reform in Fifteenth-Century England', in Renaissance and Renewal, ed. Baker, Studies in Church History 14 (1977), pp. 193–211 at 210–11.

were maintained in all religious houses and they were mainly successful in nominating reforming bishops to carry out the royal policies. Again, following the example of Henry V, Henry VII introduced into England a new religious order or, rather, a reformed wing of the Franciscan order known as Observants, that had emerged in northern Europe at the end of the fourteenth century. As in the case of the Carthusians and Brigittines the Observants attracted late vocations, men who had already achieved academic standing and whose members retained close connections with the royal court. However, when the King's divorce and the Act of Supremacy severed England's ties with the papacy, they refused to disavow their obedience to the pope. Their houses were at once suppressed and they were forced to flee abroad.[45]

One of the major areas in which there has been a significant advance in research since Knowles's day is that of the study of women religious. In his four volumes there are less than fifteen pages devoted to nuns, with a few additional passing references to individual houses; and he includes Eileen Powers's *Medieval English Nunneries* (1922) only once, in the bibliography of his first volume.[46] While undoubtedly most informative in its groundbreaking coverage of two and a half centuries, her book in retrospect is heavily marked by the influence of G. G. Coulton and by Hamilton Thompson's *Visitations*. To be fair, although her chapter on 'the machinery of reform' is replete with vivid incidents of nuns' reported misdemeanours, her concluding remarks are restrained and limited to the observation that the main problems were due to 'a growing worldliness and to minor breaches of the rule'.[47]

Miss Power made use of the writings and registers of several of the reforming Tudor bishops mentioned above whose practical concern for the nuns in their respective dioceses has recently attracted renewed attention. Bishop Fox at Winchester, for example, produced and published in 1517 a vernacular translation of the Rule of St Benet; he inserted additional commentary of his own to ensure that the nuns were able to understand what they professed, to put it into practice, to read it daily and teach it to their sisters.[48] Equally attentive to the needs of his nuns, John Alcock, during his tenure of the see of Ely (1486–1500), delivered a sermon at a profession ceremony in an unnamed convent; it too was soon in print,

---

[45] See Knowles, *Religious Orders*, iii. 206–11. See also K. Brown, 'Wolsey and Ecclesiastical Order: The Case of the Franciscan Observants', in *Cardinal Wolsey, Church, State and Art*, ed. S. J. Gunn and P. G. Lindley (Cambridge, 1991), pp. 219–38.

[46] Knowles, *Monastic Order*, p. 740.

[47] E. Power, *Medieval English Nunneries* (Cambridge, 1926), p. 498.

[48] For details of Fox's translation and of his concern for the welfare of the three nunneries in his diocese see Greatrex, 'On Ministering to "Certayne Devoute and Religiouse Women": Bishop Fox and the Benedictine Nuns of Winchester Diocese on the Eve of the Dissolution', in *Women and the Church*, ed. W. J. Sheils and D. Wood, Studies in Church History 27 (1990), pp. 223–35.

entitled the *Spousage of a Virgin to Christ*.[49] He solemnly warned his hearers that 'this spousage must be . . . desyred with all your hole herte and free wyll' and advised them to love Christ, their spouse above all things: 'he must be in your mynde, in your soule, in your herte and in all your werkes'.[50] His simple but moving phrases expressed the ideal to which the nuns were called. The visitation records depict the frequent betrayal of that ideal. It would be wrong, however, to suppose that the ideal was no longer alive; it would be closer to the truth to recognize that human nature lives in a state of perpetual tension between the two, the ideal and the reality.

Research and writings on late medieval women religious have experienced a quickening in pace and an expansion in scope in the last decade. Studies of individual houses and groups of houses have resulted in monographs, articles and unpublished theses exploring an impressive variety of themes: these include economic organization and estate management; family connections; patrons and benefactors; monastic art and architecture; intellectual pursuits, attainment and writings; prosopographical analyses; and the contrasts in conditions pertaining within male and female houses. These same themes apply also with regard to the research currently being pursued in the study of the religious houses and orders of men. Thanks to the *Monastic Research Bulletin* we are kept informed of new publications and research projects, and of the scholars and students involved.

Exercising his legatine powers of visitation, Cardinal Wolsey issued a set of constitutions for the Augustinian canons in 1519; and after a meeting with the Black Monks at Westminster in 1521, he prepared statutes for them.[51] These aroused vigorous objections from the monks on the grounds of their severity, as if Benedictines were to be identified with Carthusians, Brigittines or Observants; if the statutes were enforced, the monks argued, vocations would dry up.[52] There is more truth in their statement than they may have realized. The weakness in the Benedictine Rule, what differentiates it from the rules of the three orders named, lies in the breadth of its appeal, for it addresses and welcomes not only the contemplative, the mystic and the hermit but also the stumbling plodder willing to persevere.

In order to find and then listen to the voices of religious men and women in late medieval England we need to read more intently what they read and wrote, to hear the music with which they were familiar and to look more closely at what they beheld and contemplated: the paintings, sculpture and stained glass which encapsulated images of their view of the world and of

---

[49] John Alcock, *Desponsacio virginis Christo*, printed in English by Wynkyn de Worde at Westminster in 1498 (STC 286). It has recently been reprinted in facsimile as no. 638 in the series *The English Experience* (Amsterdam, 1974). I am grateful to Dr Yvonne Parrey for drawing my attention to this work.

[50] Ibid., A.ijr, A.iijr.

[51] *Chapters*, ed. Pantin, iii. 117–22 and Knowles, *Religious Orders*, iii. 158–60.

[52] *Chapters*, ed. Pantin, iii. 123–4.

RECENT PERSPECTIVES IN MONASTIC HISTORY

their place in it.[53] In order to find and better understand these men and women we also need to know them by name as individuals in so far as this is possible. The prosopographical method with its quantitative approach is particularly applicable to the investigation of a single religious order and individual religious houses or groups of houses within a specific area. Computer databases are already being used in such projects and will soon greatly facilitate our researches.[54]

Finally, we must bear in mind that opinions expressed about the religious by their contemporaries varied, and that the same individual could and did hold apparently contradictory views. Erasmus's berating of the monks and nuns of his day for elevating their man-made rules above the precepts of the Gospel, for example, should be tempered by his statement in a letter to the Minoresses at Denney where he described them as the 'blessed Virgins who, dead to the world, already on earth spend their life as though in heaven'.[55]

The effect of post-modernism has been to remove past certainties about the nature and study of history, even about the possibility of historical knowledge itself in terms of objectivity and fact. In consequence, we should all be aware that in reconstructing the past we are at the same time constructing it. What we dare to hope is that if we avoid the perils of Scylla and Charybdis, that is, of neither overstressing nor ignoring the failings of the religious orders, our constructions will come ever closer to the truth. Our ultimate responsibility as monastic historians is to those long-dead monks and nuns; in the words of Eleanor Searle, in her presidential address to the Medieval Academy of America, we must 'try to "get them right" as far as we can'.[56]

---

[53] The bibliography for these areas of monastic research is continuing to lengthen at an impressive rate. See especially D. Bell, *What Nuns Read: Books and Libraries in Medieval English Nunneries* (Kalamazoo, MN, and Spencer, MA, 1995). See also the references in Vincent Gillespie's contribution below pp. 75–95. Some of the monographs regularly produced by the British Archaeological Association Transactions are devoted to the works of art, the architecture and archaeology of cathedral priories and other religious houses; they provide a wealth of information on the state of recent research.

[54] Dr Peter Cunich is currently working on a monastic database for England and Wales in the sixteenth century and a biographical register of ex-religious in England and Wales c.1530–1603.

[55] This is letter no. 1925 in *Opus epistolarum Des. Erasmi Roterodami*, ed. P. S. and H. M. Allen (12 vols., Oxford, 1928) where only a short extract has been printed. It is given in full by S. Knight in Appendix XVIII of *The Life of Erasmus* (Cambridge, 1726), xlvi–lviii. Written in Latin, it takes the form of a sermon, exhorting the abbess and her nuns to strive for purity of heart and to support the church with their prayers. The phrase is on liv: 'o beatae virgines, quae, saeculo mortuae, jam in terris caelestem quodammodo vitam agitis', and continues '& abditae cum sponso Christo deliciamini'.

[56] E. Searle, 'Possible History', *Speculum* 61 (1986), pp. 779–86 at 779. I have taken the liberty of substituting the plural 'we' for her 'I' in the quotation. See also G. Spiegel, 'History and Postmodernism', in *The Postmodern History Reader*, ed. K. Jenkins (London, 1997), pp. 260–73, esp. 261–2.

Education and Learning

A Novice's Life at Westminster Abbey in the Century before the Dissolution

BARBARA HARVEY

It is widely agreed that the Benedictine noviciate in the Middle Ages contained little of the specific training in spiritual life and rigorous testing of vocation characteristic of noviciates in the post-Tridentine world. During the time of probation, from clothing to profession, and in the subsequent period when he was still in custody or under tutelage, the medieval novice was instructed in the complexities of the Divine Service and the customs of the monastery and learnt how to behave in choir, chapter, refectory and dormitory. He would indeed be introduced to works encouraging him to shun evil and turn towards what was good. But our sources suggest that the emphasis among the Benedictines was more often on the externals of behaviour than on religious observance in a deeper sense.[1] And when, with the decline of memory work in the years around 1300, some of these traditional employments demanded less time, the novice trod the lower slopes of the primitive sciences – grammar, logic, and philosophy – and, in the larger houses, even those of theology, in a programme of studies that he might one day be permitted to carry further at a university. Both before and

I gratefully acknowledge the permission of the Dean and Chapter of Westminster to use their muniments and the help received from Dr Richard Mortimer, the Keeper of the Muniments, Miss Christine Reynolds, Assistant Keeper, and Dr Tony Trowles, Librarian. I am greatly indebted to Dr James Clark who has generously shared with me his knowledge of the Benedictine noviciate in the later Middle Ages, and of custody in particular; and I owe many debts of a scholarly kind, relating to the subject-matter of this article, to Professor Joan Greatrex.

In the text and footnotes of this article, the year of account beginning on 29 September is often in use. Thus 1440–41 = 29 September 1440 to 28 September 1441.

[1] *Chapters*, ed. Pantin, i. 38; ii. 49–50; *Visitations of Religious Houses in the Diocese of Lincoln*, ed. A. H. Thompson, 3 vols., Canterbury and York Society, 17, 24, 33 (3 vols., 1915–27), i. 56; *Customary of the Benedictine Abbey of Eynsham in Oxfordshire*, ed. A. Gransden, Corpus Consuetudinum Monasticarum 2 (1963), pp. 43–57 (a text including vivid instructions for novices on how to expectorate). For succinct comment, see Knowles, *Religious Orders*, ii. 232–3. The fundamental text is *The Rule of St Benedict* (henceforward RB), cap. 58. For the novices' reading at Durham in the early fifteenth century, see R. B. Dobson, *Durham Priory, 1400–1450* (Cambridge, 1973), pp. 67–8; and in a Rhineland context in the same period, *Consuetudines et observantiae monasteriorum Sancti Mathiae et Sancti Maximini Treverensium ab Johanne Rode abbate conscriptae*, ed. P. Becker, Corpus Consuetudinum Monasticarum 5 (1968), p. 182.

after this change in the syllabus of the cloister school, he participated in the Divine Service with a regularity that might never be required of him again and was expected to observe other parts of the Rule with a fidelity no longer demanded of fully fledged members of the community. Ahead – unless he was already a priest at the time of his conversion to the monastic life – lay ordination to the priesthood, and it is also widely agreed that this great event signified the end of the entire period in custody. The *Rites of Durham* place it seven years after profession, but in practice both at Durham Cathedral Priory and elsewhere the interval in the later Middle Ages was now normally shorter: at Christ Church, Canterbury, it was four or five years.[2]

For a different conception of the noviciate, we can look not only to the post-Tridentine orders, including the Benedictines themselves in that period, but also to the Franciscans, who, having been in the first instance compelled by Honorius III to make use of a noviciate, subsequently explored the possibilities of the months of probation as a period of intense spiritual formation in which a scholar never looked at his books and other kinds of professional training had no part. It was at the next stage that the newly professed Franciscan prepared specifically for his apostolate in the world; but at both stages the goal for the individual was perfection of life.[3] David of Augsburg (1200 × 1210–1272), who was master of the Franciscan novices at Ratisbon and widely read outside as well as within Franciscan circles, especially in Germany and eastern Europe, wrote, and no doubt spoke, of two noviciates, both dominated by the search for perfection. One of the two, he explained in his *Formula noviciorum*, ends with the promise of obedience and stability in the religious life made at profession; the second, only when the novice is able to show in deeds as well as words that there will be no wavering, but constancy in his pursuit of spiritual progress. Then, with his whole being devoted to the love of God, great will be his part in the harvest of souls; and to an observant novice, David of Augsburg held out promise of this consummation in the fifth year.[4]

[2] *Rites of Durham . . . written 1593*, ed. J. T. Fowler, Surtees Society 107 (1903), p. 96; Dobson, *Durham Priory*, p. 63; idem, 'The Monks of Canterbury in the Later Middle Ages, 1220–1540', in *History of Canterbury Cathedral*, ed. P. Collinson, N. Ramsay and M. Sparks (Oxford, 1995), p. 123.

[3] M. Bihl ed., 'Statuta Generalia Ordinis, edita in Capitulis generalibus celebratis Narbonae, an. 1260, Assisii an. 1279 atque Parisiis an. 1292', *Archivum Franciscanum Historicum* 34 (1941), pp. 13–94 at 40; J. H. Moorman, *History of the Franciscan Order from its Origins to the Year 1517* (Oxford, 1968), pp. 148–50; and for noviciates more generally, A. Huerga, 'Noviciat', in *Dictionnaire de spiritualité ascétique et mystique*, ed. M. Viller, F. Cavallera, J. de Guibert *et al.* (17 vols., Paris, 1937–95), vol. xi 484–98.

[4] David of Augsburg, *De exterioris et interioris hominis compositione secundum triplicem statum, incipientium, proficientium et perfectorum*, Liber I, commonly known as *Formula noviciorum*. Around 370 MSS are listed in the edition for Quarachi (1899), and a further 50 in M. W. Bloomfield *et al.*, *Incipits of Latin Works on the Virtues and Vices, 1100–1500 A.D.* (Cambridge, MA, 1979), pp. 351–2, no. 4155; see also ibid., p. 232, no. 2655, and p. 490, no. 5676. For David of Augsburg's Latin works, and problems of authenticity, see D. Stöckerl, *Bruder David von Augsburg: Ein Deutscher Mystiker aus*

The Benedictines already had, in a sense, two noviciates, one being the time of formal probation which ended with profession; the other, the ensuing period when custody continued, though in a variety of forms. They were, moreover, great, if silent, borrowers from the friars, and we should perhaps ask, not whether their ideas on the use of these periods were influenced from the thirteenth century onwards by those of the friars, but how far the influence extended. As for Westminster Abbey, which provides the case history to be considered here, if it did not follow the example of Christ Church, Canterbury, and appoint Franciscans as claustral lecturers, it did on occasion invite Carmelites as well as Franciscans and Dominicans to preach in its church.[5] More remarkably – since, despite the survival of a very large number of manuscripts containing the *Formula noviciorum*, only a few are known to have associations with monasteries in England – in the fifteenth century, two copies of this work are associated with Westminster Abbey.[6] Possession of a book does not prove that it was read. Yet in the present case we can perhaps assume that the community at Westminster now included monks who from time to time looked outside their own order for guidance on these matters.

The century under consideration begins conveniently, though fortuitously, with the election of Edmund Kyrton to the abbacy in 1440, but it has an untidy end. The date of the Dissolution of the monastery is, of course, known from the deed of surrender, executed on 16 January 1540. However, a considerable number of monks left the community – whether voluntarily or involuntarily, it is impossible to say – in the course of the year 1534–35, and, inevitably, monastic life itself was affected by this change.[7] The quality of the surviving evidence is already in decline by that date, but the decline is

---

dem *Franziskanerorden*, Verffentlichungen aus dem Kirchen-Historischen Seminar München 4 (Munich, 1914), pp. 190–210. The *Formula noviciorum* no doubt owed much of its success to the fact that it was often attributed to St Bonaventura or St Bernard or to other authors better known than David himself; see A. Ryez, in *Dictionnaire de spiritualité ascetique et mystique*, ed. Viller *et al.*, iii. 43.

[5] Thomas Ashwell, OC, on Palm Sunday 1445 (WAM 19694); Robert Kyry, OFM, on Good Friday 1450 (WAM 19699); William Goddard, OFM on Good Friday, 1474 (WAM 1970); and an unnamed Franciscan B. Th., in 1477, probably on Good Friday (WAM 19724). For practice at Canterbury, see Dobson, 'Monks of Canterbury', p. 109.

[6] Hereford Cathedral Library, MS O. VI. 7, fols. 1–104; Balliol College, Oxford, MS 264; and see R. A. B. Mynors and R. M. Thomson, *Catalogue of the Manuscripts of Hereford Cathedral Library* (Cambridge, 1993), pp. 41–2, and R. A. B. Mynors, *Catalogue of the Manuscripts of Balliol College Oxford* (Oxford, 1963), pp. 283–4. For Evesham Abbey's copy of the *Formula noviciorum*, see *English Benedictine Libraries: The Shorter Catalogues*, Corpus of British Medieval Library Catalogues 4 (1996), ed. R. Sharpe, J. P. Carley, R. M. Thomson and A. G. Watson, B30. 47. For the only known printed copy in an English Benedictine library (at Monk Bretton), see ibid., B55. 52. I am indebted to Professor Richard Sharpe for the information that in the early sixteenth century Syon Abbey possessed several copies of the work, and for other bibliographical details.

[7] Compare the lists in WAM 18825 and 23968 with that in WAM 18827.

uneven and obscures our view of some aspects of that life a year or two before others are affected – the exact year of new professions, for example, is hard to determine after 1532, but the despatch of monks to the university is still in sight after that date. At each juncture, the discussion will take in as much as possible of the 1530s, but it will never take in quite as much of that troubled decade as we could wish.

In accordance with a common practice, the abbot and convent of Westminster recruited with an optimum figure for the total number of monks in mind; and from the late fourteenth century until the beginning of the sixteenth, their chosen number was forty-eight. Then, however, Henry VII required the abbey to recruit three additional monks to serve his chantry.[8] Given the existence of an optimum figure amounting in effect to a quota, recruitment was intimately related to mortality in the existing community. But since the abbey had a preference for receiving novices in batches, and these were sometimes as large as six, seven or even eight, the chronology of recruitment was irregular and, as at Durham Cathedral Priory, where a similar system obtained, two or three years might well pass without a clothing.[9] In late medieval England, where monastic numbers were in general declining, it was a confident monastery that imposed a delay on would-be-novices waiting to be clothed. But not quite so much confidence was needed if they were waiting in the almonry school. At Westminster, as at Durham, it seems likely that a significant number of recruits came from this school, itself greatly enlarged in the case of Westminster during the years around 1400.[10] By whatever routes the new entrants came – and we can assume that there was more than one – it was anticipated in the monastery that when the community was at its ideal strength of forty-eight, it would include forty priests and eight who were novices in the sense that they were not yet priests.[11]

In only four cases is the age at clothing or profession recorded. John Islip, who became in due course prior and then abbot, was born on 10 January 1464 and was thus sixteen years old when, on St Benedict's day (21 March) 1480, he began, in his own words, to live 'under the ordinance of religion' –

[8] CCR, Henry VII II.1500–1509, no. 389 (p. 139); B. Harvey, Living and Dying in England, 1100–1540: The Monastic Experience (Oxford, 1993), pp. 73–4.

[9] Dobson, Durham Priory, pp. 55–6. The chronology of recruitment at Westminster Abbey can be observed from c.1390 to c.1535 in E. H. Pearce, The Monks of Westminster (Cambridge, 1916), pp. 124–91. Note, however, that a monk normally appears here in the year of his profession and not that of his clothing, if the two were different.

[10] Harvey, Living and Dying, p. 74; Dobson, Durham Priory, pp. 60–1; Dobson, 'Monks of Canterbury', p. 118. On the enlargement of the almonry school at Westminster during the abbacy of William Colchester (1386–1420), see R. Bowers, 'The Almonry Schools of the English Monasteries, c.1265–1540', in Monasteries and Society in Medieval Britain: Proceedings of the 1994 Harlaxton Symposium, ed. B. J. Thompson, Harlaxton Medieval Studies 6 (Stamford, 1999), pp. 177–222 at 213–14.

[11] WAM 24068*.

a phrase probably signifying clothing rather than profession.[12] But in this period a monk who was clothed at sixteen would not have been more than seventeen, if as much, when professed, since in the late Middle Ages these two events normally occurred within only a few months or even weeks of each other. Later, in 1501, we are told that three monks who had just made their profession and now testified that it had been made freely were, respectively, seventeen, nineteen, and twenty-one years old.[13] Age at profession evidently varied, as indeed it had done in the past. Circumstantial evidence, however, points to a significant drop in the normal age at Westminster in the second half of the fifteenth century and suggests that it may have been eighteen or thereabouts for most of the period under consideration.[14]

Clothing and profession were identical events for all. But is it true at Westminster that custody ended in another event that was the common experience of all but the small minority of monks who were already priests at entry, namely ordination to the priesthood? From the mid-thirteenth century onwards, we have evidence pointing to a different conclusion. The latest customary to survive from this monastery was compiled in or about 1266, and at one point the compiler deals with the situation of novices who have learnt all they need to learn from their master. They may move, he says, to another place in the cloister and use books from the seniors' library. However, 'even if they are priests', they will not necessarily write anything or have a carrell.[15] The passage is not robbed of significance if the novice to whom it relates was a priest at entry: on the contrary, its significance is enhanced, since novices of this kind tended to be older than others at entry and correspondingly harder to detain in custody, once they had learnt everything the master of the novices had to teach them.

In the early fifteenth century, a different kind of source points to the existence of novices who were ordained. By this date, the wage system was a prominent feature of Benedictine life, and nowhere more so than at

[12] The whole passage, which occurs in Islip's memoranda book covering the years 1492–9 and was itself written in 1492, is of great interest in the context of this article: '[J. I.] . . . erat in vigilia sancti Barnabe apostoli vltimo preterito xxviij° annorum etatis et fuit in die sancti Benedicti in xlª vltimo preterito sub ordine religionis per xii^{im} annos vnde per septem annos erat claustralis et per quinque annos capellanus domini abbatis. In die Circumcisionis Domini anno etatis sue xxii^{do} primo celebravit missam in ecclesia Westm'. WAM 33290, fol. 1r; cited in Pearce, *Monks*, p. 167. See also below, p. 58.

[13] WAM 12890 v. The monks in question were Robert Downes (aged 17), John Marshall (21), and William Eles (19). Thomas Jaye made a similar affirmation on the same occasion, but his age is now illegible. See Pearce, *Monks*, pp. 178–9.

[14] Harvey, *Living and Dying*, p. 121. See also J. Hatcher, 'Mortality in the Fifteenth Century: Some New Evidence', *EcHR*, 2nd Series 39 (1986), pp. 19–38 at 27, where 18 is the presumed age of the monks of Christ Church, Canterbury, at profession in the period 1395–1505; and Dobson, *Durham Priory*, p. 61.

[15] *Customary of the Benedictine Monasteries of Saint Augustine, Canterbury, and Saint Peter, Westminster*, ed. E. M. Thompson, Henry Bradshaw Society 23, 28 (2 vols., 1902–4), ii. 168; See also ibid., p. 28.

Westminster, for here a monk who was a priest was now entitled to a sum total of £10 or £11 a year – quite enough, in secular society at this date to keep a small household in considerable comfort. All the wardens of the royal anniversaries observed at the abbey contributed largely to these payments. Among them, however, the warden of the anniversary of Richard II and Anne of Bohemia tended to note the status of recipients in unusual detail, and it is in his accounts that we find occasional references – implied rather than explicit, but clear enough, even so – to recently ordained priests as still novices. Thus in 1422–23, three monks who had been ordained in the course of the year are described as 'priests', and six others juxtaposed with them are described as 'other novices'; similarly, in the following year, two newly ordained monks are described as 'junior priests', and eight others as 'other novices'.[16]

A century later, the wage system at Westminster again sheds light on the duration of custody. Following what was probably a common practice, the abbot and convent of this period appointed senior monks to receive the wages to which novices were entitled, and to spend them on their behalf. Among Benedictines, monks acting in this capacity were known as 'tutors', and the tutorial system enabled novices to enjoy the material advantages of the wage system without themselves committing the irregularity of actually possessing wages. Equally, a failure to appoint tutors could place the monks in question at a disadvantage, as some rebellious members of the community at Malmesbury Abbey pointed out to visitors in 1527: since, they said, they had no tutors, they had no one to buy clothes and other necessities on their behalf.[17] From Westminster, there survive some of the accounts kept by senior monks apparently acting as tutors, and these show that junior monks who were already priests might be caught up in an arrangement of this kind. They show, too, that tutorial expenditure might embrace more than the 'necessities' of a material kind that the monks of Malmesbury probably had in mind. In 1502–3, for example, the prior, William Mane, was still administering the wages of Thomas Gardyner and Thomas Stowell, although both had been ordained in 1501, and his outlay included a number of payments to the grammar school master on their behalf – presumably for services rendered – and, in the case of Stowell, a payment to Richard

---

[16] WAM 23999–4000. The new priests named in 1422–23 had entered the monastery in 1420–21, and the six other novices in 1421–22. The new priests named in 1423–24 had entered in 1421–22, and three of the eight other novices in 1421–22 and five in 1423–24. See Pearce, *Monks*, pp. 138–42.

[17] *Chapters*, ed. Pantin, iii. 132. However, the status of these monks is uncertain. For tutors in the sense described in the text, and for the master of the novices as tutor, at Durham Cathedral Priory, see *Rites of Durham*, ed. Fowler, pp. 96–7; at Spalding Priory, *Visitations of Religious Houses*, ed. Thompson, ii. 343; and at Notley [Nutley] Abbey, an Augustinian house (ibid., p. 260). At St Augustine's, Canterbury, in the early fourteenth century, the assistant to the master of the novices is referred to as *tutor* (*Customary*, ed. Thompson, i. 260), and for the term at Westminster Abbey in the mid-thirteenth century, see ibid., ii. 93–4.

Caston, who may have been master of the novices at the time.[18] In 1506–7, Thomas Brown, the chamberlain, was evidently tutor to John Langham, who had been ordained in 1504–5, and his outlay on Langham's behalf included 3s. 4d. to an unnamed priest for books, and an identical sum to the precentor for a carrell.[19] Gardyner had been a student at Oxford and also, for a short time, at Cambridge, but he left the university in 1500.[20] Clearly, in 1501 he and Stowell, and five or six years later Langham, were engaged in claustral studies of one kind or another, and at the time each was still in custody. Were all three exceptional cases, spared the responsibility of handling their own wages despite the fact that each was ordained, the better to give themselves to study? Or has the fortuitous survival of some very unusual sources drawn to our attention examples of what was in fact the normal practice at Westminster in this period, namely the extension of custody beyond ordination? To the accounts of Prior Mane and Thomas Brown, we can add one or two other similar sources, apparently relating to the same situation, but not more.[21] Yet given the earlier references to monks who were in custody despite their priestly status, we may perhaps conclude that the extension of custody beyond ordination was the normal practice in this monastery.

Nevertheless, ordination was a momentous event in a monk's life. 'The priesthood is a great dignity', wrote Robert Joseph to John Feckenham, a fellow-monk of Evesham who was about to be ordained; and Feckenham, he added, would need to adopt a new bearing, a new countenance, a new way of life, and put away the things of a child.[22] At Westminster, it is the party following the First Mass, where the new priest entertained his friends to wine

---

[18] WAM 33288, fols. 21v–22r. Caston is referred to as master of the novices in 1500 (Pearce, *Monks*, p. 165). For Stowell, see ibid., p. 177, and for Gardyner, references in n. 20 below.

[19] WAM 18793, 1r, 3v. 141v. For Langham, see Pearce, *Monks*, p. 179.

[20] Pearce, *Monks*, p. 175; Emden, *BRUO*, ii. 743; and see below, p. 67.

[21] For John Islip's account, apparently in a tutorial capacity, for 'James Martin' (correctly Martin James) in 1493, see WAM 33290, fol. 15r. James had been professed in 1487–8 and ordained priest on 17 December 1491 (Pearce, *Monks*, p. 173; Reg. Richard Hill, 1489–96 (GL, MS 9531/8, 2nd Series, fol. 5r). For Islip's accounts, evidently in this capacity, for, respectively, John Warde (professed in 1482–83 and ordained in 1487–8) and Henry Duffeld (professed 1479–80 and ordained 1485–86), see WAM 30457. For his accounts for Thomas Brown (professed in 1485–86 and ordained in 1492), see WAM 33290, fol. 13r; and for Brown's ordination, GL, 9531/8, 2nd series, fol. 7r. The prolongation of the periods spent in custody by Warde and Duffeld is no doubt explained by the fact they were both students at Oxford, where Duffeld died in the period covered by Islip's account (Pearce, *Monks*, 166–7, 170–71). Prior Mane's management of the wages of Humphrey Litlyngton in 1501–2 is explained by Litlyngton's illness and subsequent death. Litlyngton was professed in 1473–74 and ordained in 1478–79. See 33288, fols. 20v–21r; Pearce, *Monks*, pp. 165–6

[22] *The Letter-Book of Robert Joseph, Monk-scholar of Evesham and Gloucester College, Oxford, 1530–3*, ed. H. Aveling and W. A. Pantin, Oxford Historical Society, New Series 19 (1967), pp. 107–8.

and farthing loaves at the expense of the obedientiaries, that our sources do more to bring to life.[23] Yet the tendency of the surviving sources here to record whatever cost money and omit the rest should not deceive us: the sense of a new beginning was no doubt present at Westminster, as at Evesham, at this juncture. Indeed, the principal challenge in describing a novice's life here at this time is in the need to hold this and the continuing constraints of custody in an appropriate tension. Claustral studies, which occupied much of a novice's time between profession and ordination and, for many, continued for a longer period, provide a coherence that would otherwise be lacking in such a situation. In the following account, we shall discuss, first, the time of probation, extending from clothing to profession; next, the period from profession to ordination, which was variable over the century under consideration, and, finally, claustral studies.

On one occasion, our sources describe a batch of newly professed novices as 'opyn profeshed': the phrase is used of a number who had what was evidently a celebratory breakfast with the prior on 24 October 1512.[24] If, as these words imply, the ceremony of profession was distinguished as 'open', or 'public' profession, we can conclude that the earlier and more informal ceremony of clothing was regarded by the monks of this period as a private form of profession – it was indeed this ceremony to which John Islip referred when he said that he began to live under the ordinance of religion at the age of sixteen.[25] No formal postulancy preceded clothing and tonsuring in Benedictine houses of this period. Yet by whatever route he entered, the new novice was not quite a stranger to the monastery on the day when these events occurred. Although the preliminary examination of candidates to confirm their seriousness of purpose and establish their educational attainments has left no trace in the surviving sources at Westminster, the general level of claustral studies here suggests that the educational component – to venture for the time being no opinion about the rest – was not perfunctory.[26] Whatever the required standard, the examination no doubt preceded the formal reception in chapter of the candidate's petition for clothing. And there were other things, too, that could not be left until the day of clothing

---

[23] The conventional contribution to each of these events was 1s. $7\frac{1}{2}$d or 1s. $11\frac{1}{2}$d. per obedientiary. However, in 1532, the monk-bailiff, who normally contributed 1s. $7\frac{1}{2}$d., actually spent 2s. $10\frac{1}{2}$d. (the cost of three gallons of wine and eighteen farthing loaves) on the occasion of Robert Crome's First Mass and the same again on that of John Alen (WAM 23025, fol. 8; Pearce, *Monks*, pp. 188–9).

[24] WAM 33325, fol. 64v.

[25] Above, pp. 54–5; Dobson, *Durham Priory*, p. 62.

[26] See also Prior Eastry's expectation at Canterbury in 1324 that entrants would be familiar with *termini grammaticales* and grounded in singing and reading (*Literae Cantuarienses*, ed. J. B. Sheppard, 3 vols., Rolls Series 85 (1887–9), i. 126–7; Dobson, 'Monks of Canterbury', p. 120. Examining committees may have been common; for the requirement that one be instituted at Ely, in 1300, see *Ely Chapter Ordinances and Visitation Records, 1241–1515*, ed. S. A. J. Evans, in *Camden Miscellany XVII*, Camden Society, 3rd Series 17 (1940), pp. 14–15.

itself: the trying on of clothes for size in the chamberlain's department, the assignment of beds in the dormitory, and instruction in the basic rules of deportment which had to be mastered if the new entrants were to survive their first day with credit. In an earlier period at St Augustine's Abbey, Canterbury, three days were allowed for these and other preliminaries, and the new entrants slept for this period in the hostelry.[27] We should probably envisage an arrangement of this kind at Westminster in our period.

The interval elapsing between clothing and profession is not explicitly recorded at this date. It was evidently shorter than the precise year recorded in the thirteenth century, but such case histories as we can piece together suggest that, as at Christ Church, Canterbury, it consisted of months rather than weeks. At Christ Church, where John Stone records the precise interval in the case of those clothed and professed between 1469 and 1534, seven or eight months were apparently normal.[28] At Westminster, John Islip, clothed, as we have seen, on 21 March 1480, was evidently professed by 29 September in this year, since he shared, as only professed monks did, in the distribution of the surplus issues of Queen Eleanor of Castile's foundation for the year of account ending on the latter date. For him, probation lasted at most five or six months; and the same may be true of the seven other novices who were professed in this year and quite possibly formed, with Islip, a single batch at entry.[29] In 1506, four novices – Christopher Goodhaps, William Holand, John Malvern and Henry Winchester – were clothed on or about 12 May. Their probation lasted at least until mid-October, as we learn from the account of Thomas Brown, their tutor, which covers most of the intervening period, but the rate at which they subsequently received wages suggests that they were professed by 25 December.[30] In their case probation lasted not less than five months or more than eight.

[27] *Customary*, ed. Thompson, i. 5–7. The period is to be envisaged as three days counting both the first and the last. For admission procedure in the case of candidates of mature age, see ibid., i. 254–8. See also *Customary of the Benedictine Abbey of Bury St Edmunds in Suffolk*, ed. A. Gransden, Henry Bradshaw Society 99 (1966), pp. 68–9. For the elaborate wardrobe of William Breynt, a new entrant at Westminster, in 1493, see WAM 33290, 18v, and B. F. Harvey, *Monastic Dress in the Middle Ages: Precept and Practice* (Canterbury, 1988), p. 28. For the necessity of a public profession, see F. D. Logan, *Runaway Religious in Medieval England, c.1240–1540* (Cambridge, 1996), p. 19.

[28] See *Christ Church, Canterbury. I. The Chronicle of John Stone, monk of Christ Church, 1415–1471. II. List of the Deans, Priors, and Monks of Christ Church Monastery*, ed. W. G. Searle, Cambridge Antiquarian Society Publications, Octavo Series 34 (1902), pp. 190–96. The actual range, however, was wide. See also Dobson, 'Monks of Canterbury', p. 122; for the few months of the probationary period at Durham Cathedral Priory, 1400–50, Dobson, *Durham Priory*, p. 62.

[29] WAM 23874–5; Pearce, *Monks*, pp. 168–9. For the precise year prescribed in RB, cap. 58 as the norm at Westminster in the thirteenth century, see *Customary*, ed. Thompson, ii. 224.

[30] WAM 18793, fols. 8, 12, 31–39r. The date of entry is implied in WAM 24241*, where it is recorded that four unprofessed novices received wages from Henry VII's

Who, then, instructed newly clothed novices, and what was the syllabus during the few months of their probation? The master of novices is rarely identified at Westminster before the sixteenth century. Then, however, he is sometimes named in the bishop of London's ordination lists as the person presenting monks of Westminster for ordination. To the names of the three who can be identified in this way – Henry Jones (1507–8), Robert Davers (1515), and Thomas Gardyner (1519–29) – we can add those of William Vertue, who is identified as master in clothing bills for novices, which can be dated 1533 × 35, and Richard Caston, who was master of the novices and keeper of the vestry at John Islip's election to the abbacy in 1500.[31] Vertue, like Gardyner, had studied at Oxford. In the monastery, all were busy men who held other offices concurrently with the mastership of the novices: Jones was kitchener; Davers, precentor, Gardyner was both chamberlain and kitchener; and Vertue, perhaps the last such official ever to hold the office, was warden of the Lady Chapel. We must conclude that the master of the novices now took little part in the actual instruction of novices: his task was to co-ordinate the work of others and it is possible that several others were involved. One of these may have been the master's deputy, the 'sowthe master', to whom Thomas Brown gave 12d. on behalf of the four unprofessed novices mentioned in 1506.[32]

The traditional place for novices and their master was the west cloister walk, and the structure here which was described as a *domus* on its repair in 1482–83 may have been used by the master and his assistants in the course of their duties.[33] It was here that the novices of our period received instruction in the office and liturgy, including the chant, and the customs of the monastery – subjects which no doubt continued to form the staple syllabus for the months of probation long after a much wider range of subjects had been introduced into the studies which followed profession. If much of their work at this stage was done in a group, we can assume that even before profession novices did some of their work, individually, in carrells in this

foundation for the final twenty weeks of the year of account ending on 29 September 1506. See also Pearce, *Monks*, p. 182.

[31] For Jones, see Reg. Richard FitzJames, 1506–22 (GL, MS 9531/8, 4th Series, fol. 23r, and 9531/9, fol. 156r); for Davers, ibid., 2nd Series, fols. 170v., 171r; for Gardyner, ibid., fols. 178, 179, and Reg. Cuthbert Tunstall (GL, MS 1951/10, 2nd Series, fols. 3r, 4v, etc.). For Caston, see Pearce, *Monks*, p. 165; and for Vertue, WAM 32042B, 32278. Davers presented novices for admission in 1516–17 and may still have been master of the novices. However, he is described on these occasions as precentor (GL, MS 9531/ 9, 2nd Series, fol. 173).

[32] WAM 18793, fol. 12r. See also the 'sowght chamberer/chamberas' who is clearly the sub-chamberlain mentioned ibid., fol. 23v. (I am grateful to Dr Roger Dalrymple and Professor Anne Hudson for help in wrestling with possible meanings of *sowthe*.) For the novice master's *socius* in an earlier period, see *Customary*, ed. Thompson, ii. 94.

[33] WAM 23558. For a late fourteenth-century reference to the seat of the master of the novices *in claustro*, see Pearce, *Monks*, p. 96. The west cloister known to novices in the late Middle Ages was less spacious than previously, since the new abbot's house constructed in the 1370s and 1380s encroached on the west side.

part of the cloister. Each new batch of novices slept in the *cella*, or enclosure, assigned to them within the monks' dormitory. This was equipped with shelves as well as beds and had a window hung, as we are told in 1500–1, with curtains of blue buckram.[34] Given the situation of the dormitory at first-floor level, and the height of the windows above its own floor level, the curtains were scarcely needed for privacy. They were for warmth and comfort, and they convey a sense of a certain kindness about the arrangements made for new novices in the last decades of the monastery's history. So, too, does the special treatment extended to Christopher Goodhaps in 1506. Goodhaps was ill during his time of probation and spent at least six weeks in the infirmary – a very long stay for a period in which the infirmarer discharged most of his patients in two weeks or less.[35] Had he been out of custody, he would probably have been sent as a convalescent to Hampstead or Hendon, where the abbey had houses for this purpose; but such a degree of relaxation of the regular life would have been considered inappropriate in the case of a novice. Instead, Goodhaps was evidently discharged with an injunction to the master of the novices that he be kept warm, for his tutor's account shows that he was provided with a fire – most likely a brazier standing in his carrell – and with a pair of lined boots with double soles. At 2s. 2d., the boots were nearly twice as expensive as boots for a healthy novice in this period.[36]

Although it was perfectly lawful for a novice to sever his ties with the monastery at any point between clothing and profession, for without profession, there could be no apostasy, the late medieval view of clothing as itself a kind of profession made it harder than it would otherwise have been for him to enjoy the liberty in this respect that the canonists intended him to have.[37] And there were other pressures on him to stay. With several teachers, a tutor to collect and spend the wages, as well as a master keeping an eye on all the arrangements, the new novice of this period could justifiably conclude that he had a number of well-wishers in the community who were anxious for him to persevere. Some novices, moreover, if educated in the almonry school, may have owed that advantage to monks who had nominated them for free places there, in accordance with a widespread convention that places in almonry schools were appropriately filled in this way.[38] We do not know how many actually departed at this stage, but the

---

[34] WAM 18789. Thirty yards (*virgate*) of buckram were purchased. Curtains for the novices' beds are also mentioned (WAM 18784).

[35] WAM 19483; Harvey, *Living and Dying*, p. 105 (Table III. 2).

[36] WAM 18793, fol. 12r. Two pairs of boots purchased in 1493 for a novice, William Breynt, cost 2s. 4d. (WAM 33290, fol. 18r).

[37] Logan, *Runaway Religious*, pp. 10–25.

[38] Bowers, 'Almonry schools', pp. 194–9, 213–16. Payments made from the goods left by Br. Richard Excestre, a former prior of Westminster, on his decease in 1396 or 1397 suggest that he had been paying the fees of two boys at the almonry school at the time of his death (WAM 6603).

buoyant numbers of the community in the fifteenth century and the early sixteenth suggest that few did so. Down to the 1530s, and except briefly in the aftermath of high mortality, the number of professed monks never fell significantly below the optimum figure of forty-eight. Such stability would have been very difficult, indeed impossible, to achieve had there been many losses between clothing and profession, since it was the number clothed that was carefully related by the monastery's recruitment policy to the short-fall of total numbers.[39]

After profession, progress through the orders of acolyte, subdeacon, deacon and priest provided landmarks in a novice's life. The monks of Westminster possessed the liberty of going to any bishop of their choice for orders;[40] but it seems clear that, setting aside old enmities, they normally, though not invariably, went in this period to the bishop of London. When, therefore, the ordination lists of this bishop are defective or non-existent, and notably during the long episcopate of Thomas Kempe (1450–89), so is our knowledge of the progress of monks of Westminster through the orders. In the following paragraphs, we shall attempt to piece together the course of events in the period 1440–41 to 1531–32, the last year in which the evidence will support an enquiry of this kind. One hundred and ninety novices were professed in this period, and to some extent we can chart the progress through the orders of sixty-eight of this total number (36%). The sixty-eight entered either in the 1440s or from the 1480s onwards.[41] Throughout the entire period, however, we normally know the year of ordination to the priesthood, since on singing his First Mass the new priest received gifts from all the major obedientiaries of the monastery, who faithfully recorded this outlay in their accounts.[42] Patchy though it is, the evidence suggests that the chronology of orders at Westminster changed in important ways in the course of this period.

The chronology of ordination could be affected at any stage in the individual case by a number of variables – by the progress made in claustral studies, by conduct in a more general sense, by illness, and by residence at the university, to mention only the most important. We find, therefore, that each batch of novices had a typical chronology of advancement through the orders, but that each tended to have an exceptional member or two who proceeded at a different pace. It was perhaps illness that led to Thomas Barton's withdrawal as a candidate for the priesthood at the sede vacante ordination in the diocese of London on 5 June 1501, for which his name was entered, and his subsequent departure for Oxford that delayed his priesting

---

[39] Above, p. 54.
[40] Acta Stephani Langton Cantuariensis Archiepiscopi AD 1207–1228, ed. K. Major, Canterbury and York Society, 50 (1950), pp. 70–1; History of Westminster Abbey by John Flete, ed. J. A. Robinson (Cambridge, 1909), p. 62.
[41] For the names, see Pearce, Monks, pp. 150–91. It should be emphasized that information about many of the sixty-eight is incomplete.
[42] Above, pp. 57–8.

until 20 December 1505.[43] The delay meant that he was priested exactly five years after his ordination as deacon and more than four years after the first of the novices who had entered, as he did, in 1498–9. Yet in general, age was probably the main influence on the rate of progress through the orders in this monastery, and a particularly strong influence on the timing of ordination to the priesthood. For this reason, the breaking of ranks among those who had probably entered as a single batch was always more conspicuous at this final stage of progress through the orders than at any earlier one. The batch of 1498–99 illustrates this point. The five novices in question were ordained subdeacon on the same day (19 September 1500), and four of the five were ordained deacon on the same day (20 December 1500). But the five were priested severally, on a total of four different occasions.[44] Throughout this period, the monastic community needed new priests as soon as it could get them – that is, as soon as the novices in question reached the permissible age. In practice this probably means that down to c.1470 monks of Westminster were ordained at the age of twenty-four but from that time onwards at the lower age of twenty-two.[45] The close link between attainment of the minimum age and ordination meant that the interval between profession and priesting varied significantly in the individual case. But the continuance of custody after ordination makes such a practice much less strange than it would otherwise appear.

Despite the practice, if we are right, of presenting monks for ordination to the priesthood at the minimum canonical age, the master of the novices and his assistants, and the abbot and prior with whom, in normal periods, decisions rested, had considerable room for manoeuvre. Moreover, they had more room from c.1470 than previously, for the age at which novices were normally professed now fell and probably did so by a considerable margin, from around twenty-one to around eighteen.[46] They seem to have used their liberty to introduce a longer interval than previously existed between profession and the conferment of the first orders, those of acolyte and subdeacon. An interval at this point can be discerned in the 1440s, but it was not then as long as the year or more that we find at the end of the fifteenth century and in the early sixteenth. The six novices, for example, who were professed in 1517–18 waited at least a year before they

[43] *Sede vacante* register, 1501–2 (GL, MS 9531/8, 4th Series, fol. 1r); *Sede vacante* register, 1505–6 (ibid., 4th Series, fol. 16r).
[44] For the four, and Barton, who probably formed a single batch at entry, see Pearce, *Monks*, pp. 177–8; and for their progress through the orders, Reg. Thomas Savage, 1496–1501 (GL, MS 9531/8, 3rd Series, fols. 12v, 13r, 14r, 15; 4th ser., fol. 10r, and references in n. 43 above); Reg. William Warham, 1502–3 (GL, MS 9531/8, 4th Series, fols. 10r, 16r). With the exception of Thomas Stowell, who may have been an acolyte at entry, all received this order on 13 June 1500. John Knolle was ordained deacon on 27 March 1501. William Marsh, one of the four, whose priesting is not recorded in these sources, sang his First Mass in 1501–2.
[45] Harvey, *Living and Dying*, pp. 119–21.
[46] Ibid.

were made acolyte on 24 September 1519, and of the eight who entered in 1523–24, six did not become acolytes until 23 December 1525.[47] In this late period, moreover, there was a tendency to present novices for the orders of acolyte and subdeacon on separate occasions, and for three of those professed in 1501–2 – John Langham, William Overton and John Cornyshe – the gap was more than a year: from 24 September 1502 to 23 December 1503.[48] We must see these changes in the larger context represented by the interval between profession and ordination to the priesthood, which itself changed in this period. Notwithstanding fluctuations from decade to decade, this was significantly longer for most of those who were professed after 1470 than for their predecessors. On a very rough estimate, those who were professed in the period 1440–70, not being already priests, could normally look forward to the lapse of between three and four years before they would sing their First Mass. For most of those professed between 1470 and 1532, however, the interval was more likely to be four to five years and for those professed in the 1470s, nearly six.[49] These figures reflect the fact that the normal age at profession of a monk of Westminster in this period dropped by a larger margin than the normal age at ordination. But we must ask how the longer period in custody before ordination was used and why a perceptible interval was inserted between profession and the conferment of the first orders and, in due course, between the first and second of these.

The fall in the normal age at clothing and profession which, *mutatis mutandis*, may have occurred quite generally in English Benedictine houses in the course of the fifteenth century, has not yet attracted the attention it deserves. To some extent it may represent a very slow response to the notorious practice of the friars in admitting candidates to profession at a

---

[47] For the six of 1517–18, see Pearce, *Monks*, pp. 185–6, and for their ordination as acolytes, Reg. Richard FitzJames, 1506–22 (GL, MS 9531/9, 2nd Series, fol. 178r). For the six of 1523–24, see Pearce, *Monks*, pp. 187–8, and Reg. Cuthbert Tunstall, 1522–30 (GL, MS 9531/10, 2nd Series, fol. 6v). The two exceptions, Armell Hurley and Richard Henley, were made deacon on 23 December 1525 and may already have received the lesser orders before their entry into the monastery (ibid., fol. 6v).

[48] Reg. William Warham, 1502–3 (GL, MS 9531/8, 4th Series, fols. 7v, 10v). It is not certain that John Cornyshe was already a monk in September 1502, although, evidently, he soon became one. For the three, see also Pearce, *Monks*, pp. 179–80. William Eles, another of the ten ordained acolyte on 24 September 1502, became subdeacon on 11 March 1503 (GL, MS 9531/8, 4th Series, fol. 8v). Two others, William Bothe and John Fulwell, were probably priests at entry. For Bothe's priest's share from Richard II and Anne of Bohemia's foundation in 1501–2, see WAM 24070; for Fulwell (Pearce, *Monks*, pp. 179–80).

[49] Sixty-four monks were professed in the earlier period and one hundred and twenty-six in the later. In both periods the actual range of intervals was very wide. The pattern in the case of those professed in 1530–32 was different from that of their predecessors in the previous decade: four of the five novices professed in these two years for whom we have evidence were apparently ordained priest after an interval of two years or less (Reg. John Stokesley (GL, MS 9531/11, fol. 128v; Pearce, *Monks*, pp. 188–9).

relatively early age, which had long attracted hostile comment.[50] Yet it must also reflect a positive willingness on the part of the communities in question to begin the teaching of the primitive sciences, and especially grammar, at a more elementary stage than had been normal in the cloister for some time. This was perhaps a response to a more recent development, namely the decree of the Provincial Chapter in 1444, requiring each monastery to employ a well qualified master – either a secular or a monk – to teach the primitive sciences, or at least grammar.[51] At Westminster and, no doubt, in many other houses, the practice of taking in novices in batches made it difficult to ensure continuous employment for such a master. But the recruitment of novices who were relatively young and would spend a relatively long time in claustral studies could ease this situation by providing the master with teaching in years when there were no new recruits, and this consideration may have helped to bring about the drop in age in this house and elsewhere. If so, in lowering the normal age of their novices at clothing and profession, the monks of Westminster expressed a degree of serious commitment to claustral studies at this time.

The spacing out of the orders lends itself to a similar interpretation. It seems unlikely that at this late date only those who had received an acolyte's or subdeacon's orders served altars in these capacities, or that it was considered necessary always to have a complement of acolytes and sub-deacons for this purpose. Indeed, it is likely that seculars, including pupils at the grammar school in the almonry, often served private masses in the abbey church and the daily Lady-Mass.[52] But by introducing a space between profession and ordination as acolyte and another between the latter and ordination as subdeacon, the master of the novices and his assistants made each stage one at which novices could be examined, if need be, in their understanding of religious observance and the more academic parts of the cloister syllabus, or their progress scrutinized in less formal ways. Something of the kind, however informal, must always have been needed as novices progressed through the orders: but the monks of this period may have taken it more seriously than many of their predecessors.

An examination system, however, is one thing, intellectual achievement and a true response to the demands of religious observance quite another. The actual quality of claustral studies at Westminster in this period, including the directed studies in which most novices probably participated throughout their period in custody, is hard to assess. Suitable books,

---

[50] Logan, *Runaway Religious*, pp. 12–13.

[51] *Chapters*, ed. Pantin, ii. 205; Knowles, *Religious Orders*, ii. 295.

[52] Bowers, 'Almonry Schools', pp. 208–9. I am indebted to Professor Richard Pfaff for advice on the substantive point. See also the notional complement of seven deacons and seven subdeacons at any one time, envisaged at Ely in 1314 in order to avoid straining the wage fund by imposing on it the burden of too many priests' shares (*Ely Chapter Ordinances*, ed. Evans, p. 43).

however, and competent teachers were essential ingredients of success, and something can be said about the supply of each.[53]

In the late fourteenth century and the early fifteenth, Westminster Abbey had been a place of active, if, on the whole, unexciting, scholarship, and in Cardinal Langham's library it acquired one of the best private libraries of that period.[54] In the mid-1370s, Adam Easton, though not expecting that the monastic library at Westminster would itself possess a copy of Wyclif's works, thought it quite possible that the abbey's current students at Oxford would know how to lay hands on one: clearly, he expected them to be *au fait* with current controversies there.[55] In the early fifteenth century, too, scholarship at Westminster was touched by topical events. It was probably during the abbacy of William Colchester (1386–1420) that the abbey, or a particular monk with an interest in the matter, acquired the works on the Schism that Leland saw at Westminster shortly before the Dissolution.[56] In our period, no acquisition as topical as these has come to light, and some of the books acquired by the monastery's student monks reflect the traditional character of higher studies at Oxford in this period. Thomas Barton, for example, who was professed in 1498–99 and subsequently graduated in theology at Oxford, possessed a printed text of Robert Holcot's *Quæstiones* on the Sentences of Peter Lombard.[57] It must be said, too, that in building a library (in the sense of book room) c.1450, the monks of Westminster were scarcely in the van of developments: they were, for example, behind the monks of Durham (1414 × 1418) and far behind the monks of Worcester (c.1376–77).[58] Yet in the long term, one result of the construction of the library was perhaps a significant increase in the number of books of all kinds now available in this official way at Westminster, in comparison to the number housed formerly in cupboards in the cloister, since the space for this was now available. Further, the catalogue compiled by Thomas Millyng

---

[53] On the education of novices and junior monks, see now J. G. Clark, 'Monastic Education in Late Medieval England', in *The Church and Learning in Late Medieval Society: Essays in Honour of Barrie Dobson*, ed. C. M. Barron and J. Stratford (Stamford, 2002), pp. 25–40. I am extremely grateful to Dr Clark for allowing me to read this important article in advance of publication, but have not attempted to explore its implications in the following attempt to piece together education at Westminster.

[54] *English Benedictine Libraries*, ed. Sharpe *et al.*, B105.

[55] *Chapters*, ed. Pantin, iii. 76–7.

[56] *English Benedictine Libraries*, ed. Sharpe *et al.*, B108. Colchester himself attended the Council of Constance in 1414.

[57] A. Coates and K. Jensen, 'The Bodleian Library's Acquisition of Incunabula with English and Scottish Monastic Provenances', in *Books and Collectors, 1200–1700: Essays presented to Andrew Watson*, ed. J. P. Carley and C. G. C. Tite (London, 1997), pp. 237–59 at 250. For Barton, who was sent to Oxford as a scholar on Henry VII's foundation at Westminster, see Pearce, *Monks*, p. 177, and Emden, *BRUO, 1501–40*, p. 29.

[58] *English Benedictine Libraries*, ed. Sharpe *et al.*, pp. 611, 652; *Medieval Scribes, Manuscripts and Libraries: Essays presented to N. R. Ker*, ed. M. B. Parkes and A. G. Watson (London, 1978), pp. 223–5.

when the library was built made those in existence at the time more accessible than previously.[59]

We can be confident that the novices of this period were permitted to use the monastery's main library. But they had special needs. The wage system made it possible to satisfy these, to some extent, out of the novices' own resources, and perhaps encouraged studies that had a more individual focus than had been possible in some earlier periods. Thomas Brown's purchase in 1506–7 of books from a priest for the novice John Langham shows us this system in operation. But Brown's account also points to the existence of an internal market in books in the monastery, for it records the purchase of a book for Langham from Thomas Sall, an older monk who had been professed in 1485–86.[60]

As for teachers, some would have been needed to teach grammar, and the lower the age of the novice at entry, the greater this need. Moreover, the decree of the Provincial Chapter in 1444, encouraged the view that a teacher whose energies were focused on this subject was needed. At Westminster, Prior Mane's expenditure on behalf of Thomas Gardyner and Thomas Stowell seems to show that the master of the grammar school in the almonry was now employed on occasion for this purpose. It is surprising to find that Gardyner still had anything to learn from him, for he had spent two years at Oxford and a shorter time at Cambridge. If, as seems likely, he was engaged in the arts courses there, it might be expected that he would no longer need the services of a grammar schoolmaster on his return to Westminster.[61] Given the master's employment to teach a monk such as Gardyner, it is easy to believe that he was also asked to teach less advanced pupils. But more advanced instruction in the arts and in elementary theology was also needed, and circumstantial evidence, namely the dovetailing of claustral studies at Westminster with studies at the university, in the case of monks who were sent there, suggests that it was available.

Between 1440–41 and 1534–35, the last year in which we can regard the community at Westminster as one that was capable of functioning normally in this respect, forty-one monks were sent to Oxford or Cambridge, and in two cases spent time at each. With the addition of John Amondesham, who was already at Oxford in 1440–41 and would continue there for a further seven years, the number is forty-two. Twenty-nine of the forty-two (69%) began their university studies after 1490, and twenty-four in or after 1500.[62]

[59] *English Benedictine Libraries*, ed. Sharpe *et al.*, p. 611. For Millyng, later (1469–74), abbot of Westminster, see Pearce, *Monks*, pp. 152–3, and Emden, *BRUO*, ii. 1282–3.

[60] WAM 18793, fol. 41v; Pearce, *Monks*, p. 171.

[61] Pearce, *Monks*, p. 175; Emden, *BRUO*, ii. 743. For Prior Mane's outlay, see above, p. 56.

[62] At the university [29 September] 1440 × [28 September] 1445: J. Amondesham; 1445 × 1450: J. Amondesham, T. Ruston, R. Teddington; 1450 × 1455: T. Ruston, R. Teddington; 1455 × 1460: T. Crosse, T. Millyng, T. Ruston, R. Teddington, R. Westminster; 1460 × 1465: J. Bayndon, T. Crosse, T. Millyng; 1465 × 1470: T. Clifford, W. Lambard, ? J. Stanes; 1470 × 1475: J. Stanes; 1475 × 1480: None; 1480 × 1485: R. Blake, H. Duffeld; 1485 × 1490: R. Blake, W. Borrow, H. Duffeld;

In the long term, however, the rate of professions scarcely changed: though uneven from year to year, it was, on average, about two a year in the period 1440 to 1490 considered as a whole, and in the period 1490 to 1535 considered in the same way. In fact the trickle of students from Westminster to Oxford dried up for a period of more than ten years after the return of John Stanes to the monastery in 1471 – a strange development, we may think, given the academic credentials of Abbot Thomas Millyng (1469–74), who had been admitted as doctor of theology at Oxford and incorporated as such at Cambridge.[63] The quickening of interest in university studies in the monastery in the decades around 1500 is unmistakeable. It began before the formal initiation of Henry VII's foundation there in 1504 and probably before this even reached the drawing board, as it no doubt did several years before the latter date. But without Henry's intervention, the monastery might never have possessed as many graduates in theology as are in fact mentioned in the final decades of its existence. As part of his detailed provisions for his chantry in the new Lady Chapel, which was itself to be built at his expense, Henry decreed that a succession of monks should be educated in theology at Oxford or Cambridge, incept as bachelors there, and serve on their return as priests of his chantry, and no fewer than twelve of the twenty-four monks who were sent to the university in or after 1500 were supported by his foundation for part of their career there, if not for the whole.[64] Nine of the

1490 × 1495: R. Blake, W. Borrow, H. Duffeld, J. More, J. Warde; 1495 × 1500: W. Borrow, W. Fenne, T. Gardyner, W. Southwell; 1500 × 1505: T. Barton, W. Bothe, W. Breynt, W. Fenne, T. Jaye, W. Southwell; 1505 × 1510: T. Barton, W. Bothe, W. Breynt, E. Flete, W. Fyttze, N. Hendon, T. Jaye, N. Lindsey; 1510 × 1515: D. Dalianns, ? A. Dunstan (alias Kitchin), W. Fyttze, N. Hendon, N. Lindsey, W. Vertue, ? H. Winchester; 1515 × 1520: R. Benet, D. Dalianns, A. Dunstan, J. Lawrence, N. Lindsey, H. Winchester; 1520 × 1525: R. Benet, D. Dalianns, A. Dunstan, T. Essex, J. Lawrence; 1525 × 1530: ? E. Brice, H. Charyte, T. Essex, T. Lovewell, J. Wheathampstead; 1530 × 1535: J. Alen, E. Brice, H. Charyte, R. Cheseman, J. Forster, J. Godeluke, T. Lovewell, R. Tamworth, J. Wheathampstead. W. Fenne spent part of the years 1499–1501, and T. Gardyner part of the year 1499–1500 at Cambridge; and R. Tamworth spent his sole year of university studies there. With these exceptions, all in the above list were students at Oxford.   All appear in Pearce, Monks, and all except T. Clifford, J. More and N. Lindsey in Emden, BRUO or Emden, BRUO, 1501–40. However, for Thomas Whethamsted [Wheathampstead] in Emden, BRUO, 1501–40, p. 620, read John Whethamsted. A student monk probably resided at the university for considerably less than the entire year. For some actual periods in the fourteenth century, see B. F. Harvey, 'The Monks of Westminster and the University of Oxford', in The Reign of Richard II: Essays in Honour of May McKisack, ed. F. R. H. Du Boulay and C. M. Barron (London, 1971), pp. 108–30 at 121–2; and for periods of residence by some student monks of Ely priory at Cambridge in the fourteenth century, J. Greatrex, 'Rabbits and Eels at High Table: Monks of Ely at the University of Cambridge, c.1337–1539', Monasteries and Society in Medieval Britain, ed. Thompson, pp. 312–28 at 319–20.

[63] Pearce, Monks, pp. 152–3; Emden, BRUO, ii. 1282–3.

[64] CCR, Henry VII II.1500–1509, no. 389 (pp. 139–40). Henry VII's scholars were Barton, Benet, Bothe, Charyte, Dalianns, Dunstan, Essex, Forster, Jayie, Lindsey, Lovewell, Winchester.

twelve incepted in theology or were admitted to oppose, but only three other students whom the monastery sent to the university in this period are known to have done likewise.[65]

Many of the student monks of Westminster were already priests when they left the monastery for the university. Indeed, this is probably true of twenty-two of the forty-two (52%) who have been mentioned, and among the twenty-two were four of the students supported by Henry VII's foundation.[66] Yet it had been Henry's intention that his students should begin their university studies as soon as they were professed. Clearly, the monastic community itself liked to give priority to claustral studies at this stage. It is noticeable, too, that the interval between ordination and the beginning of university studies, though variable in the individual case, tended to be quite a long one, lasting five years or more. In the great majority of cases the twenty-eight apparently held no office, and certainly no major one, during the interval: they were *claustrales*. But it seems unlikely that monks would have been plucked from the cloister and sent to the university after the lapse of several years had they not been engaged in study of a serious kind as *claustrales*: the interval would otherwise have been too long for a resumption of studies to be practicable, the risk of failure at the university too great.

Supplications for graces by monks of Westminster while they were at the university enable us to bridge the gap between hypothesis and fact, for these sometimes include references to years spent in claustral studies before the monks in question proceeded to the university or during vacations and other periods spent at home in the monastery, and do so successfully. Thus in 1459, when Thomas Ruston was granted a grace to oppose, his supplication included eight years in philosophy and five in theology, with many long vacations in each subject. Ruston had been ordained in 1440 and was at Oxford 1448–56. Clearly, he expected five years of claustral study to count towards his grace and was not disappointed.[67] In 1507, William Breynt claimed six years study at Oxford and five elsewhere when he supplicated for leave to oppose and was given the necessary grace. Breynt had been professed in 1493–94 and ordained in 1498–99. His five years elsewhere

[65] The nine were: Barton, Benet, Charyte, Dalianns, Dunstan, Essex, Jaye, Lindsey and Winchester. Bothe died c. five years after beginning his university studies. Of the monks sent to the university for the first time in or after 1500, but not on Henry VII's foundation, Breynt was admitted to oppose in 1507, Southwell incepted as bachelor of theology in 1506, and Wheathampstead supplicated to incept as bachelor of theology in 1533. J. Lawrence supplicated for the bachelor degree in canon law in 1524 and was admitted in 1531. As far as we know, of those sent 1440–1500, including J. Amondesham, Amondesham himself, T. Ruston, and T. Millyng were the only ones to incept in theology or be admitted to oppose.
[66] Essex (sent in 1522), Charyte (1525), Lovewell (1525), and Forster (1532). In addition, Lindsey (?1509), Winchester (1511) and Benmet (1516) were probably sent to the university in the year of their ordination. For Bothe (1503) see n. 48 above.
[67] Oxford, Bodl., University of Oxford, Register of Congregation, Aa 5, fol. 17r; Emden, *BRUO*, iii. 1612. For Ruston, see also Pearce, *Monks*, pp. 145–6.

were evidently years of claustral study at Westminster that began before he was ordained.[68]

Who, then, apart from the grammar school master, taught the novices of Westminster Abbey during their period in custody, which, if we are right, normally extended well beyond ordination? By the mid-fifteenth century, the monks of Christ Church, Canterbury, had long followed the practice of appointing a claustral lecturer to teach the primitive sciences and elementary theology from among their own university-educated monks, and, as we have seen, before this post could be filled in this way, they employed friars for the same purpose.[69] At Westminster Abbey the records of this period show no trace of either practice. But the appointment of a monk to such an office on his return from the university could have occurred without leaving a trace in the surviving records, since he may have received no fee or stipend for his services. Nor were the possible candidates for such a post exclusively university-educated monks. If, in the late fifteenth century and the early sixteenth, the abbey produced no scholar as versatile as William Sudbury or possessing the grammatical skills of Thomas Merks,[70] it attracted some recruits of a scholarly disposition who apparently spent not even the briefest period at either Oxford or Cambridge. Indeed, these may have preferred Westminster to other monasteries at entry because it seemed to offer them the right kind of environment. The most interesting among them is Ralph Langley, who entered the monastery in 1465–66, waited five years for ordination to the priesthood, and, as far as we know, never attended a university. Yet it was almost certainly Langley's intellectual distinction that persuaded the warden of Eleanor of Castile's foundation to give him the wages (40s. per annum) of a senior monk and a priest within two years of his entry; and his appointment as a preacher on Palm Sunday and Good Friday in 1477 and 1478 indicates high standing as a scholar, and probably as a theologian, in the community.[71]

We must be careful not to idealize arrangements for the noviciate at Westminster in this period. It is, for example, possible that novices in custody after ordination, or even before this event, were given light administrative jobs of the kind that were necessary to any well run department but have left few traces in the obedientiary accounts of this period; performed *gratis* by novices in custody, they could easily have

[68] Oxford, Bodl., University of Oxford, Register of Congregation, G, fol. 48r. See also Emden, *BRUO, 1501–40*, p. 68, s.n. Brent; and for Breynt, see Pearce, *Monks*, p. 175.
[69] Above, p. 53. For the monk-student of Glastonbury Abbey recalled from Oxford in 1366 to be claustral lecturer, see *Chapters*, ed. Pantin, iii. 55.
[70] For Sudbury, see Emden, *BRUO*, iii. 1813, and Pearce, *Monks*, p. 113; for Merks, *Formularies which Bear on the History of Oxford, c. 1204–1420*, ed. H. E. Salter, W. A. Pantin and H. G. Richardson, Oxford Historical Society, 2 vols., New Series 4–5 (1942), i. 182–5, 195–203; Emden, *BRUO*, ii. 1263–4, and Pearce, *Monks*, p. 116.
[71] For the distribution, see WAM 23848, 23850, 23852; for the sermons, WAM 19724–5; and for Langley's career, Pearce, *Monks*, pp. 160–61.

passed without notice. To use such novices in this way would not have involved them in forinsic cares – a point of much concern earlier to the General Chapter.[72] And the intellectual harvest of claustral studies at Westminster in this period was apparently small. It was perhaps the student in Thomas Gardyner who caught the eye of Henry VII when, in 1507, he appointed him prior of Blythe, and later, on his return to Westminster, made Gardyner acceptable as a priest of Henry's chantry, despite the fact that he had not incepted in theology or come near to doing so. His surviving works, the fruit of the years immediately following his return, consist of 'The Flowers of England', a short chronicle extending from the reign of Brutus to that of Henry VIII, and a genealogical roll demonstrating the descent of Henry VIII from Cadwallader, Alfred, Hugh Capet and William the Conqueror.[73] In the roll, Gardyner made didactic use of a very old form of historical narrative, in support of the house of Tudor, and his work is of interest for this reason. But, like the chronicle, it has little intrinsic merit.

Nevertheless, the attempt made at Westminster in the course of the fifteenth century to restructure the noviciate, though on a modest scale, is noteworthy; so, too, if we are right, the serious character of claustral studies at this time and in the early sixteenth century. These probably embraced more than the primitive sciences. After all, what Henry VII found to criticize in the community at Westminster was not a total neglect of theology, but its lack of graduates in this subject. The developments of this period are the more remarkable given the internal crises which beset the community in the mid-fifteenth crentury, when two incompetent abbots, Edmund Kyrton (1440–62) and George Norwich (1463–67), had to be encouraged into early retirement or resignation.[74] Clearly, whatever momentum change possessed at Westminster at this time was provided by the

---

[72] *Chapters*, ed. Pantin, i. 38, 50.

[73] For the *Flowers of England*, with extracts taken from the text in Trinity College, Dublin, MSS E. 1. 15 (no. 513) and E. 5. 22 (no. 633), see, J. Gilbart Smyly, 'Thomas Gardiner's History of England', *Hermathena* 43 (1922), pp. 235–48, and for Gardyner's status as a priest of Henry VII's chantry, ibid., p. 239. Oxford, Bodl., Rawl. MS D. 1020, fols. 1–32 is an imperfect copy of *The Flowers*. For a mid-sixteenth-century copy of the genealogical roll, see Oxford, Bodl., MS Eng. hist. e. 193, and O. Pächt and J. J. G. Alexander, *Illuminated Manuscripts in the Bodleian Library Oxford* (3 vols., Oxford, 1974), iii. 1186 and plate cxi; and for genealogical rolls as a form of historical writing, M. T. Clanchy, *From Memory to Written Record: England 1066–1307* (2nd edn., London, 1993), p. 142, and plate XIII. (I am indebted to Dr Nigel Ramsay for the reference to the article in *Hermathena* cited above, and for other information about Gardyner that he has generously shared with me.)

[74] For Kyrton, see V. H. Galbraith, 'A Visitation of Westminster in 1444', *EHR* 37 (1922), pp. 83–8, and for a reference in 1467, some five years after Kyrton's resignation, to the residue of unpaid debts incurred during his administration, WAM 5432, cited in Pearce, *Monks*, p. 130. For the grounds of Norwich's retirement in 1467, see R. Widmore, *Enquiry into the Time of the First Foundation of Westminster Abbey* (London, 1743), pp. 191–9, and for Norwich's career, Pearce, *Monks*, pp. 141–2.

community itself and not by its abbots. Equally, both the decline of interest in university studies to vanishing point in the 1470s and the revival of interest which becomes conspicuous in the 1490s may represent the changing views of the community of monks, articulated perhaps in chapter, on how best to educate its younger members and to use their years in custody.

However they were determined, the arrangements made for novices at Westminster in this period seem far removed from the mental and spiritual world of David of Augsburg. Yet the association of two copies of his treatise with Westminster Abbey may have a lesson for us. Each was acquired in the first instance by a monk in his private capacity. One, in a codex dating from the late fourteenth century and containing more than twenty works of a devotional, homiletic, or moral kind, was acquired by John Breynt but later belonged *ad communia armaria* [Westm'].[75] Breynt was professed as a monk of Westminster c.1373 and died in 1418, and we can assume that on his death, the customary rule that books purchased by individual monks from their own resources should be added to the monastic library on their decease took effect. Some of the authors and putative authors represented in his codex, including St Bernard and Hugh of St Victor, would certainly have been prescribed reading for novices in this period, as in earlier ones, and it is possible that Breynt was master of the novices for a time. John Stanes, the owner of the second copy of the *Formula noviciorum*, was professed in 1462–63, sent to Oxford c.1470 but did not stay there long, and died in 1485.[76] By 1460, the monastic library had been removed from cupboards in the cloister to a room, and catalogued on its removal.[77] Presumably, therefore, Stanes had only to consult the catalogue to become aware that the monastery already possessed this work. Evidently, he wanted a copy of his own, and we cannot rule out the possibility that he was himself involved for a time in the instruction of the monastery's novices. At his death the customary rule probably brought this copy, too, of the *Formula* into the monastic library.

These episodes remind us of the importance that private collections of books might have in a monastery, both in the intellectual and spiritual formation of the monks in question, and as sources, eventually, of works for the main monastic library that it might not otherwise have acquired.[78] But, whether or not John Breynt or John Stanes had any formal part in the education of novices at Westminster, their books also hint at the traffic in

---

[75] Hereford Cathedral Library, MS O. VI. 7, fols. 1v, 306v; Mynors and Thomson, *Manuscripts of Hereford Cathedral Library*, pp. 41–2. Among the items are Pseudo-Bernard, *Meditationes*, for which see Bloomfield, *Incipits of Latin Works on the Virtues and Vices*, no. 3126, and Hugh of St Victor, *De VII Vitiis* (ibid., no. 5431). On novices' reading, see also above, n. 1; for Breynt, Pearce, *Monks*, p. 114.

[76] WAM 19976; Pearce, *Monks*, p. 159; and n. 62 above.

[77] *English Benedictine Libraries*, ed. Sharpe et al., p. 611.

[78] For a conspicuous example, see Dobson, *Durham Priory*, pp. 361–2.

ideas within the community that may have influenced the use made of a novice's period in custody. If so, they have a special value, for in this late period, as in every earlier one, much that happened at this stage of a monk's life is normally hidden from our sight.

Syon and the New Learning

VINCENT GILLESPIE

In a letter to Eustochium, Jerome tells how he was struck down by illness in Antioch in 374. In his fever and delirium, he had a vision of being arraigned before the judgement seat. When asked who he was, he answered that he was a Christian. 'You lie', came the reply: 'you are a Ciceronian, for where thy treasure is, there is thy heart also'. This triggered Jerome's withdrawal into the desert wilderness.[1] For many Christian humanists who led lives of scholarly endeavour such as Erasmus, the example of Jerome's dedication to Christian letters and scholarship, grafted on to a Ciceronian concern for style and expression formed the basis of their concept of *literae humaniores*, just as Augustine's combination of Platonic learning, Christian scholarship and active ministry in the episcopate appealed especially to those, like John Fisher, who chose the active life.[2] Jerome was indeed a 'vir

This chapter forms part of an overlapping and interlocking series of papers delivered in 1999 which explore aspects of the intellectual life of the Syon Brethren as witnessed by the *registrum* of their library, preserved in Cambridge, Corpus Christi College, MS 141. The fullest of these discussions of the *registrum* is found in my 'The Book and the Brotherhood: Reflections on the Lost Library of Syon Abbey', *The English Medieval Book: Essays in Memory of Jeremy Griffiths*, ed. A. S. G. Edwards, V. Gillespie and R. Hanna (London, 2000), pp. 185–208. A more provocative account of the mystical holdings is found in my 'Dial M for Mystic: Mystical Texts in the Library of Syon Abbey and the Spirituality of the Syon Brethren', in *The Medieval Mystical Tradition: 6*, ed. M. Glasscoe (Cambridge, 1999), pp. 241–68. The present chapter re-uses and develops material from both these discussions, and adds new material to both, but it is notably more sceptical about the humanist attainments of the Brethren than 'The Book and the Brotherhood'. The *registrum* has been previously edited by M. Bateson, *Catalogue of the Library of Syon Monastery Isleworth* (Cambridge, 1898) [hereafter cited as Bateson, *Catalogue*] and has been re-edited by me as volume IX (2000) of the Corpus of British Medieval Library Catalogues under the general editorship of Richard Sharpe. The standard (and masterly) discussion of the Syon libraries is now C. de Hamel, *Syon Abbey: The Library of the Bridgettine Nuns and their Peregrinations after the Reformation* (s. l., Roxburghe Club, 1991). There is a cursory account of the library in D. N. Bell, 'Monastic Libraries, 1400–1557', in *The Cambridge History of the Book in Britain III. 1440–1557*, ed. J. B. Trapp and L. Hellinga (Cambridge, 1999), pp. 229–54, esp. pp. 245–7.

[1] Jerome, *Epistula ad Eustochium* (*ep.* 22), ed. I. Hilberg, *Corpus Scriptorum Ecclesiasticorum Latinorum* 54 (1996), 143–211, § 30 (pp. 189–91). This famous letter includes Jerome's question 'What has Horace to do with the Psalter?' (§ 29, pp. 186–9). See also E. F. Rice, *St Jerome in the Renaissance* (London, 1985).

[2] See R. Rex, *The Theology of John Fisher* (Cambridge, 1991), esp. chap. 1: 'Humanism

bonus dicendi peritus', a model of Christian scholarship, eloquence and forensic rhetoric.

As an enclosed order charged with the spiritual welfare of a large community of even more severely enclosed nuns, the example of Jerome already loomed large in the lives of the Syon brethren even before he had become one of the icons of Christian humanism. His guidance on forms of life for women recluses offered great assistance for the brethren in their role as a kind of *en suite* spiritual harem for the sisters.[3] Beyond that guidance, the brethren were bound by the Rule of St Saviour to 'enteende oonly to dyuyne office and studie 7 prayer'.[4] The four deacons (who together with thirteen priests, eight lay brethren and sixty nuns made a community of eighty-five representing the apostles, St Paul and the disciples) were meant to symbolize the four great doctors of the church: Augustine, Ambrose, Gregory and, of course Jerome (all four of whom are represented in the surviving early sixteenth-century catalogue of the brethren's library, Augustine and Jerome more richly than the others, and Ambrose rather thinly). Thomas Betson, librarian and scribe of that great catalogue, was one of those four deacons and, to judge from the preponderance of material from or attributed to Jerome in his *A Ryght Profytable Treatyse* (printed by Wynkyn de Worde in 1500) may well himself have born the diaconate of Jerome. The frontispiece of the book is a woodcut of Jerome and his lion (a story catalogued as present in several books in the library).[5]

One of the first generation of brethren, Simon Wynter, made an early

and Scholasticism in Late Fifteenth-Century Cambridge', and chap. 3: 'Fisher and the Christian Humanists, 1500–1520'. On early English humanism generally, the standard survey remains R. Weiss, *Humanism in England during the Fifteenth Century*, Medium Aevum Monographs 4 (3rd edn., Oxford, 1967). See also J. B. Trapp, 'The Humanist Book', in *Cambridge History of the Book*, ed. Trapp and Hellinga, pp. 285–315.

[3] The standard history of the house remains G. J. Aungier, *The History and Antiquities of Syon Monastery, the Parish of Isleworth and the Chapelry of Hounslow* (London, 1840), which should be supplemented by M. B. Tait, 'The Brigittine Monastery of Syon (Middlesex) with Special Reference to its Monastic Uses' (unpublished D.Phil. Thesis, University of Oxford, 1975).

[4] *Regula salvatoris*, ed. S. Eklund, Den Heliga Birgitta Opera Minora 1, Samlingar utgivna av Svenska Fornskriftsällskapet, Andra Serien, Latinska Skrifter, 8/1 (Lund, 1975), cap. 13; J. Hogg, *The Rewyll of Seynt Sauioure and Other Middle English Brigittine Legislative Texts*, vols. 2–4, Salzburger Studien zur Anglistik und Amerikanistik (Salzburg, 1978– 80), ii. 38. For discussion, see R. Ellis, *Viderunt eam filie syon: The Spirituality of the English House of a Medieval Contemplative Order from its Beginnings to the Present Day*, Analecta Cartusiana 68 (1984), chap. 3 (The Syon Additions).

[5] *STC* 1978, repr. in facsimile (Cambridge, 1905); R. Ellis, 'Further Thoughts on the Spirituality of Syon Abbey', *Mysticism and Spirituality in Medieval England*, ed. W. F. Pollard and R. Boenig (Cambridge, 1997), pp. 219–43. On Thomas Betson see A. I. Doyle, 'Thomas Betson of Syon Abbey', *The Library*, 5th Series 11 (1956), pp. 115–18. Betson probably entered Syon in or around 1481 and may have been involved with the library up to his death in 1516. A vernacular version of the *Miraculum de leone* (*PL*, xxii. 210–14; *BHL* 3872) is found, for example, in item M17 in the Syon *registrum* ('De leone sancti Ieronimi in fine libri in anglicis').

fifteenth-century translation of a life of Jerome that was composed for Margaret, duchess of Clarence, an early spiritual client of the order. According to Wynter's life, Jerome had turned from 'bokys of Poetys and Philysophres' to 'holy bokys'. Jerome's influence on two heathens so changed them that 'levynge all þe vanytees of þe worlde [they] went yn-to þe monasterye', while two young Romans saved from execution by Jerome, 'castynge from theym all wordly bysynesse, entred yn-to þe monasterye . . . entendynge to prayere and to penaunce and to holy lyuynge'.[6] The trajectory enacted by Jerome and described by Symon Wynter is exactly that followed by many of his Syon colleagues and successors. Section M of the catalogue has multiple entries for *Vitas patrum* collections celebrating the eremiticism of the early fathers, and throughout the catalogue collections of austere and high-minded moral and ascetic apothegmata abound.

Yet the catalogue as a whole is also ample witness to the Ciceronianism of the brethren in their secular lives: there are plenty of classical texts preserved, especially in Section A of the collection given over to the *Artes* and the reading texts of the liberal arts, mostly no doubt reflecting their earlier training in grammar, rhetoric and the emerging discipline of the 'humanities'. Most comprehensively represented are the works of Cicero with a variety of humanist commentaries, but there are also editions of Virgil, Horace, Sallust, Lucan, Ausonius, Statius, Ovid, Seneca (including the tragedies), Pliny, Aulus Gellius and Lucian. Some of these printed editions reflect the university studies in the humanities undertaken by the swathe of Cambridge graduates who were drawn to Syon from 1485 onwards: Richard Reynolds, Curson (a brother at the Dissolution in 1537), Richard Whitford, Stephen Sawndre and John Steyke who died in 1513. In the revision of the original catalogue, for example, some older grammatical reading texts (reflecting the training and tastes of the brethren from the first fifty years of the house's life) are replaced by new humanist editions.[7] In A49,

[6] On Margaret's links with Syon (and those of other noble benefactors), see G. R. Keiser, 'Patronage and Piety in Fifteenth-Century England: Margaret, Duchess of Clarence, Symon Wynter and Beinecke MS 317', *Yale University Library Gazette* 60 (1985), pp. 32–46. The Life of Jerome is cited from New Haven, Yale University Library MS 317, these quotations on fols. 17v–18v, and cited by Keiser, 40. Much information about benefactors can be drawn from the Syon *Martiloge* in BL, Add. MS 22285, fols. 70v–71r, which contain a list of 'Nomina specialium benefactorum et amicorum'. Some powerful early friends of Syon are mentioned in F. R. Johnston, 'Joan North, First Abbess of Syon, 1420–33', *Birgittiana* 1 (1996), pp. 47–65; *The Incendium Amoris of Richard Rolle of Hampole*, ed. M. Deanesly (Manchester, 1915), pp. 91–130; and Tait, 'Brigittine Monastery of Syon', passim.

[7] As will be discussed in more detail below, Betson's original register of books was added to until the mid-1520s, and a radical rearrangement was begun by the erasure of old entries and the insertion of new (largely printed) texts into the vacated library marks. Later still, preparations were made for a wholesale reordering of the collection, perhaps in expectation of some change in its physical location or the manner in which it was stored. So even the single register that survives today probably witnesses at least three distinct phases of library development, reordering and curatorial activity within no

Geoffrey of Vinsauf's *Poetria nova* is replaced by Richard Reynolds' copy of the Paris 1511–12 edition of Lucan. In A63 Leland's grammar text is replaced by the Paris 1496 edition of the *Metamorphoses* with the commentary of Raphael Regius, given by Richard Whitford. The most emblematic substitution is the replacement in A70 of an archetypal collection of 'medieval' grammar school reading texts (Cato, Avianus, Pamphilus, Horace, Maximian, Statius and Claudian) by Richard Reynolds's copy of the *Silvae* of Jodocus Badius Ascensius in the Lyon 1492 edition.

However, earlier (manuscript) copies of similar classical and grammatical works remind us that it was not an exclusively humanist endeavour to read and emulate the masterpieces of classical style. The core of the early library after the first professions in 1420 was, after all, the magnificent and diverse collection of at least 111 volumes given by John Bracebridge, a Cambridge graduate who had enjoyed a successful career as a grammar master in Lincoln diocese before resigning in 1420, perhaps to become one of the original professed priests, although he does seem to have been the only graduate in the community at the 1428 election for the confessor-general, which is in contrast to the striking 'graduateness' of the later community.[8]

Similarly catholic juxtapositions are found in Section C of the catalogue, where modern 'humanist' translations of Aristotle by Leonardo Bruni and others, Ficino's versions of Plato and Plotinus (C7 and C3), commentaries by Jacques Lefèvre D'Etaples (C1) and Hermolaus Barbaro's version of Themistius Peripateticus (C16) rub bindings with much older works by Walter Burley or Averroistic commentaries owned by Bracebridge, all probably refugees from earlier courses in natural philosophy. There is very little evidence of an interest in Greek or Hebrew in the holdings listed in the catalogue, which does not seem to have responded to or reflected the developments in teaching those languages underway in the universities from 1510 onwards. There are translations from Greek texts, and some printed editions, such as the *Aratea* in the 1499 Aldine edition of Firmicus Maternus (B10) included Greek texts alongside translations by Thomas Linacre. There is also a 1502 edition of Ambrosius Calepinus's Latin and Greek dictionary (A38). John Fewterer had a 1524 Hebrew bible concordance, which survives with Syon markings but which was not included in the catalogue (which may have fallen into disarray by that date).[9] There were two copies of a triplex psalter (though one of these belonged to John

---

more than a quarter of a century. The catalogue as it is now preserved in Corpus 141 is identified in the new edition as document SS1. The edition also includes as document SS2 items erased from the collection and reconstructed from the imperfectly corrected original index and from ultra-violet recovery of erasures. See also 'The Book and the Brotherhood'.

[8] Aungier, *History and Antiquities*, p. 52; Bateson, *Catalogue*, p. xxiii; Tait, 'Brigittine Monastery of Syon', p. 246, traces his career as a grammar master in Lincoln diocese. Entered in the *Martiloge* of the house for 27 March (BL, Add. MS 22285, fol. 6r), he is described as 'sacerdotis et bachalarii in theologia'.

[9] Now Oxford, Merton College, 76 b. 11.

Bracebridge, one of the brethren of first profession, so cannot be considered a witness to humanist commitment to biblical language study), and a few editions of Scripture that included Greek texts. So the signals from the catalogue are very mixed.

A collection dominated by printed books from the period 1470 to 1525 may *de facto* have to be a Christian humanist collection. But given the background and training of many of the post-printing brethren, one needs to be cautious about attributing to the collection a deliberate intellectual character that may partly be the result of accidents of chronology and printing history: brethren may have bought the editions they did because that was what was available at the time they were studying. So although there is evidence to suggest that the later brethren were recipients of the intellectual monuments of the New Learning at the end of the fifteenth and the beginning of the sixteenth centuries, it is much harder to say if they were active participants because of the varied ways in which books came to be part of their collection. Basing his assessment on their library holdings, M. B. Tait argues in his excellent study of the intellectual ethos of the house, that 'for the Brigittines the New Learning was represented principally by its contributions to the study of theology and philosophy . . . the renaissance at Syon was still at the elitist stage and was very much a religious phenomenon'. More recently, Christopher de Hamel spoke of the Syon collection as 'the envy of any library of renaissance scholarship, including texts by Coluccio Salutati, Leonardo Bruni, Poggio, Cardinal Bessarion, Platina, Poliziano, and Pico della Mirandola, and translations from the Greek by Hermolaus Barbarus, Gaza, Erasmus and others, with works by Petrarch, Boccaccio, Savonarola and Reuchlin'.[10] All this is true, and it is clear in particular that efforts were made to keep abreast of the best of new scholarship on Scripture and on the patristic authors of East and West. It is also true, however, that many of these accessions can be attributed to the personal libraries of two men: Richard Reynolds, 'the only English monk well versed in the three principal languages' according to Pole, and John Fewterer, confessor-general up to the eve of the Dissolution. But there are reasons to be sceptical about the level of intellectual engagement shown by the remaining Syon brethren in the last fifty years of the house's existence.[11] As de Hamel says, 'to receive a gift is not at all the same as commissioning a book'.[12] And a collection that is largely donated by the brethren themselves rather than actually acquired as a result of a deliberate and consistent acquisition policy may, in the most cynical reading, be no more than the accumulated intellectual detritus of its donors' previous lives before they followed the example of Jerome and

---

[10] Tait, 'Brigittine Monastery of Syon', p. 338; de Hamel, *Syon Abbey*, pp. 79–80.

[11] See my 'Dial M for Mystic' (above, n. 1) for a sceptical look at the reputation of the Syon brethren for contemplative prowess.

[12] de Hamel, *Syon Abbey*, p. 80.

withdrew to the monastery.[13] Although Syon was the venue for some famous humanist set pieces, not least a remarkable argument between John Fisher and Richard Pace, apparently over the inspired nature of the Septuagint, what is remarkable about these vignettes is that the Syon brethren appear to play no overt part in them. Major intellectual figures like Whitford, who served in the *familia* of Fisher prior to his profession, chose instead to produce low-key, impeccably orthodox but narrowly ascetic and austere handbooks of moral improvement. The Syon brethren only emerge into public view over the matter of Henry's divorce from Catherine of Aragon, when they staunchly took the Queen's line, at least initially. But although others, like Pace, may have used the resources at Syon for works of Christian humanist scholarship, there is no sign of significant literary or polemical activity from the brethren themselves.[14]

Books ought to have been an important part of the intellectual life of the Syon brethren. The *Regula salvatoris* allowed books to be received 'as many as be necessary to doo dyuyne office and moo in no wyse', but also provided that 'Thoo bookes they shalt haue as many as they wylle in whiche ys to seruen or to studye'.[15] This is implicit in the early history of the house, founded in 1415 with the first professions in April 1420. The urgent need for books had been recognized by Henry V in the provisions he made in his will for his twin foundations of Sheen and Syon. Henry left his books of meditation and those useful for preaching the Gospel to be divided equally between Syon and Sheen, stipulating that the preaching books should all go to Syon because the Brethren there are required to preach and the Carthusians are forbidden so to do.[16] Henry's emphasis on preaching books

---

[13] For the 'cynical' view, see R. Lovatt, 'The *Imitation of Christ* in Late Medieval England', *TRHS*, 5th Series 18 (1968), pp. 97–121: 'the Syon library, impressive though it seems, had a more fortuitous character, and was basically little more than the sum of the libraries of its benefactors' (p. 112).

[14] Rex, *Theology of John Fisher*, pp. 148–61. On Whitford, see the account by James Hogg in *Dictionnaire de spiritualité* 16 (1994), cols. 1410–18. For discussion of the literary output of Syon, see, for example, J. T. Rhodes, 'Syon Abbey and its Religious Publications in the Sixteenth Century', *JEH* 44 (1993), pp. 11–25; G. R. Keiser, 'The Mystics and the Early English Printers: The Economics of Devotionalism', in *The Medieval Mystical Tradition in England: 4*, ed. M. Glascoe (Cambridge, 1987), pp. 9–25. The foundational survey of this material remains James Hogg's 'The Contribution of the Brigittine Order to Late Medieval English Spirituality', *Spiritualität Heute und Gestern*, Analecta Cartusiana 35/3 (1983), pp. 153–74.

[15] CUL, MS Ff. 6. 33. fols. 62v–63r., reproduced by Hogg, ii. 49–50. For the Latin text see cap. 21, sections 227–8: 'Libri quoque, quotquot necessarii fuerint ad divinum officium peragendum, habendi sunt, plures autem nullo modo. Illos autem libros habeant, quotquot voluerint, in quibus addiscendum est vel studendum' (Eklund, p. 127). The vernacular version, cap. 18, sections 227–8, is substantially the same (Eklund, pp. 204–5).

[16] P. and F. Strong, 'The Last Will and Codicils of Henry V', *EHR* 96 (1981), pp. 79–102. Bridget is included in the list of saints from whom suffrages are requested at the beginning of the will (Strongs, p. 89). N. Beckett, 'St Bridget, Henry V and Syon

is a signal that the vocation of the Syon brethren was seen from the outset as different from that of the Carthusians.

This respects Bridget of Sweden's intention that the Brigettine brethren should openly and simply expound the Sunday gospel in the vernacular for the benefit not only of the nuns but also of the laity. Brethren were allowed three days off choir duty when they were rotaed on to preach 'to recorde hys sermon'.[17]

Henry's royal benefaction ought to be seen as the founding collection of the Syon Abbey library. But, as with much of the history of this richly fascinating and challenging collection, nothing is quite as simple as it looks. The books appear never to have arrived. The surviving catalogue of the library of the Brethren, drawn up and partly revised by Thomas Betson in the very early years of the sixteenth century, makes no mention of the royal books. Indeed early benefactions to the library are not specifically mentioned in the *Martiloge* until the record of a community decision reached in 1471, where the status of proto-benefactors goes instead to Thomas Grant, canon and precentor of St Paul's and to his parents.[18]

The death in 1471 of Thomas Grant, whose twenty-six donations recorded in the catalogue constitute a substantial collection of multi-work miscellany manuscripts, prompted the addition of special provision in the *Martiloge* for benefactors to the library. The service of the dead with nine readings and a requiem mass are to be said for those who provide books for 'librarie sororum vel librarie fratrum' or those who provide books for common use. On the brethren's side, the service is to be said by the priest brother who currently holds the deputed office of *custos librorum* or *librarie*, a post whose existence is confirmed from other documentary sources, notably the Library Ordinances of 1482.[19] The 1471 document implies the existence

Abbey', in *Studies in St Birgitta and the Brigittine Order*, ed. J. Hogg, Analecta Cartusiana 35/19 (1993), ii. 125–50.

[17] The Syon Additions for the Brethren (Guildhall manuscript) record in a short chapter headed 'Of the offices of the prechours' that 'Eche of the prechours schal besyde the sermon day haue thre hole days at lest oute of the quyer to recorde hys sermon', ed. Hogg, iii. 122. The preaching office of the Syon brethren has been carefully and thoughtfully studied by S. Powell, 'Preaching at Syon Abbey', *Working Papers in Literary and Cultural Studies* 29 (Salford, 1997); see also her 'Syon, Caxton and the Festial', *Birgittiana* 2 (1996), pp. 187–207, which discusses Syon's possible involvement with printed sermons. Tait, p. 214, notes that Bonde, Fewterer and Reynolds all served as university preachers at Cambridge before joining the order.

[18] *Martiloge*, fol. 17v: (*De exequiis pro benefactoribus librariarum. Capitulum 7*). The decision is dated 7 September 1471, and grants prayers 'inspeciali pro anima magistri Thome Graunte et pro animabus Iohannis et Helene parentum eius. In generali vero pro animabus eorum omnium qui librarie sororum vel librarie fratrum aliquem vel aliquos libros ad communem usum eorundem pro Dei honore ampliando contulerunt.'

[19] A surviving 1482 ordinance for the making of books refers to 'the kepers of the libraris of the bretherne and [Sys]terne Sydes there', printed by R. J. Whitwell, 'An Ordinance for Syon Library, 1482', *EHR* 25 (1910), pp. 121–3. The 1471 addition of an obsequy for donors to either of the two libraries is recorded in the *Martiloge*, fols. 4r–v and

of at least three collections of books at Syon: the library of the sisters; the library of the brethren and the collection of books held for common (and probably liturgical) use. Earlier Syon documents imply the emergence of a book culture early in the life of the house: the vernacular *Additions* to the Rule for the Sisters and for the Brethren, dating from the first half of the fifteenth century (though surviving only in much later copies), both include specific prescriptions against the mistreatment of books and require silence in what is explicitly called 'the lybrary'.[20] But prior to the 1471 agreement, over half a century of (not inconsiderable) manuscript library and literary acquisitions and activity apparently went unrecorded and uncelebrated. Inventories and registers earlier than the early sixteenth-century Betson catalogue should have existed, if only to fulfil the visitation injunctions that that such registers should be inspected by the diocesan bishop.[21] But no such earlier registers survive, nor do any obvious signs of earlier cataloguing, pressmarks or other indications of curatorial activity that can be said with any confidence to predate Betson's period as *custos librarie*. So the period after the 1471 *Martiloge* decision emerges as a decisive one in the history of the library of the brethren, and this renaissance in the library may have been the work of a recent recruit to the house.

Thomas Westhaw, third confessor-general, descibed in the *Martiloge* as 'doctor theologie', had been a fellow of Pembroke Hall, Cambridge in 1436. He was rector of All Hallows London and had moved to Syon by 1468, becoming confessor-general from 1472 to his death in 1488.[22] This period marks such a change and development in the library collection, including building works in 1479 on the fabric of the library, the profession in 1481 of Thomas Betson who acted as *custos librarie* and the arrival in 1482 of Thomas

17v–18r. The *Martiloge* also grants prayers for the souls of benefactors of books for 'common use', fol. 17r. De Hamel has suggested (pp. 60–61) that Grant was donating books to various institutions well before his death (including the copy of Bridget's *Revelations* now in BL, Add. MS 22572, given to Canterbury College, Oxford, and suggesting an (unsurprising) interest in the cult of the saint during his lifetime), but the entry in the Syon *Martiloge* dated 27 September follows close upon his death on July 8 1471 (not 1474 as some sources, including de Hamel, report it).

[20] Whitwell, 'An Ordinance for Syon Library', p. 121; Hogg, *Rewle of Seynt Sauioure*, iv.72 (the Additions for the Sisters). The relevant entries are usefully collected by M. C. Erler, 'Syon Abbey's Care for Books: Its Sacristan's Account Rolls 1506/7–1535/6', *Scriptorium* 39 (1985), pp. 293–307.

[21] The Bishop is to enquire 'quomodo custodiuntur et reperantur libri studiales inter fratres et si inter eos habeatur Inventorium seu Registrum eorundem librorum', Cambridge, St John's College, MS 11 (A.11), fol. 45v; Hogg, *Rewle of Seynt Sauioure*, ii. 144. Similar provisions appear in the vernacular Additions (Aungier, *History and Antiquities*, p. 278), but only this Latin version specifies books 'inter fratres'.

[22] The tradition that Westhaw was a Carthusian of Sheen before moving to Syon (mentioned in 'Dial M for Mystic' above, n. 1) is based on a reference to him in the Paston Letters. But, as I mentioned in that article, it was customary to refer to both Henrician foundations as 'the King's great work at Sheen' because of their geographical closeness, so the absence of any indult allowing transfer from Sheen to Syon suggests that this reference is the result of a common conflation or confusion.

Raille to care for the books, that it is tempting to suggest that it is Westhaw's reaction to the state of the Brethren's library holdings that may have prompted the reform of the collection in the wake of the 1471 *Martiloge* resolution.[23] Westhaw was himself a bibliophile, owning several collections of early printed *sammelbände* and contributing over fifty books to the collection.[24] It may be that the library at Syon was not the well-organized intellectual treasure house in the first half century of the house's existence that it was later to become and that the real heyday of the collection coincides quite precisely with the advent of printing and, perhaps incidentally, with the growth of the New Learning in England.

The absence of *ex libris* marks, curatorial marks, or earlier pressmarks on surviving Syon books suggests that Thomas Betson's task in drawing up the new *Registrum* was largely undertaken *ab initio*, and the skill and ingenuity of his design and execution of the new catalogue served the community well. The main stint of copying the new catalogue was completed around 1504, but some of the later additions are also in Betson's hand so he seems to have remained involved after this date. It is not clear when Betson gave up his work on the catalogue, or if he continued to supervise the work of the other scribes whose hands appear in the manuscript. He may have handed over during the first decade of the century. Even after his hand is replaced in entries into the catalogue, and even after his death in 1516, the collection continued to grow with the addition of new printed books. Some of these were added onto blank pressmarks in Betson's catalogue; others were simply not catalogued (as we have seen, some surviving books owned by John Fewterer (died 1536) do not feature in the catalogue at all, including, intriguingly, a Hebrew Concordance printed at Venice in 1524).[25] Books continued to be added to the catalogue at least until the mid-1520s, but Betson's meticulous standards of description, layout and detail were not uniformly sustained by those responsible for later additions.

Betson was a remarkable librarian, and perhaps a passionate one. In his sole surviving published work, *A Ryght Profytable Treatyse*, printed by Wynkyn de Worde in 1500, his parting shot is a colophon that reads '¶ Lerne to kepe your bokes clene &c.'. To gauge from the thirty or so books surviving from the Brethren's library, his descriptions in the catalogue were notably accurate (though not always exhaustively complete). He produced

---

[23] Erler, 'Care for Books', p. 298. Raille's duties at Syon are discussed in detail by de Hamel, *Syon Abbey*, pp. 83–91.

[24] See also N60, 61, 62 and 65.

[25] See n. 9 above, and also Oxford, Bodl. 8 A 11 Th (a copy of the Venice 1509 *opuscula* of Agepetus, with other works on the psalms by Reuchlin (Tubingen, 1512) and Nicholas Denyse (Paris, 1509), with the name of John Fewterer on the title page, and with characteristic Syon tags and nail holes on the lower board corresponding to the usual position of the Syon book label). A copy of the Hagenau 1501 edition of Pelbàrt Temesvári, *Stellarium Coronae beatae Mariae uirginis* with a Syon label on the lower board, giving the donor as Curson, is now in the collection of Dr A. I. Doyle. It appears not to have been in the catalogue in any of its recensions.

an index to the collection as he catalogued it that is so detailed that it allows modern users greater insight into the holdings. The index often adds crucially elaborative detail that allows the modern editor to clinch an identification or to link several occurrences of the same work.

Betson's catalogue already contains significant numbers of printed books even in its first recension, and it may be that his custodial activity was partly prompted by the increasing tide of printed books that necessitated revision, expansion and rearrangement of whatever inventories or *registra* preceded him. At the latest after his death in 1516, other hands took on the role and at some point in the 1520s the catalogue seems to have been abandoned. New marginal library marks added by a hand later than Betson's suggest that there may have been some intention to rearrange the collection to bring cognate materials more closely together. These added pressmarks might suggest that the Betson catalogue was being marked up for eventual absorption into a new *Registrum*. But there is room for doubt about whether this was ever executed: only one of the surviving books carries any sign of the 'new' pressmarks.[26]

As it survives today, the catalogue offers remarkable evidence of the continuing efforts to accommodate and incorporate new accessions and to reorder and perhaps dispose of older, superseded or less useful volumes. This gives a fascinating insight into the life of a major monastic collection as it embraced the change from script to print. As in Section A (discussed above), the items removed and apparently not reassigned elsewhere in the collection are interesting and potentially significant. It is, though, impossible to say with confidence whether such removals from the catalogue were the result of deliberate withdrawal of stock; the recognition of irredeemable loss through loan or damage; or the result of the texts being superseded, perhaps by printed editions or more comprehensive holdings.[27] The truth is probably a combination of all these factors, though I suspect that printed editions of collected *opera* seriously lessened the utility of some of the older manuscript miscellanies of patristic materials, and that printed canon law, with its superior finding aids and cross-referencing, rendered older manuscript collections less attractive. Lawyers, in my experience, always want the newest edition of everything, and the rearrangement of the law sections (T and V) was carefully and thoughtfully executed with few books disappearing altogether (though a canonical miscellany is replaced by a printed *Summa angelica* in T18). Thus the collection of English episcopal legislation that was originally in T22 is replaced by a printed vocabulary of canon law terms, maybe because its functions were now catered for by the multiple copies of Lyndwood's *Provinciale* which remained in the collection.

[26] However the evidence of surviving Syon books suggests that it was never common practice at Syon to put press or library marks in their books or on the book labels, even in the heyday of Betson's time as librarian.
[27] See the discussion of Section A above, and n. 9.

Both older copies of the Ottobonian constitutions are discarded, as are two copies of the constitutions of 'Iohannes episcopus Eboracensis' (the work of John Thoresby). Given Syon's later prominence in the debate over the King's divorce, the wholesale restocking of their canon law library proved to be both good librarianship and political prescience. Indeed it seems likely that this was one of the most heavily used sections of the library in the twenty years prior to the Dissolution.

Elsewhere in the catalogue, some authors attested in the index seem to have disappeared from the collection altogether. Bernardus Silvestris, who in Betson's original catalogue was represented in three separate books, no longer features in the catalogue in its final recension. The only copy of William of Conches (in C18 alongside Bernardus Silvestris) disappears to be replaced by a volume of Aristotelian *problemata* whose *secundo folio* agrees with editions printed in Venice in 1501 and 1505, the gift of John Fewterer. The only copy of Claudian goes, as does a copy of the Revelations of Elizabeth of Hungary in English. John Howden's thirteenth-century poem the *Philomela*, influential on the development of the English cult of the name of Jesus, goes to be replaced by the 1516 London edition of the *Nova legenda Angliae*, given by its printer Wynkyn de Worde. Both copies of Matthew of Vendôme, the only copy of Petrus Riga's *Aurora*, most of the works of Ovid (with the exception of the morally correct but textually discredited *De vetula*): all these go. But the balance is partly offset by the arrival of a printed text of the *Metamorphoses* given by the future wretch of Syon and former fellow of Queen's College, Cambridge, Richard Whitford. Also lost is a copy of 'Astrolabius poeta', perhaps Abelard's verses to his son, and an English *Consolation of Philosophy* (probably Chaucer's translation), though Boethius is still well represented in other copies including one with the influential glosses of Nicholas Trevet. A manuscript copy of the sermons of Bernadino of Sienna goes to be replaced by a printed copy of the same at R65. A manuscript copy of Pseudo Denys the Areopagite's mystical theology is discarded, but a printed copy of his complete works is added at D118 in the edition of Strasbourg 1501 which contains among much else no less than four Latin versions of the mystical theology in the translations of Sarracenus, Grosseteste, Ambrogio Traversari and Marsilio Ficino. It is hard to find a clear and purposeful pattern to these removals and additions, though randomly scattered copies of Aristotle disappear to be replaced by con-solidated humanist editions and commentaries. Noted printed humanist accessions include the *opera* of Virgil (in one of three 1490s editions all sharing the same *secundo folio*: A62); and two copies of the great Venice 1493 edition of Ptolemy, Zael, Bethem and Messahala (B47 and B55); the *opera* of Plato (C7, the Venice 1491 edition, containing thirty-nine works and a life of Plato by Ficino) and Plotinus (C3, the Florence 1492 edition with Marsilio Ficino's commentary). One of the later brethren, John Steyke, who died in 1513, seems to have had a modest but genuine interest in printed books of science and astronomy: among his fifty or so donations are copies of Euclid's *Elementa* and a run of eight books (B44–51) including Pliny, Ptolemy in the 1493 omnibus edition, the ten tracts on astronomy by Guido Bonnetti in the Augsburg 1491 edition, the Venice 1497 edition of the *Mathesis* and a print of Boethius's *De institutione arithmetica*. Little printed medicine is added to the quite extensive collections of urinaries and other diagnostic aids in Section B of the catalogue: whereas medicine was a clear emphasis in the holdings of the library in its manuscript phase, this is replaced by more speculative philosophy and science in its printed phase.

Perhaps the most mysterious effect of the post-Betson rearrangement of the catalogue is the disappearance of nearly all the works attributed to the Syon brethren themselves. In H34 Nicholas the deacon's sermons on Matthew chapter 1 are replaced by Fewterer's Basel 1494 edition of Thomas Aquinas on John. Symon Wynter's alphabetical collection of 'materia predicabilis' in L41 gives way to Lawsby's gift of a manuscript copy of the *Rosarium theologiae*, the reduced version of the alphabetical Wycliffite *Floretum*: very much a change of like for like; preaching aid for preaching aid; manuscript for manuscript. The sermons of Richard Bellyngham are removed without replacement from P34 and 35; likewise those of Thomas Bulde in P42 and 42 and R19. Hugo Damlett and Roger of Syon, both donors of books (the former not certainly a brother), both have their sermons deleted. The only Syon priest whose work survives into the final recension of the catalogue is Symon Wynter, with four volumes of *sanctorale* and *temporale* sermons, two copies of a vernacular sermon on the famous Syon pardon and commentaries on Marian antiphons. Why is this? Were their works buried with them? Were home grown sermons de-accessioned into the library of the sisters for improving reading or into some other intermediate collection? Although the reasons are murky, the policy is clear and ruthlessly applied.

One of the most comprehensive purges was, by accident or design, carried out on the works of John Wyclif. Four out of the six manuscript copies of Wyclif's works, scattered in miscellanies throughout the collection and offering some important attestations of rare works by him, such as a previously unknown commentary on Aristotle's *Metheorum* (C15: now also attested from a catalogue in the Carolinum Library in Prague), or a letter from Wyclif to John of Gaunt (K37) do not survive in the catalogue's final version. The view taken of him may be deduced from Betson's index entry for one of these lost texts: 'de sacramento altaris cum aliis de quibus cavendum est' (S6, fol. 11). But two copies of William Woodford's fourteenth-century attack on Wyclif's views survive the collection's reorganization. D75, given by William Catesby who died in 1510, also contains other anti-Wycliffite texts.

One of the reasons for Syon's foundation had been to stand as a bulwark of orthodoxy in the Lancastrian campaign against Lollardy. It is odd to see Lollard materials being apparently discarded at a period when the fight for catholic orthodoxy was once again hotting up. The library did have copies of Henry VIII's 1521 *Asssertio septem sacramentorum aduersus Martinum Lutherum* (O23), and John Fisher's *Assertionis Lutheranae confutationis* in the Antwerp 1523 *editio princeps* (S2), as well as Leo X's bull *Exsurge domine* of 15 June 1520 (S32). There was also a copy of *Malleus maleficarum* in S72, and a copy of Colet's *Sermo ad clerum* in a composite Reynolds volume (N26). But none of Fisher's later anti-Lutheran polemics are found in the catalogue, and the Syon brethren seem to have had no public or explicit role in the battle against heresy led by Fisher and his circle. There is no work by Thomas More recorded in the catalogue.[28]

Books arrived in both houses and libraries at Syon from external benefactors; they arrived with priests entering the order as brethren; and, judging by the donations attributed to the brethren in Betson's catalogue, they also continued to arrive for the use of those brethren after they had entered the order. This seems to have been the case particularly in the late fifteenth and early sixteenth centuries, a period of great growth in the size of the library collection, when a number of the brethren had arrived not only with substantial and impressive academic reputations but also with sub-stantial and impressive academic libraries. The pattern of recruitment, especially in the later years of the fifteenth century and into the sixteenth century, shows a high percentage of graduate entrants, and some very high-powered academic recruits, including several former heads of house at Oxford and Cambridge. Many of these men brought all or part of their books with them on profession (some made selected donations to their *alma mater* on resignation). Stephen Sawndre, for example, fifth confessor-general from 1497 to his death in 1513, was previously a fellow of Pembroke Hall, Cambridge and left three books to them on his resignation, probably to join Syon. Betson's catalogue records eighteen of his books in the brethren's collection. John Trowell, who left Merton College, Oxford as sub-warden in 1491, left the college three books and gave Syon twelve. Even in its early years, when the library seems to have been less substantial and wide-ranging, the house benefited from the generosity of its brethren.

Moreover, Syon brethren had embraced the potential of the printing press early.[29] Books printed in the 1460s and early 1470s are easily identified in the

---

[28] Though the copy of the *opuscula* of Lucian in G12 probably includes the translation of the *dialogi* by Erasmus and More (pr. Paris 1506, and subsequently). The rest of G12, given by Reynolds, contains editions by Erasmus of Lorenzo Valla's annotations on the New Testament; his translation of the *Hecuba* and *Iphigenia in Aulis* of Euripides; and the *Exempla* of Marcus Antonius Coccius Sabellicus, in the Paris 1509 edition (which preceded his profession in 1513).

[29] It should be noted, however, that some of these early prints will have entered Syon in the personal libraries of Brethren professed after this period. Nevertheless, the 'printed' quality of the Syon collection is striking. M. C. Erler, 'Pasted-in Embellishments in English Manuscripts and Printed Books', *The Library*, 6th Series 14 (1992), pp. 185–206, comments that Syon 'appears to be the only English religious institution whose espousal of the new technology of printing is extensive enough to be described as

surviving catalogue. Among the earliest printed books are a 1469 edition of Bessarion (B55), a 1470 Cicero (A45) and a Strasbourg c.1470 Valerius Maximus (K13), along with several volumes of *sammelbände*. Identified books come from presses across the length and breadth of Europe. As so many of the later accessions to the Brethren's library were printed books, it is possible in some cases to identify donations associated with particular priest-brethren which cannot have come into the house with them on their profession because their publication post-dates that profession, and this is a way of factoring out those books that were the accumulated baggage of earlier academic or secular careers. This baggage includes, for instance, the large number of Sentence commentaries, the preponderance of Aquinas and Scotus along with Alexander of Hales and the eloquently complete absence of any work by Ockham. All this points to the influence of set-texts from late fifteenth-century university syllabuses that were still weighted towards scholastic writers of the *via antiqua*.[30]

Stephen Sawndre, confessor-general from 1497–1513, resigned his Cambridge fellowship in 1478. He perhaps brought with him what is now D30 (the Cologne 1475 edition of Augustine of Ancona's *De ecclesiastica potestate*) and D35, the Venice 1477 edition of the *quodlibets* of Scotus edited by Thomas Penketh, a text firmly associated with the old 'scholastic' learning. But he must have subsequently acquired or been given C17 (the Venice 1491 print of Antonius Andreae's *quaestiones* on the *Metaphysics* of Aristotle) and A10 (Perotti's *Grammatica* and his *Ars epistolandi*, whose *secundo folio* agrees with the editions of Paris 1488 and Lyon 1492).

Richard Terenden, a fellow of New College, Oxford, in 1473, has books printed at Nuremberg in 1475 (H41), Venice 1480 (T54), Nuremberg 1484 (K49–51), 1485 (L46), Nuremberg 1487 (E60–63), Strasbourg 1490 (M99), Nuremberg 1498 (T66) and Strasbourg 1501 (T62), some of which will certainly have been acquired after his profession. He seems to have been systematically acquiring new printed books for over twenty years. Among his acquisitions are some significant books: the four-volume Bible with the postills of Nicholas of Lyre, printed by Koburger in Nuremberg 1487; the 1490 Strasbourg edition of the *Legenda aurea*; and several canon-law texts such as the Strasbourg 1501 edition of Durandus's *Rationale diuinorum*

adapting a continental model', both in relation to its own publications and its familiarity with continental printing though its library. See also M. Lane Ford, 'Importation of Printed Books into England and Scotland', in *Cambridge History of the Book*, ed. Trapp and Hellinga, pp. 179–201, who recalls that Graham Pollard argued for the import of printed books into England as early as July 1466.

[30] See Rex, *Theology of John Fisher*, pp. 13–29, and the chapters on university books by E. Leedham-Green and K. Jensen in *Cambridge History of the Book*, ed. Trapp and Hellinga. See also the chapters on theology (J. I. Catto) and the arts faculty (J. M. Fletcher) in *The History of the University of Oxford II. Late Medieval Oxford*, ed. J. I. Catto and T. A. R. Evans (Oxford, 1992). M. Lane Ford, 'Private Ownership of Printed books', in *Cambridge History of the Book*, ed. Trapp and Hellinga, pp. 205–28, discusses the book needs of students at different levels of the university curriculum.

officiorum or the 1498 Nuremberg edition of the *Summa angelica* of Angelo de Clavisio.

Richard Reynolds, the most prolific donor to the later collection with ninety-four volumes attributed to him in the catalogue, had been a fellow of Corpus Christi College, Cambridge, and where he seems to have carried out his external noviciate at Syon, completing his Cambridge doctorate after profession. He is recorded as donor of books printed after entering Syon in 1513, such as his Venice 1516 edition of Bessarion (C5). His copy of the sermons of Gabriel Biel (R38) has a *secundo folio* which agrees with Hagenau editions printed in 1510 and 1519, so it is unclear if he acquired it pre- or post-profession, but his copy of Johannes Raulyn's quadragesimal sermons (S24–5) was the Paris 1519 edition, and his copy of Raulyn's penitential sermons must post-date the *editio princeps* in Lyon in 1518. His copy of Thomas Ringstead's commentary on the book of Proverbs was in fact the Paris 1515 edition that attributed the work to Robert Holcot (G23), while his copy of Petrus de Natalibus's *Cathologus sanctorum* was the Lyon 1514 edition (M85). Of all the Brethren, his pattern of book acquisition suggests that his collection of books is the closest to the model of an English Christian humanist library as might be exemplified by the library of John Fisher.[31]

Another substantial late donor to the collection was John Fewterer, fellow of Pembroke Hall, Cambridge, still active in Cambridge as late as 1515, and confessor-general during the troubled years leading up to the suppression (he died in 1536), whose donations included the massive nine-volume edition of Jerome edited by Erasmus and printed in Basel in 1516 (H49–53) and Iohannes Oecolampadius's index to the Erasmus Jerome (H54) which was not published until 1520, and predated his election as confessor-general by only three years. It is likely that he acquired both after joining the Brethren. He also gave two volumes of the incomplete Basel 1521 edition of the works of Bede (I2–3). Fewterer in particular seems to have actively acquired printed books well into the mid-1520s, when the upkeep of the surviving catalogue seems to have been abandoned (or was perhaps transferred to another catalogue, of which no trace survives). His copy of the works of Fulgentius and Iohannes Maxentius (O43) has a *secundo folio* that agrees with the editions from Hagenau of 1520 and Cologne of 1526. If it was the latter, this would be the latest datable accession to the catalogue, but even the earlier edition would post-date his arrival at Syon. Other donors in the 1520s included Henry VII, who gave a copy of his 1521 *Asssertio septem sacramentorum aduersus Martinum Lutherum* (O23), and one Langton, probably not a member of the community as his name does not occur in the *Martiloge*, who gave the Erasmus New Testament paraphrases (Basel 1522: H57), his paraphrases on the Acts of

---

[31] Fisher's library has been helpfully reconstructed by Rex, *Theology of John Fisher*, pp. 192–203.

the Apostles (Basel 1524: I54), and Theophylact of Constantinople's *Enarrationes in quattuor euangelia* (Basel 1524, in the translation by Oecolampadius: H58). Another post-1520 accession was the Basel 1521 edition of Tertullian (N43), with no donor identified in the catalogue (perhaps a purchase for the community). But it is probably significant that there are relatively few recorded donations of post-1515 editions (Betson died in 1516), and very few recorded donations by Brethren after 1520. Accessions or purchases may gradually have stopped being recorded in the 'Betson' catalogue. Indeed, as we have seen, several volumes have survived which were known to have been owned by Fewterer in Syon but which are not recorded in the catalogue in its final phase. This might account for the paucity of interest in Hebrew or Greek evinced by the surviving entries in the *registrum*, though there is little compelling evidence to support what would be an adventitiously convenient upsurge of interest in biblical language study coinciding precisely with the falling into decline or neglect of the library register.

An earlier confrater, Lawsby, who died in 1490, presumably acquired his copy of the pseudo-Bonaventuran *Meditationes vitae Christi* only shortly before his death as the *secundo folio* given by Betson agrees with the edition printed in [Paris] and dated by ISTC [c.1490] (GW 4743). Thomas Westhaw, the reforming third confessor-general, had been a fellow of Pembroke Hall, Cambridge, until at least 1445–6. He vacated as Rector of All Hallows the Great (London) in 1459, perhaps to transfer to Syon, where he became confessor-general from 1472 to his death in 1488. Among his gifts were several collections (or *sammelbände*) of Cologne editions all printed in the early 1470s, and therefore certain to have been acquired during his time at Syon.

The networking and academic reputation of the post-1471 brethren may have placed them conveniently to benefit from the advent of the New Learning in England and may have helped them to identify, target and acquire or receive by gift many of the new editions and studies that flooded out of Europe's presses at this time. As Syon was not formally allowed to accept gifts of money (although sums are recorded in the *Martiloge*, perhaps as valuation of land or gifts in kind), and as all financial surpluses had to be disposed of at each year's end it seems possible that gifts of books would have been encouraged, especially in return for the kinds of external pastoral and spiritual duties undertaken by some of the Brethren.[32] But it is considerably more difficult to assess what the Brethren would have done with the books once they had them.

Despite the rigour of their lives (comparable in severity to the

---

[32] See also de Hamel, *Syon Abbey*, pp. 59–60, 88, who also notes that John, Duke of Bedford marked his laying of the foundation stone for the new site at Isleworth by giving the house 'duos pulchros libros officii sororum et vnam legendam' (p. 64); *Martiloge*, fol. 14v.

Carthusians), the Brethren of Syon do not seem to have had a contemporary reputation as mystics or mystagogues, or even as mystographs. Nothing in the *Martiloge* suggests special renown or expertise of a contemplative kind among the Brethren. (Indeed the entire order boasts only two saints in its six-hundred-year-history, one of whom was the English martyr Richard Reynolds, whose heroism was political rather than mystical).[33] Part of this is no doubt because we know rather little about the careers and backgrounds of the Brethren, especially the non-graduate brethren and all the Brethren in the first fifty years of the house's existence. Nor do we know much about the extent and range of their spiritual guidance of lay people. But this is of course a circular argument: their obscurity may be well deserved. It is unlikely in a house so well connected, so keen on self-publicity and so well frequented by the chattering classes of its day that reputations for contemplative or visionary excellence would not have become known. Perhaps this is the silence of the dog that did not bark. Why, for example, are so many of the contemplative, meditative and devotional texts known to have been in Syon ownership written by Sheen Carthusians?[34] We can only be guided by the austerity of their published works and the aspirations of their way of life.

Among the later Brethren, there is some evidence to suggest that they continued to acquire a few printed mystical texts until quite late in the house's history. The Paris 1510 edition of the *Speculum spiritualium* (M36) was added by William Barnarde (died 1517). Edyman, master of Corpus Christi College, Cambridge, in 1515, gave a copy of the Paris 1513 edition of *Liber trium uirorum et trium spiritualium uirginum*, edited by Jacques Le Fèvre d'Etaples, which included the *Pastor* of Hermas, the *Liber uisionum* of Robert d'Uzes, Hildegard of Bingen's *Scivias*, the life of Elizabeth of Schönau, and Mechtild of Hackeborn's *Liber specialis gratiae* (M121). Another copy of the same edition was at M107, given by Selby. Another printed text was a 1512 edition of Gregory of Nyssa and Gregory Nazianzen in N3, and a further edition of Gregory Nazianzen, printed at Strasburg in 1508 (O54), both editions given by John Fewterer.

But the number of contemplative, mystical or paramystical accessions during this period is swamped by the number of printed sermons, printed canon law and, most notably, more directly humanist editions, especially among the books of Richard Reynolds and John Fewterer.

Indeed if the Syon Brethren had a reputation, especially in the later

---

[33] However, the Carthusian Maurice Chauncy's c.1570 account of the martyrdom of Reynolds and the London Carthusians describes him as 'insignis ille raraeque sanctitatis et doctrinae', recording that (true to the preaching vocation of the Syon Brethren) he preached a 'godly and noble sermon' to the crowd while awaiting his turn on the scaffold: M. Chauncy, *The Passion and Martyrdom of the Holy English Carthusian Fathers: The Short Narration*, ed. G. W. S. Curtis (London, 1935), pp. 96–7.

[34] This subject is explored in greater detail in my 'Dial M for Mystic' (above n. 1).

years of the house, it was for previous secular academic brilliance rather than mystical or spiritual excellence: Richard Whitford entered the order after a career in academic and ecclesiastical administration, including service with John Fisher, and with the accolade of letters and a dedication from Erasmus in his edition of the dialogues of Lucian. Richard Reynolds was reputed to be one of the finest scholars of his day, but proved his heroic virtue not in mystical endeavours but on the gibbet at Tyburn, alongside the Carthusian martyrs of the London house. The supply of recruits to Syon from careers in education, administration and as secular clergy (especially in and around London) is well documented. In the early sixteenth century (and perhaps from as early as the 1470s) Syon seems particularly to have functioned as sheltered housing for retiring academics, whereas in the early years a university education was less prized: at the 1428 election for confessor-general, only John Bracebridge, the largest single benefactor to the library with 111 volumes, is recorded as a graduate, and most of his career prior to Syon had been spent as a grammar master in Lincoln diocese. But the fact that John Blacman, advisor of Henry VI and owner of one of the finest private collections of contemplative books in England, chose to enter the Carthusians as a *clericus-redditus* reminds us that other paths were open to those in retreat from public life. John Colet, for example, built for himself a retreat in the grounds of Sheen Charterhouse that was subsequently used by Cardinal Pole and Cardinal Wolsey.

The reading typified by Syon books, and recommended by Betson on the authority of his titular saint Jerome is of the kind provided by Thomas Gascoigne's miscellany of scriptural and patristic extracts (N58–9) and the eremitic miscellanies found widely in the catalogue. There are, as de Hamel says, works by a range of benchmark humanist writers. But they are of a consistently high-minded theological bent. Marsilio Ficino, for example, is mainly represented by his editorial and translation work on the texts of Proclus, Plotinus and Plato. Theodore of Gaza is likewise well represented as a translator and editor of printed editions. Poggio, Gaguin, Mapheus Vegius and Marcus Vigerius are usually represented in a single work or in a single volume. Valla's edition of Sallust is at A77 and the 1505 Erasmus edition of Valla on the New Testament was at G12 in a volume of Erasmian editions given by Reynolds.[35] Christofero Landini's *Camuldulensian Disputations* is represented in a Strasbourg 1508 print belonging to Reynolds (O20). Boccaccio is present in a single edition of both the *Genealogiae deorum gentilium* and the *De montibus* (C6, a composite volume given by Reynolds); Petrarch in a printed *De remediis utriusque fortunae*, and a manuscript collection containing that, the *Secretum*, *De vita solitaria* and his commentary on the penitential psalms (N37). And many humanist authors such as Nicholaus Perottus, Agostino Dati, Johann Reuchlin, Dionysius Nestor, and

---

[35] See n. 28 above.

Heinrich Bebel are represented primarily by 'primer' works of grammatical or rhetorical instruction. There was a single copy of Reuchlin's De uerbo mirifico (G24, in a volume given by Fewterer) but this is the only trace of Christian Cabbalism. Even Pico, a model of the synthetic humanism that brought together the best of patristic and new learning, is represented only by a two-volume edition of his opera (O41–2) given by Reynolds (the Strasbourg 1504 edition).

The Syon library did, however, contain many of the monuments of Christian humanist patristic scholarship: the 1516 Erasmian Jerome (H49–54); the eleven-volume 1505 opuscula of Augustine (O79–87); the 1512 opera of Origen (G52–3); the works of Ambrose (N76–8 and O29–31, both, in the Basel 1492 editio princeps); and Tertullian (N43, in the Basel 1521 edition); of Athanasius and the Victorines (e.g. the opera of Hugh in the Paris edition of 1506 at I34 and N86, both given by Fewterer). It also contained many printed texts and commentaries on the Bible, especially Nicholas of Lyra and Hugh of Saint-Cher. The library also contained most of the major biblical works by Erasmus, and some of the innovatory editions of Jacques LeFèvre D'Etaples (e.g. I4 on the Pauline epistles). But there are also many copies of much older commentaries and of the Common Gloss, and it would be difficult to characterize its holdings in biblical scholarship as distinctively humanist. Rather, like the collection as a whole, it is eclectic and chronologically layered, reflecting the tastes, interests, acquisitions and set texts of several generations of brethren. There are, for example, many manuscript and printed copies of hard-core 'scholastic' texts, including quantities of Thomas Aquinas, and many of these 'scholastic' texts survived the later purging and rearrangement of the catalogue. The single largest genre in the library's holdings of printed books is sermons, reflecting the distinctive preaching function of the Brigittines.

The size and extent of the library holdings at Syon may perhaps be giving a false impression of interest among the brethren in mystical humanist texts, especially as the their own literary output is heavily tilted towards ascetic adaptations of mystical texts like David of Augsburg and emasculated rules of life for nuns and lay people. However generously interpreted, the publications of the English Syon Brethren cannot support a claim for serious and extensive engagement with the literature of contemplative and para-mystical aspiration. Even allowing for the fact that Betson's A Ryght Profytable Treatyse was aimed at entrants to religion and at a secondary audience of laymen, Betson's spiritual aim is modest (and characteristically Brigittine given Bridget's own ascetic view of the world). A similar experience is found in reading Thomas Prestin's (or Prestius's) vernacular version of David of Augsburg's De exterioris et interioris hominis compositione (of which there were multiple copies of the Latin text in the library).[36]

---

[36] e.g. M24; M57; M78. Thomas's translation of this work is edited by P. S. Jolliffe, 'Middle English Translations of De exterioris et interioris hominis compositione', Mediaeval Studies 36 (1974), pp. 259–77.

William Bonde, the most mystical of all Syon authors, shows the influence of Christian humanism's scholarly attention to patristic texts in his careful scholarly apparatus to his works. But Reynolds, the most impressively humanist of all the Brethren judging by his books, is deafeningly silent, and Fewterer's literary output is a blend of late medieval affective spiritualities.[37] Perhaps, because the order was brought to England as part of a campaign to uphold rigour and orthodoxy against heterodox thought and teaching, it may be that the early Brethren in particular deliberately played safe with the materials they produced, especially those which might circulate outside the enclosure, or played safer still by not producing any materials of that kind at all. Their caution might have been reinforced by the threats of neo-Lollardy and Lutheranism.

Certain broad trends are discernible in the growth and development of the collection of the Syon Brethren as witnessed by the *registrum*. Script gives way to print, or is at least increasingly heavily outnumbered; manuscript miscellanies gave some way to collected *opera*; *antiqui* give way to *moderni*; Christian humanist learning shows signs of supplementing if not entirely supplanting the old wisdom; scholasticism is firmly of the *via antiqua* in both manuscript and printed holdings; secular learning in science and classical languages continues into the sixteenth century (though Greek and Hebrew texts are very thinly represented); vernacular materials remain scarce (less than thirty items in total). When they are singled out for attention, Syon's printed biblical and patristic holdings seem in the mainstream of Christian humanism, but in the wider context of the catalogue, they are in fact surrounded by many older and pre-humanistic texts and commentaries. In any case, was a real and informed choice of intellectual school possible for a potential buyer within the range of available printed editions? It is surely much more likely that, especially in the years before 1500, printed editions were acquired as and when they became available, and their ownership is probably not reliable evidence of a positive intellectual allegiance, though it may reflect a particular intellectual caste and training. There is no sign among the book holdings of the Syon Brethren of consistent engagement with contemporary debates on biblical inspiration, for example, despite the fact that John Fisher and Richard Pace, two leading protagonists, had strong connections with Syon, Pace having stayed there for some time in 1527.[38] In the preference for *via antiqua* schoolmen over Ockham and the nominalists, the Syon library (perhaps cumulatively) reflects the humanism of late fifteenth-century Cambridge and the libraries of men like Fisher. Or perhaps it merely basks in the acquired glory of the embedded libraries of Reynolds and Fewterer. What any of the Brethren actually did with the books is another matter altogether.

In Thomas Betson's A *Ryght Profytable Treatyse*, printed in 1500, Betson

---

[37] See Hogg, 'Contribution', passim, and n. 13 above.
[38] Rex, *Theology of John Fisher*, pp. 148–61.

cites Pseudo Jerome's *Regula monachorum* (a copy of which was in the library at O55) to establish a paradigm of behaviour that must have been amenable to this book-loving man:

> Lete none see you from the seruyce of god or unoccupyed. In redynge of propheytes, epystles, gospelles, sayntes lyues and other dedes of vertue doynge, hauynge euer bokes in your handes, studyenge or wrytynge þat peple seynge you may saye: Beholde here the seruaunt of god and the lanternes of the world.[39]

The literary output of the Syon Brethren is modest indeed considering the intellectual firepower it could muster in the last fifty years of its existence. But the pattern of book acquisition in the post-1471 library suggests that the exhortation to study and reading may have been more widely respected, and that that reading was generally more Christian than Ciceronian.[40] Certainly the library had a reputation, and was a place of resort for scholars. This is supported by the famous report of the Venetian Gasparo Spinelli concerning his visit to Syon in July 1527 to meet Richard Pace, dean of St Paul's, where he describes him as 'leading a blessed life in that beautiful place', surrounded by such a quantity of books that Spinelli had never seen the like of before. Pace is reported as making himself competent as a Hebrew and Chaldean scholar, as part of his study of corruptions in the Latin text of Scripture.[41] But it is precisely books such as these that are most eloquently absent from the Syon catalogue. And, by the date of Spirelli's visit, maintenance of Betson's *registrum* had been abandoned.

---

[39] STC 1978, repr. in facsimile (Cambridge, 1905), sig. c iv v.

[40] For example, none of the books discussed in D. R. Carlson, *English Humanist Books: Writers and Patrons, Manuscript and Print, 1475–1525* (Toronto, 1995) is attested in the library of the Syon Brethren.

[41] Rex, *Theology of John Fisher*, pp. 149–52; *I diarii di Marino Sanuto*, ed. F. Stefani, G. Berchet and N. Barrozzi (58 vols., Venice, 1879–1903), xlv. 631; Tait, p. 340; R. Rex, 'The Earliest use of Hebrew in Books Printed in England: Dating some works of Richard Pace and Robert Wakefield', *TCBS* 9 (1990), pp. 517–25. J. Wegg, *Richard Pace: Tudor Diplomat* (London, 1932).

Franciscan Learning in England, 1450–1540

JEREMY CATTO

Unlike the older religious orders, the friars of fifteenth-century England have not had the posthumous satisfaction of a late-flowering respect among modern historians for their learning and intellectual achievements. The sharp contrast between the impressive literary record of their predecessors from the age of Grosseteste to that of Wyclif, and their own meagre, virtually non-existent contribution in the age of the Renaissance, has been, and remains, a mystery. Leland's famous description of the Greyfriars library at Oxford just before its dissolution in the autumn of 1538 only confirms a century's accumulation of negative evidence: 'at the Franciscans' house there are cobwebs in the library, and moths and bookworms; more than this – whatever others may boast – nothing, if you have regard to learned books. For I, in spite of the opposition of all the friars, carefully examined all the bookcases in the library.'[1] True, the remaining bookworms, if we can take them seriously, do rather imply that there had been books about not long before, which may have been disposed of like the plate and the lead on the convent roof, out of necessity or the desire to thwart the King's commissioners; the latter possibility may be the reason why so many books of the various Cambridge friaries, only two of them apparently seen by Leland, ended up in the Ottobuoni collection in the Vatican.[2] But at some point between the visits of Dr Thomas Gascoigne to the Greyfriars library, datable to between 1432 and 1458, and that of Leland, the destruction of an elaborate instrument of instruction and scholarship was accomplished, an instrument to which the book collection was essential. We must bear in mind the possibility that it may have been accomplished not by long-term decay but by rapid and deliberate action shortly before the dissolution of the convent itself.

---

[1] J. Leland, *Collectanea*, ed. T. Hearne (6 vols. in 4, London, 1715), iii. 60. Leland's Latin is quoted by K. W. Humphreys, *The Friars' Libraries*, Corpus of British Medieval Library Catalogues 1 (1990), p. 229; I have used the translation of A. G. Little, *The Grey Friars in Oxford*, Oxford Historical Society 20 (1891), p. 62 n. 4.

[2] N. R. Ker, 'Cardinal Cervini's Manuscripts from the Cambridge Friars', *Xenia medii aevi historiam illustrantia oblata Thomae Kaeppeli OP*, ed. R. Creytens and P. Künzle (Rome, Edizioni di storia e letteratura, 1978), pp. 51–71, repr. in N. R. Ker, *Books, Collectors and Libraries*, ed. A. G. Watson (London, 1985), pp. 437–58; J. Carley, 'John Leland and the Contents of English Pre-Dissolution Libraries: The Cambridge Friars', *TCBS* 9 (1986), pp. 90–100.

Against this unpromising background the humanistic interests of individual friars can hardly outbalance the literary inactivity of their fellows, particularly as they did not bear fruit in compositions from English friars' hands. Henry Standish, the friar castigated by Thomas More for his criticism of Erasmus's edition of the Greek New Testament, was probably more interested in philology than in scholastic philosophy, though his opponents presented him as a champion of the so-called Old Learning; but he has left no writings. The Greek learning of the Cambridge friar Richard Brinkley is often adduced in this context. Brinkley was at Cambridge from 1489 and a doctor of theology of both Oxford and Cambridge; from 1518 to 1526 he was minister provincial. His notes in a Greek psalter and Greek New Testament now at Caius testify to his interest in Greek biblical scholarship: he borrowed the latter manuscript from the Oxford Franciscan convent. He also borrowed from Bury St Edmunds a Hebrew psalter. Perhaps it was at his behest that the Cambridge convent acquired printed texts of Photius and of the letters of Aeneas Sylvius Piccolomini (later Pope Pius II). But he evidently did nothing with his learning, and he seems to have been unknown to Erasmus. Nor to all appearances did he have any followers. His interests were individual in an order that had become intellectually original through co-operative learning; they seem to have had no point of contact with the traditional, and continuing, work of the friars. They cannot help us to understand the state of mind of his contemporaries.[3]

The fate of the Oxford convent must not be seen, of course, in isolation. It was only one of the Franciscan *studia* in the English province; the Greyfriars convent at Cambridge was equally ancient, and received English and foreign friars in similar proportion to its Oxford sister up to its dissolution; and there were other *studia* of the order in each of the seven custodies, especially London, Norwich and York, as well as a semi-detached Observant house of recent foundation at Greenwich.[4] Nor should the Franciscans be treated separately from the other orders of friars. The Dominicans, Carmelites and Austin friars were also in principle bodies of learned preachers and scholars, all of whom, like the Franciscans, owed the regulation of their educational provisions to the decrees of Benedict XII in the 1330s. They too had *studia* in the same cities as the Friars Minor, where in principle, and in the fourteenth century at least in practice too, foreign friars might be assigned for their advanced education.[5] That intellectual activity among all the orders of friars

---

[3] On Standish see Thomas More, *Letter to the University of Oxford*, ed. and trans. D. Kinney, *The Complete Works of St Thomas More* (15 vols., London, 1963–), xv. 130–49; on Brinkley, J. H. Moorman, *The Grey Friars in Cambridge, 1225–1538* (Cambridge, 1952), pp. 155–6.

[4] J. H. Moorman, *A History of the Franciscan Order to 1517* (Oxford, 1968), pp. 124, 444; W. J. Courtenay, *Schools and Scholars in Fourteenth-Century England* (Princeton, 1987), pp. 61–77.

[5] Moorman, *History of the Franciscan Order*, pp. 366–7; Courtenay, *Schools and Scholars*, pp. 63, 70, 76.

in England seems to have left few traces in the last century of their existence must be a significant circumstance for understanding the specific position of the Franciscans. By the same token, the evidence of intellectual renewal among the Franciscans of Italy and Spain to which the preaching of St Bernardino of Siena and the reforming energy of Francisco Ximénez de Cisneros, founder of the University of Alcalá, bears witness, applies equally to the Dominican friars whose preachers, like St Vincent Ferrer, and reformers such as Savonarola are comparable to the Franciscans. It is no longer necessary after the work of several scholars, most notably Barrie Dobson, to draw attention to the achievements of the monastic orders, whether in England or abroad, during the Renaissance, achievements which did not prevent the destruction of their monastic houses under Henry VIII; and for that matter it was only by a whisker that several secular foundations, including the colleges of Oxford and Cambridge, escaped a similar fate. Had they too failed to avoid the wholesale bonfire of corporate bodies contem-plated in the 1540s – their own libraries did not entirely escape it – our perspective on the end of the English Franciscans would be radically different.

This is the context in which it is necessary to examine the practical system of education and evangelization within which the learning of the Franciscans had flourished. Their learning had always been subordinate to the apostolic purpose of the order; Franciscan theology, as developed by Bonaventure and Duns Scotus, was defined as a practical not a speculative science guided by the Franciscan doctrine of the primacy of the will over the intellect. In its dominant Scotist form, the theology of the Franciscan masters looked to the idea of God's freedom and its perfection in love as the principle of the created universe, manifested above all in the Incarnation of Christ.[6] The operation of the human intellect could never be satisfied by its contemplating a purely rational or natural order: constantly thrown up against the impenetrable mysteries of *theologia Dei* beyond its comprehen-sion, it must adopt a stance of humility before the intuitive wisdom of babes and sucklings, and find its fulfilment in works of charity including preaching and hearing confessions. The massive intellectual achievement of the fourteenth-century Friars Minor could never be measured by their literary remains, university lectures circulating in book form and model sermon collections; it is lost to historians in the personal encounters, in public in the pulpit or privately in conversation or the confessional, between trained and learned friars and their clientèle. Its foundations, however, are clear enough. A network of *studia*, headed by the university convents at Oxford and Cambridge, gave the friars instruction in arts subjects and elementary theology at least as good as that provided for secular students, as the

---

[6] For a brief summary see J. I. Catto, 'Theology and Theologians, 1220–1320', *A History of the University of Oxford I. The Early Oxford Schools*, ed. J. I. Catto (Oxford, 1984), pp. 505–11, esp. pp. 507–8.

extensive knowledge of natural science manifested by William Woodford in his biblical commentary of 1373 goes to show; he had acquired it, evidently, in the London Greyfriars.[7] These *studia* were accessible to foreign friars through the process of assignation by the Chapter General of the order. In this way Nicholas Comparini could come from Assisi to Norwich in 1337, bringing books with him as well as conveying texts back to his home province in due course; the Norwich *studium* at this time was clearly a lively centre of learning and debate.[8] Well-stocked libraries were essential to the Franciscan strategy of transmitting sound learning to the laity; but they were only the beginning of an elaborate attempt to put every form of text to maximum use, of which the most striking initiative was the *Registrum Anglie*, a kind of union catalogue of patristic and other texts available in a wide variety of English monastic libraries. To judge by the complaint of at least one late fourteenth-century secular student, the friars at Oxford and perhaps elsewhere were inclined to keep the immediate benefits of their organized learning to themselves, denying others access to the often unique texts in their library.[9] But the result of their project, by the beginning of the fifteenth century, was the creation of a cadre of supremely well-qualified preachers and confessors, whose services were in constant popular demand. It made the friars, especially the Franciscans, distinctly unpopular with *bien-pensant* opinion among the secular clergy, which only underlined their impact on the wider population.

Did the traditional structure of Franciscan education survive into the fifteenth century and beyond? The Oxford University registers and the Cambridge grace books yield the names of numerous friars after 1450 who studied theology and became bachelors and doctors; indeed the Oxford registers allow more friars to be identified from these years than in any previous generation. There is also evidence of the assignment of foreign friars to both Oxford and Cambridge at least as late as the 1490s. In nearly every case, however, the entry in the grace book or register is the only evidence of a particular friar's career: after graduation they disappear from the record. A few became Irish or Welsh bishops, such as Richard Edenham, bishop of Bangor, and others seem to have abandoned their vows for careers as secular clergy. They are the exceptions. One can only conclude, in the case of the majority, that they remained in their convents and quietly

[7] Catto, 'Wyclif and Wycliffism in Oxford, 1356–1430', in A History of the University of Oxford II. Late Medieval Oxford, ed. J. I. Catto and T. A. R. Evans (Oxford, 1992), pp. 196–8.

[8] W. J. Courtenay, 'Nicholas of Assisi and Vatican MS Chigi B.v.66', Scriptorium 36 (1983), pp. 260–63.

[9] R. H. and M. A. Rouse, Registrum Anglie de libris doctorum et auctorum veterum, Corpus of British Medieval Library Catalogues 2 (1991) and 'The Franciscans and Books: Lollard Accusations and the Franciscan Response', in From Ockham to Wyclif, ed. A. Hudson and M. Wilks, Studies in Church History, Subsidia V (Oxford, 1987), pp. 369–84.

pursued their pastoral vocations: for the most part, they would only turn up in the historical record if they were concerned with property transactions or accused of some offence, and their anonymity therefore might be taken as a sign of the success of their pastoral work on the traditional basis of personal poverty and advanced theological training. Certainly one cannot assume, given the complete lack of systematic documentation from any convent, that the silence of the record implies the desuetude of the system. The steady stream of Franciscans and other friars though the Oxford and Cambridge schools would hardly have flowed had it not produced obvious value for the considerable sums of money involved.

The continuity of Franciscan education need not, of course, imply that it was still informed by the ideas of Bonaventure and Scotus. So far as I know, a notebook of indisputably Franciscan origin which might throw light on theology teaching in either the Oxford or the Cambridge convent in this period does not survive. The closest we get is the logic notebook of an Austin friar, Thomas Penketh, who studied at Oxford sometime in the early 1460s; this is now Corpus Christi College, Oxford, MS 126. It includes *quaestiones* by an earlier Augustinian doctor, William Russell, of a distinctly Scotist character, as well as a text of Antonius Andreae's equally Scotist commentary on the *Metaphysics*. In the 1470s Penketh was lector in Padua, where he brought out the *editio princeps* of the Sentences commentary and of the quodlibetal questions of Scotus, and of Antonius Andreae's *Metaphysics*, though whether he used his own manuscript text of that work has not been established. He was evidently one of the leading Scotus scholars of the day, and in his way a precursor of the great humanist editors of the next generation, who included Erasmus.[10] His work also provides evidence of the predominantly Scotist outlook of the Oxford schools in the fifteenth century, and if the schools as a whole looked to Duns Scotus as their guiding spirit, the Franciscan school must *a fortiori* have taught his philosophy. Fortunately there is more direct evidence of the teaching of the school. Friar John Foxholes took the degree of bachelor of theology at Oxford in 1451; he went on to lecture on logic according to the ideas of Scotus at the convent of San Paolo in Monte at Bologna. His expositions of the commentaries of Scotus and Antonius Andreae were popular in the late fifteenth century, and were printed more than once.[11] It is clear from the work of Penketh and Foxholes that the philosophy of Scotus flourished in Italy in the late fifteenth and early sixteenth centuries, and also that they owed some of their inspiration to English Franciscan teaching, and especially to its original home in Oxford, where two Franciscan friars, William Vavasour and Petrus Pauli of Nyköping in Sweden were transcribing texts of Scotus and Antonius

[10] Catto, 'Theology after Wycliffism', *Late Medieval Oxford*, ed. Catto and Evans, pp. 269–70.

[11] Ibid., pp. 270–71; G. J. Etzkorn, 'John Foxal OFM: His Life and Writings', *Franciscan Studies* 49 (1989), pp. 17–24.

Andreae as late as 1491.[12] Even later, in 1505, an Italian friar at the Oxford convent, Girolamo da San Marco, published a work on Aristotelian mechanics and two years later a guide to Scotist logic.[13] An analogous development occurred among the French Franciscans, who used the revised textbook of Guillaume de Vaurouillon (or Vorillon), a Scotist commentary on the Sentences composed perhaps in the 1430s, which addressed current questions and which was printed for more general circulation at the end of the century.[14] Though the evidence is sparse, it is consistent: it was possible, as in Paris, for young Franciscans to be trained in an up-to-date version of the traditional philosophy of their order in Oxford, and almost certainly elsewhere in England, as late as the first decade of the sixteenth century.

The dominance over the Oxford schools which the Franciscan philosophy of Duns Scotus had achieved by the end of the fourteenth century was probably not fortuitous. It was more accommodating than its rivals to the need felt by many thinkers of that epoch to find room for mystical theology and the art of contemplation within the confines of the academic discipline. Jean Gerson, lecturing at Paris on mystical theology in November 1402, had urged his confrères in the theology faculty to read the classics of the contemplative art, as had their greater predecessors Augustine, Hugh of St Victor and Thomas Aquinas.[15] His advice was congenial to English theologians familiar with the Franciscan masters. One of the modern classics of contemplation was the book attributed to St Bonaventure but probably written by another Franciscan, John de Caulibus, the *Meditationes super vitam Christi*; its phenomenal popularity in Latin and in several vernaculars in the fifteenth century testifies to the enduring hold of Franciscan spirituality on readers of widely different intellectual attainments.[16] John Foxholes himself emphasized the purpose of theology as a practical art tending to the increase of charity when he explained that the intention of his commentary on Scotus's exposition of Porphyry was to make more fruitful the work of preachers.[17] While at Oxford he copied out a text of the *Meditationes* in his

---

[12] Oxford, Corpus Christi College, MSS 227 and 228.

[13] Girolamo da San Marco, *Opusculum de universali mundi machina ac metheoricis* (London, 1505) and *Compendium praeclarum quod parva logica seu summule dicitur* (Cologne, 1507).

[14] William of Vorillon, *Super quattuor libros Sententiarum* (Venice 1496 and other editions). See F. Pelster, 'Wilhelm von Vorillon, ein Skotist des 15 Jahrhunderts', *Franziskanische Studien* 8 (1921), pp. 48–66; Ignatius Brady, 'The *Liber de Anima* of William of Vaurouillon OFM', *Medieval Studies* 10 (1948), pp. 225–97 and 11 (1949), pp. 247–307.

[15] Jean Gerson, *De mystica theologia lectiones sex*, ed. P. Glorieux, *Oeuvres complètes de Jean Gerson* (10 vols., Paris, 1960–75), iii. 255–6.

[16] *Meditaciones de passione Christi*, ed. Sister M. J. Stallings (Washington, Catholic University Press of America, 1965); on its English translation by Nicholas Love O.Carth. see now *Nicholas Love*, ed. S. Ogura, R. Beadle and M. G. Sargent (Cambridge, 1997).

[17] *Expositio questionum doctoris subtilis Joannis Scoti in universalibus Porphyrii edita a magistro Joanne Anglico ordinis minorum* (Venice, 1512), fol. 63.

own hand, together with Bonaventure's *Legenda maior*, the standard life of St Francis, Richard Rolle's *Form of Living* and the brief tract of Friar Henry Chambernoun, *Doctrina in via perfectionis*. The manuscript, now Hereford Cathedral MS P.1.9, must have remained at Greyfriars when he left for Bologna after 1451, as it is annotated by Gascoigne.[18] The Scotism of Foxholes was not therefore merely a dry academic shell: it is likely that Scotus's emphasis on the Incarnation as an eternally predestined event, and not the consequence of original sin, and on Mary's immaculate motherhood, a relation outside human causality, provided for his fifteenth-century disciple the intellectual backbone for popular devotion: more precisely, for the Franciscan devotion centred on the humanity of Christ which was purveyed in the pseudo-Bonaventuran *Meditationes* and in numerous Franciscan sermons.

It was perhaps on this popular and diffused level that the genuine, continuing theological sophistication of the fifteenth-century friars is most palpable, though even there it is only visible in fleeting glimpses. The best-established channel of diffusion was the sermon; friars had transformed and popularized preaching, which reached its apogee in the fifteenth century in the great open-air sermons of St Bernadino of Siena and St John Capistrano. Among the mass of fifteenth-century sermon-cycles of English origin, it has been difficult to isolate the Franciscan variety. One such set, perhaps preached about 1415, has been attributed to the Franciscan author of the tract *Dives and Pauper*; another was preached by Friar Nicholas Philip in various places between 1430 and 1436, providing solid evidence of Franciscan preaching tours on a large scale; in mid-century the sermons of Dr John Brackley, John Paston's confidant and a Franciscan of Norwich, were probably never collected but were evidently numerous.[19] William Goddard the elder, minister provincial of the Franciscans whose career stretched from the late 1440s, when Bishop Pecock angrily denounced his preaching, to the 1490s, was reputed a great preacher in his time, though no sermons of his can now be identified.[20] Surviving sermons exhibit a well-digested learning of a traditional kind in which Franciscan devotional themes, developed in accordance with Franciscan theology, predominate. Even the carols or devotional poems which were written to be sung by preaching friars and their audiences were composed with theological orthodoxy in view: among many anonymous pieces, a collection of 166 poems written about 1490 by Friar James Ryman of the Canterbury convent

[18] See R. A. B. Mynors and R. M. Thomson, *Catalogue of the Manuscripts of Hereford Cathedral Library* (Cambridge, 1993), p. 69.

[19] A. Hudson and H. L. Spencer, 'Old Author, New Work: The Sermons of MS Longleat 4', *Medium Ævum* 53 (1984), pp. 220–38; A. J. Fletcher, 'The Sermon Booklets of Friar Nicholas Philip', *Medium Ævum* 55 (1986), pp. 188–202; on Friar Brackley's preaching see his letter to John Paston in *Paston Letters and Papers*, ed. N. Davis (2 vols., Oxford, 1971–6), ii. 221–2, no. 618, probably quoting an actual sermon.

[20] On Goddard see Emden, *BRUO*, ii. 776.

survives.[21] The popularization of theology, therefore, does not imply any intellectual degeneration. There is no reason to assume that the almost anonymous friars whose names appear in the Oxford and Cambridge registers, and are not heard again, were defective either in intelligence or education. Anonymity, after all, was part of their religious discipline.

There is no reason, therefore, to believe the rhetoric of Erasmus, Thomas More or Dr John London, the leading Oxford enforcer of Thomas Cromwell's reformation, when they turned their scorn on Scotist logic or rejoiced to see the 'leaves of Duns' fluttering in the breeze of New College quadrangle. It was, indeed, ignored at the time by dozens of lecturers on the text of Aristotle, who now referred to the new printed editions of Scotus brought out by Penketh and others and imported in large numbers into England. Dr John Case, the exceptionally learned and entirely up-to-date Aristotelian scholar of Elizabethan Oxford, singled out Scotus as one of his masters, and his contemporary Samuel Daniel could write that 'Erasmus, Reuchlin and More brought no more wisdom into the world with all their new revived words than we find was before, it bred not a profounder divine than Saint Thomas . . . a more acute logician than Scotus'.[22] That was in 1602. Daniel was a post-Reformation, post-Franciscan link in the chain of theological learning which stretched back to Bonaventure and beyond, in which the anonymous friars of the century before the Reformation, in Oxford and elsewhere, played a humble but nevertheless essential role.

[21] J. Zupitza, 'Die Gedichte des Franziskaners Jakob Ryman', *Archiv für das Studium der neueren Sprachen und Literaturen* 89 (1892), pp. 167–338. See A. G. Little, 'James Ryman – a Forgotten Kentish Poet', *Archaeologia Cantiana* 54 (1941), pp. 1–4, and D. L. Jeffery, 'James Ryman and the Fifteenth-Century Carol', in *Fifteenth-Century Studies*, ed. R. F. Yeager (Hamden, Conn., 1984), pp. 303–20. I am grateful to Dr Linne Mooney for the latter reference.

[22] J. McConica, 'Humanism and Aristotle in Tudor Oxford', *EHR* 94 (1979), pp. 291–317; see also pp. 301, 315. The quotation from Daniel is in *A Defence of Ryme*, ed. A. C. Sprague, *Samuel Daniel: Poems and a Defence of Ryme* (Cambridge, MA., 1950), p. 145.

MENDICANT LIFE

The Grey Friars in York, c.1450–1530

Michael Robson

The Grey Friars or Friars Minor reached York about 1230 and had settled at Castlegate by 1243.[1] They were supported by the citizens and enjoyed an enduring popularity across the city. This chapter focuses on the life of the community as it moved into its third century and explores four features: the friars' integration in the life of the city; their ministries of preaching and hearing confessions; their role as intercessors; and finally their observance of the vow of poverty. Despite the loss of the friars' archives, there are sufficient sources to permit the reconstruction of aspects of their conventual life in the last phase of its history.

In many cities the ownership of the friary was vested in the secular authorities, who gave the friars the use of the site and its conventual buildings.[2] In the wake of the 'economic distress' that afflicted York between the 1460s and 1480s,[3] the friars turned to the lord mayor and commonalty for assistance, recognizing them as their founders[4] and patrons.[5] Agreement was reached on 21 September 1487, whereby the civic authorities agreed to pay the friars an annual pension of 20s. for a *Dirige*, Mass and other suffrages. As elsewhere in the English province,[6] civic dignitaries attended Masses in friaries on special occasions and four aldermen were deputed to make arrangements with the guardian, reserving suitable places for civic officials in the church. The text of the agreement uses the phrase 'for the tyme being

---

I am grateful to Dr Joan Greatrex for her valuable comments on an earlier draft of this chapter.

[1] *Fratris Thomae vulgo dicti de Eccleston tractatus de adventu Fratrum Minorum in Angliam*, ed. A. G. Little (Manchester, 1951), p. 45. See also M. Robson, 'A Prosopographical Study of the Greyfriars of York, c.1230–1538', *Medieval Prosopography* 22 (2001), pp. 1–29.

[2] E. Doyle, 'William Woodford OFM: His Life and Works together with a Study and Edition of his *Responsiones contra Wiclevum et Lollardos*', *Franciscan Studies* 43 (1983), pp. 17–187 at 160.

[3] R. B. Dobson, 'Urban Decline in Late Medieval England', *TRHS*, 5th Series 27 (1977), pp. 1–22 at 12, 19–21, explains the economic hardships experienced by York in the 1480s.

[4] BL, Harley MS 1408, fol. 66r. The friars had regarded Henry III, the donor of the new site, as their founder.

[5] A. G. Little, 'The Grey Friars of Beverley', in *VCH Yorks.*, iii. 264–6, shows that the friars appointed new patrons in the fourteenth and fifteenth centuries. See also B. J. Thompson, 'Monasteries and their Patrons at Foundation and Dissolution', *TRHS*, 6th Series 4 (1994), pp. 103–25.

[6] Corporation of London, Records Office, Letter Book M, fol. 224r.

standes patronez and ffoundours'; this formula was absent from the text's ratification on 21 January 1488, which bore the seal of the civic authorities, the minister provincial and the local friary.[7] The Latin text for the second agreement employs an unconditional tone and speaks of the civic authorities as the 'patroni et fundatores ecclesie sive domus predicte'. The sum of money was to be administered by the chamberlains, whom the guardian was to approach for payment two or three days after the Mass, which was celebrated at the high altar.[8]

There were three categories of friar in the community. First, there were novices, that is, those newly admitted to the fraternity. In each custody one friary was designated for the formation of the novices and, where necessary, a second friary.[9] Novices were drawn into the network of intercession associated with the friary and small sums of money were paid for their prayers.[10] On 12 March 1495 a testator left 6d. to each novice present at his funeral.[11] Despite the injunction against contact with laymen and religious of other orders, there arose the practice of novices attending funerals outside the friary.[12] Secondly, the ranks of the non-priests included brothers, and those who had graduated from the novitiate en route to the priesthood. These friars also attracted recompense for attendance at funerals and prayers.[13] Thirdly, although most friars were moved from one friary to another in the custody of York, some had a lengthy stay in the county town. The son of Robert, a fletcher and parishioner of St Michael, Spurriergate in York, John Harwood is recorded as a member of the community across a thirty-year period between 26 August 1458 and 26 February 1489.[14]

Throughout the period the friars remained fully integrated into the civic and ecclesiastical life of York. They participated in celebrations, such as the visit of Princess Margaret Tudor on 16 July 1503, who was travelling to Scotland to join her husband, James IV. All four orders took part in the

---

[7] *York Civic Records: II*, Yorkshire Archaeological Society, Record Series 103 (1941), pp. 30–31, 33, reads the text as 'foundors'. *The York House Books, 1461–1490*, ed. L. C. Attreed (Stroud, 1991), pp. 591–2, 606–7.

[8] York City Archives, G4a, which specifies that the suffrages should be carried out after the feasts of St Juliana, virgin, on 23 February, and the beheading of St John the Baptist, on 29 August.

[9] M. Bihl, 'Statuta generalia ordinis edita in capitulis generalibus celebratis Narbonae an. 1260, Assisii an.1279 atque Parisiis an.1292. (Editio critica et synoptica)', c.1, nos.7–9, *Archivum Franciscanum Historicum* 34 (1941), p. 40.

[10] Testamentary dispositions should not be regarded as proof that there were novices in a particular year. They do, however, reflect the expectation that there would be novices in the community.

[11] *Testamenta Eboracensia*, ed. J. Raine, 5 vols., Surtees Society 4, 30, 45, 53, 79 (1836–84), iv. 102–7.

[12] *Testamenta Eboracensia*, ed. Raine, v. 70–71.

[13] Ibid., 192.

[14] Borthwick Institute of Historical Research [hereafter Borth. Inst.], Probate Register 20, fol. 200r–v; Register 4, fols. 91r, 223r; Register 5, fols. 336r–v, 357v–358r.

grand procession, which met her at Micklegate Bar.[15] The friars' spacious church was a regular venue for ordinations, some of which were celebrated by two former friars of York, John Kegill, bishop of Philippopolis (1441–59), and William Duffield, bishop of Ascalon (1531–39).[16] Two friars, John Kegill and Thomas Richmond, were rectors of Holy Trinity, Goodramgate (1444–54)[17] and St Cuthbert (1457–58).[18] Further evidence of the friars' pastoral and social connections with the city emerges from wills. William Rok, a plumber and parishioner of Holy Cross, left Friar William Awne 20d. on 12 October 1448[19] and John Melton, formerly a soldier and parishioner of Aston, York, gave Friar Thomas Fox one mark on 1 April 1455.[20] Joanne Halifeld, a widow and parishioner of St Michael, Spurriergate, left 16d. to Friar Andrew on 26 September 1479.[21] On 4 November 1478 Thomas Neleson, a merchant who was buried in the priory of Holy Trinity, left 20s. to Friar John.[22]

From the moment that St Francis of Assisi heard the Gospel during Mass he perceived that his vocation was to revive the spirit of Christianity for his contemporaries. His followers quickly developed into a band of itinerant and talented preachers, whose theological knowledge and fervent preaching earned them respect and admiration. Their zealous commitment to preaching both in the cities and the countryside was praised by Frederick Visconti, archbishop of Pisa (1253–77), who announced that through the grace of God two new orders had been raised up in the last days, the Dominicans and Franciscans.[23] While reforming bishops in England freely conceded that some parochial priests were hampered by an incomplete grasp of Latin,[24] their episcopal colleagues heaped praise on the friars. On 30 May 1267 Walter Giffard, archbishop of York, thanked God that the friars had been sent 'ad salutem animarum et subsidium praelatorum'.[25]

When the friars began to build their own churches in the 1240s, they appeared to rival the parochial clergy, whose sacramental jurisdiction and income were seriously diminished. By 1250 the parochial clergy's complaints

[15] R. Davies, 'Margaret Tudor of York', Yorkshire Archaeological Journal 7 (1881–2), p. 314.
[16] Borth. Inst., Register 28, fols. 194v–197v. Duffield held three ordinations between 11 March 1536 and 24 February 1537.
[17] Borth. Inst., Register 19, fol. 185v; Register 20, fol. 5v.
[18] Ibid., fol. 10v.
[19] Borth. Inst., Probate Register 2, fol. 381r.
[20] Ibid., fol. 319v.
[21] Borth. Inst., Probate Register 5, fol. 151r. This may have been John Andrew, who had just completed his term as guardian of the community.
[22] Borth. Inst., Probate Register 5, fol. 212v. No surname is supplied.
[23] Les sermons et la visite pastorale de Federico Visconti archevêque de Pise (1253–77), ed. N. Bériou, Sources et documents d'histoire du moyen âge publiés par l'École française de Rome 3 (2001), no. 3, p. 658.
[24] S. Gieben, 'Robert Grosseteste on Preaching, with the Edition of the Sermon Ex rerum initiatarum on Redemption', Collectanea Franciscana 37 (1967), pp. 100–41 at 112.
[25] Historical Papers and Letters from the Northern Registers, ed. J. Raine, Rolls Series 61 (1873), pp. 9–10.

against the mendicants had already focused on five points: tithes, burials, preaching, confessions and Masses celebrated in mendicant churches.[26] Relations between the bishops and friars were regulated by *Super cathedram* on 18 January 1300, which obliged the minister provincial or the *custos* to submit to the bishop the names of friars for a licence to preach and hear confessions. Numerous friars were licensed in the diocese of York, although they were named less regularly in the episcopal registers after the Black Death. Despite the paucity of documentary evidence for bouts of renewed friction between the secular clergy and the friars, tensions found expression in religious art. Misericords carved between 1445 and 1520 in the collegiate churches of Ripon and Beverley and in the parish church of St Mary at Beverley depict the fox, a symbol of mendicant preachers, preaching to sundry fowl. In Beverley Minster there are two friars, Dominican and Franciscan, representing the two communities of the town, with a fox between them. In St Mary's two foxes holding croziers appear to be receiving instruction from a superior. They are depicted wearing hoods replete with geese.[27] Nonetheless, some secular priests continued to favour the friars, including Robert Clifton, prebendary of Wistow, who enlisted the prayers of John Depying and John Kingston in his will of 24 February 1503.[28]

York provided the friars with a substantial population for their twin ministries of preaching and hearing confessions. Friars were invited to preach in the city's churches, as the experience of William Melton[29] and Thomas Richmond in 1426 confirms.[30] The expansion of the grounds of the friary in 1268 presupposed that people would assemble to hear the friars' sermons in the open air.[31] The friars' own church was designed to facilitate this ministry and the laity of the city and its environs went there to hear sermons and to confess their sins. In 1371–2 the friars complained that the butchers were dumping offal, blood and dung in the Ouse, close to walls of the friary. They added that the fear of disease was keeping people away from their church, which was invaded by an unpleasant odour. They protested that many people were ceasing to attend Greyfriars for Mass and devotions.[32] William Woodford bears witness to the large number of people who made their confessions in the friars' churches during Lent, especially between

[26] *Salimbene de Adam, Cronica*, ed. G. Scalia, Scrittori d'Italia 232–3 (Bari, 1966), pp. 610–16.
[27] B. Chapman, *Yorkshire Misericords* (Beverley, 1996), pp. 3–5, 43–9, 52–3. M. H. Bloxam, 'Some Account of the Friary of Llanvaes, near Beaumaris, and of the Tomb of the Princess Joan, Daughter of King John, and Wife of Llewelyn, Prince of North Wales', *Archaeologia Cambrensis*, 4th series 6 (1875), pp. 137–44, 138.
[28] Borth. Inst., Probate Register 6, fol. 25r.
[29] *York Memorandum Book, II*, ed. M. Sellars, Surtees Society 125 (1915), pp. 156–9.
[30] *The Records of the Northern Convocation*, ed. G. W. Kitchen, Surtees Society 113 (1907), pp. 145–7.
[31] *CPR, Henry III, VI. 1266–1272*, pp. 260–61; Little, 'The Grey Friars of York', p. 288, VCH *Yorkshire*, iii. 287–91.
[32] *CCR, Edward III, XIII. 1369–1374*, p. 438.

Passion Sunday and Easter Sunday.[33] In addition to the licences issued for a deanery and the diocese, friars served as confessors to some citizens of York, such as Dame Joan Chamberleyn, whose will of 9 January 1502, identified John Makeblith as her confessor.[34]

From the outset friars preached in the city and its churches as well in the adjacent territory, which was known as a *limitatio*. Each friary had its own boundaries, established by the Provincial Chapters,[35] within which friars carried out their ministry and sought alms; these borders were carefully devised to prevent the activities of one friary impinging upon those of an adjacent community. The General Chapter of 1260 decreed that each friary should regard the places nearest to it as its own territory, regardless of whether they crossed the boundaries of a diocese or realm.[36] The *limitatio* of York covered a large territory in the three Ridings of Yorkshire. Professor R. B. Dobson reflects that the ministry of friars, whose base was urban, was appreciated beyond their immediate vicinity.[37] A barometer of the mendicants' influence is the support of testators as far afield as Leeds in the early sixteenth century.[38] The friars embarked upon preaching tours, especially during the seasons of Advent and Lent.[39] Friars of all four orders, for example, were accustomed to preach in Leeds and their visits were noted by a testator on 27 June 1448.[40] In addition, the practice of making annual visits to towns and villages appears in both contemporary literature[41] and testamentary dispositions. The vicars of Laxton on 20 October 1427[42] and Batley on 23 July 1435 mention the friars' sermons.[43]

The success of the friars' work as preachers and confessors was based upon their solid theological preparation. The school at York served the friaries in the custody and achieved international recognition from Benedict XII, when

---

[33] Doyle, 'William Woodford', p. 146.

[34] *Testamenta Eboracensia*, ed. Raine, iv. 200–2.

[35] Bihl, 'Statuta generalia ordinis edita in capitulis generalibus celebratis Narbonae an. 1260', c. 10, no. 17, p. 303.

[36] F. Delorme, 'Diffinitiones capituli generalis O. F. M. Narbonensis (1260)' no. 12, *Archivum Franciscanum Historicum* 3 (1910), pp. 491–504 at 503.

[37] Dobson, 'Yorkshire Towns in the Late Fourteenth Century', *Thoresby Society* 59 (1985), pp. 1–21 at 6.

[38] G. D. Lumb, 'Testamenta Leodiensia, 1514–1521', *Thoresby Society* 9 (1889), pp. 80–83, 88–9, 162, 167–8, 174–7.

[39] A. J. Fletcher, *Preaching, Politics and Poetry in Late-Medieval England* (Dublin, 1998), pp. 41–57, 49, shows that Friar Nicholas Philip preached many of his sermons in Lent and Passiontide in the 1430s.

[40] W. Brigg, 'Testamenta Leodiensia', *Thoresby Society* 2 (1891), p. 101.

[41] Giovanni Boccaccio, *The Decameron*, translated by G. H. McWilliam (2nd edn., Harmondsworth, 1972), pp. 469–77. Friar Cipolla, a friar of St Anthony, made an annual visit to Certaldo, promoting devotion to St Anthony. Some members of the parish were enrolled in the order's confraternity and paid an annual subscription, which was collected by the friar.

[42] Borth. Inst., Probate Register 2, fols. 547r, 650r.

[43] R. B. Cook, 'Wills of Leeds and District', *Thoresby Society* 22 (1915), pp. 238–9.

on 28 November 1336 he named twenty-one custodial *studia*, whose masters were deemed adequately prepared to lecture at the *studia generalia*.[44] Friars bearing the names of Dutch, German, and Italian cities were ordained at York, probably while they were attending the school. In the larger friaries the teaching duties of the lector were split, as at York, although it remains unclear how the subjects were divided. Two lectors and three cursors at York were licensed to preach and hear confessions in the diocese on 30 August 1398.[45] Dobson's observation that the prominent mendicants of York remained learned to the end[46] is supported by the continuation of the practice of sending friars to the universities. Four friars of York appear in the incomplete records of Cambridge University between 1473 and 1522: Henry Scherwyn,[47] William Swynborn,[48] Thomas Slater[49] and William Duffield[50] and three at Oxford University between 1500 and 1535: William Vavasour,[51] John Porrett[52] and William Walker.[53] Thomas Thomson (Tomsun) spent time at both universities before supplicating for his B.D. at Oxford in 1535.[54]

The practice of friars of all four orders attending funerals began at an early date and certainly before the middle of the fourteenth century. On 18 August 1508, Martin Collins, treasurer and canon residentiary of York Minster, left 10s. to each friary in York to take part in his funeral in the minster.[55] Friars were sometimes invited to the homes of the deceased where they celebrated a vigil for the faithful departed. Vested in albs and copes and carrying processional crosses, they made their way to the church with prayers and hymns on their lips. On 28 December 1453 Adam Skelton, who left 6s. 8d. to each mendicant community, asked the friars to come to his house and precede his body to the church of St Nicholas in Micklegate for burial.[56] Such instructions were left on 28 December 1509 by Sir John Gilliot, the alderman

---

[44] M. Bihl, 'Ordinationes a Benedicto XII pro Fratribus Minoribus promulgatae per bullam 28 novembris 1336', *Archivum Franciscanum Historicum* 30 (1938), c. 9, no. 14, p. 349.

[45] *A Calendar of the Register of Richard Scrope, Archbishop of York, 1398–1405*, ed. R. N. Swanson, Borthwick Texts and Calendars 11 (York, 1985), no. 729, p. 12.

[46] Dobson, 'Mendicant Ideal and Practice in Late Medieval York', in *Archaeological Papers from York presented to M. W. Barley*, ed. P. V. Addyman and V. E. Black (York, 1984), p. 120.

[47] J. R. H. Moorman, *The Grey Friars in Cambridge, 1225–1538* (Cambridge, 1952), p. 208.

[48] Ibid., pp. 214–15.

[49] Ibid., p. 208.

[50] Ibid., pp. 172–3.

[51] A. G. Little, *The Grey friars in Oxford*, Oxford Historical Society 20 (Oxford, 1892), p. 130.

[52] Ibid., pp. 277–8.

[53] Ibid., p. 284.

[54] Ibid., p. 290.

[55] *Testamenta Eborancensia*, ed. Raine, iv. 277–9.

[56] Borth. Inst., Probate Register 2, fol. 293r

and former lord mayor, who was buried in St Saviour's church.[57] On 9 January 1502 Dame Joan Chamberleyn made bequests to all four orders going in procession with their crosses from her home to St Mary's Abbey for burial; the communities of friars were asked to use 'sich oracions and prayers as shal be thoght to theym most expedient'.[58] The will of Brian Palmes of Naburne, sergeant at law, on 31 October 1519 invited the friars to meet his body at the cross between Fulford and York, accompanying it to St George's church.[59]

Regional variations in requests for burial among the mendicants are observed by Jenny Kermode, who explains that only 4% of testators in York, Beverley and Hull sought burial among the friars compared with 10% in Norwich.[60] Incomplete lists of people interred at the York Greyfriars were compiled in the late fifteenth century by John Wriothesley, garter king-of-arms,[61] and in the late seventeenth century by James Torre.[62] Testators were accustomed to make arrangements for burial, specifying the exact location.[63] There were several requests for burial beside a spouse, parent or sibling and this pattern is exemplified by the Salvin (Salvane, Salvayn) family. On 26 October 1420 Sir Roger, a knight of York, asked for burial in the church.[64] Gerard, probably his son, was buried there, along with his own sons, John[65] and Henry, who requested burial in the choir, beside his brother, on 15 September 1464.[66] Dame Margery, widow of Sir John, knight, asked to be buried on the north side of the church before the image of the Blessed Virgin Mary; her will was proved on 24 January 1496.[67] William Cerff, rector of Rowley in the East Riding, requested burial in the choir before the statue of St Francis and named six friars whom he asked to celebrate a trental for him in his will of 26 February 1489.[68] A few chaplains and chantry priests sought burial in the Greyfriars, including John Ardeslaw, chantry priest of St Peter in the parish of All Saints, Pavement, on 4 June 1459.[69]

---

[57] *Testamenta Eboracensia*, ed. Raine, v. 12–17.

[58] Ibid., v. 200–2.

[59] Ibid., v. 103–7.

[60] J. Kermode, *Medieval Merchants: York, Beverley and Hull in the Later Middle Ages* (Cambridge, 1998), p. 142.

[61] C. G. Young, 'Notices Concerning Religious Houses in Yorkshire, with the Names of their Founders, and of Persons Buried Therein', *Collectanea Topographica et Genealogica* 4 (1837), pp. 77–9.

[62] York, York Minster Library, Dean and Chapter, LI [Torre, 1691], fols. 873–6, BL, Harley MS 1408, fol. 65r.

[63] GL, MS 9531/9, fols. 203v–205r. On 23 April 1510 Katherine Langley Bowes of Barking in Essex asked for burial at the London Greyfriars in the chapel where her 'lord Willoby' and his wife were buried; 'Master Doctor [John] Cutler knewith ye place in ye said chapel which I have assigned for me.'

[64] *Testamenta Eboracensia*, ed. Raine, i. 413.

[65] Young, 'Notices Concerning Religious Houses in Yorkshire', p. 78.

[66] Borth. Inst., Probate Register 2, fol. 431v, *Testamenta Eboracensia*, ed. Raine, ii. 263.

[67] *Testamenta Eboracensia*, ed. Raine, iv. 116–17.

[68] Borth. Inst., Probate Register 5, fols. 357v–358r.

[69] Idem, Probate Register 2, fol. 406r.

The friars offered their benefactors perpetual remembrance in martyrologies and necrologies. Each friary was required to keep a benefactors' book in which they faithfully enrolled all the names;[70] liturgical calendars from the friaries of Richmond (Yorkshire)[71] and Exeter have survived.[72] The reading of benefactors' names was associated with the meeting of the domestic chapter[73] and this is exemplified by the friary at Beverley, where the chapter was held on Fridays.[74] On 15 September 1396 Robert of Howm, a parishioner of Holy Trinity, Goodramgate, left money to each house of friars in York and asked them to inscribe his name in their martyrologies.[75] The contents of such documents are demonstrated by the necrology of the friary of St Francis at Udine, in the Veneto, which includes the names of both benefactors and some friars as well as details regarding the celebration of anniversaries and prayers to be recited at the place of burial.[76] Three elements of the martyrology at York emerge from the testamentary dispositions. First, there was the request for Masses, some of them to be celebrated daily with a solemn Mass annually.[77] Secondly, some testators gave precise instructions about the type of Masses to be celebrated,[78] even down to details about the hour of the Mass and the weekly rotation of celebrants.[79] Thirdly, the devotions to be performed at the graves of those interred in Greyfriars were specified. Each Friday, for example, the community was accustomed to assemble at Sir Brian Rocliff's grave, where they sang the antiphon *Jhesu*. Sir John, his son, issued elaborate instructions for the prayers to be said at his own grave each Tuesday, with details of psalms and collects and the posture of the friars present.[80]

Despite the order's espousal of evangelical poverty and its wish to distinguish itself from religious who enjoyed estates and endowments, the friary drew small amounts of rent from houses in York and other towns[81] and kept some poultry.[82] William Woodford lamented that few friaries were free

---

[70] Bihl, 'Ordinationes a Benedicto XII pro Fratribus Minoribus', c. 13, nos. 1–4, p. 360.
[71] Oxford, Bodl., Rawl. liturg. MS e.1, fols. 3r–14v.
[72] Oxford, Bodl., Bodley MS 62, fols. 8r–13v, which contains two *memoranda* for anniversary Masses.
[73] Doyle, 'William Woodford', p. 171.
[74] *North Country Wills, 1383 to 1558: II*, ed. J. W. Clay, Surtees Society 116 (1908), pp. 104–6.
[75] Borth. Inst., Probate Register 1, fols. 100v–101r.
[76] G. Luisetto, *Archivio Sartori: documenti di storia e arte francescana*, ii/2 (Padua, Basilica del Santo, 1986), pp. 1732–36.
[77] *Testamenta Eboracensia*, ed. Raine, v. 191–3.
[78] *Testamenta Eboracensia*, ed. Raine, iv. 28; York City Archives, G70: 36.
[79] *Testamenta Eboracensia*, ed. Raine, v. 321–2.
[80] Ibid., 319–23.
[81] L. M. Goldthorp, 'The Franciscans and Dominicans in Yorkshire', *Yorkshire Archaeological Journal* 32 (1935), p. 289.
[82] *Churchwardens' Accounts of St Michael, Spurriergate, York, 1518–1548*, ed. C. C. Webb, Borthwick Texts and Calendars 20 (York, 1997), pp. 92, 99.

from debt and poverty.[83] The practice of grouping the friars with the poor and the sick is exemplified by the will of Roger Parke of St Mary Senior, Bishophill, on 14 November 1463. His bequest to the city's mendicants was followed by gifts to the hospital of St Thomas outside Micklegate and the poor lepers in the same suburb.[84] In 1487 the civic officials awarded the friary an annual grant of 20s., which was still being paid on the eve of the Dissolution.[85] The friars made annual visits to parishes for alms; testators affirm that this practice took place *ex consuetudine*.[86] The limiters or *quaestores* remained active in Yorkshire, as parishioners of Dewsbury,[87] Wakefield,[88] Rudby[89] and Sigglesthorne[90] confirm between 28 September 1498 and 8 March 1527. There is encouragement for the view that sometimes the limiter accompanied the preacher on his annual round of visits.[91]

The figure of William Vavasour raises the question of the relationship between the conventual life sketched by the general constitutions and the personal observance. Were there elements of the *vita privata*, nurtured and sustained by gifts from relations and testators? Unlike his other confrères, Vavasour's name was mentioned by a number of testators of York in the 1520s and 1530s. John Marshall, a parishioner of St Mary at Castlegate, left him five marks and a gilded spoon to pray for him. Vavasour was appointed as an executor of the merchant's will on 15 December 1524.[92] He witnessed the will of Thomas Threpeland, vicar of Christ Church, King's Court, on 12 June 1529. Although the friar was not expressly named in the will, Threpland left money to the Greyfriars for Masses.[93] John Besby, an alderman, gave 5s. to Vavasour for his burial in his will on 23 July 1535 and a further 10s. for supervising it.[94] All three testators were members of the guild of Corpus Christi, as was Vavasour. It is not clear whether the friar followed the traditional practice of handing in any gifts given to him. Occasional bequests from an earlier date were manifestly intended for the

---

[83] Doyle, 'William Woodford', p. 178.

[84] Borth. Inst., Probate Register 4, fol. 58v.

[85] J. S. Purvis, 'Four Antiquarian Notes', in *Yorkshire Archaeological Journal* 2 (1967–70), p. 52.

[86] Borth. Inst., Probate Register 5, fol. 132r. On 4 November 1478 John Smyth de Oremsby left 40s. to the mendicant orders collecting alms in his parish on an annual basis.

[87] *Testamenta Eboracensia*, ed. Raine, iv. 168–71; ii. 137–8. On 21 December 1447 the will of Richard Wintworth of Everton, Nottinghamshire, left the limiters of the four orders of friars visiting Everton 3s. 4d.

[88] *Testamenta Eboracensia*, ed. Raine, v. 73–6.

[89] Borth. Inst., Register 27, fols. 143v–144r.

[90] Idem, Probate Register 9, fol. 375r.

[91] Boccaccio, *Decameron*, pp. 469–70.

[92] *Testamenta Eboracensia*, ed. Raine, v. 191–3.

[93] *York Clergy Wills, 1520–1600: II. City Clergy*, ed. C. Cross, Borthwick Texts and Calendars 15 (York, 1989), pp. 9–10.

[94] Borth. Inst., Probate Register 11, fol. 147r.

individual friar rather than the community.[95] Furthermore, there is some evidence that poverty was felt more keenly by some friars than others.[96] In the second half of the fifteenth century there is more evidence of gifts being given to individual friars. The sources do not provide a clearer answer to the question of observance, although there are indications of the *vita privata* in some friaries along with evidence of corporate relaxations.

At the end of the fifteenth century friars in Yorkshire were in touch with currents of reform within the local church[97] and their own fraternity. The friars of the Observance, based on a more rigorous application of the Rule of St Francis, reached England in 1482, when a community was established at Greenwich. The pope ordered that three of the convents of the Grey Friars or Friars Minor Conventual should be handed over to the Observants, resulting in the transfer of the friaries at Canterbury, Southampton and Newcastle.[98] Observant communities were subsequently established at Richmond (Surrey) and Newark, but plans to found a community at Wakefield in the later 1520s came to nothing, despite the hopes of one testator.[99] One point of contact between the Observants and the Grey Friars occurred at ordinations. On 18 September 1501 three Observants from Newcastle were ordained in Greyfriars at York, along with six friars of the local community. The advent and progress of the Observant reform in England attracted some of the friars. John Baker, at York when ordained priest on 24 September 1496, became an Observant at an unknown date before 1532. Another recruit was John Lambert, who was at York when ordained priest on 2 June 1509. He too joined the Observants before 1534. Many testators grouped the Observants with the other four orders of friars.[100] Although Thomas Wentworth of North Elmsall left sums of money to all four orders on 1 April 1522, he instructed his executors to set aside funds for the maintenance and repair of the Observant friaries of Newark and Newcastle.[101]

One way of ascertaining the vitality of a religious community lies in the process of recruitment of friars for ordination, although this does not take into account non-clerics. At the close of the fifteenth century and the

[95] GL, MS 9171/1, fols. 26v–27r. On 1 July 1375 John Berlyngham, merchant of London, left Gilbert Pecham 40s 'ad proprium suum usum'.

[96] Ibid., fols. 239r–240r. On 6 May 1390 Matilda, widow of alderman Stephen Cavendish of London, asked for her body to be lowered into the earth by the four friars 'qui sunt maxime egentes in domo eorum London'.

[97] *Testamenta Eboracensia*, ed. Raine, ii. 114–15, n.

[98] See also Little, 'Introduction of the Observant Friars into England', PBA 10 (1921–23), pp. 455–71, and 'Introduction of the Observant Friars into England: A Bull of Alexander VI', PBA 27 (1941), pp. 155–61, K. D. Brown, 'Wolsey and Ecclesiastical Order: The Case of the Franciscan Observants', in *Cardinal Wolsey: Church, State and Art*, ed. S. J. Gunn and P. G. Lindley (Cambridge, 1991), pp. 219–38.

[99] *Testamenta Eboracensia*, ed. Raine, v. 229.

[100] Ibid., 55–7.

[101] Ibid., 144–6.

opening of the sixteenth there were signs of buoyancy in the community. There were forty-three friars ordained at York in the 1490s, the second-best total since the 1420s. But even that figure was surpassed when the number climbed to sixty-seven in the first years of the sixteenth century. This peak was never matched in the years remaining before the Dissolution: numbers of ordinands fell to thirty-four between 1510 and 1520, and a decade later there were only fourteen. These statistics cannot be separated from demographic factors, such as the unusually high incidence of mortality in the diocese of York in 1505, 1508 and 1512–13.[102] Furthermore, this deterioration may have been the result of the circulation of new ideas about religious life as well as the praise heaped upon the Observants, who were beginning to attract wider support. An internal source reveals that there was a crisis of recruitment among the Greyfriars in England. At the General Chapter at Troyes in May 1504, the minister provincial reported that 400 friars had died since 1500 and only forty new friars had been admitted.[103] These statistics put the evidence from York in a broader context.

The friars remained at the heart of the life of the city throughout this period. At least eight of them were admitted to the guild of Corpus Christi[104] and the guild or fraternity of St Francis attracted occasional support from testators.[105] The friars' ministry of preaching and hearing confessions in York and its environs continued unbroken. Claire Cross's analysis of the extant wills by secular priests in the diocese shows that between 1520 and 1540 a third of them turned to the friars for suffrages.[106] The appeal of the friars' life brought a steady flow of recruits in the second half of the fifteenth century. While the number of ordinands did not match those of the previous eighty years, the city's population was diminishing, from approximately 14,000–15,000 in 1377 to 6,000–8,000 in 1524–5.[107] Ordinations between 1500 and 1510 reached levels unsurpassed for a century. This peak was immediately followed by a diminution of the friars ordained in the 1520s. When the royal officials arrived on 27 November 1538, they did not find an aged community, but one which included five novices and some younger priests, one of whom, Gilbert Berkeley, was appointed bishop of Bath and Wells in 1560.

[102] P. J. P. Goldberg, 'Mortality and Economic Change in the Diocese of York, 1390–1514', *Northern History* 24 (1988), pp. 38–55 at 42, 47.

[103] *Regesta ordinis fratrum Minorum conventualium, 2 (1504–1506)*, ed. G. Parisciani, Fonti e studi Francescani, no. 7 (Padua, 1998), no. 300, p. 69.

[104] *The Register of the Guild of Corpus Christi in the City of York*, ed. R. H. Skaife, Surtees Society 57 (1872), pp. 28, 32, 47, 74, 109, 145, 176.

[105] Borth. Inst., Probate Register 2, fols. 272v, 537v, 546r, 600r–v; Register 3, fol. 575v.

[106] C. Cross, 'Monasticism and Society in the Diocese of York, 1520–1540', *TRHS*, 5th Series 38 (1988), pp. 131–45 at 140.

[107] Kermode, *Medieval Merchants*, pp. 8–9.

Mendicants and Confraternity in Late Medieval England

R. N. Swanson

The role of the mendicant orders in late medieval English religion is still relatively obscure. While literary 'anti-fraternalism' has attracted attention,[1] ties between the mendicants and the laity remain shadowy. Arguably, a key method of establishing such links was through the concept of confraternity, creating arrangements that have left a considerable scatter of evidence. However, mendicant confraternity cannot be treated in isolation: it must be set among other processes for distributing spiritual privileges, what might be called the 'indulgence business', of which confraternity is clearly a constituent. Indeed, to establish a formal boundary between mendicant confraternity and the pre-Reformation indulgence business is almost impossible. Mendicant confraternity must therefore also be considered in relation to indulgences in general, as one component of lay piety as a whole.

By the late Middle Ages, ideas of confraternity had expanded far beyond the early association with monastic houses.[2] The monastic and other regular orders still admitted brethren and sisters, and others had followed their lead. Several secular cathedrals had confraternities, of two different types. The first was a small and socially exclusive body, its members admitted by formal grant of the dean and chapter. Alongside, several cathedrals sought contributions to their fabric funds by creating apparently nominal bodies whose members received particular spiritual privileges in return for their donations. These groups were seemingly unstructured, and lacked formal

I am grateful to the British Academy and the Leverhulme Trust for funding for projects of which this is a by-product.

[1] Notably P. R. Szittya, *The Antifraternal Tradition in Medieval Literature* (Princeton, 1986).

[2] For early English monastic confraternity, D. Postles, *Lay Piety in Transition: Local Societies and New Religious Houses in England, 1100–1280*, Friends of the Department of English Local History, University of Leicester, Friends' Papers 1 (Leicester, 1998), pp. 30–40. See also W. G. Clark-Maxwell, 'Some Letters of Confraternity', *Archaeologia* 75 (1924–25), pp. 19–37, and idem, 'Some Further Letters of Confraternity', ibid., 79 (1929), pp. 180–85; E. Bishop, *Liturgica historica: Papers on the Liturgy and Religious Life of the Western Church* (Oxford, 1918), pp. 349–61. On terminology, C. H. Barron, 'The Parish Fraternities of Medieval London', in *The Church in Pre-Reformation Society: Essays in Honour of F. R. H. du Boulay*, ed. C. H. Barron, and C. Harper-Bill (Woodbridge, 1985), p. 17, although the distinction made there does not always hold.

administration; but they still functioned nominally as confraternities, like that of St Andrew at Wells, or St Chad at Lichfield.[3]

In the fifteenth century, the concept of confraternity also covered much of the business associated with the main institutions that raised funds through pardoners or similar collections. The guild of Our Lady at Boston thus distributed its indulgences as a confraternity.[4] The Roman hospitals of St Thomas and the Holy Trinity, or Santo Spirito in Saxia, also had confraternities which sought members in return for annual donations. Such ties must have been very loose indeed. While St Thomas seemingly had a full network of pardoners in England (probably most of them lessees, whose main interest lay in the potential profits), Santo Spirito apparently had just one representative collecting throughout the whole kingdom. Membership in that confraternity was apparently registered, but what followed from that is unclear.[5]

These cases are only part of the range of collections made in late medieval England, which altogether amounted to business operations of considerable scale. The mendicant associations must be set alongside such structures, even placed in competition with them.[6] Usually, following historiographical stereotype and presuppositions created by Chaucer's Pardoner (or, from the sixteenth century, John Heywood's equally corrupt exemplars),[7] this business is simply bundled under the heading of indulgences. That, however, is a misnomer, except in a very general sense. The spiritual privileges on offer were rarely identified in temporal terms;[8] they frequently include the right to choose a confessor to grant full absolution at death (many of the letters

---

[3] Both types await their historians. For the fabric-funding bodies see e.g., *Wells Cathedral: Fabric Accounts, 1390–1600*, ed. J. C. Colchester (Wells, 1983), pp. 6, 10–12, 17–19, 225, 29–31, 36, 38–39; R. N. Swanson, *Catholic England: Faith, Religion, and Observance before the Reformation* (Manchester, 1993), pp. 202, 218–21; Clark-Maxwell, 'Further Letters', p. 182.

[4] 'gilde sive confraternitatis': Nottingham, Nottingham University Library [NUL], Mi.F1/8.

[5] St Thomas merits further investigation. For now, see M. Harvey, *England, Rome, and the Papacy, 1417–1464: The Study of a Relationship* (Manchester, 1993), pp. 53, 60–61, 65–66, 79–80. For Santo Spirito, Chester, Cheshire Record Office, CR 63/2/681; Oxford, Bodl., Arch Ab.8 (18),(20); Clark-Maxwell, 'Some Further Letters', p. 198.

[6] For competition between friars and pardoners, see A. Williams, 'Relations between the Mendicant Friars and the Secular Clergy in England in the later Fourteenth Century', *Annuale Medievale* 1 (1960), pp. 81–82; and John Heywood's *Play Between the Pardoner and the Frere, the Curate and Neybour Pratte*, written c.1520, in *A Select Collection of Old English Plays, Originally Published by Robert Dodsley in the year 1744*, ed. W. Carew Hazlitt (15 vols., 4th edn., London, 1874), i. 199–238.

[7] *The Riverside Chaucer*, ed. L. D. Benson (3rd edn., Oxford, 1988), pp. 34, 194–96, 201–2; Heywood's corrupt Pardoner appears at his worst in *The Four P.P.*, in *Select Collection*, ed. Hazlitt, i. 331–88.

[8] There are some statements of temporal value: Clark-Maxwell, 'Some Letters', p. 41; NUL, Mi.F1/7; London, Lincoln's Inn Library, MS Hale 179, fols. ii, 225. The latter suggests that a cumulation of papal indulgences might be assumed in all confraternity grants.

conferring the privileges state the words of absolution); they also often allowed ecclesiastical burial even in interdicted places, unless personally excommunicate. Most privileges conferred participation in spiritual good works, whether of an order or an institution.

It follows, then, that mendicant confraternity cannot be treated in isolation. It merges into, sometimes becomes indistinguishable from, the wider range of spiritual benefits offered by a host of institutions, which might well merge in the minds of the purchasers. The situation is exemplified in a Liskeard confraternity document, which combines a range of episcopal and papal indulgences (amounting to fourteen years and 400 days of pardon) with benefit from masses celebrated in assorted religious houses, and what amount to the privileges of confraternity with the Dominicans of Truro and the Franciscans of Bodmin.[9]

Against this background, mendicant confraternity raises several questions, about how the privileges were distributed, and about the perceptions associated with them. In this array of products – each with its own brand identity – what, if anything, made mendicant confraternity different? How did it appeal, when compared to the other privileges being marketed? Such questions cannot be successfully answered, because the evidence available for assessment is generally insufficient. Usually, it amounts to mere scraps and fragments. Particularly unfortunate is the lack of material to indicate mendicant appreciations, or administrative arrangements. The paucity of mendicant sources, especially accounts, effectively makes it impossible to consider confraternity from their perspective. The two known account fragments, from the Cambridge Franciscans of 1336, and York in the 1530s, contain no explicit references.[10] As confraternity receipts apparently counted as accidental income, no details appear in the *Valor ecclesiasticus* of 1535. While several mendicant confraternity letters survive, the main evidence for mechanisms comes from literary and controversial comments.

Amid all the possibilities, a standard is needed against which mendicant confraternity can be tested. The obvious model is monastic confraternity, which remained valid throughout the period. The underlying concept of participation in the merit secured by spiritual good works was apparently shared across the range of orders, although the precise format of the grants (and the quality of the documents) varied greatly. A Carthusian confraternity letter from Hinton in 1525 is simple in its wording, offering participation in the convent's spiritual good works (listed straightforwardly as masses, prayers, fasts, vigils, abstinences, alms, 'ceterisque divinis excerciciis'), plus commemoration as done for a member of the convent on notification of

[9] R. M. Haines, *Ecclesia Anglicana: Studies in the English Church of the Later Middle Ages* (London and Toronto, 1989), pp. 198–99. He questions its date and authenticity, ibid., pp. 195–97, but I have no reservations about it.

[10] J. R. H. Moorman, *The Grey Friars in Cambridge, 1225–1538* (Cambridge, 1952), pp. 242–45, see also 70–75; J. S. Purvis, 'Four Antiquarian Notes', *Yorkshire Archaeological Journal* 42 (1971), pp. 52–53.

death.[11] This is a far cry, in decoration, verbosity, and precision, from Westminster Abbey's grant of confraternity to members of the Stanley family in January 1528. This promised them participation in the spiritual merits of the abbey and all associated houses, and all houses of the order, in masses, psalms, and prayers, vigils, discipline, afflictions, fasts and alms, as well as 'aliis omnibus beneficijs spiritualibus a nobis vel per nos . . . faciendis'. At death their souls would receive absolution, each priestly monk would say a private mass, and each monk of lower rank a psalter. Moreover, when the next mortuary roll was sent out for a dead monk after hearing of their deaths, their names would be included, allowing them to be absolved in each of the houses visited; and their names would be inscribed in Westminster's martyrology, with those of deceased brothers and sisters, so that they could be annually commemorated.[12]

The promise of post-mortem commemoration may be the most significant clause in such confraternity grants, especially given the emphasis on Purgatory in late medieval religion. Equivalent clauses appear in a document of 1469 granting confraternity with St Mary's Abbey, York,[13] and in a Cistercian grant of 1500.[14]

Such arrangements concerned specific individuals, and it may be natural to envisage monastic confraternity in terms of grants to individuals. However, there was another version of confraternity, more widely distributed. Thirteenth- and fourteenth-century monastic fund-raising documents show that participation in the spiritual benefits of a house's good works was sometimes integrated into the gift exchange of such campaigns: a donor was awarded the benefits of confraternity. It seems unlikely that this was acknowledged by a personalized document; it probably gained implicit inclusion among the 'benefactors' in appropriate commemorative prayers. An early fourteenth-century document issued by Tonbridge Priory, seeking funds for rebuilding after a fire, authorizes the proctor to publish indulgences (amounting to 230 days), and promises fraternity to the donors, with participation in masses, prayers, alms and other spiritual acts performed by the convent.[15]

Turning at last to the mendicants, how did their confraternity system operate? It is, perhaps, necessary to eliminate one aspect of devotion involving the mendicants before turning to confraternity itself. This is the popular belief that burial in a mendicant habit secured salvation. There is in

[11] Truro, Cornwall Record Office [CRO], AR 27/10. This, as a letter from a particular house, seems very different from the letters issued by the order's central authorities: see Clark-Maxwell, 'Further Letters', p. 185. The wording of the Hinton letter is in fact evocative of mendicant letters.

[12] Chester, Cheshire Record Office, DLT/2173 (not individually numbered).

[13] Stratford on Avon, Shakespeare Birthplace Trust [SBT], DR 37/91/3.

[14] NUL, MiF1/4.

[15] Oxford, Bodl., Kent rolls 8, doct. k. See also *Charters of St Bartholomew's Priory, Sudbury*, ed. R. Mortimer, Suffolk Records Society, Suffolk Charters 15 (1996), no. 124; Cambridge, King's College Archives, GBR/278.

fact surprisingly little evidence for this in late medieval England, although it clearly has affinities with earlier monastic conversion *ad succurendum*.[16] The failing may be a failing of the sources, the silence covering a burgeoning practice, but there is no hard evidence. Yet the belief was criticized by Wyclif and his followers, although Woodford responded by denying that the promise of salvation was offered as a blanket consolation; while 'Friar Daw', responding to 'Jack Upland', similarly denies the charge – although leaving open the possibility of some such suggestion from the Carmelites.[17] Given the paucity of the appropriate sources, there is the possibility of an overlap between this devotional practice and membership of a mendicant confraternity; but there is nothing to indicate any formal connection. It is quite possible that confrères sought burial in the habit, as Sir John Meaux did in Yorkshire in the late fourteenth century,[18] but there is no necessary link.

As for the confraternity system, letters survive from all four major orders: the Augustinians, Dominicans, Franciscans, and Carmelites. Other orders which contemporaries treated as mendicants (the Crutched Friars, Trinitarians, and Mercedarians – even though these last had no formal establishments in England) were also active, but may fall into a different category. All three leave some signs of involvement, although the Trinitarians are by far the best documented.[19] No confraternity letters survive from the houses of England's Franciscan Observants, but it seems that they did issue them. Moreover, John Arundell of Cornwall obtained a letter from the Irish house at Youghal in 1515, while a commissary general of the order also offered confraternity within England.[20] One oddity which merely needs to be mentioned here is the presence in England of collectors for the Palestinian Franciscans in the late fifteenth century; they too distributed letters.[21]

[16] On this practice, J. Burton, *Monastic and Religious Orders in Britain, 1000–1300* (Cambridge, 1994), p. 217.

[17] E. Doyle, 'William Woodford OFM: His Life and Works together with a Study and Edition of his *Responsiones contra Wiclerum et Lollardos*', Franciscan Studies 43 (1983), pp. 17–187 at 140–41; *Johannis Wyclif, Tractatus de blasphemia*, ed. M. H. Dziewicki, Wyclif Society (1893), pp. 20–21 – see also *John Wyclif's Polemical Works in Latin*, ed. R. Buddensieg (2 vols., London, 1883), i. 35 n.h. For 'Jack Upland' and 'Friar Daw', *Six Ecclesiastical Satires*, ed. J. Dean (Kalamazoo, MI, 1991), pp. 125, 165.

[18] A. G. Little, 'Franciscan letters of Confraternity', *Bodleian Library Record* 5 (1954–56), p. 18. For tomb monuments showing burials in the habit, ibid., pp. 19–20. There is nothing to suggest that such burial was as popular in England as in some parts of the continent; but it may have occurred without being stipulated in a will. For stimulating comment see C. M. N. Eire, *From Madrid to Purgatory: The Art and Craft of Dying in Sixteenth-Century Spain* (Cambridge, 1995), pp. 105–13.

[19] For Trinitarians and Crutched Friars, see below. The Mercedarians are attested by a questorial licence of 1532, covering the jurisdiction of the dean and chapter of York (York Minster Library, H3/1, fol. 171r) and one confraternity document (Clark-Maxwell, 'Some Further Letters', p. 201 – but I cannot find this in his list).

[20] Little, 'Franciscan Letters', pp. 18–19; below, n. 110; CRO, AR 27/6. See also Clark-Maxwell, 'Some Further Letters', pp. 189–90, 210.

[21] Stafford, Staffordshire County Record Office [SRO], D603/A/ADD/725, granting participation in the benefits of the brethren at Bethlehem, Mount Calvary, the

To talk of 'mendicant confraternity' suggests something easily definable; but it actually remains rather vague. For one thing, the term 'confraternity' is rarely used by the mendicants; usually what is offered if simply described as participation in the spiritual benefits.[22] In addition, there are clearly differences in the circumstances and nature of the grants, so that a blanket definition is inappropriate. There is an immediate distinction to be made on the basis of the visual format of the documents, which indicates two different types of basic grant, presumably with distinct distribution methods. Unfortunately, this difference is rarely apparent in archive catalogues, or sometimes in the secondary literature.[23] To differentiate between them, and the structures they reflect, they will here be called 'specific confraternity' and 'open confraternity'.[24]

Letters of 'specific confraternity' were specially written for the recipient. They are normally (from the extant examples) made out in the name of the prior or minister provincial,[25] although some were issued by heads of individual houses.[26] The documents are written in a uniform hand throughout, the script usually not being very ornate but nevertheless formal, and usually (but not always) bear a full dating clause. Exceptions include a grant from the Franciscans of Bedford dated simply by year (1444), although this appears to be a 'specific' letter.[27] Similarly, a grant from the Carmelites of Norwich, despite its decoration and careful production, is dated only to

---

Holy Sepulchre, and elsewhere. See also Clark-Maxwell, 'Some Further Letters', pp. 189, 210.

[22] See comment in Clark-Maxwell, 'Some Further Letters', p. 193. A vocabulary of confraternity appears in some Dominican documents: below n. 75; London, Lincoln's Inn Library, MS Hale 179, fols. ii, 225.

[23] Clark-Maxwell, 'Some Letters', pp. 19–60; idem, 'Some Further Letters', pp. 179–216, almost makes the distinction, but without quite formulating it; his list gives the impression that all the letters are the same. Of secondary writers, D. W. Whitfield, 'An Early Letter of Fraternity', *Franciscan Studies*, New Series 14 (1954), pp. 387–91, does not raise the issue; Little, 'Franciscan Letters', notes the difference (p. 15), without differentiating in his list (pp. 20–25). The discussion and descriptions of Augustinian letters in F. Roth, *The English Austin Friars, 1249–1538*, Cassiciacum: Studies in St Augustine and the Augustinian Order (American Series) 6–7 (2 vols., New York, 1961–66), i. 212–14 – see also list of references at 212 n. 433 – gives no detail on their format.

[24] Early sixteenth-century Carmelite records mention confraternity letters in both 'common' and 'full' forms. The distinction is unclear, but from the context both might be types of what I am calling 'open confraternity': R. Copsey, 'The Visit of the Prior General, Peter Terrasse, to England in 1504–1505', in *Carmel in Britain: Essays on the Medieval English Carmelite Province*, ed. P. Fitzgerald-Lombard (2 vols., Rome, 1992), i. 190.

[25] For examples see BL, Stowe ch. 605; NRO, Phi/567; PRO, C270/35/1. Clark-Maxwell, 'Some Further Letters', pp. 209–12, lists the documents by issuing authority, but has not differentiated between the 'specific' and 'open' grants.

[26] NUL, MS Mi.F1/3: Robert Jacsone, prior of the Derby Dominicans, 1489.

[27] Oxford, Bodl., Bedfordshire charter 26.

1517.[28] Several of these letters also carry the name of another friar at the bottom, but exactly what function that reflects is not revealed. Possibly he instigated the grant from the provincial authorities; in some instances he does appear to have been the head of a house.[29]

The 'open confraternity' letters are very different. These were presumably mass-produced: prepared in advance of distribution, they left blank space for the recipient's name, and sometimes to complete the dating clause. In format they match (*mutatis mutandis*) the many similar documents issued by other collecting agencies from the fourteenth to the sixteenth centuries, to secure funds for English and continental institutions, solicit donations for crusades, and support projects like the papally sponsored campaign of 1439–40 to fund Greek attendance at the proposed discussion on reunion of the Orthodox and Catholic churches.[30]

Among the surviving examples, mendicant grants of specific confraternity may outnumber the open confraternity letters; but without a full census, this is not certain. Even so, the relative survival rates cannot in themselves validate conclusions about distribution processes, although there are some oddities concerning the survival of some open confraternity letters that will require further comment in due course.[31]

Before passing to consider the mechanisms for dealing with the two types of confraternity, it is worth noting here how the Trinitarians, as quasi-friars, dealt with their documents. They certainly issued open confraternity letters in abundance (and did actually say that they admitted to fraternity); their documents are amongst the most prolific survivors. They do not seem to have issued documents which precisely parallel grants of specific confraternity, but there are hints that they ran a two-tier system. Forms issued in the late fifteenth century by the authority of Robert, minister of Knaresborough, describe him as vicar general and provincial of the whole order in England;[32]

---

[28] Oxford, Bodl., Norfolk ch. 302. This may be a form letter: the handwriting for the names does look slightly different.

[29] For example NUL, MS Mi.F1/3, seemingly not a form, has under the seal flap 'per f. Thomam Cotys'; PRO, C270/32/10 (Austin friars, 1404), has a note at the bottom right: 'fr. Robertus Blak' (not obviously a form, but suggestive differences in ink colour and hand hint that it may be). Roth identifies some of the Augustinians in these cases as local priors, who 'countersigned' the documents (*English Austin Friars*, ii. 277*, 324*, 355*, 362*).

[30] For representative examples, BL, Stowe ch. 604 (St Mary, Newton, Cambridgeshire, 1448), 607 (funds for the Greek delegation, 1439), 611 (Holy Trinity and St Thomas, Rome, 1478), 619 (Burton Lazars, 1512); PRO, C270/32/13 (Hospitaller collections for crusade funds, 1480). The mass production is presumed, but is evident elsewhere, as in the indulgence publicity documents produced at Hereford c.1320 to stimulate donations to build a shrine for St Thomas Cantilupe: Hereford, Cathedral Archives, 1447, 3214. The easy shift to print for confraternity documents may point in the same direction.

[31] See below, p. 134.

[32] Matlock, Derbyshire Record Office, D2375/204/5 (dated 1480); Oxford, Bodl., Yorkshire charter 65 (dated 1491): 'miseracione divina vicarius generalis et

usually Trinitarian letters were issued by the minister of the house in his own right.[33] One of these 'provincial' Trinitarian letters also bears the name of another friar, Laurence.[34] This links it with mendicant 'specific confraternity' grants – although it also has affinities with a Carmelite 'open confraternity' letter of 1512, which also bears a friar's name.[35]

Another Trinitarian grant raises the possibility that a distinction between 'specific' and 'open' confraternity is mistaken, for it shows that 'open' letters were sometimes produced in deluxe form. This is Hounslow's grant to the future Henry VIII in 1508.[36] Its wording essentially matches other Hounslow grants, but there any similarity ends.[37] Visually it is very different from all other Trinitarian (or, indeed, mendicant) letters: larger, and decorated with heraldic devices, Tudor emblems, and gold, its closest match for calligraphy and decoration is Westminster Abbey's 1528 confraternity grant to the Stanleys. It is so abnormal that it cannot in itself overthrow the suggested distinction between the two types of confraternity.

Rather more worrisome in advocating the distinction is another document, this time issued by the Franciscans, as part of a campaign to distribute spiritual privileges in 1479.[38] Most documents associated with that campaign are 'open confraternity' letters; the majority of those known were issued in the name of heads of individual houses. This letter was issued by the minister provincial, and is not a form on which the names of the recipients have later been entered. Addressed to the members of the fraternity of St Mary at Aylesbury, en masse, its purpose seems more normal and 'ordinary' than the special case of the Hounslow letter for the future Henry VIII, and accordingly more of a threat to the distinction between types of letter. Yet although less impressive than the Hounslow letter, the Aylesbury grant may once have been quite a splendid document.[39]

provincialis tocius dicti ordinis in Anglia'. Another Knaresborough grant of 1480 lacks the provincial title: C. Wordsworth, 'On Some Pardons or Indulgences Preserved in Yorkshire, 1412–1527', *Yorkshire Archaeological Journal* 16 (1902), p. 418.

[33] Clark-Maxwell, 'Some Further Letters', p. 193.

[34] Oxford, Bodl., Yorkshire charter 65 (not a particularly special document, carrying a note of an annual subscription of 2d). An intermediary friar is also named on the (non-provincial) Knaresborough grant of 1480: Wordsworth, 'Some pardons in Yorkshire', p. 418.

[35] NUL, MS Mi.F1/7, with the note 'per me fratrem Th. Vicars'.

[36] BL, Stowe ch. 617.

[37] It is slightly different, as it recites only a general absolution, provided on the front of the document, and lacks the different absolutions to be offered annually or *in mortis articulo*. However, WAM 6653, a Hounslow form of 1503, likewise has only a single absolution (on the dorse).

[38] On this campaign, see below, p. 134.

[39] Worcester, Worcestershire Record Office, BA 2309/17 (not individually numbered), addressed to '[V]enerabilibus ac devotis in Christo viris Thome Belle, Johanni Elys, et Thome Hempman, omnibus que confratribus et consororibus fraternitatis beate Marie in villa Aylysbury'. Unusually, it is sealed on strings rather than a tag, and drawn up as an indenture. The once elaborate decoration has been cut away. The pope's name is

The grants of 'specific confraternity' suggest a distinct distribution method, but its exposure is virtually impossible. No mendicant records show the system in operation; but hints exist in late fourteenth-century literature, specifically in Chaucer's *Summoner's Tale*, and some of the anti-fraternal writings of the period.

The *Summoner's Tale* shows a friar and a married couple who have joined his confraternity: the friar has brought back a special letter, sealed with the convent seal. This process matches that outlined in *Piers the Plowman's Crede*, where the letters were offered in exchange for significant donations.[40] However, the precise details of the administrative processes to secure and issue the grant are not indicated.

Despite their formality, the letters of specific confraternity are in many ways less interesting than the 'open confraternity' grants. However, their careful preparation does suggest some appreciation and a sense of purpose and commitment, with some overlap with traditional monastic confraternity. An awareness that such confraternity was a privilege to be granted only occasionally appears in some instances where priors provincial of the Augustinian friars were authorised to issue only a specified number of grants when they entered office.[41] However, it seems unlikely that this would be the total number of grants allowed during their term of office, and they were perhaps authority to make grants at their own nomination. In that respect they are akin to the authority granted to papal representatives in England (and other favoured recipients) to issue specific numbers of identified dispensations and licences during their terms of office.[42] Rather similar is the sense of privilege conveyed in the records of Peter Terrasse's visitation of the English Carmelites in 1504-5. The register of his activities likewise records individual grants of confraternity, many of which were probably 'specific'.[43] However, there are cases which leave room for doubt, especially when confraternity was granted to rather large groups, such as 'the burgesses, bailiffs and commoners of the town of Ipswich of either sex and whether secular or clergy'.[44]

With the 'open confraternity' letters we enter very different waters. These

---

scratched out, suggesting (despite the inherent contradiction) that the grant was still considered valid in Henry VIII's later years.

[40] Dean, *Six Ecclesiastical Satires*, pp. 17–18.

[41] Roth, *English Austin Friars*, i. 214. For the order as a whole, see also D. Gutierrez, *The Augustinians in the Middle Ages, 1357–1517*, History of the Order of St Augustine 1/2 (Villanova, PA, 1983), p. 194.

[42] See for example *CPL IV, A.D. 1362–1404*, pp. 305–6.

[43] Copsey, 'Visit of Peter Terrasse', pp. 190–91, 196, 199, 200, 201. In several of these cases, the head of a house acted as intermediary in the grant.

[44] Ibid., pp. 190, 195. Some of these suggest parallels with the Franciscan grant to the guild of St Mary at Aylesbury, but with no actual documents the similarity remains speculative. A Burton Lazars grant of 1463 to the inhabitants of East and West Hagbourne, Oxfordshire, once had a schedule listing the beneficiaries: PRO, C270/32/5 (the detached list might be C270/32/11).

documents take mendicant confraternity into the open market, into mass production and commodity dealing. For the Dominicans and Franciscans, these may be very localized collections, associated with individual houses rather than a provincial structure. (Extant letters from the Augustinians and Carmelites are too few to integrate into this system convincingly.) Possibly the letters should be appreciated primarily as confessional licences (similar letters were sometimes called 'confessionals'),[45] giving the right to choose a confessor and receive absolution, but still securing participation in the orders' spiritual merit. (A Trinitarian publicity document from the 1520s might be invoked here: its concern in pushing the product is primarily with the confession and burial privileges on offer, rather than participation in the merit from good works; yet the Trinitarian letters do promise such participation.)[46]

Details of the distribution mechanisms remain a matter for speculation. The exempt status of the main mendicant orders here allows their activities to avoid detection: while ordinary pardoners were subject to the diocesan (and sometimes peculiar) authorities, who would grant collecting licences and discipline those collecting without authorization, the mendicants (and others) evaded such constraints. Yet the lack of registration perhaps confirms that the main orders did normally use friars as collectors, rather than questors.[47]

The most likely organizational structure for the mendicants' distribution of open confraternity letters would be through the network of local collectorates (the Franciscan 'limitations', for instance), within each of which an individual friar was the principal alms collector.[48] Such localized collecting may explain why it was the wardens of particular houses who issued Dominican and Franciscan grants of 'open confraternity',[49] but precise geographical ties between the houses and the people named on the forms are generally elusive. Moreover, some forms were issued by provincial authorities.[50]

---

[45] See the printed forms for Santo Spirito in Sassia: 'Visum est presens confessionale per me Walterum Stone, legum doctorem': Oxford, Bodl., Arch Ab.8 (18), (20).

[46] The publicity document is transcribed in Lichfield Record Office, B/A/14i, fol. 69v. SBT, DR 37/91/5 (Thelsford, 1476) promises 'in omnibus ieiuniis, vigiliis, abstinenciis, peregrinacionibus, elemosinis, ceterisque bonis et suffragiis in dicto nostro ordine factis et faciendis eisdem [i.e. the recipients] in domino participamus'. The other privileges are also described.

[47] Nevertheless, questors were sometimes used: see below, pp. 132–3.

[48] A. Williams, 'The "Limitour" of Chaucer's Time and his "Limitacioun"', Studies in Philology 57 (1960), pp. 463–78.

[49] For example SRO, D1743/F17, D593/A/1/32/16–18 (John, Guardian of the Stafford Franciscans, 1479 – see also below, p. 134–5); Exeter, Devon Record Office [DRO], 2527M/CL1 (John, prior of the Exeter Dominicans, 1485); NUL, Mi.F1/1–2 (John, warden of the Nottingham Franciscans, 1479 – both dated 4 April, but they differ in size and writing). These were all linked to special campaigns: see below, pp. 134–5. See also London, Lincoln's Inn Library, MS Hale 179, ff. ii, 225, issued in 1520 by Henry Osborn, prior of the Oxford Dominicans.

[50] PRO, C270/32/15, issued in 1485 by John Payne, Dominican prior provincial in England. See also the letter for the fraternity of St Mary at Aylesbury, above, p. 128.

More precise evidence for activity is almost completely absent. A possible indication – of uncertain reliability and validity – may be Chaucer's portrait of the Friar in his *Summoner's Tale*. Here we have a friar out collecting alms, and jotting down (and erasing) the donors' names as he goes round.[51] This certainly suggests a similarity with the requirement that questors for other institutions should maintain lists of donors,[52] but it does not actually show letters of confraternity being issued; William Woodford's discussion of the practice suggests that this refers simply to ordinary alms-gathering, rather than confraternity distributions.[53] Nevertheless, the possibility of integrating Chaucer's friar into the 'open confraternity' system merits further thought, given other possible parallels between mendicant collectors and questors.

Anti-mendicant writings – notably the complaints of Jack Upland – claimed that mendicants farmed out their limitations to the highest bidder.[54] If 'open confraternity' involved an annual subscription to retain membership and its privileges, then the limiter might be the obvious person to undertake such collecting.[55] With that in mind, might the licences found in episcopal registers admitting friars as confessors and preachers in accordance with the papal decree, *Super cathedram*, be deemed equivalent to ordinary questorial licences?[56]

This is all speculative, but this is a subject for which the obscurity of the evidence means that speculation unavoidably piles on speculation. Whether

---

[51] *Riverside Chaucer*, ed. Benson, p. 129, lines 1741–44, 1757–59.

[52] For requirements that questors return names, T. Madox, *Formulare Anglicanum* (London, 1702), p. 149; Oxford, Bodl., MS Tanner 211, fols. 5v, 28r.

[53] Doyle, 'William Woodford', p. 150.

[54] Dean, *Six Ecclesiastical Satires*, p. 125.

[55] I know of no evidence to support this statement in relation to the four main mendicant orders, the closest approximations being only chance remarks. Wyclif makes an imprecise throwaway reference to 'fraternitatis redditibus' (Buddensieg, *Wyclif's Polemical Works*, i. 213), but this might merely mean receipts from distribution of letters. One of 'Jack Upland''s questions alleges that the friars 'desire that other riche men axen you letteris for a certeyne summe bi yere' (Dean, *Six Ecclesiastical Satires*, p. 125 – this phrase not in the original Latin questions, or the 1536 printed edition: Doyle, 'William Woodford', p. 79 [q.23]). The Friar in one of John Heywood's plays says that 'I come not hither for money nor for rent' (Hazlitt, *Select Collection*, i. 199). The comment nevertheless suggests regular collections, from the same people each time. Notes of annual subscriptions appear on some letters issued by the Trinitarians (e.g. Worcester, Worcestershire Record Office, BA 8965/5(ii): Thelsford, 1492, priced 4d.) and by bodies like Burton Lazars hospital (e.g. SBT, DR.37/91/14: 1504, also 4d.). An unlikely possibility – but not utterly to be excluded – is that a fee for 'open confraternity' was paid in annual instalments (like membership fees for other guilds, including the 'confraternity' of the Boston guild). The collecting machinery might then still depend on the local limiter on his rounds.

[56] On such licences, Williams, 'Limitour', pp. 470–76; Williams, 'Relations', pp. 29–43. The argument in B. Z. Kedar, 'Canon Law and Local Practice: The Case of Mendicant Preaching in Late Medieval England', *Bulletin of Medieval Canon Law* 2 (1972), pp. 17–32, would work against this suggestion.

the limiter formally leased the collecting rights, as 'Jack Upland' asserted, cannot be determined from available evidence; the mendicants' financial arrangements remain extremely obscure. The charge that limiters did farm perhaps first appeared in some manuscripts of the *Canterbury Tales*.[57] A similar charge was emphatically denied by the Franciscan William Woodford, writing in 1395, at least with respect to his order and the Dominicans.[58] Yet it resurfaced when the accusations fed into the anti-fraternal criticisms of *Jack Upland*, produced around 1400,[59] in turn evoking a riposte in *Friar Daw's Reply*.[60] Upland later returned to the attack, but added nothing new.[61] He may have been drawing on continental experience, as leasing of collectorates occurred there among fifteenth-century Augustinians even if it was unknown in England.[62] Daw's response claims that Upland was simply mistaken, having drawn a false parallel between limiters and the pardoners of the leading London hospitals.[63] The error's source may actually lie elsewhere. A hint in Upland's work suggests that the charge is indeed a misunderstanding, perhaps deliberate, used to berate the friars. Upland refers to *five* orders of friars; a reference firmly deflated by his respondent with the comment that there were actually only four 'foundid in the lawe'.[64] This reply, however, overlooks the anomalous status of both the Crutched Friars, and the Trinitarians, as quasi-mendicant orders.[65] The former were probably too few in England to explain the misperception and confusion over the limiters (although there is evidence that they distributed 'open confrater-nity' letters, possibly through questors);[66] but the larger number of Trinitarian houses, and their higher profile in the indulgence trade, may provide an answer. Although formally Augustinian canons, the Trinitar-ians were often considered a fifth order of friars because they solicited alms for the redemption of captives. While their collecting arrangements are generally no easier to elucidate than those of the other orders, they were more firmly under episcopal jurisdiction. They certainly farmed out some collections; and questors can be identified in episcopal records, paying fees

[57] *Riverside Chaucer*, ed. Benson, p. 27, ll. 252a–b.
[58] Doyle, 'William Woodford', pp. 111–12, 137. Doyle considers his qualified response 'evidently a piece of diplomatic evasion' (p. 112).
[59] For date, Doyle, 'William Woodford', pp. 90–91. For leasing, Dean, *Six Ecclesiastical Satires*, p. 125.
[60] Dean, *Six Ecclesiastical Satires*, p. 165, although he perhaps misses the point.
[61] *Upland's Rejoinder*, ibid., p. 211, ll. 233–4.
[62] Roth, *English Austin Friars*, i. 226. See also Williams, 'Limitour', pp. 477–78.
[63] Dean, *Six Ecclesiastical Satires*, p. 164 (ll. 478–83).
[64] Ibid., pp. 122, 152. Langland also refers to five orders: William Langland, *Piers Plowman: The C-Text*, ed. Derek Pearsall (2nd edn., Exeter, 1994), pp. 154 (VIII, 191), 177 (IX, 345), 250 (XV, 81).
[65] For these orders see *MRH*, pp. 203–11.
[66] Below, p. 133.

for their licences.[67] Their tours of parish churches are attested by a publicity document of c.1520, detailing the spiritual privileges available to their benefactors. That proclamation firmly states that the collectors 'be no questers but religious men approved',[68] suggesting that members of the order did participate in the quests – a suggestion supported by the occasional naming of friars on the documents.[69]

The scant evidence for the Crutched Friars supports the picture presented by the Trinitarians. They too acquired questorial licences, which suggests a structured marketing system, linked to individual houses. In July 1519 and March 1521, the Colchester house obtained licences for collections within York Minster's peculiar jurisdiction – so collections were doubtless occuring elsewhere in the diocese, and presumably in jurisdictions between York and Essex.[70] That these two licences are the only ones recorded for collecting which must have been extensive is not surprising: questorial licences are very imperfectly registered after 1400. More impressive evidence for the Colchester collections comes from the printing of their confraternity certificates. Two such copies survive, dated 1523, leaving space for the month (and presumably precise date) to be added later.[71] The printing of the precise year suggests a considerable market, and annual reprints; otherwise it would be left incomplete, to be entered at sale.[72]

The Crutched Friars may also have used questors, rather than (or in addition to) their own members. Accordingly, three men were granted a collecting licence on behalf of the London house within the diocese of Hereford in 1527; in 1532 the same bishop's register identifies Humphrey Wood as the questor (he also acted for several other institutions in Hereford diocese around this time).[73]

The patchy surviving evidence leaves questions unanswered and un-answerable, notably about the intensity of any order's marketing methods. Rarely do sufficient letters survive to permit real comparisons or assessments,

---

[67] Madox, *Formulare Anglicanum*, p. 149; NRO, 9/14, fols. 25r, 79v. Proctors are also occasionally identified in episcopal registers and elsewhere, and presumably were not members of the order. See for example *Registrum Caroli Bothe, episcopum Herefordensis, A.D. MDXVI–MDXXXV*, ed. A. T. Bannister, Canterbury and York Society 28 (1921), pp. 355–58 (and one unnamed at p. 359).

[68] Lichfield Record Office, B/A/14i, fol. 69v. A (biased) glimpse of Trinitarians at work may be provided in *Piers the Plowman's Crede*: the Franciscan, disparaging the Carmelites, calls them 'Robertes men'. This is glossed as 'robbers', but might also be meant to invoke the questors for St Robert of Knaresborough, one of the most active Trinitarian houses. Dean, *Six Ecclesiastical Satires*, p. 10 (for the gloss, p. 72).

[69] Oxford, Bodl., Yorkshire charter 65; Wordsworth, 'Some Pardons in Yorkshire', p. 418.

[70] York, York Minster Library, H3/1, fol. 101r.

[71] J. Fraser, 'A Pynson Indulgence of 1523', *Sussex Archaeological Collections* 50 (1907), pp. 109–13.

[72] See also Boston letters, giving the century but not the year: PRO, C270/32/18; WAM, 6655; or NUL, Mi.F1/7, which has the century printed, but completed by hand for 1512.

[73] Bannister, *Registrum Bothe*, pp. 358, 360; see also below.

and much must be extracted from single copies and their individual idiosyncracies. Such caveats make anomalies noticeable, and worrying. For the Franciscans, for instance, letters of 'open confraternity' bunch very markedly in 1479: more letters survive for that year than any other. This reflects the aftermath of a papal bull of that year, and a special distribution of confessional letters.[74] Similarly, there is a cluster of Dominican letters in 1485, linked with a confessional licence granted by Pope Innocent VIII.[75] That raises questions about the marketing in other years. Should we see mendicant 'open confraternity' not as something generally available, but as a short-term response to immediate crises that stimulated concerted fund-raising efforts in which participation in spiritual privileges was a 'special offer' inducement? This is probably something that will never be adequately resolved. The open confraternity letters printed for the Dominicans of Oxford in 1520 referred expressly to papal privileges granted to donors to the order, 'manus adiutrices porrigentibus pro fabricis ecclesiarum domorum et aliis eorum necessariis secundum ordinis suppetentiam', implicitly tying the grant of confraternity to relief of such needs for the individual house.[76]

Whatever the orders' distribution arrangements, the actual letters sometimes show unexpected sophistication and refinement, and a clear appreciation of marketing strategies. While manuscript reproduction obviously imposed limitations, it did not preclude aiming at market niches. The letter distributed by the Stafford Franciscans in 1479 survives in three different versions. Two, presumably intended for general distribution, are simply addressed 'In Christo sibi karissimi', and written on one side only, but one was intended for a married couple, leaving space for both names to be entered

---

[74] Little, 'Franciscan Letters', p. 16, and list at pp. 23–24; also Clark-Maxwell, 'Some Further Letters', pp. 189, 193, 211.

[75] These also use a vocabulary of confraternity. Clark-Maxwell, 'Some Further Letters', pp. 188–9; Exeter, Devon Record Office, 2527M/CL1 ('quilibet confratrum et consororum'); SBT, DR 37/91/7 ('singulis confratribus confraternitatis utriusque sexus ordinis nostri').

[76] London, Lincoln's Inn Library, MS Hale 179, ff. ii, 225. Irish evidence may support this contention. In 1357 the Kilkenny Franciscans established a confraternity precisely to fund a new bell tower and church repairs: E. B. Fitzmaurice and A. G. Little, *Materials for the History of the Franciscan Province of Ireland, A.D. 1230–1450*, British Society for Franciscan Studies 9 (Manchester, 1920), p. 139. Equivalent short-term arrangements may explain the grants authorized to benefactors of the Carmelite convents of Ipswich, Yarmouth, and Norwich in 1504: Copsey, 'Visit of Peter Terrasse', p. 190. A distinction would be needed between such 'short-term' confraternities and the ties established by permanent guilds or fraternities which were associated with mendicant houses, but possibly not through confraternity: see Barron, 'Parish Fraternities', p. 23. English funding campaigns like that for Kilkenny were supported by episcopal indulgences and authorized collections: see for example B. Nilson and R. H. Frost, 'The Archiepiscopal Indulgences for the City of York, 1450–1500', in *The Church in Medieval York: Records edited in Honour of Professor Barrie Dobson*, ed. D. M. Smith, Borthwick Texts and Calendars 24 (York, 1999), nos. 4, 14.

but with 'his consort' included in the pre-written matter. The third version, on a larger piece of parchment, and with an absolution on the dorse, was aimed more precisely, being addressed 'Venerabile in Christo patri ac domino' – rather inappropriate for its eventual purchaser, a mere chaplain. Evidently, the distributors did not always appreciate the niceties of their wares.[77]

While the mendicants are generally obscure players in the confraternity and indulgence business, and are perhaps overshadowed by the fuller evidence and seemingly more dynamic business acumen of institutions like St Anthony's Hospital, London, or the Boston Guild, they clearly were not passive players. The Franciscan and Dominican letters of 1479 and 1485, and later activities of the Austin friars, show a conscious and determined exploitation of funding opportunities.

The Austin friars (at least, those of Cambridge) may have been aggressively marketing a plenary indulgence in 1494,[78] but no major campaign is adequately documented before 1516. Then Pope Leo X authorized collections linked with an indulgence, for ten years.[79] A printed form letter of January 1518 offered plenary remission a pena et culpa in return for donations for rebuilding both St Peter's at Rome and the Austin friars' convents in England, with numerous other spiritual benefits. The gist of a confraternity letter lingered, with participation in the order's spiritual good works and post-mortem commemoration.[80] As with the Colchester Crutched Friars in 1523, printing the year on the form suggests expectations of high sales, apparently justified. In the first five years in which the indulgence was offered total receipts – presumably after expenses – were almost £2300, from which the friars received £1144 13s. 9½d.[81] The purchasers' motivations cannot be assessed: were they supporting the friars, or St Peter's, or just acquiring the privileges?

This foray into collecting continued later, possibly in breach of the bull, or following its renewal. In 1526 the prior provincial authorized a blanket grant of participation to the members of the guild of St John, Wakering, which presumably benefited both institutions through the distribution of the letters.[82] Four years later, the Hereford episcopal register shows them actually

---

77 SRO, D593/A/1/32/16–18. See also R. N. Swanson, 'Letters of Confraternity and Indulgence in Late Medieval England', *Archives* 25 (2000), p. 53.

78 Roth, *English Austin Friars*, i. 431–32; ii., no. 966.

79 Ibid., ii., no. 1020.

80 CRO, AR 27/8. For the indulgence see also W. E. Lunt, *Financial Relations of the Papacy with England, 1327–1534*, Publications of the Mediaeval Academy of America, 74 (Cambridge, MA, 1962), pp. 609–10. Individual houses may have organized the collections, but whether they used questors is unclear. For a collecting licence, Bannister, *Registrum Bothe*, p. 355.

81 Lunt, *Financial Relations*, pp. 610–11. This must be read alongside Roth, *English Austin Friars*, ii., nos. 1020, 1040–41. The sums recorded may not account for all the receipts, as one of the administrators was charged with peculation in 1522: ibid., ii., no. 1041.

82 Clark-Maxwell, 'Some Further Letters', pp. 191, 212 [I have not seen this]. This grant, in conjunction with the Franciscan grant to Aylesbury's guild of St Mary in 1480

using a questor. Humphrey Wood was then joint proctor with Thomas Bradley for the Ludlow house for collections whose purposes match those of 1516.[83]

Mendicant enterprise also appears in the ready adoption of print for their letters. Evidence does not survive from every order; but that may be merely a matter of survival. The indulgence trade rapidly appreciated the potential for mass reproduction of documents like the 'open confraternity' letters, and it is probably no accident that the first extant example of English printing is actually an indulgence letter.[84] Printers may also have appreciated the value of such jobbing work to maintain their cash flow, alongside the printing of books. Certainly the wide range of such ephemera printed by Richard Pynson suggests that they were an important element in his business.[85]

Printed mendicant confraternity documents are scarce, no matter what the original print runs.[86] Differences between the handwritten Carmelite letter of 1448 and that printed in 1512 may reflect the new technology: the latter is visually more impressive, wordier, and appears more consciously a marketing device.[87] Its history also is demonstrably wrong. It asserts that Pope Julius II had ratified privileges granted by previous popes ranging from Hadrian II (867–72) to John XI (931–6), a fictitious Sergius V (perhaps a printing error for Sergius IV), and Innocent IV (1243–54) – but the Carmelite order did not exist until the thirteenth century![88] Historicity presumably mattered less to the purchaser than the benefits being offered. These were a temporal indulgence calculated at over 5000 years, and a share in 'all the masses, prayers, fasts, vigils, preachings, abstinences, indulgences, and all the other good works' performed by the province's friars.[89]

Of course, analysis of the distribution of mendicant confraternity letters addresses only one side of an equation. The orders could prepare any number

(above, p. 128), raises the possibility that fraternities often attracted members via such letters, which no longer survive. Wholesale participation in mendicant confraternity privileges almost certainly cost less than a formal papal pardon, or even episcopal indulgences.

[83] Bannister, Registrum Bothe, pp. 359. Lunt (Financial Relations, p. 611) is emphatic that the collection of 1517–22 was the last papal indulgence administered in England, but was not aware that Leo X's bull was valid for ten years. This leaves a problem with later collections: was the grant renewed or extended, or did the friars ignore the restriction?

[84] L. Hellinga, Caxton in Focus: The Beginning of Printing in England (London, 1982), pp. 81–82; P. Needham, The Printer and the Pardoner: An Unrecorded Indulgence printed by William Caxton for the Hospital of St Mary Rounceval, Charing Cross (Washington, DC, 1986), p. 32.

[85] A proper study of such ephemeral printing is needed, despite the obvious problems. Its contribution to Pynson's career is ignored in J. H. White, 'Richardus Pynson de parochia Sancti Clementis Danorum', Fifteenth-Century Studies 8 (1983), pp. 275–90.

[86] For a summary list (probably incomplete, listing issues rather than individual copies) see STC ii. 2–9.

[87] SRO, D593/A/1/32/13; NUL, Mi.F1/7.

[88] NUL, Mi.F1/7.

[89] NUL, Mi.F1/7.

of letters, but the effort was wasted if no one wanted them. Purchasers were absolutely essential: their acquisition of confraternity privileges reflects their appreciations of the mendicants, and the orders' role in society.

It is no easy task to assess those issues. The evidence is again scattered, fragmentary, and incoherent, inviting speculation rather than permitting clear argument. Thus, the absence of formal evidence for the existence of the Third Orders in England – despite the production of English versions of the Franciscan Rule – has generated suggestions that mendicant confraternities should be considered as equivalent to the tertiaries.[90] It is not clear whether this claim applies primarily to 'specific' or 'open' confraternity, or to both. The seemingly informal links between orders and confrères – especially in the open confraternities – makes the suggestion tentative at best.[91]

There are two possible lines of approach here. On one hand, several purchasers treated mendicant privileges as one element in a general collection of spiritual benefits, acquiring whole collections of indulgences and similar documents which just happened to include mendicant letters. In the collection built up by Henry and Katherine Langley, mendicant letters sit alongside the Saintes Cathedral indulgence, support for the Hospitallers at Rhodes, and other good causes.[92] Similarly, John Arundell in Cornwall acquired a set of miscellaneous documents;[93] while in Warwickshire the collection of John Archer and Alice his wife included confraternity from the Dominicans of Warwick and St Mary's Abbey, York, with letters from the hospitals of Walsoken and St Thomas and Holy Trinity, Rome, and the Burton Lazars pardon.[94] Such hoards suggest indiscriminate acquisition rather than deliberate choice. Clearer evidence of random acquisition appears in the early sixteenth-century account books of the Willoughby family. Donations to mendicants appear scattered among domestic, charitable, and devotional payments, including those to pardoners for a range of

[90] D. W. Whitfield, 'The Third Order of St Francis in Mediaeval England', *Franciscan Studies*, New Series 13/1 (March 1953), pp. 57–58; Roth, *English Austin Friars*, i. 212–13. The attempt by J. V. Fleming ('The Summoner's Prologue: an Iconographic Adjustment', *Chaucer Review* 2 (1967–68), pp. 101–5) to assimilate the confraternity of the Summoner's Tale with the Third Order and continental-style confraternities (or possibly the normal guilds) is misleading. Some English lay devotional fraternities did meet in friaries, and had ties with mendicant spirituality (Barron, above, n. 2), but these are fundamentally different from the links reflected in confraternity letters.

[91] See also the comment of J. Smet, *The Carmelites: A History of the Brothers of Our Lady of Mount Carmel* (3 vols. in 4, Darien, IL, 1975–82), ii. 222, applicable to the continental context, where the Third Orders and small confraternities linked to individual houses flourished: 'Lowest in the scale of commitment and affiliation with the Order were those who were only given letters of confraternity which entitled them to a share in the spiritual goods of the Order in view of some benefit bestowed'. The different English situation may require some revision of that assessment.

[92] For example PRO, C270/32/12–18.

[93] N. Orme, 'Indulgences in Medieval Cornwall', *Journal of the Royal Institution of Cornwall*, New Series 2/1 (1991–92), pp. 153, 163 (not a full list of Arundell material).

[94] SBT, DR.37/91/3, 5–10.

institutions, and for guild memberships. The only clear reference to mendicant confraternity occurs in 1520, with a payment of 12d. for brotherhood with the Coventry Carmelites.[95] The ordering of the accounts makes such acquisitions seem routine, and again indiscriminate.

Even if a deliberate concern to be associated with the mendicants cannot be identified from such evidence, their letters and spiritual privileges were obviously desired. Their effective distribution fits the mendicant confraternities firmly into the wholesale marketing of such benefits, to take advantage of (but not necessarily exploit) the widespread concern with Purgatory and penitential obligations. This popularity explains why the letters were one of the Wycliffite targets, on practical and theological grounds. Wyclif himself condemned them as simony,[96] and also challenged them on the basis that the prayers would not help those predestined to damnation.[97] Similar charges about the sinfulness of the recipients appeared in the questions to which William Woodford responded in 1395, together with comment that the friars themselves might not be all that meritorious anyway.[98] On the other hand, they were also challenged for not making the letters (and presumably the prayers) more generally available: if they were efficacious, it was uncharitable not to make them more easily accessible.[99]

Individual and deliberate reactions to the mendicants' promises appear in the provisions made by testators concerning the spiritual privileges. Here the promise in the confraternity letters of commemoration when notified of the death, comes into its own,[100] although not all letters carried such an explicit promise, or required notification of the death.[101] The

---

[95] HMC: Report on the Manuscripts of Lord Middleton Preserved at Wollaton Hall, Nottingham (London, HMSO, 1911), p. 332. This payment is my only solid evidence that surviving confraternity letters were actually bought. The 12d. paid to the Coventry Carmelites in April 1524 (ibid., p. 365) is entered as a 'rayward'. A payment of 12d. for a Dominican letter is mentioned in Clark-Maxwell, 'Some Letters', p. 60, without a reference.

[96] Johannis Wycliffe Dialogus, sive Speculum ecclesie militantis, ed. A. W. Pollard (London, 1886), p. 79.

[97] Ibid., pp. 25–26.

[98] Doyle, 'William Woodford', pp. 168–70. Woodford justifiably responds that similar arguments were applicable to all forms of confraternity. 'Friar Daw' responds to the same question with charges that it undermines the whole system of prayers, by laity and regulars: Dean, Six Ecclesiastical Satires, p. 173. See also Pearsall, Piers Plowman, pp. 176–77.

[99] Doyle, 'William Woodford', p. 138. Woodford squirms somewhat. The challenge to confraternity is very similar to aspects of the Wycliffite challenge to indulgences in general.

[100] For example SBT, DR 37/91/2 (Austin friars, 1384): 'cum obitus alicuius vestrum in capitulo nostro locali fuerit nobis nunciatus, id pro vobis devote fiet quod pro fratribus nostris defunctis in communi ibidem fieri consuevit'.

[101] SBT, DR 37/91/7 (Warwick Dominicans, 1485), grants participation in spiritual good works 'in vita pariter et in morte', without requiring notification of the death or promising special commendation. This seems characteristic of letters issued under a

demand for notification was criticized in the late fourteenth century, with claims that those who did not give notice were denied the prayers.[102] How a death was to be notified is rarely specified, yet it had implications for the fate of the confraternity letters. If notification were merely by report, the letters would stay with the purchaser's heirs, to be kept or destroyed as they saw fit, like any other ephemera. However, actual surrender of the letters may have been required, as stipulated for instance in the Franciscan grant of specific confraternity to the fellows of Pembroke College, Cambridge, in 1475.[103] If this did happen, as a task perhaps enjoined on executors, the documents had to be handed over – but how this worked for multiple grants like those to Pembroke College and Aylesbury's fraternity of St Mary is hard to imagine. Individuals occasionally ordered the return of the letters in wills, as Christopher Horbury of Wakefield did in 1480 for his letters from the Augustinians of Tickhill and the Trinitarians of Knaresborough.[104] Robert Est at York in 1467 apparently had letters from each of the mendicant houses in York, and from the Carthusians at Mount Grace and Hull.[105] Similar provisions appear in the wills of John Benyngfeld and William de Ergh, respectively in 1395 and 1414.[106] Many other testators left bequests and identified themselves as brethren or sisters of one or more mendicant orders; for example William Ernton, who left 6s. 8d. to the London Dominicans in 1435, or the references to the Augustinians by Margaret Dolowe in 1456 and to the Carmelites by William Alygh in 1496.[107]

Not all, however, managed to secure confraternity whilst they lived. Apparently, the spiritual privileges of mendicant confraternity could also be acquired after death, and some testators made bequests for that purpose. Adam Brusshcombe of London in 1390 sought admission by all four orders,[108] while in 1520 Henry Atkyn left a bequest to the London Crutched Friars to cover his burial and his admission as a 'broder off there chapeter'.[109] Given such instances, it is equally likely that executors enrolled the deceased among the confraternity, to satisfy the catch-all residual bequest

confessional licence from Pope Innocent VIII: see also Clark-Maxwell, 'Some Further Letters', pp. 188–89; DRO, 2527M/CL1.

[102] This is the version to which William Woodford responded: Doyle, 'William Woodford', pp. 171–72. It is phrased differently in 'Jack Upland'.

[103] Reproduced in Clark-Maxwell, 'Some Letters', pl. VI (at p. 42), from Cambridge, Pembroke College Archives, Box A, 23.

[104] *Testamenta Eboracensia*, III, Surtees Society 45 (1864), p. 259; also in Roth, *English Austin Friars*, ii. 366*.

[105] *Testamenta Eboracensia*, III, p. 160.

[106] GL, MS 9171/1, fol. 350v; 9171/2, fols. 315v–316r. (I owe these Guildhall references to Dr Jens Röhrkasten.)

[107] GL, MS 9171/3, fol. 444r–v; 9171/5, fol. 223v; 9171/8, fol. 134v. On bequests see also Little, 'Franciscan letters', pp. 18–19.

[108] GL, MS 9171/1, fol. 211r.

[109] GL, MS 9171/9, fols. 154v–155r.

'for the good of the soul', although any such dealings are elusive.[110] Burial at a friary may also have been treated as conferring confraternity, without the preliminary administrative work.[111]

Some wills may, however, give a wrong impression. Death could be the point where a previous commitment was simply reinforced, even if the words suggest a new connection. In 1456 Harry Bobyngton left a bequest to the London Dominicans to record his name among their confrères; but noted that he had actually joined the confraternity under a previous prior provincial.[112]

The return of mendicant confraternity letters at death meshes into the general concern for post-mortem commemoration, and makes the mendicant provisions very like those for other commemorative bodies, including ordinary guilds. In the 1420s, John Thurston of London required his executors to notify his death to groups which would pray for him, identifying six by name, 'and suche other places that I have writinges of, so that I may [have] the prayers and suffrages of the places and gyldes aforsaid as a brother ought to have.'[113]

Presumably when letters were surrendered the names were checked against an existing register, or were newly registered among those for whom a house should pray. The originals then became obsolete, perhaps simply accumulating, to be destroyed only when the friaries were dissolved. Yet, as ephemera, they might have been destroyed anyway. Like many other obsolete medieval documents, some were recycled to provide seal tags, explaining why fragments of one confraternity letter appear as tags on another, issued by the Knaresborough Trinitarians in 1465.[114]

What, finally, can be said in conclusion? This chapter aimed to set mendicant confraternity in a broad context. Its practice clearly fits into a habit of acquiring spiritual benefits from varied sources. In personal collections, there is nothing to mark out membership of mendicant or monastic confraternities from links with other bodies offering similar privileges: they are simply another element in the preparation for Purgatory. Yet mendicant confraternity cannot just be submerged into the concern for

[110] A curious bequest in the will of Richard Clerke of Lincoln (1528) may be directed to executors: 'To the Frerys Observantes of Newarke, where it please them [= the executors?] by the meanys of good frere Barton to get me a letter of brotherhode for me and my wyff, to bestowe it as the father ther for the tyme beyng shall thynke moste convenient' (Lincoln Wills, volume II: A.D. 1505 to May, 1530, ed. C. W. Foster, Lincoln Record Society 10 (1918), p. 89). Why a letter should be obtained after death is unclear. Clarke also left bequests to the Trinitarians of Hounslow and Knaresborough, without declaring himself a confrere (ibid., p. 90).

[111] Little, 'Franciscan Letters', p. 19.

[112] GL, MS 9171/5, fol. 209v, see also 226r.

[113] PRO, Prob. 11/20, fol. 181v. Other bequests included 20s. to the Sheen Charterhouse for a trental, 'and to have me remembred amongs their praiers as a brother'. See also Swanson, 'Letters', p. 56 n. 102.

[114] WAM, 6658*, and Swanson, 'Letters', p. 56 and n. 104.

the afterlife. Admission to specific confraternity does suggest a more deliberate desire for ties with the friars, and the testamentary references suggest that confraternity membership did matter; at least to those who singled it out for mention. At that point, however, much would depend on the executors, on those left behind. A worrying aspect of dealing with mendicant confraternity letters is precisely the number still in family collections: they evidently were not returned to the issuing houses. Was the relevant death notified by some other means; or were the survivors too preoccupied to worry about another's soul? Or was it the case, as William Woodford commented in 1395, that the prayers were offered even without the letters being returned?[115]

At the Henrician Reformation, both mendicant and monastic confraternity disappeared, as provision for Purgatory was systematically dismantled. While they had existed, however, they were important elements in religious life, aspects of a neglected but extensive and highly important process of gift exchange and charitable giving which was, arguably, a fundamental component of medieval English Catholicism.

---

[115] Doyle, 'William Woodford', p. 171. He seems a touch evasive, perhaps differentiating between letters that specifically promised prayers for individuals, and general prayers for members of the confraternity as a whole.

WOMEN RELIGIOUS

Yorkshire Nunneries in the Early Tudor Period

CLAIRE CROSS

In his poem 'On Nun Appleton House' Andrew Marvell imaginatively recreated an episode in the history of Nun Appleton Priory where Isabel Thwaites had been dispatched for her education in the early sixteenth century. Seeing a rich prize within their grasp the nuns set about enticing the young heiress into joining the order. If the austerities of their life repelled her, they promised 'the rule itself to you shall bend'. Once professed, she could count on rapid promotion: 'Our abbess too, now far in age,/ Doth your succession near presage'. Yet, despite their best efforts, the young girl rejected these blandishments, and fled the convent to wed William Fairfax of Steeton. The tale, however exaggerated in the telling, still contains a kernel of truth. Gentry families at this time did indeed regard local nunneries as finishing schools and were more than content for unmarriageable daughters to remain there as nuns, where good birth undoubtedly advanced their chances of high office. The intention of this chapter is to explore, so far as the fragmentary sources will allow, the relationship between Yorkshire nunneries and secular society in the early Tudor period.[1]

Just one century in the high Middle Ages saw the foundation of twenty-five nunneries in Yorkshire beginning with Clementhorpe the Benedictine priory established by Archbishop Thurstan immediately outside the walls of York in 1125, and ending with the Cistercian house of Ellerton-on-Swale definitely in being by 1227 but so poorly endowed and documented that not even the name of its benefactor has been preserved. In total the county contained nine Benedictine nunneries, Arden, Marrick, Nunburnholme, Nunkeeling, Nun Monkton, Thicket, Wilberfoss, Yedingham and Clementhorpe; twelve Cistercian nunneries, Basedale, Ellerton-on-Swale, Esholt, Hampole, Handale, Keldholme, Kirklees, Nun Appleton, Rosedale, Sinningthwaite, Swine and Wykeham; single houses of Cluniac nuns at Arthington and Augustinian nuns at Moxby; the important Gilbertine

[1] *Andrew Marvell: The Complete Poems*, ed. E. Story Donno (Harmondsworth, 1972), pp. 78–83; summaries of the sources on which this chapter is based are contained in *Monks, Friars and Nuns in Sixteenth Century Yorkshire*, ed. C. Cross and N. Vickers, Yorkshire Archaeological Society, Record Series 150 (1995), pp. 403–6, 512, 516, 521–608; the spelling of all quotations has been modernized.

double house for nuns and canons at Watton and St Leonard's Hospital served by a small number of sisters as well as brothers. After this quite remarkable development northern landowners lost interest and erected no new religious houses for women throughout the whole of the rest of the medieval period.[2]

Of all these many foundations only two attracted substantial bene-factions: Watton had an income a little in excess of £360 at the Dissolution with St Leonard's Hospital, with revenues of almost £310, approaching Watton in wealth, though most of this sum financed the master, the monastery and the sick and infirm and only a very small proportion went to the sisters. Apart from Watton and St Leonard's, virtually all the nunneries were poor, some very poor indeed, and none came within striking distance of possessing lands worth £200 a year, the sum which Parliament in 1536 made the distinguishing mark between the greater and lesser monasteries. On the assessments given in the *Valor ecclesiasticus*, excluding Watton and St Leonard's Hospital, only six Yorkshire nunneries could count on a clear annual income in excess of £50, the most prosperous being Swine in the corn lands of the East Riding valued at over £82, followed by Nun Monkton and Nun Appleton in the Vale of York with a little over £75 and £73 respectively, Clementhorpe in the suburbs of York with £68, Hampole near Doncaster with £63, and Sinningthwaite, again in the Vale of York and not far from Nun Monkton, with exactly £60 a year. At the other end of the scale eleven houses, Wilberfoss, Yedingham, Thicket, Basedale, Kirklees, Ellerton, Handale, Esholt, Arden, Arthington and Nunburnholme somehow managed to survive on incomes of under £22. The most impecunious of all the houses was Nunburnholme valued at a mere £8 15s. 3d. per annum in 1536. Yet despite their poverty these priories maintained the religious life for more than three centuries and at the Dissolution they supported approximately 230 nuns. Since according to Eileen Power there may not have been as many as 2000 nuns in the entire country in 1534, Yorkshire alone apparently harboured around an eighth of all the nuns in England.[3]

Monastic historians have long recognized that by the late Middle Ages religious houses were very consciously cutting their coat according to their cloth, with the richer abbeys admitting more religious than the less well endowed priories and consequently keeping numbers remarkably constant. This certainly held true for Yorkshire nunneries. Watton with forty-one nuns and sisters and eight canons emerged at the Dissolution as far and away the biggest nunnery in the county. Swine with twenty nuns and Hampole and Nun Appleton each with nineteen in 1539, though half the

[2] J. E. Burton, *The Yorkshire Nunneries in the Twelfth and Thirteenth Centuries*, Borthwick Papers 56 (1979), pp. 38–45; B. Golding, *Gilbert of Sempringham and the Gilbertine Order, c. 1130–c. 1300* (Oxford, 1995), pp. 214–17.

[3] E. Power, *Medieval English Nunneries, c. 1275 to 1535* (Cambridge, 1922), pp. 1–3; E. Power, *Medieval Women*, ed. M. M. Postan (Cambridge, 1975), p. 87.

size of Watton, were even so considerably larger than the other surviving eleven nunneries which after the closures of 1536 and the ensuing transfers still only maintained convents of between nine and thirteen nuns.

The initial letter of a royal charter granted to Esholt nunnery in 1485 shows the prioress and eight nuns kneeling before an image of the virgin and child, the only known contemporary picture of any Yorkshire religious. This would seem to have been an exact delineation of the convent: at its surrender in 1539 Esholt held precisely nine nuns. Some priories had even fewer nuns than this. Of the nine houses dissolved in 1536 the number of nuns at Nun Monkton was not recorded but Sinningthwaite and Clementhorpe had nine, and Moxby and Rosedale eight, Arden, Ellerton and Keldholme a mere six and Nunburnholme three. On an income of under £9 Nunburnholme would have had difficulty supporting even three nuns, which raises the question of how such a tiny number could adequately have performed the liturgy.

These very small, poorly endowed houses, which on all rational grounds could well have been expected to have expired generations earlier, survived into the 1530s largely it seems because of the support of families which had a practical interest in their continuation. Whereas by and large in Yorkshire the male religious orders seem to have been recruiting from the middle echelons of society by the late Middle Ages, the nunneries had not lost their aristocratic connections and a sprinkling of representatives from northern noble families, and very many more from gentry families appear on the pensions lists at the Dissolution. Katherine Nandyke, the last prioress of Wykeham, where Elizabeth Percy had been a nun until 1539, in 1541 left the countess of Northumberland a silver cross, a standing maser and a corporax in compensation 'for such costs and charges as I put her good ladyship unto'. Watton Priory at this time included Anne Ellerker, a close relation of Sir Ralph Ellerker of Risby, Agnes Ellerker, Eleanor Constable, Dorothy Vavasour, and Joan Roose, while Joan Hurtskie, the daughter of William Hurtskie, though less well connected derived at least from the parish gentry. Isabel Ward, who surrendered Clementhorpe to the Crown in 1536, was also related to the Ellerker family. The prioress of Marrick in 1539, Christabel Cowper, seems to have been the aunt of Christopher Thormonby of Thormanby, gentleman. Nunkeeling in the same year in addition to the prioress, Christiana Burgh, contained members of the Stapleton, Sidgwick, Mettam and Thomlinson families. At its dissolution in 1536 the prioress of Nun Monkton was Joan Slingsby, who secured a not inconsiderable pension of £13 6s. 8d. Through a series of dynastic accidents Elizabeth Lutton, professed at Yedingham in about 1512, on the death of her grandfather, William Lutton, in 1530 became a contender for the Lutton inheritance. Agnes Aislaby, originally a nun at the very poor house of Ellerton, who after its dissolution in 1536 chose to transfer to Nun Appleton, on the death of her father, Richard Aislaby of Whitwell, gentleman, in 1542 received

£6 13s. 4d., two cows with their calves, two silver spoons and his second-best bed.[4]

While gentlemen's daughters undoubtedly formed a sizeable proportion in most convents and predominant one in some, the Yorkshire houses were also attracting nuns from prosperous urban families. Elizabeth Lord, the last prioress of Wilberfoss, was the daughter of Robert Lord of Kendal: her sister, Mary, married the goldsmith, George Gale, who served as mayor of York in 1534 and 1536. Margaret Whitfeld, the daughter of a York alderman, went from a similar background to be a nun at Swine. When her mother, Isabel Whitfeld, died in 1534 she set aside £3 6s. 8d. to be kept by her brother and delivered to the nun as she might require it.[5]

As a member of the most affluent Yorkshire nunnery apart from Watton, Margaret Whitfeld should not have been in need of financial support from her family, but certain northern houses may have depended upon subventions from secular sympathizers for their very existence. At Wilberfoss in 1537 Dame Agnes Barton gained a feather bed, a coverlet, blanket, pair of sheets and 8d. from William Gurnell, parson of Full Sutton who also gave Dame Ellen Reide 6d., a ewe and a lamb. The feather bed which in 1527 John Lawton of Thirsk bequeathed after the death of his wife to his daughter a nun at Arden would have constituted a welcome amenity to a house which had an income of only £12 a year. At the even poorer priory of Nunburnholme John Tonge, bailiff of Nunburnholme, in July 1521 willed 10s. and four ewes to Dame Joan Pellerayn, 8s. and four ewes to Agnes Williamson and 16d. and two ewes to their sisters Margaret Craike, Ellen Harper, Agnes Robinson, Margaret Somerby and Cecily Thomlynson.[6]

The most indigent houses needed considerably more than these sporadic benefactions to stave off insolvency and some clearly resorted to extreme measures to make ends meet. In 1534 the archbishop of York found it necessary to warn the prioress and convent of Sinningthwaite against committing simony through accepting girls into the community for money or a pact, though he allowed the prioress to take a voluntary offering at a nun's profession. He also prohibited the house from granting any corrodies, pensions or liveries, or letting any granges or demesnes without previously obtaining his consent. In the following year he licensed the prioress to pawn

---

[4] An analysis of the social antecedents of late medieval Yorkshire monks is included in C. Cross, 'The Origins and University Connections of Yorkshire Religious, 1480–1540', *The Medieval Church: Universities, Heresy, and the Religious Life. Essays in Honour of Gordon Leff*, ed. P. Biller and B. Dobson, *Studies in Church History*, Subsidia 11 (1999), pp. 282–6; F. D. Logan, *Runaway Religious in Medieval England, c. 1240–1540* (Cambridge, 1996), pp. 89–96; Borth. Inst., Prob. Reg. 11, pt. II fols. 559v–560r (Nandike); ibid., fol. 573v (Hurtskie); ibid., fol. 647r (Aslabie); Prob. Reg. 15, pt. I, fol. 68r–v (Thormonby); Prob. Reg. 18, fol. 152v (Ward).

[5] Borth. Inst., Prob. Reg. 13, pt. II, fol. 705r (Lord); Prob. Reg. 11, pt. I, fol. 105r–v (Whitfeld).

[6] Borth. Inst., Prob. Reg. 9, fol. 374v (Lawton); Prob. Reg. 9, fol. 195r (Tonge); Abp. Reg. 28, fol. 174r–v (Gurnell).

silver vessels up to the value of £15 to repair buildings that had fallen into decay. At Esholt, where the nuns had turned to an even more desperate expedient, the archbishop in September 1535 forbade the prioress, Joan Jenkynson, from keeping an alehouse within the precincts. Like other very small houses at this time these nuns were clearly experiencing major problems in raising revenues to maintain the community at even a subsistence level.[7]

The very small Yorkshire houses with convents of half a dozen or so sisters also had great difficulty in producing from within their ranks nuns of sufficient calibre to govern the community and several had to look for help to other houses of their order. In 1526 the archbishop confirmed Katherine Chapman, previously a nun at Clementhorpe, as prioress of Thicket and another nun from the same community, Mary Marshall, went to be prioress at Rosedale in the same year. The pregnancy of Joan Fletcher, originally a nun of Rosedale, who had become prioress of Basedale at the age of thirty in 1524, led to her enforced resignation in 1527 and replacement by Elizabeth Roughton of Keldholme. In 1534 a third Clementhorpe nun, Elizabeth Kilbourne, was brought in to fill the vacancy at Nunburnholme caused by the deposition for a great scandal of the prioress, Isabel Thwing.[8]

Instances of sexual immorality occurred in Yorkshire nunneries with depressing regularity in the late fifteenth and early sixteenth centuries, affecting no fewer than nine houses, Watton, Swine, Nun Appleton, Yedingham, Kirklees, Esholt, Nunburnholme and Sinningthwaite as well as Basedale. Perhaps as many as fifteen nuns actually had babies while others came under vehement suspicion of living unchaste. Archbishop Lee showed no mercy to these errant nuns ordaining in 1535 that the prioress of Esholt should for two years imprison Dame Joan Hutton in some secret chamber in the dorter where none of her sisters or any secular persons could speak with her without licence, administer such discipline as was customary in the sisters' presence in the chapter house and furthermore undertake that she fasted on bread and ale every Wednesday and Friday. However unsuited to the religious life nuns might prove to be, they could not escape; the archbishop also compelled two other nuns, Joan Fletcher and Elizabeth Lutton, who had not only had children but had subsequently attempted to abscond, to return to their convents. Although not even the relatively wealthy nunneries seem to have been immune to these infractions of the rule, slackness of observance seems to have been concentrated within the smaller and poorer communities.[9]

---

[7] Borth. Inst., Abp. Reg. 28 fols. 89v, 95r–96r, 99r–v; S. M. Jack, 'Of Poverty and Pigstyes: The Household Economy of some of the Smaller Religious Houses on the Eve of the Dissolution', *Parergon*, New Series 1 (1983), pp. 69–91.

[8] PRO, SP 1/102, fols. 89r, 90r; Borth. Inst., Abp. Reg. 27, fols. 27v, 68v–69r, 77r, 82r, 86v; Mon. Misc. 7.

[9] PRO, SP 1/102, fols. 88r–97v; Borth. Inst., Abp. Reg. 28, fols. 91v, 92r, 95r–96r, 99r–v; Mon. Misc. 7; G. W. O. Woodward, *The Dissolution of the Monasteries* (London, 1966),

With some justification, therefore, the ecclesiastical authorities placed particular emphasis on the enforcement of enclosure at visitations of Sinningthwaite, Nunburnholme and Esholt in the summer of 1534 and the spring of 1535. In the ensuing injunctions for Sinningthwaite and Nunburnholme the archbishop commanded the prioresses to lock the cloister doors from compline till 6.00 a.m. in summer and 7.00 a.m. in winter so that no sisters might go out and no outsiders might come in. At Esholt he gave orders for a strong wall to be built on the south side of the church where the sisters worked and where they had access to the waterside and the bridge. In the daytime the prioresses should allow no sisters to leave the precinct without permission and then they might go out only in the company of another discreet sister. In the future no secular or religious persons might have recourse to the nuns apart from their parents or near kinsfolk.[10]

Elsewhere episcopal concerns seem to have lain largely with the physical welfare of the nuns. On 1 August 1534 officials sent injunctions to Nun Appleton which, apart from an order forbidding lay people other than servants from coming into the hall when the sisters were having their dinner or supper, concentrated exclusively on the nuns' well being. They instructed the prioress to provide good and wholesome bread and ale for the community of the same quality as she had herself, to see that as many spoons were laid on the convent table as there were sisters present, to supply lighter food for sick nuns, to appoint a laundress to wash the sisters' clothes and to ensure that the convent had a fire in the hall from All Saints' day till Good Friday according to the custom of the house.[11]

At Sinningthwaite and Nunburnholme the visitors also clearly felt anxiety over the nuns' sustenance, commanding the prioresses to see that they had their dinner at eleven or soon after and their supper at five and that they ate communally at one table and not severally in their chambers. Measures to promote more efficient economic management and better internal government feature prominently in these injunctions but they reveal disappointingly little about the Opus Dei. Apart from admonitions for the observance of poverty and chastity according to the rule of St Benedict, for part of the rule to be read daily in the chapter house and for silence to be kept in the cloister, frater and dorter and prohibiting the absence from divine service of the prioress or her sisters except for sickness or other just cause, they contain nothing on the liturgy. Perhaps contemporary churchmen may not have expected a great deal from women religious but, if silence can be taken as a guide, they appear to have thought that whatever their individual shortcomings even

---

pp. 39–49; J. E. Burton, 'The Election of Joan Fletcher as Prioress of Basedale, 1524', Borthwick Institute Bulletin 1 (1975–8), pp. 145–53; Logan, Runaway Religious, pp. 89–96, 264.

[10] Borth. Inst., Abp. Reg. 28, fols. 95r–96r, 97r, 99r–v.

[11] Borth. Inst., Abp. Reg. 28, fols. 99r–v.

in the very small houses the nuns were satisfactorily performing the divine office.

The records disclose very little about the intellectual state of the Yorkshire nunneries. The nuns would have sung their service in Latin, but officials assumed that they had little understanding of the language, invariably issuing their injunctions in English. In comparison with the number of late medieval books associated with Barking, Dartford and Syon the tally for the Yorkshire nunneries is meagre in the extreme. Swine, next to Watton the largest of the nunneries, in the late fourteenth or early fifteenth century received eleven books from the local vicar which in addition to Peter Comestor's *Historia scolastica*, the encyclopaedia and another work of Isidore of Seville, a volume of Ambrose, a glossed version of St Mark's Gospel, clerical manuals and service books significantly included a book of St Brigit and 'liber beate Matildis virginis vocatus liber spiritualis gracie'. Two of the convent's books, the copy of Ambrose and the 'Pistil of Love', still survive, as does a Latin psalter from Hampole. Marrick also certainly owned one English book, 'The Dream of the Pilgrimage of the Soul'. In 1481 Jane Fisher, a nun at Dartford Priory quite exceptionally obtained a licence to learn Latin grammar, but there is no evidence at all for any Yorkshire nuns attaining even the rudiments of classical learning in the Tudor period.[12]

Next to furnishing an outlet, less expensive than marriage, for the superfluous daughters of reasonably affluent sectors of Yorkshire society, the laity may have most valued the nunneries for their activities in the sphere of education. As early as the thirteenth century Marrick Priory was providing some elementary teaching for the laity and by the fourteenth century Arden, Arthington, Esholt, Hampole, Keldholme, Moxby, Nun-burnholme, Nunkeeling, Rosedale, Sinningthwaite and Clementhorpe all had reading schools. A school of this sort was being held at Swine in the fifteenth century and incidental mentions of schools occur at Wilberfoss in 1484 and at Nun Appleton in 1489. Wilberfoss and Esholt were known to be running what could be regarded as finishing schools for well born girls in the reign of Henry VIII and it seems highly likely that other nunneries were continuing to do the same not least as a means for supplementing their revenues.[13]

Unspectacular, modestly endowed, some burdened with debt and

[12] M. R. James, *A Descriptive Catalogue of the Manuscripts other than Oriental in the Library of King's College, Cambridge* (Cambridge, 1895), pp. 34–5; N. R. Ker, *Medieval Libraries of Great Britain: A List of Surviving Books*, Royal Historical Society Guides and Handbooks 3 (2nd edn., London, 1964), pp. 95, 129, 184; P. Lee, *Nunneries, Learning & Spirituality in Late Medieval English Society. The Dominican Priory of Dartford* (Woodbridge, 2000), p. 158.

[13] J. A. Hoeppner Moran, *The Growth of English Schooling 1340–1548: Learning, Literacy and Laicization in Pre-Reformation York Diocese* (Princeton, 1985), pp. 238, 249, 253, 257, 262, 263, 265, 268, 271, 274, 277, 278; *LP*, xii/2, 549.

tarnished by scandal, the Yorkshire nunneries still appear to have been performing a necessary function in local society in the early sixteenth century. Largely it seems because Cromwell's officials discovered virtually all the nuns wished to persevere in religion, the crown only confiscated nine nunneries in 1536, Arden, Nunburnholme, Nun Monkton, Clementhorpe, Ellerton, Keldholme, Rosedale, Sinningthwaite and Moxby, all of which held fewer than ten nuns, and at the time of the Pilgrimage of Grace the rebels may have temporarily restored Clementhorpe, Nunburnholme, Sinningthwaite and Arden. The state then permitted the remaining nunneries, their ranks augmented by transfers from the dissolved houses, to continue for three further years before abolishing them all in 1539.[14]

Female monasticism in the county withered quietly way over the course of the sixteenth century. Some of nuns like Joan Fletcher and Elizabeth Lutton must have rejoiced to have gained their freedom at last. Even though expressly forbidden to do so when expelled from their houses, some married in the reign of Edward VI. Margaret Bashfurth, a former nun of Moxby, subsequently excused herself to the Marian authorities by claiming that she had continued single for thirteen years before marrying Roger Newstead, a gressman of Thormanby. Forcibly divorced in 1555 she returned to her husband on Elizabeth's accession. Unlike Margaret Bashfurth, who did not qualify for a pension on the surrender of her house in 1536, the former prioress of Thicket, Agnes Beckwith, with an annuity of £6 13s. 4d., could not credibly claim that poverty had driven her to wed Gilbert Parr of York. Since she allied herself to one of the supervisors of her father's will, Brian Spofforth, rector of Barton in Ryedale, Agnes Aislaby's family may even have had a hand in her disposal. A minimum of seven nuns chose to marry, and given the very great difficulty of tracing women who changed their surnames, this is almost certainly an underestimate.[15]

The majority of the former nuns, nevertheless, observed their vows and stayed chaste. Some of the prioresses who obtained adequate pensions lived in considerable state. Elizabeth Lord, the former prioress of Wilberfoss, after the Dissolution joined her sister and brother-in-law in York where she mixed with the top ranks of the civic hierarchy. At her death in 1551 she asked to be buried near her brother's stall in Holy Trinity, Goodramgate, and left approaching £100 in money and plate. Though nothing like as wealthy, Isabel Ward, the last prioress of Clementhorpe, had her own household in

---

[14] G. W. O. Woodward, 'The Benedictines and Cistercians in Yorkshire in the Sixteenth Century' (Unpublished Ph. D. Thesis, Trinity College, Dublin, 1956), pp. 311, 315, 316–17.

[15] Borth. Inst., Chanc. AB 6, fol. 22v; Chanc. AB 7, fol. 32r; Prob Reg. 11, pt. II, fol. 647r (Aslabie); A. G. Dickens, *The Marian Reaction in the Diocese of York: Part II, The Laity*, Borthwick Paper 12 (York, 1957), pp. 16–19.

the parish of St Mary, Bishophill Junior, bequeathing silver spoons and a silver goblet to her Ellerker cousins in her will of 1569.[16]

Where the records give any indication of their beliefs, most of the former nuns, as might well be anticipated, remained conservative in religion. Although she made her will well into the reign of Elizabeth I Christiana Burgh, formerly prioress of Nunkeeling and then resident in Richmond, still in 1566 bequeathed her soul in the traditional manner 'to Almighty God and to our blessed lady St Mary and to all the holy company of heaven' while Isabel Ward similarly in 1569 called for the prayers of the virgin and saints. Some former prioresses certainly kept in contact with their communities. In addition to giving Mistress Isabel Percy a basin and 5s. in gold in 1541 Katherine Nandyke bestowed a further 6s. 8d. a piece upon 'eight of my sisters that was professed in Wykeham abbey'. In 1550 the impecunious Joan Harkey, assigned a pension of only £3 when she surrendered her house in 1536, left a shilling each to four of her former nuns, Dame Alice Tomsone, Dame Cecily Swale, Dame Agnes Aislaby and Dame Elizabeth Parker. In 1566 Alice Syggeswicke and Isobel Bane, both former members of Nunkeeling, received bequests from their one time prioress, Christiana Burgh.[17]

Some of these nuns may even have preserved some sort of community life. In 1543 Katherine Foster, the former prioress of Sinningthwaite, bestowed her best gown upon her former nun, Alice Sheffield, and appointed her one of the executors of her will. Christabel Cowper may perhaps have been living with another of her nuns when in 1555 Roger Watson of Farlington, a former monk of Rievaulx, left 12d. 'to her that was prioress of Marrick and her sister, Dame Anne'. According to a tradition which long persisted in the locality Jane Kyppax, the former prioress of Kirklees, retired with four of her sisters to Paper (or Papist) Hall in Mirfield. Elizabeth Thorne, once a nun of Swine, in 1557 gave her house in Hull for life to her sister in religion, Elizabeth Patricke. A least one former nun died a witness to her faith. Pursuivants searching Arthington Hall in 1586 discovered the former Arthington nun, Isobel Whitehedde, sick in bed. On her refusal to reveal the priests' hiding place they carried her off to York Castle where she died on 18 March 1587.[18]

Medieval monasticism in Yorkshire finally came to an end with the death of Isabel Coxon, a young nun of twenty-two when expelled from Hampole in 1539, who was still being paid her pension of £2 per annum in 1602. Had the Tudors not severed ties between the English church and Rome and had there

[16] Borth. Inst., Prob. Reg. 13, pt. II, fol. 705r–v (Lord); Prob. Reg. 18, fol. 152v (Ward).
[17] Leeds Record Office, RD/AP1/43/19 (Harkay); RD/AP1/8/140 (Burghe); Borth. Inst., Prob. Reg. 11, pt. II fols. 559v–560r (Nandike); Prob. Reg. 18 fol. 152v (Ward).
[18] Borth. Inst., Prob. Reg. 11, pt. II, fol. 715v (Foster); Prob. Reg. 14, fol. 179v–180v (Watson); Prob. Reg. 15, pt. I, fol. 357v (Thorne); S. J. Chadwick, 'Kirklees Priory', *Yorkshire Archaeological Journal* 16 (1902), p. 322; *The Troubles of our Catholic Forefathers related by themselves*, ed. J. Morris (London, 1877), p. 328.

been no Protestant Reformation it seems highly unlikely that the Yorkshire nunneries could have remained unscathed. Indeed only Wolsey's absence from his archiepiscopal see may have saved the smaller houses from the dissolutions he effected elsewhere to finance his educational foundations. Yorkshire had far too many, poorly endowed nunneries in the Middle Ages: the wonder is that they all survived so long.

Patterns of Patronage to Female Monasteries in the Late Middle Ages

MARILYN OLIVA

Discussions about the patronage of monasteries in the late Middle Ages usually focus on the ties established and maintained between a religious house and its founders and their heirs. Founders' motives varied, but most, like Margery de Creyk who founded Flixton Priory, a small female house in the county of Suffolk, endowed and continued to patronize their foundations for prayers for the salvation of their souls and those of their relatives, both living and dead.[1] In addition to the spiritual benefits founders reaped by establishing religious houses, patrons also derived a certain amount of social prestige from their foundations. They were, in a very real way, symbols of status, physical manifestations of patrons' wealth and the connections associated with it, which had enabled them to establish these monastic houses in the first place. Succeeding generations could carry on their predecessors' gift-giving to their foundations to ensure the continuation of the intercessory prayers as well as to enjoy the social kudos associated with their ancestors' religious houses.

By the later Middle Ages, however, connections between founders' families and monasteries rarely applied because later generations had either died out or lost interest.[2] Monasteries in general, moreover, had ceased to attract the patronage of the wealthy and powerful whose religious philanthropy had turned toward establishing private foundations, like chantries and chapels, or to the large and relatively new monasteries, like Syon Abbey and the Charterhouse.[3] Patronage of institutions like these

---

[1] BL, Stowe Charter 291, for de Creyk's foundation charter where she states her motives for founding a small house of nuns in the parish of Flixton. This charter is printed in William Dugdale, *Monasticon Anglicanum*, ed. J. Caley, H. Ellis and B. Bandinel (6 vols. in 8, London, 1817–30), vi. 593–4.

[2] J. Burton, *Yorkshire Nunneries in the Twelfth and Thirteenth Centuries*, Borthwick Papers 56 (York, 1979), pp. 18, 20–21, 26; Knowles, *Religious Orders*, ii. 283–7; B. J. Thompson, 'Monasteries and their Patrons at Foundation and Dissolution', *TRHS*, 6th Series 4 (1994), pp. 103–23.

[3] G. McMurray Gibson, *The Theater of Devotion: East Anglian Drama and Society in the Late Middle Ages* (Chicago and London, 1989), p. 20, for East Anglia specifically; and J. T. Rosenthal, 'Kings, Continuity and Ecclesiastical Benefaction in Fifteenth-Century England', in *People, Politics and Community in the Later Middle Ages*, ed. J. T. Rosenthal and C. Richmond (Gloucester, 1987), pp. 161, 168–69, for England in general.

continued to garner prayers and prestige for these donors and enhance the public visibility for the institutions themselves.

But if patronage of monasteries had become passé among medieval England's social elite, in the diocese of Norwich, at least, members of lower social groups – parish gentry and yeoman farmers – continued actively to support the diocese's relatively small and poor female monasteries in a variety of ways. This chapter examines some of the ways in which people of lesser social status patronized the convents and shows that their support entailed more than giving gifts of land and money. This analysis suggests further that certain aspects of such patronage could have conferred on parish gentry and yeoman farmer families a level of prestige among their peers similar in quality to the prestige upper status groups derived from their support of private institutions and fashionable monastic ones.

The diocese's eleven female monasteries do not at first glance seem to have been the kinds of places that would have attracted the attention of potential patrons, rich or poor.[4] The eleven female convents in this diocese, which included the counties of Norfolk and Suffolk, were poor and small. In 1535 they were worth between £23 and £67, and housed throughout this later period an average of ten nuns per house. The two exceptions to this pattern were Campsey Ash and Shouldham Priories. Campsey Ash was valued at £182 and Shouldham at £138, and while Shouldham averaged ten nuns in this period, Campsey Ash maintained an average of twenty. Except for Carrow Priory, which was sited in the suburbs of the city of Norwich – the diocesan seat – these were rural foundations, located in rather desolate and marginal areas, like the western fens of Norfolk and the eastern lowlands of Suffolk.

Despite their size and poverty – or perhaps because of these characteristics – these convents and the nuns who lived therein were, along with the diocese's mendicant houses, the most common beneficiaries in the wills of people of parish gentry and yeoman farmer status. Their bequests, like those of other social groups who made bequests to any of the church's institutions, were always accompanied by a request for intercessory prayers. These bequests and supplications for prayer were inscribed in wills that were most often registered in one of the diocese's five probate courts – the four archdeaconry courts of Norfolk, Norwich, Sudbury, and Suffolk – and the consistory court of Norwich. Over three thousand wills were analysed in an attempt to discern the extent of parish gentry and yeoman farmers' patronage of these female houses. This analysis revealed certain patterns.

First, these testators preferred friars to any other religious group. Sixty-five percent of parish gentry bequests to religious institutions were to friaries, despite the fact that they comprised less than half the number of male houses

---

[4] For the following descriptions of the size, wealth, and location of these convents see: M. Oliva, *The Convent and the Community in Late Medieval England: Female Monasteries in the Diocese of Norwich, 1350–1540* (Woodbridge, 1998), chap. 1.

in the diocese.[5] All of the yeoman farmer testators in the archdeaconry of Norwich who made bequests to male religious made them to one or more of the mendicant houses. Similarly, in the archdeaconry of Suffolk, of the 155 people who left gifts to religious houses, 123 gave to houses of friars.[6]

But while friars were the most popular recipients of this type of patronage by members of these social groups, the nuns ranked second. Bequests to the nuns from these two social groups significantly outnumbered those to male monasteries even though the population of monks and canons outnumbered the nuns by a ratio of 5:1, and despite the fact that there were sixty-three male houses and only eleven female ones. Among parish gentry will-makers, for example, only 14% left anything to a male monastic house, while 21% made bequests to one or more of the female houses. Testators of yeoman farmer status showed a similar preference: 4% left a gift or sum of money to a male house; 15% made bequests to nuns.[7]

This disparity between gifts to nuns and those to their male monastic counterparts may have had to do with the ideal of poverty and peoples' perception of genuine religious lifestyles. Local contemporaries must have seen the friars, despite their negative portrayal in medieval literature, as more deserving of their patronage than other male religious. Perhaps testators so valued the friars because they appeared to live truly spiritual lives of poverty and thus their prayers were considered to be more efficacious than those of the local monks and canons. Why else would the majority of these testators have made bequests to the friars and sought their prayers?

These will-makers must have thought of the nuns in a similar way. Their appeal was perhaps also the simplicity and poverty of their lives, the services their convents provided, and the absence of the kinds of scandals that plagued their male counterparts.[8] Such qualities would have signalled to people that, like the friars, these were holy women who devoted their lives to prayer and good works; hence the nuns' popularity as beneficiaries and as celebrants of intercessory prayers.

Second, testators' giving tended to be localized. For example, Alice Bocher of Thetford left the prioress and nuns of the priory there 3s. 4d. and an acre of land.[9] A man who lived in the parish of Redlingfield gave 20s. and a flat piece of silver to the prioress and nuns there.[10] And Galfrido Wode, rector of Asshe, left all of his goods to the nuns close by at Campsey Ash Priory.[11]

---

[5] Ibid., p. 175.

[6] Ibid.

[7] Ibid., p. 176.

[8] Ibid., pp. 139–56 for the services nuns provided despite their relatively small annual budgets; and ibid., pp. 31–2, 73, 104, 137–8 for the scandals that plagued many of the diocese's male monasteries in this period of time.

[9] NRO, Archdeaconry of Norwich Register Fuller-alias Roper, fol. 96, dated 1483.

[10] Suffolk Record Office [SRO], Ipswich, William Stevenson Fitch, *Suffolk Monasteries* (4 vols., unpublished manuscript, undated), ii. 23.

[11] NRO, Norwich Consistory Court, 10 Hyrnyng, dated 1416.

Examples of bequests to neighbouring religious houses overwhelm those of gifts to houses farther away by a significant margin. This pattern seems to have pertained to bequests to mendicant and male monastic houses as well.[12]

Wode's bequest of all his personal property was not uncommon, but it was also not typical. Most gifts were small and though the majority of them were made to a convent as a whole, individual nuns also appeared as recipients. Testators left the nuns minor sums of money like the 40d. that Thomas Beaufeld left to each nun at Carrow Priory in 1504, 20d. for his 'keeping', with another 20d. to be dispensed to each nun on his burial day.[13] Or people gave small parcels of land, like Richard Colpyll, who bequeathed to the nuns at Bruisyard Abbey his tenement in the same parish.[14] Not infrequently bequests accompanied directions for repairs to one or another of a convent's buildings. William Pratte of Hehale, for example, gave 16s. to Bruisyard, 'out of which every lady is to have 4d. and the remainder to go toward repairs.'[15] Thomas Canon of East Dereham made a similar gesture when he left 10s for repair of the church of the Thetford nuns.[16]

While these acts of patronage were valuable to patrons for the prayers they insured, and to the convents for the material support the bequests afforded – however minor they might have been–testamentary gifts did not necessarily confer upon a patron the kind of status that large donations of money or land garnered for wealthier benefactors. For the most part these gifts were small, quickly utilized, and lacked the show and dazzle of newly carved church benches, new leaded-glass windows, or the construction of a new building. Although perhaps testators discussed the disposal of their goods or the content of their wills with family and friends beforehand, most testamentary bequests were private donations, not necessarily common knowledge, and not public gestures of largesse. And in medieval England life was by necessity public in nature, where visible displays of piety and ritual, and open and elaborate demonstrations of status defined the social and cultural terrain.[17] What garnered prestige for people then were public displays of generosity, wealth, and power.[18] Two things then could function for members of parish gentry and yeoman farmer groups as more public

---

[12] For example of localized giving by testators, see N. Tanner, The Church in Late Medieval Norwich, 1370–1532 (Toronto, 1984), pp. 119–21.

[13] NRO, Norwich Consistory Court, 491–2 Popy.

[14] SRO, Suffolk Archdeaconry Register, vol. 10, no. 65, dated 1524.

[15] Fitch, Suffolk Monasteries, iii. 148.

[16] NRO, Archdeaconry of Norfolk, 99 Grey, dated 1466.

[17] See for example, M. James, 'Ritual, Drama and Social Body in the Late Medieval English Town', Past and Present 98 (1983), pp. 3–29; M. Keen, 'Chivalrous Culture in Fourteenth-Century England', Historical Studies 10 (1976), pp. 1–24; M. Rubin, 'Corpus Christi Fraternities and Late Medieval Piety', in Voluntary Religion, ed. W. J. Sheils and D. Wood, Studies in Church History 23 (1986), pp. 97–109.

[18] M. D. Sahlins, 'On the Sociology of Primitive Exchange', in The Relevance of Models for Social Anthropology, ed. M. Banton (London, 1965), p. 158 for how 'the publicity of primitive life' governed emotions and exchanges of gifts and goods.

gestures of patronage that could enhance their standing among their peers, or help them finesse the social divide: one, burial in a convent's church or cemetery; and two, the profession of a family member into one of these houses as a nun.[19]

Place of burial was significant in death and in life in the Middle Ages: in death because a secure and sanctified location contributed to one's safe passage to the world beyond, and in life for its sign of status on earth.[20] And a significant percentage of people who made bequests to the diocese's female houses amongst these two lesser social groups requested burial in a conventual church or cemetery. Some, like Richard Boydbale, simply asked to be buried in the 'chaple of the nuns of Blackborough Priory', without reference to a tombstone or other marker of his final resting-place.[21] Other requests were more detailed and no doubt attracted more public attention. William Walsingham wanted to be interred in the church of the nuns at Carrow, 'before the door of the chapel of St Ann.'[22] Robert Bylnye of Brakendale's choice clearly involved a public display when he asked for burial in the churchyard of St James of Carrow, ordering two images of St Mary and St John to be made and placed in the walls of the church.[23] Elizabeth Yaxley's grave was even more elaborate. She wanted to be buried in the church of Our Lady at Carrow, at the end of the high altar, before the image of Our Lady, and she ordered a stone to be laid over her.[24] Markers like these were the kinds of public display that symbolized the prestige of those buried and ensured that they were not forgotten by those left behind whose prayers would help their standing in the afterlife.[25]

Tombstones and other grave-markers signalled the status of the dead, but other public demonstrations of patronage could confer prestige on the living, the most obvious being to have a female family member enter a local convent as a nun. Though this idea is nearly impossible to prove, and many factors, including financial ones, influenced one's decision to enter religious

---

[19] See P. Coss, 'Knights, Esquires and the Origins of Social Gradation in England', *TRHS*, 6th Series 5 (1995), pp. 155–78 for a discussion of the gradations of social ranks and the definitions of gentleman, valet, knight, and esquire, many of whom comprised the parish gentry. The fluidity of these ranks would have facilitated the actions by which members garnered prestige amongst each other and also moved up – or down – the social scale.

[20] V. Harding, 'Burial Choice and Burial Location in Later Medieval London', in *Death in Towns: Urban Responses to the Dying and Dead, 1000–1600*, ed. S. Bassett (Leicester, 1992), pp. 119–35.

[21] NRO, Norwich Consistory Court, 11 Hyrnyng, dated 1416.

[22] NRO, Norwich Consistory Court, 115 Gelour, dated 1474; also noted in Walter Rye, *Carrow Abbey, otherwise Carrow Priory; near Norwich, in the County of Norfolk; its Foundation, Buildings, Officers, and Inmates with Appendices* (Norwich, 1889), p. xviii.

[23] Rye, *Carrow Abbey*, p. xxiii.

[24] NRO, Norwich Consistory Court, 104 Platfoot, dated 1530; also in Rye, *Carrow Abbey*, p. xxviii.

[25] R. Dunn, '"Monuments Answerable to Mens Worth": Burial Patterns, Social Status and Gender in Late Medieval Bury St Edmunds', *JEH* 46 (1995), pp. 237–55.

life in the Middle Ages, it is nevertheless worth considering that a woman's profession to religious life may well have had significance for people beyond her own kin group. The culture of Medieval England was one in which religion and the church profoundly influenced peoples' lives, pervading their day-to-day existence as well as framing their concepts of life beyond death. And despite intermittent problems and discontent, most people – even in the later Middle Ages – still adhered to and valued the mores and culture the church had created. That people sought involvement in the religious culture of medieval England can be seen in their deathbed requests as well as in lifetime donations of money, land, or goods to any of the various religious institutions that adorned the landscape. For parish gentry and yeoman farmer families who lacked the means to make large donations, having a daughter, sister, or aunt become a nun constituted a significant act of patronage that ensured the family perpetual prayers. Such an act also could have enhanced the family's status among their neighbours and friends who shared the social and cultural values of the church, and who saw participation in their religious culture as spiritually and socially advantageous. As a gift and an act of patronage, moreover, having a daughter or sister enter religious life defined a gift in the most classic way: as something that is not inert, but rather continues to contribute in a positive way to both the donor and the recipient.[26]

Among this diocese's population of nuns, in fact, those from parish gentry and yeoman farmer families far outnumbered nuns from any other social group. As I have shown elsewhere, of the 553 nuns who lived in the diocese between 1350 and 1540 who can be identified by name, at least 64% came from these two lower social groups.[27] And family pride in their religious relatives is reflected in parents' and siblings' wills. John Harleston, for example, left to his sister Marieta, a nun at Flixton, his 'best hide'.[28] To his daughter Alice, a nun at Thetford, Nicholas Fermer left a brass pot and three acres to sing a trental.[29] Parents and siblings further demonstrated appreciation and respect for their religious kin by requesting their services as executors of their wills, a service crucial to testators who relied on their executors to carry out their deathbed requests. Isabel Babour, a nun at Carrow, was named executor of her mother's will in 1460.[30] And Lawrence Draper asked the same of his sister Alice, a nun at Thetford.[31]

Acquiring the skills necessary to act as an executor undoubtedly raised the profile of the nuns who did so. While their noviciates were less rigorous than those of monks and canons, nuns were still expected to learn the rudiments

[26] M. Mauss, The Gift, intro. S.S. Evans-Pritchard and trans. Ian Cunnison (New York, 1967), pp. 21, 45, 54–5.
[27] Oliva, Convent and Community, pp. 52–60.
[28] NRO, Norwich Consistory Court, 36 Doke, dated 1437.
[29] NRO, Archdeaconry of Norfolk Register Shaw, fol. 188, dated 1508.
[30] NRO, Norwich Consistory Court, 206 Brosyard.
[31] NRO, Norwich Consistory Court, 199 Heydon, dated 1382.

of reading, and perhaps even writing. Mastering these could lead to the acquisition of a monastic office; and success in executing its duties – which usually entailed keeping annual accounts – led to appointment to a higher office.[32] As opportunities like these were less available to lay women of these two social groups, it is not unreasonable to suggest that when a nun succeeded in attaining such skills, her accomplishments were a step up for her and by association her family. And so, just as taking up a clerical benefice or joining a religious order functioned as a mechanism for social advancement for men and their families, it is possible that becoming a nun could achieve similar ends for a woman and her family.[33]

That families valued their religious daughters and sisters for their prayers and other services, however, does not necessarily mean that others did, although most of the women who became nuns in this diocese entered convents close to their homes, making it more likely that their actions would be known to neighbours and friends who lived nearby.[34] And, in addition to the number of testators without kinship ties to nuns who made bequests to them, a significant number also requested nuns' services as executors of their wills, a sure indication that people in general recognized and valued these nuns as well.[35]

This recognition by non-family members of a woman's status as a nun, moreover, often extended to an acknowledgement of her family, as the wording of testators' bequests to individual nuns indicates. Elizabeth Clere, for example, left 20s. to Mary White, who she specified as the daughter of William Whyte.[36] Similarly, Thomas Bokenham left a 'carte full of faggot wood to Dame Agnes Sherman, my wife's daughter, who is a nun at Carrow'.[37] And Sir John de Repp left one of his cups to 'the daughter of John de Plumstede, a nun at Bruisyard'.[38] While expressions like these could also be read simply as formulae, or just a clear means of identifying a particular recipient, such identification nevertheless reveals that testators made the association between a nun and her family.

Did this association, though, necessarily equate with the social enhancement of a nun's family? It may well have. Consider the words of Thomas

---

[32] Oliva, *Convent and Community*, pp. 107–8 for evidence of a career ladder for nuns in the diocese of Norwich as well as nuns of convents elsewhere in England.

[33] M. Bennett, 'Sources and Problems in the Study of Social Mobility: Cheshire in the Later Middle Ages', *Transactions of the Historical Society of Lancashire and Cheshire* 128 (1978), pp. 66–7.

[34] M. Oliva, 'Counting Nuns: A Prosopography of Late Medieval English Nuns in the Diocese of Norwich', *Medieval Prosopography* 16 (1995), pp. 66–7.

[35] Oliva, *The Convent and the Community*, pp. 27, 150.

[36] Rye, *Carrow Abbey*, p. xxi.

[37] PRO, Prerogative Court of Canterbury, Prob. 11/9, fols. 133v–134v. Thanks are due to Dr Claire Noble for her assistance with this, and the PRO document cited in note 4 below, dated 1491.

[38] F. Blomefield, *An Essay Toward a Topographical History of the County of Norfolk* (11 vols., London, 1805–10), viii. 150.

Godsalve, of Norwich. He made a bequest to 'Katherine Bloomfield, some-time nun of Campsey, daughter to my late wife . . . whom I esteem to be a woman of much virtue and honeste desiring her honestly to pray for me'.[39] Similarly, when Agnes Thorpe made a bequest to Agnes Warner, nun of Carrow, she identified her as 'daughter of William Warner, who I value for keeping a placebo, dirge and mass required for my soul, those of my friends and all Christians'.[40] These people obviously treasured the nuns they named as beneficiaries, and by association the families from which they came. That testators referred to these and other nuns in such ways suggests that the nuns' families derived a certain amount of prestige from those around them whose wills included bequests to their daughters, sisters, and other female kin.

Identifying patterns of gift-giving and discerning which gifts functioned as symbols of status and prestige for medieval England's lesser social groups is no easy task. But parish gentry and yeoman farmers, like members of any social group, did things to garner prestige and status among their peers.[41] Making testamentary bequests to their local female monastery was not only also a generous act, it was also one that guaranteed intercessory prayers. But perhaps the more public gestures of patronage discussed here – burial in a convent's cemetery or church, and having a daughter or sister become a nun in one of the diocese's female houses – functioned for these parish gentry and yeoman farmer families as a means by which their social standing was enhanced. These acts of patronage certainly were in any case consistent with the favour members of these two social groups displayed toward the nuns and their houses in the diocese of Norwich through their testamentary bequests throughout the later Middle Ages.

---

[39] NRO, Norwich Consistory Court, 275–286 Mingay, dated 1542.
[40] PRO, Prerogative Court of Canterbury, Prob. 11/13, fols. 211v–223v, dated 1503.
[41] For example, building moated manor houses: L. Cantor, 'Castles, Fortified Houses, Moated Homesteads and Monastic Settlements', in The English Medieval Landscape, ed. L. Cantor (Philadelphia, 1982), pp. 126–53, esp. 133, 138.

Monasteries and Society

Monasteries, Society and Reform in Late Medieval England

BENJAMIN THOMPSON

It has always been difficult to think about late medieval monasteries in isolation from what happened to them in the 1530s. Nor was it easy, for four centuries, to write about the Dissolution without confessional blinkers, albeit that different attitudes could be adopted within the broad church of Anglicanism.[1] That the religious were incorrigibly corrupt was the first, and official, version of the state of the monasteries; on the basis of the lurid findings of the 1535–6 visitors, the colourful rhetoric of the Act of 1536 dissolving the smaller houses alleged 'manifest sin, vicious, carnal and abominable living'.[2] Although this was the orthodox view inculcated into English people until at least a century ago,[3] it never commanded universal assent, even among Anglicans, because of the manifest mendacity of the methods by which the evidence for corruption was acquired.[4] A broad

---

[1] See in general R. O'Day, *The Debate on the English Reformation* (London and New York, 1986), esp. pp. 31–101, although the Dissolution receives little explicit coverage. See for example the work of the non-juror Collier and the Tractarian Canon Dixon in n. 6.

[2] 27 Henry VIII, c. 28, *Statutes of the Realm*, Record Commission (11 vols. in 12, London, 1810–28), iii. 575ff.

[3] As seems clear from the debate in 'The Norfolk Monasteries at the Time of the Suppression by Henry VIII', ed. A. Jessopp, *Norfolk Antiquarian Miscellany* 2, ed. W. Rye (Norwich, 1883), pp. 442–3. See for example Gilbert Burnet, *History of the Reformation of the Church of England* (1679–1715), ed. N. Pocock (7 vols., Oxford, 1865), i. 305–7; *Three Chapters of Letters relating to the Suppression of Monasteries*, ed. T. Wright, Camden Society 26 (1843), pp. v–vi; J. A. Froude, *History of England from the Fall of Wolsey to the Death of Elizabeth* (12 vols., London, 1856–70; 4th edn., London, 1867–70), pp. 444–55; G. G. Coulton, *Five Centuries of Religion* (4 vols., Cambridge, 1923–50), iv. 680–702. G. Baskerville, *English Monks and the Suppression of the Monasteries* (London, 1936) – a work similarly unreliable in overall perspective, but packed with fascinating and useful evidence – pp. 120–43 defends the visitation.

[4] For example Thomas Fuller, *The Church-History of Britain from the Birth of Jesus Christ untill the Year MDCXLVIII* (1655), pp. 314–19; Jeremy Collier, *An Ecclesiastical History of Great Britain, Chiefly of England: From the First Planting of Christianity in this Island, with a Brief Account of the Affairs of Religion in Ireland* (2 vols., 1708–14), ii. 108–9; John Lingard, *The History of England, from the First Invasions by the Romans to the Accession of William and Mary in 1688* (1819–30; 6th edn., 10 vols., 1854–5), v. 27; *Visitations of the Diocese of Norwich, AD 1492–1532*, ed. A. Jessopp, Camden Society, New Series 43 (1888), pp. xii–xiii, xxii, xxvii, xxxii, xxxvii, xlix–l; and most modern writers, as in the next note.

consensus has therefore rejected the more extreme claims of the visitors, and instead adopted an unflattering account of the late medieval religious as materially comfortable and spiritually redundant.[5] Such a view was always unacceptable to Catholic polemicists, and in the nineteenth century a case was made for a much more positive account of the condition of monasteries, and especially of their social role, which has been reasserted recently.[6] Yet the debate still cannot be disentangled from the Dissolution: some recent exponents of the more positive view are students of the Reformation(s), and the (paradoxical) thrust of their argument is to contrast the medieval history of monasteries with the cataclysm which befell them.[7] The events of the 1530s are seen as belonging to a particular set of circumstances in domestic and international politics, initiated from above, discontinuous with previous church history, and above all a great act of state intervention in the distribution of property; late medieval monasticism can therefore be aligned with the rosier view of late medieval religion which has emerged in the last quarter-century.[8] Because the Dissolution was so evidently a political coup rather than a natural development, what happened to the monasteries was equally evidently not what they deserved.

The problem with this view is that it ignores a counter-factual dimension; the fact that the 1530s were so turbulent does not entitle us to deduce that the Dissolution Should Not Have Happened. Because the Henrician Reformation occurred in a burst of political activity, we do not know what would have happened in less disrupted circumstances, or whither more natural developments would have led. We do know that calls for reform were mounting in the 1520s even without the looming shadow of the royal supremacy, international isolation and the consequent desperate

---

[5] For example A. Pollard, Henry VIII (rev. edn., London, 1905), pp. 337–42; G. R. Elton, England under the Tudors (1955; 2nd edn., 1974), pp. 103–6, 141–4; Knowles, Religious Orders, iii. passim, esp. pp. 51, 75, 126, 136, 459–65; A. G. Dickens, The English Reformation (2nd edn., 1989), pp. 83–7, 197, 200–1.

[6] See n. 1; Nicholas Sanders, Doctissimi viri Nicolai Sanderi, de origine ac progressu schismatis Anglicani (Cologne and Rheims, 1585), cited in Burnet, History of the Reformation, i. 4, 357; R. W. Dixon, History of the Church of England from the Abolition of the Roman Jurisdiction (6 vols., 1878–1902), i. 301–59; F. A. Gasquet, Henry VIII and the English Monasteries (2 vols., 1889–90), passim, esp. i. xvii–xxx, 325–78, ii. 490–526; J. Gairdner, Lollardy and the Reformation in England: An Historical Survey (4 vols., 1908–13), ii. 32–3; C. Haigh, Reformation and Resistance in Tudor Lancashire (Cambridge, 1975), pp. 63, 73, 118ff.; J. J. Scarisbrick, The Reformation and the English People (Oxford, 1984), pp. 6, 51–4, 74.

[7] See Haigh and Scarisbrick in the note above. This is not to say there are not also medievalists arguing for a more positive view of late medieval monasticism; see this volume, and chapters in Monasteries and Society in Medieval England: Proceedings of the 1994 Harlaxton Symposium, ed. B. J. Thompson, Harlaxton Medieval Studies 6 (Stamford, 1999).

[8] For which see also, for example, E. Duffy, The Stripping of the Altars (London and New Haven, 1992); J. Bossy, Christianity in the West, 1400–1700 (Oxford, 1985).

search for cash.[9] It is still useful to ask, therefore, what might have happened to the monasteries on the basis of their later medieval development, or, more concretely, whether that history did contribute to some aspects of the Dissolution.

It is particularly noticeable that the fate of the monasteries fits the revisionist view of the Reformation(s) less well than do other aspects of the ecclesiastical and religious history on which the new interpretation has been built.[10] Where we have been taught to think of a long-drawn-out process of reform with many episodes and changes of direction and different levels of activity – from above, but slow – the Dissolution was achieved remarkably quickly and, perhaps, relatively easily.[11] Perhaps ten per cent of the wealth of England (and Wales) was redistributed in four years flat.[12] Even if the process was driven by Cromwell's search for resources and his Protestantism, and even if it took several years initially to find an acceptable and workable procedure,[13] there remains the question of why such a rapid upheaval was possible. Even powerful states find it hard to make major social changes without some element of consent, or at least apathy. If the Reformation was slow because traditional religion was in good health and fulfilled important functions, can the same really be true of the monasteries? The events of 1536–40 suggest that the religious houses were at least vulnerable to disendowment, and certainly ripe for reform.

It may be useful to draw a distinction, albeit artificial, between religion and the church, between the substance of Christian belief and practice, and the institutions that existed to promote and provide them. Concomitantly one can distinguish reform from Reformation: renewing the church was not necessarily the same as changing religion. Although the latter will involve the former, the reverse is not the case, as much of what Henry VIII did and

---

[9] See below, n. 15; Knowles speculates very briefly on what might have been, *Religious Orders*, iii. 465–6.

[10] Indeed Duffy barely mentions the monasteries (see *Stripping of the Altars*, pp. 383–5); Haigh's latest statement does so mainly in the context of the Pilgrimage of Grace: *English Reformations* (Oxford, 1993), pp. 130–31, 140–49; Scarisbrick integrates the monasteries more into the main argument: see n. 6.

[11] The above writers emphasize the extent of opposition; but also see Knowles, *Religious Orders*, iii. 141; G. R. Elton, *Reform and Reformation: England, 1509–1558* (London, 1977), pp. 240–41; A. G. Dickens, *English Reformation*, pp. 179–80, 197; S. Brigden, *London and the Reformation* (Oxford, 1989), p. 293.

[12] The figure is impossible to pinpoint: see A. Savine, 'English Monasteries on the Eve of the Dissolution', in *Oxford Studies in Social and Legal History*, I, ed. P. Vinogradoff (Oxford, 1909), pp. 79–88; Elton still thought twenty per cent, *Reform and Reformation*, p. 247.

[13] On these points, see for example G. R. Elton, *England under the Tudors*, pp. 142–3; Elton, *Reform and Renewal: Thomas Cromwell and the Common Weal* (Cambridge, 1973), pp. 34–6; Dickens, *English Reformation*, pp. 197–200; Haigh, *English Reformations*, pp. 125–36; R. W. Hoyle, 'The Origins of the Dissolution of the Monasteries', *HJ* 38 (1995), pp. 275–305.

wanted seems to suggest.[14] Again, the fact that the reforms of the 1530s involved some Protestantizing elements – especially in the motivation of the dominant faction, and even if many of these were later reversed – makes it hard to distinguish between changes which were part of a religious reformation, and those which could have been part of a conservative ecclesiastical reform. Such reform was certainly on the agenda in the early sixteenth century, in the view of such as Colet, Longland, Pole, and indeed of Wolsey: complex though was his motivation and half-hearted his will, his acts of and plans for redistribution in the 1520s suggest the direction which might have been taken in a calmer 1530s.[15] Even without the Dissolution, therefore, medievalists are obliged to question why monasteries were thought to be in need of reform, and therefore what aspects of what did happen in the 1530s were based not just in the crises of the moment or the zeal of some evangelicals, but had longer-term roots in the nature of late medieval monasticism.

Reformers measure performance, or under-performance, by ideal standards. What were they looking for from late medieval monasteries? Essential to this is the question of the monasteries' function: what were they perceived to be *for*? In the case of institutions with nearly a millennium of history behind them, the answer is inevitably complex. Monasticism was originally a way of practising religion outside society, whether for individual hermits, or in enclosed, self-sufficient communities, as the Rule of Benedict depicted.[16] Successive waves of reformers judged the practice of their own day according to these ideals, from the early Cluniacs, through the eleventh- and twelfth-century new orders, to the later medieval Carthusians.[17] Yet for a variety of reasons it was difficult to maintain monastic isolation in practice. Quite apart from the inability of the religious to live up to demanding standards and remain 'unworldly', monasteries were fundamentally part of the societies

---

[14] For the (old) view that Henry remained a staunch Catholic, see Haigh, *English Reformations*, pp. 152–67; but see also *The Reign of Henry VIII: Politics, Policy and Piety*, ed. D. McCulloch (London, 1995), pp. 174–80; George Bernard, 'The Piety of Henry VIII', in *The Education of a Christian Society: Humanism and Reformation in Britain and the Netherlands*, ed. N. S. Amos, A. Pettegree and H. van Nierop (Aldershot, 1999), pp. 62–88: I am grateful to Dr Bernard for sending me a copy of this paper.

[15] Knowles, *Religious Orders*, iii. 141–64; Hoyle, 'Origins of the Dissolution', pp. 279–83; C. Harper-Bill, 'Dean Colet's Convocation Sermon and the Pre-Reformation Church in England', *History* 73 (1988), pp. 191–210; M. Bowker, *The Henrician Reformation: The Diocese of Lincoln under John Longland, 1521–1547* (Cambridge, 1981), esp. pp. 9–12, 16–37; Haigh, *English Reformations*, pp. 84–6; Pollard, *Henry VIII*, pp. 338–9; and see the various evidences collected in Coulton, *Five Centuries of Religion*, ii. 619–46, iv. 675. For Wolsey see below, nn. 124, 143.

[16] *RB 1980: The Rule of St Benedict in Latin and English with Notes*, ed. T. Fry (Collegeville, Minnesota, 1981), passim: reference to what is outside the monastery usually concerns maintaining a strict boundary between the two: for example caps. xxix, l–li, liii–liv, lviii–lxi, lxvi.

[17] For a sketch, see C. H. Lawrence, *Medieval Monasticism: Forms of Religious Life in Western Europe in the Middle Ages* (2nd edn., Harlow, 1989).

which provided the manpower and resources for their existence, and which expected benefits in return for them.[18] The functions of religious houses as understood by prelates, the clergy, lay benefactors, local residents, and even the religious themselves, were often rather different from those conceived by reformers and the founders of monastic orders.

Monasticism cannot therefore be measured by a single standard emanating from the religious side; quite apart from the variety of different ideals on offer, especially after the eleventh century, monasteries were multi-faceted institutions fulfilling a number of different functions, which were often particular to the time and place of their existence. This is indeed much of the explanation for the success of medieval monasticism; it retained support because it satisfied a range of different needs. If, therefore, monasteries were subject to different kinds of expectation even at their foundation, as well as in the course of their history, monasticism is clearly more complex than a single image such as the Benedictine Rule can suggest. Moreover, some of these expectations were bound to conflict, such as the desire for withdrawal against the demands by lay benefactors for tangible services.[19] Such tensions were not only developments from an original ideal – what the reformers called 'corruption'; they were present at the foundation of monasteries, which required a coalition of different interests, and therefore lay at the heart of monastic existence.

A brief glance at monasticism before the late Middle Ages illustrates this. At various times and places during the medieval period monasteries were the most serviceable churches, and so were central to the structure and functioning of the whole church; clergy living in common preserved the literacy and learning necessary to the practice of a religion of the book, and their churches were effective observers of liturgy and even providers of ministry.[20] Even periodic reforms, such as that of the tenth-century West Saxon monarchs, were part of more general ecclesiastical (and political) reforms and tended to reinforce the importance of monasteries to society.[21] This tradition of monasticism nourishing the church was realized most spectacularly in the papal reform of the later eleventh century, whose roots were in monastic reform but which applied it to the whole church.[22]

---

[18] For fuller exposition of these points, see B. J. Thompson, 'Introduction: Monasteries and Medieval Society', in Monasteries and Society, ed. Thompson, pp. 4–24.

[19] For example the problems experienced by the Cistercians in fending off benefactors' requests for prayers; Coulton, Five Centuries of Religion, iii. 65–7; Cistercian Statutes, 1256–88, ed. J. T. Fowler (London, 1890), pp. 28–30, 132.

[20] For example J. M. Wallace-Hadrill, The Frankish Church (Oxford, 1983), pp. 55–74; S. Foot, 'The Role of the Minster in Earlier Anglo-Saxon Society', in Monasteries and Society, ed. Thompson, pp. 35–58; Pastoral Care before the Parish, ed. J. Blair and R. Sharpe (Leicester, 1992). The following sketch offers large generalizations and rides roughshod over complexity and nuance, above all the question of what was denoted by a 'monasterium' in the early period.

[21] H. Loyn, The English Church, 940–1154 (Harlow, 2000), pp. 9–28.

[22] H. E. J. Cowdrey, The Cluniacs and the Gregorian Reform (Oxford, 1970).

Religious of various sorts were important in the next two centuries of the reform project, from the Cluniacs early on, through the canons who seemed initially to represent the ideal of the reformed clergy and even the Cistercians who in St Bernard and Eugenius III made their own contribution to the papacy, to the friars who took up the baton from the canons as the ideal type of ministers, personally ascetic but active in the world.[23] Yet one of the successes of the reform period was to construct a secular church capable of reaching virtually every community in Christian Europe, through the structure of dioceses and parish churches.[24] The resulting church of the later Middle Ages was emphatically not monastic in tone, leadership or character. The monasticism of the early and central Middle Ages founded the secular church of the later, with its vibrant parochial life, its schools and universities, and its secular bishops, but was not itself central to it any longer.

This might have provided the opportunity for the religious to conform to the original ascetic Benedictine ideal of withdrawal and to become properly isolated from society; perhaps the Cistercians and Carthusians were parts of a movement trying to take that path. In practice, however, outside particular periods of intense inspiration and enthusiasm such as was witnessed in the late eleventh and early twelfth centuries, the demand for seriously ascetic monasticism is usually limited. In later medieval England there were some impressively devoted ascetics, above all in the Carthusian, Observant and Brigittine houses, but they were a tiny minority.[25] While these were highly valued (and they were eventually the staunchest defenders of monasticism), they suggest that there was no extensive demand for such a form of the religious life, either from recruits or benefactors.[26] Society did not expect to support ascetics on a very great scale.

Yet it had founded a large number of monasteries, mainly in the eleventh, twelfth and early thirteenth centuries, during the great period of monastic foundation.[27] Such institutions were of various different types and had been founded for a number of different reasons. They had also experienced various different histories under various different sorts of circumstances and pressures thereafter. But they had, by and large, survived: the combination of ecclesiastical insistence on the inalienability of property once given to

---

[23] C. Morris, *The Papal Monarchy: The Western Church from 1050 to 1250* (Oxford, 1989), chaps. 3–4, 10.ii, iv, 18.i.

[24] Ibid., pp. 294–7, 536–9; J. Blair, 'Introduction', in *Minsters and Parish Churches: The Local Church in Transition, 950–1200*, ed. J. Blair (Oxford, 1988), pp. 1–19; *The Parish in English Life, 1400–1600*, ed. K. L. French, G. G. Gibbs and B. A. Kümin (Manchester, 1997), pp. 3–32; Duffy, *Stripping of the Altars*, passim, esp. pp. 131–54.

[25] As both the Black Monks and Pole asserted: see below, n. 125; Coulton, *Five Centuries of Religion*, iv. 675; Knowles, *Religious Orders*, ii. 129–36, 175–80; iii, 10–13, 206–7, 212–15; see also the Dominican nuns: P. Lee, *Nunneries, Learning and Spirituality in Late Medieval English Society: The Dominican Priory of Dartford* (York, 2001).

[26] As the 1520 reaction to reform proposals makes clear; below, n. 125.

[27] See most conveniently, D. Knowles and R. N. Hadcock, *Medieval Religious Houses of England and Wales* (2nd edn., London, 1971).

God (not in practice watertight) and the protection afforded by secular law in England from the later twelfth century meant that it was difficult even for weak institutions to disappear altogether.[28] They were left to some extent as a deposit from an earlier age, as their original functions became less important. The essential question to be addressed here, therefore, is what their role was in later medieval society. How far were they valued for what they did originally, and how far had they adapted to new needs?[29]

In 1529 a parliamentary petition suggested that if religious houses could not show that they were using their lands for the original purposes envisaged by donors, then donors or their heirs could resume those lands.[30] This presupposed that donors gave lands to the church with specific objects in mind, an assumption based in late medieval practice that had more than two centuries of history behind it.[31] In 1285 the second Statute of Westminster allowed donors or their heirs to sue churches for the recovery of land given for chantries, lights or alms if the latter had not been kept up for two years.[32] This attitude was applied to the whole church: the preamble to the Statute of Provisors of 1351, derived from a petition of 1307, asserted that extensive possessions had been given to the church in England by its founders – the kings and nobles of yore – so that the clergy would teach religion, pray, and perform works of charity for the souls of the donors and their heirs, and that these purposes were damaged by papal invasion of ecclesiastical property and benefices.[33]

The laity, moreover, had shown that they could act on these assumptions, by resuming and redistributing lands and churches belonging to the alien priories during the Hundred Years War.[34] The possessions held by

---

[28] M. Cheney, 'Inalienability in Mid-Twelfth-Century England: Enforcement and Consequences', in *Proceedings of the Sixth International Congress of Medieval Canon Law, Berkeley, California, 28 July–2 August 1980*, ed. S. Kuttner and K. Pennington, Monumenta Iuris Canonici, Series C, Subsidia, 7 (Vatican, 1985), pp. 467–78; B. J. Thompson, 'Free Alms Tenure in the Twelfth Century', *Anglo-Norman Studies* 16 (1994), pp. 236–42.

[29] As ever, much of my evidence is taken from intensive study of the religious houses of Norfolk, which involves a possible bias towards small and poor houses, especially of canons. Friars and nuns are only touched on sporadically here.

[30] Hoyle, 'Origins of the Dissolution', pp. 284–7, printed at 302–5.

[31] B. J. Thompson, 'From "Alms" to "Spiritual Services": The Function and Status of Monastic Property in Medieval England', *Monastic Studies* 2, ed. J. Loades (Bangor, 1991), pp. 250–61.

[32] *Statutes of the Realm*, i. 91–2.

[33] *Councils and Synods with Other Documents relating to the English Church, II. 1205–1313*, ed. F. M. Powicke and C. R. Cheney (2 vols., Oxford, 1964), ii. 1232–6; *Statutes of the Realm*, i. 316–18.

[34] See D. Matthew, *The Norman Monasteries and their English Possessions* (Oxford, 1962), chaps. 3–4; M. Morgan, 'The Suppression of the Alien Priories', *History* 26 (1941), pp. 204–12. The emphasis in what follows is my own: see 'The Laity, the Alien Priories and the Redistribution of Ecclesiastical Property', in *England in the Fifteenth Century:*

French abbeys, and the priories subject to those abbeys, were natural targets for suspicion, and sources of funds, during periods of warfare, and they were taken into royal hands from 1337. Subjected to lay scrutiny, a process of definition ensued over subsequent decades which attempted to distinguish which properties were supporting worthwhile divine services and which were not. Functioning convents were often supported by their patrons, who valued their divine and other services; they removed priories from the jurisdiction of the foreign mother-houses and expelled the French monks, making them independent houses staffed by English religious, who would continue to maintain suffrages for the lineage. Cells, however, whose function was to export the fruits of their (sometimes extensive) English possessions, found few supporters but many exploiters, and were gradually occupied, farmed, purchased and finally seized: in 1414, it was projected that all such cells would be resumed once the war ended, 'to the end that divine services in the aforesaid places be more fully performed by Englishmen than they were by the French'.[35] The subsequent process of redistribution, still in train in Edward IV's reign, demonstrated the fact of lay power over the church, and the preparedness of the laity to intervene in the structure and functioning of the church on the basis of their own criteria of utility. In the later Middle Ages, then, it was clear that churches had to justify their use of resources to the laity on the latter's terms.

There was, of course, a great variety of churches, and of monasteries, from great abbeys to small priories of a few canons, not to mention nunneries and friaries.[36] The greater monasteries, many of which were pre-Conquest in origin and were assumed into royal patronage in 1066, were economically and politically strong, with seats in parliament and incomes equivalent to nobles; they were an accepted and powerful part of society.[37] The Conquest both coincided with the beginning of the heroic period of monastic foundation and stimulated it in England because a new aristocracy marked their arrival with plentiful gifts to their own churches and establishment of new ones.[38] The initial waves of Benedictine and Cluniac – and later Cistercian – foundations by kings and barons and bishops produced

Proceedings of the 1992 Harlaxton Symposium, ed. N. Rogers, Harlaxton Medieval Studies 4 (Stamford, 1994), pp. 19–41.

[35] *Rotuli Parliamentorum* (6 vols., London, 1783), iv. 22.

[36] J. Burton, *Monastic and Religious Orders in Britain, 1000–1300* (Cambridge, 1994). For catalogues, see MRH, and the volumes of the VCH for more detail. A qualitative sketch of the Norfolk monasteries is in B. J. Thompson, 'Monasteries and their Patrons at Foundation and Dissolution', *TRHS*, 6th Series 4 (1994), pp. 104–6.

[37] MRH, contains income figures; for a full list from the *Valor ecclesiasticus* of 1535, see Savine, 'English Monasteries', pp. 270–88. Perhaps they also had something equivalent to the noble affinity; see the fourteenth-century fraternity-list of St Benet's, Holme: William Worcester, *Itineraries*, ed. J. Harvey (Oxford, 1969), pp. 224–5.

[38] See now E. Cownie, *Religious Patronage in Anglo-Norman England, 1066–1135* (London, 1998).

houses which were healthy, if rarely as grand as the older abbeys;[39] but in the course of the twelfth century, abetted by the onset of a diverse range of monastic orders, lesser founders established smaller institutions. The Augustinians in particular littered the landscape with houses occupied by small groups of canons that had various origins, from knights attempting to imitate their baronial superiors by establishing copycat monasteries, through townspeople re-establishing decayed churches and collectively supporting their ministers, to small groups of priests wishing to live in common.[40] The emergence of opportunities for women added to the mix, and the arrival of the friars in the thirteenth century presented another combination of different ideals, ascetic and property-less in lifestyle, but ministerial in function.[41]

Despite this diversity of institution, late medieval monasteries were often conceived as primarily chantries for their founding families.[42] The Statute of Carlisle of 1307 asserted that religious houses were founded and endowed to support works of piety and charity for the souls of the founders and their heirs.[43] Houses which were immune from secular exactions by their patrons were said to be held in return for nothing but prayers.[44] Petitions for the denization of alien priories tended to construct them as houses of prayer for the patron's lineage.[45] The damage caused to any monastery by loss of resources through mismanagement or over-taxation was sustained by founders and their salvation; in 1384 the prior of Walsingham was attempting to get himself made abbot and was thus expending the house's goods, which led to diminution of Divine Service, to the prejudice of the

---

[39] B. Golding, 'The Coming of the Cluniacs', *Anglo-Norman Studies* 3 (1981), pp. 65–77; B. D. Hill, *English Cistercian Monasteries and their Patrons in the Twelfth Century* (Urbana, IL, 1968).

[40] J. C. Dickinson, *The Origins of the Austin Canons and their Introduction into England* (London, 1950).

[41] S. Thompson, *Women Religious: The Founding of English Nunneries after the Norman Conquest* (Oxford, 1991); S. Elkins, *Holy Women of Twelfth-Century England* (Chapel Hill, NC, 1988); Knowles still provides the best introduction to the friars in England: *Religious Orders*, i, part II.

[42] See also the evidence in the first paragraph of this section, above, p. 171. Modern writers have certainly assumed such: for example Baskerville, *English Monks*, pp. 19–20; Elton, *England under the Tudors*, p. 142; F. Heal, *Hospitality in Early Modern England* (Oxford, 1990), p. 245; P. Gwyn, *The King's Cardinal: The Rise and Fall of Thomas Wolsey* (London, 1990), p. 271; S. Brigden, *New Worlds, Lost Worlds: The Rule of the Tudors, 1485–1603* (London, 2000), p. 127.

[43] *Statutes of the Realm*, i. 150.

[44] For example S. Wood, *English Monasteries and their Patrons in the Thirteenth Century* (Oxford, 1955), p. 14 n. 2; Baskerville, *English Monks*, p. 20: Michelham 'held by the service of finding thirteen canons to pray for the soul of the founder'.

[45] For example St Neot's, 1409: *CPR, Henry IV, III.1408–13*, p. 76; in full in William Dugdale, *Monasticon Anglicanum*, ed. J. Caley, H. Ellis and B. Bandinel (6 vols. in 8, London, 1817–30), iii. 479–80. See also Stoke-by-Clare, below, n. 79.

patron, the earl of March.[46] Various kinds of evidence from the time of the Dissolution itself suggest that this remained the common assumption. The confession extracted from the canons of Westacre in 1538 outlined their crimes as 'omitting the execution of observances that they were bound by their vows to their founders, the King's progenitors, to maintain'.[47] In discussing the fate of the monasteries in 1536, Thomas Starkey supposed that they existed to relieve souls through prayers and alms.[48]

How accurate this assumption was is hard to gauge in terms of what the monasteries were actually doing for their first founders and current patrons in the later Middle Ages. Although twelfth-century founders did not specify what spiritual services they were to receive, it seems likely that they were often commemorated in an annual obit, and probably mentioned daily at high mass such as chantry-founders would expect as the minimal return on their investment.[49] Some time after 1447 an inscription was placed near the tomb of the founder of Wymondham Abbey, who died in 1139: 'Pray yee for the Soul of William de Albany Founder of this Abby', and his obit was kept up to 1535.[50] There is a range of evidence, not least from the Dissolution process itself, that houses remained conscious of their first founders and major benefactors.[51]

Keeping up these suffrages, however, was not necessarily enough to justify the monasteries' existence. The problem with the currency of spiritual services was the dislocation of their beneficiaries from their means of support; property in the present was supporting good works for long-dead benefactors. Why this had come to be was complex, involving the donation of considerable quantities of (then plentifully available) land in the conquest-and-colonization period of the central Middle Ages, the role of monasteries as symbols and foci of their founding families' identity and power into the future, the development of Purgatory and its associated practices by which the living helped the dead through their punishments, the insistence of canon law on the inalienability of ecclesiastical property, and the (paradoxical) effectiveness of the common law in securing this

---

[46] CPR, Richard II, II.1381–5, pp. 383, 421; see Baskerville, English Monks, p. 46 for a nice example, John of Gaunt and Nuneaton.

[47] This was again linked to delapidation of property; Gairdner, Lollardy and the Reformation, ii. 116.

[48] Starkey's Life and Letters, ed. S. J. Heritage, EETS, Extra Series 32 (1878), pp. lv–lvi.

[49] I shall explore this problem fully elsewhere; see my 'The Church and the Aristocracy: Lay and Ecclesiastical Landowning Society in Fourteenth-Century Norfolk' (Unpublished Ph.D. Thesis, University of Cambridge, 1990), pp. 95–6.

[50] F. Blomefield, An Essay towards a Topographical History of the County of Norfolk (11 vols., London, 1805–11), ii. 524; Valor ecclesiasticus (6 vols., London, 1810–34), iii. 323.

[51] Evidence is cited at Thompson, 'Monasteries and Patrons', pp. 117–18; see particularly the visitation articles and draft injunctions, the northern compendium compertorum, and parts of the Valor ecclesiasticus, for example Suffolk: LP, viii. 76(3); x. 364 (pp. 137–43); Valor ecclesiasticus, iii. 412–37.

objective. But its effect was, as Thomas Starkey asserted, 'to conuerte ouer much possessyon to that end & purpos . . . to pray for them wych be departyd out of thys mysery'.[52] The dead did not make very good protectors in the present, and perpetual institutions therefore always needed to appeal to the living to justify themselves.

The heirs of founders and benefactors were bound in duty to secure their forebears' spiritual welfare, and might therefore have been adequate supporters of family monasteries. The dislocation of lineages in space and time, however, meant that this obligation would not last forever. Families moved their centres of gravity, and with it the primary focus of their religious patronage, as the Clares did in moving from East Anglia to the southern Welsh march in the thirteenth century.[53] Moreover, patri-monial lineages became extinct – at something like a quarter every quarter-century – leaving their priories to new lines through heiresses or royal grant; so the Clare monasteries passed to the de Burgh earls of Ulster, the Mortimers and the dukes of York through heiresses, and thus came to the Crown.[54] I have shown elsewhere that advowsons of monasteries were increasingly likely to move up the social spectrum; while the crown and higher nobility founded one third of the Norfolk monasteries, their sixteenth-century successors held two thirds of the county's monastic advowsons, the crown holding half of these or one-third of the total number of houses.[55] While this process had unfolded over centuries, the fifteenth century – perhaps the Wars of the Roses – seems to have been crucial in interrupting relationships between noble lineages and monas-teries. No Norfolk house was founded by the male ancestors of its sixteenth-century patron, and most of the latter were not resident in the county, such as (apart from the Crown), the earls of Oxford, Arundel, and Rutland, and Lords Dacre and Clinton, who between them accounted for at least ten advowsons.[56]

Later medieval patrons were therefore less and less likely to regard praying for deceased – generally long-deceased – predecessors as an adequate use of resources. Churches had to be able to offer benefits to the living, or at most the fairly recently dead, to be valued. This was particularly so when at that period benefactors increasingly preferred immediate suffrages in large numbers to perpetual benefits stretching into the future; the earl of Warwick wanted thirty trentals and 1000 masses in 1401, and even more spectacular

---

[52] *Starkey's Life and Letters*, p. lvi.
[53] J. C. Ward, 'Fashions in Monastic Endowment: The Foundations of the Clare Family, 1066–1314', *JEH* 32 (1981), pp. 427–51.
[54] GEC, *The Complete Peerage*, ed. V. Gibbs *et al.* (12 vols. in 13, 1910–59), iii. 242–6.
[55] Thompson, 'Monasteries and Patrons', pp. 119–20, 124–5.
[56] For whom see *Complete Peerage, ad loc*. Even Suffolk and Norfolk (representing another three advowsons) were not resident in the county, and Suffolk moved in 1538 to Lincolnshire; S. J. Gunn, *Charles Brandon, Duke of Suffolk, c.1484–1545* (Oxford, 1988), pp. 143–82, esp. p. 170.

numbers were requested in the following century.[57] Perpetual institutions, therefore, had to reach out to the living to secure continued support, and to fend off critical opinions of their use of resources. They needed to maintain a continuous reciprocal exchange between themselves and benefactors down the generations.

Their current patrons were the natural place to look for support in the first instance, even if they were no longer of the same family as the first founders. To attract their patronage, the religious had to be able to offer something new, over and above the benefits which were accruing to the dead. This was often not difficult: the larger houses were important constituents of noble lordships and were naturally of interest to the inheritors and grantees of those lordships. Because there was a very rough correlation between date of foundation and size and wealth of monasteries, the houses founded after the Conquest as adjuncts to the new baronies were prestigious symbols of their lords' lordship, and connected new families to an older past, especially through burials and tombs. The Fitzalan earls of Arundel initially colonized Lewes, the first Cluniac priory, when they had inherited it from the defunct Warennes in the second half of the fourteenth century; they secured the denization of its daughter-houses and cells, including Castleacre, during the alien priories crisis.[58] Thetford Cluniac Priory, founded by the Bigod earls of Norfolk who were generally buried there, was a magnet for their successors, the dukes of Norfolk, both Mowbray and Howard, the latter attempting to save it at the Dissolution.[59] Lesser families who inherited monasteries, especially near their residences, were similarly active in filling the role of patron, for instance the Lords Bardolf at Wormegay and Clifton at Wymondham and Buckenham.[60] Rosenthal calculated that forty-three per cent of the nobility were buried

[57] Lambeth Palace Library [LPL], Register of Archbishop Arundel, i, fol. 179v; John de Vere, earl of Oxford (died 1513), requested 2000 masses as soon as possible: W. St John Hope, 'The Last Testament and Inventory of John de Veer, Thirteenth Earl of Oxford', *Archaeologia* 66 (1914–15), pp. 310–11; Joan Beauchamp, Lady Bergavenny, wanted 5000; *The Register of Henry Chichele, Archbishop of Canterbury, 1414–1443*, ed. E. F. Jacob (4 vols., Oxford, 1937/8–47), ii. 535, and see p. 811; Henry VII wanted 10,000 in a month; G. Temperley, *Henry VII* (London, 1917), p. 371.
[58] CPR, *Edward III, XV.1370–74*, p. 286, *Monasticon*, ed. Caley *et al*., v. 15–16. The earl who died in 1376, and his younger brother and daughter-in-law, were buried there, and his son intended to be; thereafter they used their new college at Arundel: *Complete Peerage*, i. 244, 260; LPL, Reg. Sudbury, fols. 92v, 102; *A Collection of All the Wills of the Kings and Queens of England*, ed. J. Nichols (1780), p. 120.
[59] CPL i. 594–5; CFR, v. 227; J. Weever, *Antient Funerall Monuments* (London, 1631; 1767 edn.), pp. 828ff.; *Complete Peerage*, ix. 578–615; note that the Mowbrays abandoned the Carthusian Priory at Epworth which they had founded; and see below n. 131.
[60] Bardolf: PRO, C143/139/9; CPR, *Edward III, III.1334–8*, p. 157, CPR, *Henry V, I.1413–16*, p. 349; LPL, Reg. Courtenay, fol. 215v; Blomefield, *Norfolk*, vii. 501. Clifton: CPR, *Edward III, IX.1350–54*, p. 440; Blomefield, *Norfolk*, i. 375–7, 386; ii. 522, 525; vi. 146; *Valor ecclesiasticus*, iii. 316.

in regular houses, a proportion much higher than that of their social inferiors.[61] Members of patronal families can be linked to thirty-five grants in mortmain of property during the fourteenth century in Norfolk, roughly one per house on average; twelve of these were manors or substantial holdings, and another twelve advowsons.[62] Testators often seem to have tried to ensure that they left something beyond customary payments to churches within their lordships, especially payments for prayers and masses, and they sometimes stated this explicitly.[63] The pre-existing connection between monasteries and their patronal families made them natural partners in the giving of benefits in return for spiritual services, building on those being performed for their ancestors or predecessors.

While some patrons continued to be active supporters of their monasteries, they equally spread their spiritual investments, the more widely in proportion to the extent of their territorial holding and wealth.[64] Even more modest landowners could exercise a degree of choice between parish churches on their lands, houses of friars, cathedrals, monasteries or secular colleges.[65] The more powerful, especially titled families, had large portfolios of churches and religious houses, accumulated with the various lordships they had inherited or been granted; this was another effect of the way in which advowsons of monasteries descended through the generations. When fourteenth-century Fitzalans chose to be buried at Lewes, they were deserting

---

[61] J. T. Rosenthal, The Purchase of Paradise: Gift-Giving and the Aristocracy, 1307–1485 (London, 1972), p. 82; the figure is higher for the fourteenth century than the fifteenth. For the contrast with the gentry, see n. 65.

[62] Thompson, 'Church and Aristocracy', pp. 114–33, which also covers other forms of help. The evidence for the fifteenth century is much thinner because of the decline in numbers of mortmain licences, and probably also of perpetual grants.

[63] For example Richard Fitzalan (died 1376), 'churches in my lordships', LPL, Reg. Sudbury, fol. 93v; Thomas Beauchamp, earl of Warwick (died 1401), 'religious houses of the foundation of my progenitors, and all houses where I have confraternity', LPL, Reg. Arundel, i, fol. 180; John de Vere (died 1513), masses to be said by friars and monks in houses of his ancestors' foundation, and donations to those houses; St John Hope, 'Testament of John de Veer', pp. 310, 312–13. Long lists of religious houses often look like attempts to cover all such houses, and others; for example Elizabeth de Burgh, lady of Clare, and Edmund, earl of March, Royal Wills, ed. Nichols, pp. 22–37, 104–16.

[64] The wills in the note above demonstrate this precisely, as do most other noble wills; see those in Royal Wills and the archbishops' registers, some conveniently printed in the second volume of the Register of Henry Chichele where they are very helpfully indexed.

[65] Each member of the Bardolf family seems to have been buried in a different place; Complete Peerage, i. 418–21. The gentry were overwhelmingly buried in parish churches, with mendicants and cathedrals attracting some knights, other regular houses very few: A. Brown, Popular Piety in Late Medieval England: The Diocese of Salisbury, 1250–1550 (Oxford, 1995), pp. 35–6, 253; P. Fleming, 'Charity, Faith, and the Gentry of Kent, 1422–1529', in Property and Politics: Essays in Later Medieval English History, ed. A. J. Pollard (Gloucester, 1984), p. 50; M. G. A. Vale, Piety, Charity and Literacy among the Yorkshire Gentry, 1370–1480, Borthwick Paper 50 (York, 1976), p. 8.

the traditional family burial-house of Haughmond Abbey.[66] Moreover many individuals founded at least their own chantries, and perhaps colleges or even Carthusian houses: fifteenth-century Fitzalans were buried at Arundel College, founded by the two Earls Richard in the later fourteenth century on the basis of a purchased alien priory.[67] Members of noble families could exercise considerable individual choice over where to be buried and where to bestow other grants and forms of support. When Maud, widow of Robert de Tony proposed to found a chantry in the 1320s, she first approached the Tony priory at Westacre; but negotiations broke down and she gave the endowment instead to Coxford Priory nearby, despite the fact that Westacre at the time was mounting something of an appeal to attract chantries.[68] Even when landowners did place their chantries in family houses, they often specified that the chantry itself was to be staffed by secular chaplains.[69] Friars were another obvious divergence from family tradition, attracting both burials and intercessory payments from members of landowning families.[70]

Monasteries were therefore competing in an almost open market with other churches for patronage from their noble patrons, a phenomenon most obvious in the context of the Crown's vast portfolio of houses, few of which were able to attract the attention of their royal patron. If old connections sometimes gave the monasteries an advantage with particular families in terms of attracting payments at death and additional chantries, other factors worked in the opposite direction. The perception that monasteries were chantries for long-dead souls reduced their attraction to the living in terms of their available suffrage power for additional benefactors, especially when it was often assumed, in the context of the smaller numbers of religious after the Black Death, that the limit of a convent's mass resources could easily be reached.[71] This encouraged benefactors, including patrons, to make separate provision to avoid their suffrages being merged in those of the house in general, a trend also informed by the greater specification and individual-ization of spiritual services from the thirteenth century onwards: all benefactors expected suffrages to be focused primarily on themselves, and

---

[66] Complete Peerage, i. 240–41; MRH, p. 159; VCH Shropshire, ii. 62–5.

[67] VCH Sussex, ii. 108–9; Complete Peerage, i. 246–50.

[68] Thompson, 'Church and Aristocracy', pp. 141 n. 38, 247–9; Dean and Chapter of Norwich, Episcopal Registers, ii, fol. 80v.

[69] For example Maud Tony's chantry was for a secular chaplain in her chapel at Necton. See also the chantries prescribed by noble wills, for example Richard Fitzalan for Arundel Priory, LPL, Reg. Sudbury, fol. 93. K. L. Wood-Legh, Perpetual Chantries in Britain (Cambridge, 1965), pp. 136–54, 189.

[70] Rosenthal, Purchase of Paradise, pp. 82, 84; Fleming, 'Gentry of Kent', p. 50. For bequests, see the wills again (nn. 64–5); great testators often left money to a large number of mendicant houses, often all those within their sphere of influence; for example Robert and William Ufford, successive earls of Suffolk (died 1369 and 1381), to all friars in Norfolk and Suffolk: LPL, Reg. Whittlesey, fol. 111v, Reg. Courtenay, fol. 191.

[71] Wood-Legh, Perpetual Chantries, pp. 137–8; and see Coulton below, n. 77. For numbers see MRH, pp. 488–94.

their benefactions and even foundations were concomitantly more individual, less for the lineage as a whole.[72] Even patrons in making gifts to their
own monasteries increasingly separated out their suffrages – and their own
monks or canons saying them – from those of their ancestors, as in the
Clifton chantries at Wymondham and Buckenham.[73] Payments to religious
for prayers at death were equally very much focused on the individual who
had just died. One result of these developments was that patrons' gifts were
not as valuable to their houses as they might have been. Payments for prayers
and masses at death often went to individual religious rather than to the
general funds of the house.[74] Significant benefactions from patrons usually
came with significant additional obligations – routinely secured by conditions intended to guarantee their performance[75] – so that the house's general
endowment (core-funding in modern academic fund-raising parlance) did
not necessarily benefit. Indeed benefactions for additional intercessory
obligations often proved inadequate, leaving them to be supported from
other resources, or forgotten.[76]

Paradoxically, monasteries were of most use to patrons when they
abandoned praying for past generations altogether and focused their
suffrages on the present. It is hard to know how much this was done
informally, but that at least neglect of mass obligations was thought to be
endemic is clear from the rhetoric of complaint against it, for instance in
the legislation of the Benedictine chapters, and the inquiries of visitors.[77]
Yet this shows precisely the pressures against such abandonment, in the
ingrained respect for prayers for the dead. Moreover, ecclesiastical authorities were aware that, quite apart from the moral case against neglect in
defrauding benefactors, it was not very prudent in terms of attracting further
support by reassuring benefactors that *their* prescriptions would be honoured

[72] This is a simplification of a more complex pattern which I will discuss elsewhere; but
the generalization holds good. The increasing specification of services is discussed in
my article cited in n. 31.

[73] See above, n. 60 (the same was perhaps also true of the Bardolf proposals cited there),
and in n. 69. It was *a fortiori* true of chantries and secular colleges; see for example E. K.
Bennet, 'The College of St John the Evangelist, Rushworth', *Norfolk Archaeology* 10
(1888), pp. 368–73.

[74] As is explicit in some wills, for example *Royal Wills*, ed. Nichols, pp. 48, 99, and John
de Vere's in n. 57; Coulton, *Five Centuries of Religion*, iii. 385–7; B. Harvey, *Living and
Dying in Medieval England: The Monastic Experience* (Oxford, 1993), pp. 117, 153, 210.
The same might also apply to chantries in monasteries; Wood-Legh, *Perpetual
Chantries*, pp. 130–35.

[75] For example Wood-Legh, *Perpetual Chantries*, pp. 144–7; Coulton, *Five Centuries of
Religion*, iii. 76–8; the 1285 statute above, n. 32.

[76] Wood-Legh, *Perpetual Chantries*, pp. 93–129; A. Kreider, *English Chantries: The Road to
Dissolution* (London, 1979), pp. 73, 86–9, 236; N. P. Tanner, *The Church in Late
Medieval Norwich, 1370–1532* (Toronto, 1984), p. 93.

[77] Coulton, *Five Centuries of Religion*, iii. 69–86; *Chapters*, ed. Pantin, i. 45, 70–71, 78, 99,
241, 263; ii. 32–3, 46, 71, 84, 196–7, 204; A. H. Thompson, *The English Clergy and their
Organization in the Later Middle Ages* (Oxford, 1947), p. 296.

in future.[78] Being a sound perpetual institution whose prayers would continue indefinitely into the future was after all one of the main advantages which monasteries had over less well endowed churches. Since both royal and canon law restricted the extent to which patrons themselves might resume and re-use endowments wholesale, this only happened in times of crisis, whether general, as in the case of the alien priories, or particular, when individual houses failed. In these cases endowments were re-used to update institutions both in form, as colleges or chantries, and in terms of spiritual beneficiaries, to re-focus suffrages on the current generation.[79]

This illustrates precisely the dangers to which religious houses were exposed: in their old form, many of them were likely to be of decreasing or peripheral interest to patrons; yet it was not easy to transform them into institutions which patrons would continue to value highly. In these circumstances it is not surprising that one patronal response was to prefer the temporal perquisites of their lordship over churches to the spiritual. Monasteries provided hospitality for sometimes large households including horses, corrodies for servants, advowsons to which clerks could be recommended, places for relatives, banking facilities, and symbols of a family's antiquity and lordship.[80] This was certainly how the Crown, the greatest patron of all with perhaps one third of advowsons by the sixteenth century, treated its houses from at least the thirteenth century; the nobility to some extent followed suit, listing, for instance, advowsons on their inquisitions *post mortem* alongside knights' fees.[81] Perhaps lordship over monasteries had finally suffered the same fate as had knight service much earlier: both had originally reflected an important relationship which meant much more than its legal manifestation, but whose demise had left only a formal structure as a right to be exploited. Although, therefore, late medieval religious houses could be of some utility to their patrons, it is doubtful that this alone was adequate to justify their occupation of plentiful resources, as the contemporary view of the function of monasteries implied that it should.

[78] Explicit at Wood-Legh, *Perpetual Chantries*, p. 37. Note in this context the increasing security-measures imposed by benefactors in the late Middle Ages, at n. 75.

[79] For example Stoke-by-Clare, an alien priory which became a secular college; *Monasticon Anglicanum*, ed. Caley et al., vi. 1416–23; *CPR, Henry V, I.1413–16*, pp. 291–2. See in general Thompson, 'Monasteries and Patrons', pp. 113–17, 'Laity and Alien Priories', pp. 30–35, 39–41.

[80] Wood, *Monasteries and Patrons*, pp. 101–20; Baskerville, *English Monks*, pp. 25–9, 46–50; E. J. Gardner, 'The English Nobility and Monastic Education, c.1100–1500', in *The Cloister and the World: Essays in Medieval History in Honour of Barbara Harvey*, ed. J. Blair and B. Golding (Oxford, 1996), pp. 80–94. Thetford was a good place to stay: in 1279 the John Bigod, the patron's brother, was there with a household which cost more than the rest of the community put together, and in 1483 the duke of Norfolk was there with twenty-five horse; *Visitations of English Cluniac Foundations in 47 Hen. III (1262), 3 & 4 Edw. I (1275–6), & 7 Edw. I (1279)*, ed. G. F. Duckett (London, 1890), p. 35; *The Household Books of John Howard, Duke of Norfolk, 1462–1471, 1481–1483*, ed. A. Crawford (Stroud, 1992), pp. 449, 452.

[81] See for example above, n. 44; see also *CIP* passim.

Monasteries clearly had to appeal beyond their patrons and to offer benefits more widely to attract benefactors and protectors, often without the advantage of previous connections and obligations. In this market they were competing with secular churches, and the above disadvantages applied to them *a fortiori*: late medieval benefactors more naturally turned to secular clergy than religious for suffrages, and preferred exclusivity rather than risking their identity being submerged in the obligations incurred by a monastery through the centuries. Most late medieval patronage was focused on the parish church, the main centre of local ecclesiastical (and often social) activity. Even in the north, where the monasteries were more important to the structure of ecclesiastical provision, only one sixth of wills mentioned the possessioner religious.[82] The proportion of chantries founded in monasteries fell during the later Middle Ages, and many of these were for secular chaplains.[83]

Nevertheless, religious houses were able to attract albeit declining patronage in various ways and for various reasons. The Carthusian houses and others of the more ascetic orders were valued and respected, although comprising only a small segment of the monastic population.[84] The friars maintained their important role in urban religion, and retained the loyalty of many inhabitants, to judge by wills, for example.[85] Monastic cathedrals played an important role in their towns and dioceses, and they similarly continued to be valued, measured in terms of the bequests they attracted.[86] Other great monasteries provided a similar focus, especially when they were in towns (which had sometimes grown up around them), such as Bury St Edmunds or St Albans.[87] Even St Benet's at Holm, stuck out in the marshes

---

[82] C. Cross, 'Monasticism and Society in the Diocese of York, 1520–40', *TRHS*, 5th Series 38 (1988), pp. 131–45 at 132; I have taken the figure only up to 1535, and note the comment on p. 133 that most of these testators had monks for landlords or parochial appropriators; for the importance of monasteries in one county, see Haigh, *Reformation and Resistance*, pp. 91, 120–26. For other figures, see Brown, *Popular Piety*, pp. 28–32; Tanner, *Norwich*, pp. 222–3; Vale, *Piety, Charity*, pp. 20–22; Fleming, 'Charity, Faith', pp. 48–9; Scarisbrick, *Reformation and English People*, p. 6; Bowker, *Henrician Reformation*, pp. 48, 148.

[83] Brown, *Popular Piety*, p. 95; R. Ward, 'The Foundation and Functions of Perpetual Chantries in the Diocese of Norwich, c.1250–1547' (unpublished Ph.D. Thesis, University of Cambridge, 1999), pp. 83–7; see above, n. 69.

[84] See above, n. 25.

[85] See n. 82; other works, especially on urban piety, are listed at, for example, R. Houlbrooke, *Death, Religion and the Family in England, 1480–1750* (Oxford, 1998), pp. 111–14.

[86] For Norwich, see Tanner, *Church in Late Medieval Norwich*, pp. 12–13, 96, 120–21, 222, although note hostility between city and priory before 1450; see also for Salisbury, Brown, *Popular Piety*, pp. 49–66.

[87] J. G. Clark, 'Reformation and Reaction at St Albans Abbey, 1530–58', *EHR* 115 (2000), pp. 297–328; D. MacCulloch, *Suffolk and the Tudors: Politics and Religion in an English County, 1500–1600* (Oxford, 1986), pp. 135–6; note the various relics and the money found in the monastery at the Dissolution, suggesting continuing attraction of offerings; *Three Chapters of Letters*, ed. Wright, pp. 85, 144; M. R. James, *On the Abbey*

of the Norfolk broads, had a fraternity involving various East Anglian landowners.[88] Among other Norfolk houses, Walsingham was spectacularly successful in this period through its possession of the most-venerated image of the Virgin, as was Bromholm, to a lesser extent, with its Holy Cross.[89] The latter also illustrates another way in which monasteries could rekindle benefactors' interest, through 'bastard-feudal' patronage: the house's patrons were the earls and dukes of Suffolk as lords of the honour of Eye, but they paid it little attention, leaving the way open for the Pastons to use it as their family burial-house, as is most graphically seen in the burial of John Paston I in 1466.[90] Similarly, another gentry family, the Calthorpes, seem to have become de facto patrons of the Crown's Creake Abbey, although this did not prevent the house being dissolved for lack of canons in 1506.[91]

The monasteries' utility to society was reinforced by the fact that they could offer much else besides spiritual benefits in terms of suffrages or a vocation to the (latterly falling) numbers of those inclined to it.[92] In a few houses learning was maintained, as James Clark has shown for St Albans.[93] The greater houses provided education not just for their own inmates, either through maintaining a grammar master for the town, or through a school based in the almonry, of which around thirty have been identified.[94] The diversion of alms, in this case to the education of boys, was a trend also identified by Barbara Harvey at Westminster, where monks nominated their

of St Edmund at Bury (Cambridge, 1895), pp. 136–41, 149–50. Of course both had uncomfortable relationships with their towns, and suffered in the revolt of 1381; The Peasants' Revolt of 1381, ed. R. B. Dobson (London, 1970), pp. 236, 243–8, 254–6, 269–77.

[88]   See n. 37.

[89]   J. C. Dickinson, The Shrine of Our Lady at Walsingham (Cambridge, 1956), esp. pp. 24–47, 59–60; Valor ecclesiasticus, iii. 344, 388; The Cellarer's Account for Bromholm Priory, Norfolk, 1415–16, ed. L. J. Redstone, Norfolk Record Society 35 (1944), p. 54; W. Sparrow Simpson, 'The Pilgrimage to Bromholm', Journal of the British Archaeological Association 30 (1874), pp. 51–61; F. Wormald, 'The Rood of Bromholm', Journal of the Warburg Institute 1 (1937), pp. 31–45.

[90]   Blomefield, Norfolk, vi. 479, 482–5; also printed in The Paston Letters, ed. J. Gairdner (6 vols., London, 1904; repr. Gloucester, 1983), iv. 226–31, no. 637; and see index s.v. Bromholm and references.

[91]   'A Cellarer's Account Roll of Creake Abbey, 5 & 6 Edward III', ed. G. A. Carthew, Norfolk Archaeology 6 (1864), pp. 338–41; G. A. Carthew, 'North Creake Abbey', Norfolk Archaeology 7 (1872), p. 158; A Cartulary of Creake Abbey, ed. A. L. Bedingfeld, Norfolk Record Society 35 (1966), pp. xxii, xxx, 68–71, 113–19.

[92]   This has played an important role in writing on the Dissolution, for example esp. Gasquet, Henry VIII and Monasteries, pp. xxvi–xxxii; Heal (Hospitality, p. 245) suggests that, once it was clear that the monasteries' primary function would not save them, secondary functions became more prominent in the debate.

[93]   J. G. Clark, 'Intellectual Life at the Abbey of St Albans and the Nature of Monastic Learning in England, c.1350–c.1440: The Work of Thomas Walsingham in Context' (Unpublished D. Phil. Thesis, University of Oxford, 1997).

[94]   R. Bowers, 'The Almonry Schools of the English Monasteries, c.1265–1540', in Monasteries and Society, ed. Thompson, pp. 177–222.

own recipients of their leftover food, such as favourite servants or kin (or even dogs).[95] Nevertheless monastic alms and hospitality had a reasonable reputation in the early sixteenth century – the religious provided a network of inns – and their loss was and is often cited as a damaging aspect of the Dissolution.[96] The religious were also employers on a major scale, like any landowner; on average somewhere between three and five laymen depended for their living on each religious.[97] The property of the religious could be enjoyed in various ways by laymen, especially through leases, common in the fifteenth century, and administrative office; another feature of the relationship between Bromholm Priory and the Pastons was William Paston's position as the house's chief steward, with administrative control over its property, adjacent to his own growing estate.[98] Other facilities such as banking and corrodies were probably more unevenly available – the financial health of many houses would hardly have allowed it.[99] Indeed it is not easy to measure the extent of the monasteries' contribution in these fields, as the difficulty of estimating the extent of almsgiving shows; but the presence of literate administrators was a resource both for the Crown, which used religious as JPs and tax-collectors, and for the village, just as the parish clergy sometimes seem to have played the role of general local factotum.[100] The general process of monasteries opening out to society in the later Middle Ages was not only an unconscious trend, but also an overt ideal in the view of some monastic thinkers, for whom such utility was to provide further justification of the monasteries' existence.[101]

---

[95] Harvey, *Living and Dying*, pp. 15, 20–21, 67–9, 173–4, 191–2; for alms in general, pp. 7–33. For lady-friends and hounds, for example *Norwich Visitations*, ed. Jessopp, pp. 250; 215, 279.

[96] Savine, 'English Monasteries', pp. 228–40; Baskerville, *English Monks*, pp. 25–9; Heal, *Hospitality*, pp. 54–6, 200–1, 223–46, but note her emphasis on inns as the 'primary grid of accommodation for travellers', p. 202. Note the abbot of Evesham arguing for the preservation of his house, partly as a lodging for persons of quality, *LP*, xiii/2. 866. Gasquet, *Henry VIII and Monasteries*, ii. 500–17, 523–4, above all focused his defence of monasteries on poverty.

[97] Savine, 'English Monasteries', pp. 218–27, 264–6; for great variation see the figures of the Dissolution commissioners, ranging in Norfolk from 3:64 or 1:16: Jessopp, 'Norfolk Monasteries', pp. 450–63, where the range is from 1:16 or 3:64 to 4:6 (predictably nuns); for resident servants, see below, n. 112. Gasquet, with a different agenda, came up how many people were made destitute by the monasteries, came up with 1:10; *Henry VIII and Monasteries*, ii. 323.

[98] The *Valor ecclesiasticus* lists officials and shows the extent of leasing, although not the lessees; Savine, 'English Monasteries', pp. 150–61, 245–61; Baskerville, *English Monks*, pp. 58–64; *Bromholm Cellarer's Account*, ed. Redstone, p. 86; see above, n. 90.

[99] Baskerville, *English Monks*, pp. 33–5; Coulton, *Five Centuries of Religion*, iii. 273–85; Haigh, *Reformation and Resistance*, pp. 123–4; Harvey, *Living and Dying*, pp. 179–209.

[100] See *CPR*; for example Prior More, Knowles, *Religious Orders*, iii. 124.

[101] Clark, 'Intellectual Life at St Albans', pp. 282–90; W. A. Pantin, 'Two Treatises of Uthred of Boldon on the Monastic Life', in *Studies in Medieval History presented to Frederick Maurice Powicke*, ed. R. W. Hunt, W. A. Pantin and R. W. Southern (Oxford, 1948), pp. 374–84.

This suggests a crucial point about these various activities: both in the spiritual and the secular sphere, little that the religious did was exclusive to them. Secular churches also provided suffrages of various kinds, and space for chantries. Nor were the benefits which flowed from being perpetual and secure institutions exclusive to monasteries; so were all other churches in principle, and since in practice longevity depended on financial strength and local opinion, colleges and parish churches thrived as well as or better than religious houses.[102] Almsgiving was as much a duty of parish clergy – and indeed landowners – as it was of monasteries.[103] In the field of education monasteries had not only lost their virtual monopoly but also now only made a small contribution to a flourishing spectrum of provision which stretched from the efforts of individual parish priests through various sorts of more- or less-formalized schools to the universities, not to mention increasingly autonomous lay education in guilds and households.[104] When Matthew Parker praised Stoke-by-Clare College, of which he was dean, in 1546, in an attempt to save it from suppression, his description of its activities might equally have fitted a monastery ten years earlier: they distributed alms and hospitality daily, instructed in the word of God and taught children grammar, singing and playing.[105] Cathedrals above all show the monasteries' social functions to have been no monopoly of the religious; divided roughly evenly between secular and monastic, their nature was secondary to their fundamental role as head-church of their diocese.[106] The utility of the religious, therefore, depended on being churches serving particular people in particular places, rather than on the vows they had taken to live the enclosed life. Indeed, had they lived up to ideals of monastic enclosure, they would not have been so connected to the locality. The various functions that they fulfilled which society valued could be – and were – equally performed by secular institutions.

It may therefore be asked how different the monasteries really were from other churches in the later Middle Ages. One approach to this issue is through the traditional method of trying to assess the way of life of late medieval religious through the various visitations which survive from the last century or so of monasticism.[107] Visitations are difficult to use, and

[102] See for example works in n. 24 above.
[103] Heal, Hospitality, pp. 223–8, 246–56.
[104] For a survey, N. Orme, English Schools in the Middle Ages (London, 1973); also his From Childhood to Chivalry: The Education of the English Kings and Aristocracy, 1066–1530 (1984). For universities, the first two volumes of The History of the University of Oxford, ed. J. I. Catto, and Catto and T. A. R. Evans (Oxford, 1984, 1992), and D. R. Leader, A History of the University of Cambridge, I: The University to 1546 (Cambridge, 1988).
[105] Except, of course, for the lack of prayers for the dead; LP, xxi/1. 968.
[106] See above n. 86.
[107] I have used Norwich Visitations; see also Visitations of Religious Houses in the Diocese of Lincoln, 1420–1449, ed. A. H. Thompson, 3 vols., Canterbury and York Society, 7, 14, 21 (1915–27); Visitations in the Diocese of Lincoln, 1517–1531, ed. A. H.

perhaps not difficult to discredit in terms of the unbalanced view of imperfection which they naturally present. The *comperta* of 1535–6 above all, with their systematic listing of the sexual sins of the religious – a third of the Norwich religious were painted as guilty of some form of pollution – hardly provide the material for a balanced account of the pre-Dissolution monasteries; the fact that they were used as evidence to help get the first Suppression Act through in 1536 might therefore seem to discredit the whole process.[108] But in ignoring this particular body of evidence, it is easy to assume that one has thus exonerated the religious from all charges;[109] their vices did not have to be spectacular to be insidious. The earlier visitations offer a much more nuanced and complex picture, although equally conditioned by the circumstances of their production. Episcopal officials were looking for anything that disrupted regularity and order or created scandal, rather than investigating the quality of spiritual life *per se*. And they were dependent on what the religious chose to tell them, which often testified to tensions within the community, but might equally hide all manner of problems: *omnia bene* might suggest not so much a lack of anything wrong as low standards and expectations, or even positive conspiracy.[110]

Taken with other evidence, however, the visitations do offer insights into the nature of late monastic life. In terms both of the personal lifestyle of the religious and of the barrier between the monastery and the world, an insistent picture emerges of institutions which were not very distinctive from their surroundings, and certainly nothing like as separate as monastic

Thompson, 3 vols., Lincoln Record Society 33, 35, 37 (Lincoln, 1940–47); *Collectanea Anglo-Premonstratensia*, ed. F. A. Gasquet, Camden Society, 3rd Series 6, 10, 12 (1904–6). These have become a standard feature of modern treatments of the Dissolution; for example Baskerville, *English Monks*, pp. 72–95; P. Hughes, *The Reformation in England* (3 vols., 5th edn., London, 1963), i. 47–66, Knowles, *Religious Orders*, iii. 62–86; Bowker, *Henrician Reformation*, pp. 17–28.

[108] These are an even more enduring feature of writing on the Dissolution – and always a central part of the debate – going right back to the seventeenth century: see the works listed above at nn. 3–6. For the evidence, see *LP*, x. 364, and *Three Chapters of Letters*, ed. Wright. Fortunately, Tony Shaw of Warwick University is in the process of a serious, scholarly and balanced study of the visitation and its infamous *comperta*. The figure is taken from his MA dissertation, 'The "Compendium Compertorum" and Associated Correspondence of the Royal Visitation' (1998), p. 46 and appx. 6; I am most grateful to him for a copy.

[109] A view taken by writers cited above, nn. 4, 6; for example Jessopp in *Norwich Visitations* and 'Norfolk Monasteries'.

[110] Can the bishop really mean that nothing is worthy of reformation at Beeston Priory in 1532 when there were only three canons? *Norwich Visitations*, p. 315. The pressures on religious not to reveal anything to visitors were strong, especially when the visitors went away and they were left to the mercy of the superior for another three or six years; in some cases conspiracy is demonstrable: *Norwich Visitations*, p. 126. For colourful examples, Baskerville, *English Monks*, pp. 73–8, 87; Bowker shows that even the 1535 visitors missed some fairly strong evidence; *Henrician Reformation*, pp. 103, 106.

idealists thought they should be. Barbara Harvey has shown how at the top end, at Westminster, monks lived, many in warm private apartments, with plenty of private property from their individual wages, and had access to vast quantities of protein.[111] Complaints about the low quality of food – especially by juniors in the refectory against seniors, who ate elsewhere more often – are indeed a consistent feature of the visitations, suggesting the worst of all worlds: the standard of personal asceticism had been almost completely relaxed, yet the administrators were not always able (or willing) to supply the religious up to their expectations. Servants were another cause of trouble, and there were plenty in monasteries (including women, some-times sleeping in); there were on average at least two domestic servants for each religious.[112] Evidence from the accounts of Thetford Cluniac Priory (exempt from episcopal jurisdiction) adds to the impression that the larger and wealthier monasteries, now supporting far fewer monks than in earlier centuries, had something of the atmosphere of gentlemen's clubs, with visiting entertainers.[113] Yet even canons in very small houses assumed that they should live in comfort: when Mountjoy Priory was reduced to a single canon in 1509, he demised the whole house to Walsingham, on condition that he be provided with 'mete and drinke and a servant to wait upon hym as a gentilman haught to have'.[114]

If monks looked little different from other clergy or even laymen, this was hardly surprising given that the barrier between the cloister and society had become almost entirely permeable.[115] Not only were there plenty of laity residing in houses and coming and going; but equally, the monks were often out, sometimes taking their leisure,[116] but also for quite legitimate administrative purposes, running the monastic economy. A good proportion of the religious held obediences: at Walsingham in

---

[111] Harvey, *Living and Dying*, pp. 34–71, 77, 117, 153, 210; Knowles, *Religious Orders*, i. 287–9; ii. 240–44; Coulton, *Five Centuries of Religion*, iii. 375–94; on a more modest scale, *Bromholm Cellarer's Account*, ed. Redstone, pp. 70–73.

[112] Harvey, *Living and Dying*, pp. 149–53, is the most recent estimate, *contra* Knowles, *Religious Orders*, iii. 260–64 (ratio of 1:1); Savine, 'English Monasteries', pp. 218–27, has 1:3; Dickens, *English Reformation*, p. 81, shows great variety, as do the figures found by the Dissolution commissioners in 1536: Jessopp, 'Norfolk Monasteries', pp. 450–63.

[113] *The Register of Thetford Priory, 1482–1540*, ed. D. Dymond (2 vols., Oxford, 1995–6), i. 47–52 and see index *s.v.* Entertainers for many references.

[114] *Catalogue of Ancient Deeds* (6 vols., London, 1890–1915), A 6056.

[115] Some worries in the visitations suggest that there was still an awareness of the need to maintain the enclosure; but the actual evidence in them and elsewhere suggests that this was an aspiration honoured in the breach.

[116] Apart from visitation evidence of drinking in the town (for example C. R. Cheney, 'Norwich Cathedral Priory in the Fourteenth Century', *BJRL* 20 (1936), pp. 16, 28; *Norwich Visitations*, ed. Jessopp, pp. 116–17, 122, 147), exercise outside the enclosure was probably normal; see J. Youings, *The Dissolution of the Monasteries* (London, 1971), p. 153; Coulton, *Five Centuries of Religion*, iv. 646–7 (St Albans); at Hickling in 1526 it was regarded as unreasonable of the prior not to allow it adequately, *Norwich Visitations*, p. 211.

1526, for instance, eleven canons held offices, leaving five others and six novices.[117] Moreover, some religious from the larger houses would have been away at the university; and not insignificant was the number serving secular cures at this period.[118] Cromwell's injunctions for religious houses in 1535 put this permeability at the top of its list of abuses: no religious were to go out, and women were not to be allowed in.[119] This produced a storm of protest, because it militated against both custom and efficient administration, but the responses are indicative of how far the ideal of separation from the world had disappeared in expectation as well as in practice.[120]

It might be said that the religious houses were at least keeping up the round of observance, their fundamental function; the visitations certainly testify to an expectation that this would be so, if they also show it failing.[121] Yet the proportion of religious within each house actually attending the offices was as low as a third (as at Westminster), because a *cursus honorum* had emerged in which the younger religious and the novices did choir work, and then proceeded to offices and ultimately retirement, which exempted them from the rigours of the liturgical round.[122] At Walsingham in 1532 (a visitation which revealed much improvement on the previous decade), one canon complained that often there were scarcely four canons on one side at matins – presumably eight in all.[123] Yet Walsingham's twenty-three canons made it one of the largest houses in its diocese; for the three quarters with a complement under twelve it must have been difficult to maintain the liturgical round at all satisfactorily. The Black Monks, indeed, made no bones about the fact that regular observance was little loved: in 1519–20 Wolsey presented reform proposals to the Augustinians and Benedictines which went back not to twelfth-century ideals, but only to the papal statutes of 1336 which

---

[117] *Norwich Visitations*, pp. 170–72; see also 314–15; the prior was absent in 1526 and Edmund Warham was sub-prior.

[118] Knowles, *Religious Orders*, ii. 14–28; J. Greatrex, 'Monk Students from Norwich Cathedral Priory at Oxford and Cambridge, c. 1300–1530', *EHR* 106 (1991), pp. 555–83. For secular cures, Swanson, *Church and Society*, p. 86; P. Heath, *The English Parish Clergy on the Eve of the Reformation* (London and Toronto, 1969), pp. 175–82; Haigh, *Reformation and Resistance*, p. 122; Baskerville, *English Monks*, pp. 151–2.

[119] First, that is, after matters touching the supremacy and succession: in full in Burnet, *History of the Reformation*, ed. Pocock, iv. 218; conveniently in Youings, *Dissolution*, p. 149.

[120] Knowles, *Religious Orders*, iii. 336–7; Youings, *Dissolution*, p. 153.

[121] Complaints are generally about non-attendance at matins, which may suggest that there was little problem elsewhere (see *Norwich Visitations*, ed. Jessopp, *passim*); but it may be that during the day religious had various reasons for not being present, which at night they did not; or it may be that non-attendance at matins was endemic, so it was easy to use at a visitation to pursue a grudge against a particular brother.

[122] Harvey, *Living and Dying*, p. 77.

[123] *Norwich Visitations*, ed. Jessopp, p. 315.

themselves institutionalized gentler standards.[124] Yet even these were said to be too rigorous for most of the monks; few would be able to follow the asceticism practised by the Carthusians, Brigittines or Observants, and few even loved 'observanciam regularem' in this sad era.[125]

The visitations and the reactions to the reform proposals of 1519–20 and 1535 offer a telling indication of how the religious houses saw themselves at this period: they were not intended to be practitioners of traditional monasticism, so much as ministers of churches, living (comfortably) within institutions which they devoted much of their energy to sustaining at an economic and administrative level. It seems plausible to suggest that churches differed from each other in practice not according to their monastic profession or order, but according to their size and function.[126] Cathedrals have already been mentioned in this context, as being primarily head-churches of their dioceses and only secondarily monasteries or secular churches. The other great monasteries similarly seem to have been more important as great churches, ruling and serving their communities, as did Westminster, St Albans and Bury.[127] They employed the same architects and the same musicians as did secular churches.[128] The fact that some survived either as new cathedrals or as secular churches emphasizes the point.[129] At a lower level, parochial functions provided another fundamental connection to the locality, and reason for (at least partial) survival, as at Wymondham and Binham in Norfolk.[130] The hoped-for conversion of some middling houses into colleges by nobles hoping to preserve their mausolea, for instance the duke of Norfolk and Thetford, again suggests that it was not the monastic nature of the church that was now important.[131] The fact that Stoke-by-Clare had indeed been converted from a monastery into a secular college more than a century earlier makes the point; it had continued to fulfil its role as head-house of the honour of Clare for its successive holders,

---

[124] Knowles, *Religious Orders*, ii. 3–4; iii. 158–60; *Monasticon Anglicanum*, ed. Caley et al., vi (ii), 851–4. Knowles dates the dialogue with Black Monks as 1521–2, but Pantin 1519–20: see next note. Gwyn, *King's Cardinal*, pp. 267–353, 464–80, offers a positive view of Wolsey's reform plans.

[125] They also said that the religious could not be recalled to 'austeritatem regularis observanciae'; *Chapters*, ed. Pantin, iii. 123–4.

[126] Thompson, 'Monasteries and Society', pp. 29–31.

[127] See n. 87; G. Rosser, *Medieval Westminster, 1200–1540* (Oxford, 1989), esp. pp. 255–63.

[128] C. Wilson, 'The Designer of Henry VII's Chapel, Westminster Abbey', and M. Williamson, 'The Eton Choirbook: Collegiate Music-Making in the Reign of Henry VII', both in *The Reign of Henry VII: Proceedings of the 1993 Harlaxton Symposium*, ed. B. J. Thompson, Harlaxton Medieval Studies 5 (Stamford, 1995), pp. 125, 133–56.

[129] Knowles, *Religious Orders*, iii. 389–92.

[130] MRH uses the symbol † to designate current ecclesiastical use (see especially the Benedictines, and, rather surprisingly less, the Augustinians); for some examples, see Rose Graham, *An Essay on English Monasteries* (HA pamphlet, 1913), pp. 36–7.

[131] LP, xiv/2. 815–16.

and was playing an important role in local ecclesiastical provision, as Parker claimed.[132] The smaller monasteries with fewer than a dozen religious may have looked like colleges and chantries.[133] Indeed there is some confusion of terminology to suggest that at this lowest level there was little to distinguish between secular or monastic churches: the secular college founded at Attleborough in 1406 was described as a prior and canons in 1492, and the Ingham Trinitarian Priory could equally be described as a college – which in effect it was – and was once claimed as a friary.[134] It was never clear what order the canons (or friars) of Peterstone belonged to.[135] When Flitcham Priory was made a cell of Walsingham in 1528–30, Wolsey seems to have conceived of it as a chantry for himself.[136]

The religious houses of later medieval England look, therefore, as if they were interchangeable with secular churches of similar size, a possibility reinforced by the easy transition which a few of them did in fact make to secular status. In so far as regular churches retained a valued role in society, this does not seem to have depended on their monastic nature or any distinct monastic ethos, so much as on the fact of their existence as local churches staffed by a number of clergy. The greater importance of monasteries to ecclesiastical provision in the north suggests precisely this.[137] The monasteries were in effect attempting to return to their early medieval function as churches that did the work of the church meeting the needs of society, religious and other. If they had not been caught up in the cataclysm of the 1530s, perhaps many would have evolved less traumatically into essentially secular churches.

Nevertheless, it is that cataclysm which is at stake here, and the contribution of the monasteries' past history and current state to it. Their problem was that it was difficult to make the transition into more open, secular institutions precisely because of the baggage of monastic identity inherited from centuries of existence. They had been founded as enclosed institutions – more or less, according to their order – and there was still a small group of

---

[132] See above, nn. 79, 105.

[133] So Thompson (*English Clergy*, pp. 162–3) suggested for the Augustinians.

[134] *Norwich Visitations*, pp. 37–8; Norwich Episcopal Registers, v, fol. 2v, viii, fol. 147; *VCH Norfolk*, ii. 411. The dean of Stoke-by-Clare was described as 'prior' by Archbishop Morton's commissary in 1499, *The Register of John Morton, Archbishop of Canterbury, 1486–1500*, ed. C. Harper-Bill, Canterbury and York Society 75, 78, 89 (1987–2000), iii. 147.

[135] *VCH Norfolk*, ii. 391; Blomefield, *Norfolk*, vi. 23–4, x. 4; *CPR, Edward III, III.1334–8*, p. 300; *John Capgrave's Lives of St Augustine and St Gilbert of Sempringham, and a Sermon*, ed. J. J. Munro, EETS, Original Series 149 (1910), p. 148.

[136] *VCH Norfolk*, ii. 397; the patron also reserved chantry-benefits, H. C. Maxwell-Lyte, *A History of Dunster* (2 vols., Exeter, 1909), i. 138.

[137] Haigh, *Reformation and Resistance*, pp. 91–2, 121–2; for a vivid snapshot, J. Burton, 'Priory and Parish: Kirkham and its Parishioners, 1496–7', in *Monasteries and Society*, ed. Thompson, pp. 329–47.

houses demonstrating that the original monastic vocation was neither dead nor unappreciated by recruits or benefactors. Reformers, therefore, including conservatives, sought to remedy their perceived problems by attempting to restore them to earlier ideals, and especially to enforce a more rigorous withdrawal from the world. Such was Colet's recommendation in 1510, and similarly Longland of Lincoln attempted to re-assert an older ideal of Benedictine practice; this was also the direction of both Wolsey's and Cromwell's reform injunctions (however insincere the latter may have been in intention).[138] The secularizing movement that was taking place quietly in practice was opposed by theoretical perceptions of what monasteries *ought* to be like. Yet it was and is equally evident that no restoration of observance was possible; it was neither desired by the religious themselves – who, it was said in 1520, would apostasize *en masse* – nor was it of much social benefit since the value of regular churches had come to depend on their openness and responsiveness to social needs, not their enclosure. The monasteries in the early sixteenth century were caught in a double bind between the reforming imperative of withdrawal, and the social imperative of integration.

This helps to explain why, despite widespread awareness of the need for reform in the early sixteenth century, the church was unable to transform the monasteries – and indeed itself – sufficiently to make the case for thorough reformation look implausible. At local level, indeed, some bishops were making efforts through visitation, and were sometimes able to eradicate the more scandalous abuses and to tighten up finance and even discipline.[139] But they were never going to get very far when the aims of reform – strengthening enclosure and observance – conflicted with lay expectations that religious houses were to serve their communities in various different ways, including at a material level. Indeed secular interference – in the guise of either worldly motivation or intervention by laymen – was often one of the reasons why churchmen found improving clerical standards difficult. Quite apart from those cases where servants (and their wives) are found lording it over monasteries, monks sometimes appealed over the heads of the visitors to undermine their authority, a problem that Longland faced in the Lincoln diocese, just as it did Pecham

---

[138] J. H. Lupton, *A Life of John Colet, D.D., Dean of St Paul's and Founder of St Paul's School: With an Appendix of some of his English Writings* (London, 1887), p. 301; Bowker, *Henrician Reformation*, pp. 17–26; see above, nn. 125–6; Burnet, *History of the Reformation*, ed. Pocock, iv. 218–22; Youings, *Dissolution*, pp. 149–52. Nikke's visitations show some concern for enclosure, *Norwich Visitations*, ed. Jessopp, after p. 65.

[139] For example Knowles, *Religious Orders*, iii. 65–75; the larger monasteries of Norfolk, the cathedral priory, St Benets, Wymondham, Westacre and Walsingham, were all found to be in a poor state, but some improvement seems to be shown if the visitations are followed through, in Jessopp's *Norwich Visitations*. Bowker, *Henrician Reformation*, pp. 17–28, emphasizes rather Longland's inability to make much headway.

and Winchelsey when they tried to visit royal free chapels.[140] Some houses were of course immune to episcopal visitation altogether. Another facet of the bishops' problem, therefore, was that they did not have the power or even authority to implement radical reform: they could only attempt to make the monasteries work on their own terms, but could not restructure them or redistribute property. The canonical inalienability of ecclesiastical property they could get round, but in England property was protected by the common law and royal authority, and could therefore only be conveyed under secular auspices. The eight small Norfolk houses that were suppressed between 1449 and 1530 required secular authorization for the redistribution of their property.[141] Indeed the English church had for centuries been particularly subject to royal protection and jurisdiction.[142] The Dissolution of the alien priories, therefore, ultimately had to be carried through by the king, and ratified in parliament.

Thoroughgoing reform therefore had to come from higher up. Wolsey was the person who had the means – as well as the motive and the opportunity – to carry it out, through combining in himself the authority of both church, as legate, and Crown, as chancellor and effective first minister.[143] It may be that he got close to doing so; his 1519–20 proposals got nowhere, and his piecemeal dissolutions did not constitute a comprehensive programme, but his proposals of 1528 were potentially more radical. Removing houses with fewer than six religious and combining those with fewer than twelve might have reduced the Norfolk monasteries from thirty-six (including houses already dissolved, but excluding friars, hospitals, colleges and cells) to fewer than ten; a not dissimilar figure of eight houses were formally exempt from the Act of 1536.[144] This programme failed because events intervened, and perhaps because Wolsey had not been committed or sincere enough; had he moved earlier, he might have had time to carry it out, but his own 'secularization' in terms of his motives in dissolving houses for his own two colleges, not to mention the pressing business of running the country, had put it down his list of priorities. The fact that secular events brought him – and his reform proposals – down pinpoints nicely the church's vulnerability to secularity and its inability to reform itself. In 1529, then, the church was still susceptible to reform, and the proposals in circulation at parliament in that

[140] For servants: *Norwich Visitations*, ed. Jessopp, pp. 101–6, 113–23. Bowker, *Henrician Reformation*, pp. 23–8; Baskerville, *English Monks*, pp. 85–94; J. H. Denton, *English Royal Free Chapels, 1100–1300: A Constitutional Study* (Manchester, 1970).

[141] Thompson, 'Monasteries and Patrons', pp. 115–16.

[142] D. Hay, 'The Church of England in the Later Middle Ages', *History* 53 (1968), pp. 35–50.

[143] Gwyn, *King's Cardinal* (as above, n. 124); for the 1528 proposals, pp. 469–71.

[144] Numbers of monks are from Jessopp's *Norwich Visitations* and the supremacy and Dissolution documents, reported in *VCH Norfolk*, ii (and recognizing that numbers at the Dissolution may have fallen recently). For income, *Valor ecclesiasticus*, iii. 281–402, tabulated at Thompson, 'Monasteries and Patrons', pp. 124–5.

year show that some sections of opinion were considering a thorough overhaul of more than the monasteries.[145]

By then, however, the ground-rules were changing and new circumstances were emerging which would ensure that reform would not be conducted against a stable background. The King's great matter increasingly cut across previous norms so that reform was taken out of the hands of the conservatives and began to take quite new directions.[146] The reform that happened in the 1530s, therefore, was not the one that might have been predicted – or even perhaps the one that was needed – on the basis of earlier developments, but was partly a product of its own particular circumstances and the pressing requirements of the time. Some aspects of what did happen to monastic life, therefore, can indeed only be explained as consequences of the lurches in policy over which Cromwell presided. The removal of the few ascetic monks was driven by political needs (their refusal to accept the supremacy), more than by any general lack of respect for their way of life, although the ruling evangelical clique was prejudiced against them. In the subsequent comprehensive elimination of regular life, many houses were removed which might otherwise have survived, some of the greater houses and the nunneries prominent among them.[147] The complete removal of churches which otherwise might have been quietly secularized, maintaining their social functions, did leave some gaps, perhaps especially in almsgiving, hospitality and ministry, and certainly in the north.[148]

Nevertheless, some features of the Dissolution are less far from what might have been expected from a measured reform based on the state of the monasteries in the 1520s. Such a reform would have judged them against the criteria of social utility and effective deployment of resources which have been used here, and which were indeed claimed in the statute of 1536 –

---

[145] Hoyle, 'Origins of the Dissolution', and for whispering at this time, *LP*, iv/3. 5416, 6011; see also 1534 proposals, Youings, *Dissolution*, pp. 145–7.

[146] Haigh, *English Reformations*, part ii.

[147] A case might also be made for the friars, although less clearly, since one may wonder whether they were really necessary as a supplement to the ministry of the secular church now that the latter was functioning effectively.

[148] Hence the Pilgrimage; Haigh, *Reformation and Resistance*, pp. 118–38; *English Reformations*, pp. 145–50; M. Bush, *The Pilgrimage of Grace: A Study of the Rebel Armies of October 1536* (Manchester, 1996), passim, for example pp. 18–19, 396–8, 413–15; and now, R. W. Hoyle, *The Pilgrimage of Grace and the Politics of the 1530s* (Oxford, 2001). Almsgiving is complicated by the prejudice of the time against the able-bodied – sturdy beggars – as in the Act of 1536 (27 Henry VIII, c. 25); Thomas Starkey, *A Dialogue between Pole and Lupset*, ed. T. F. Mayer, Camden Society, 4th Series 37 (1989), pp. 60–62, 113–17; see P. Slack, *Poverty and Policy in Tudor and Stuart England* (Harlow, 1988), pp. 116–19; but this did exempt monastic doles from its prohibitions, and Cromwell himself fed more than 200 poor twice daily at his gate; John Stow, *A Survey of London*, ed. C. L. Kingsford (2 vols., Oxford, 1908), i. 89. It is hard to see much damage in employment: the lands were taken by the nobility and gentry (who had had some control over them before).

asserting that monastic wealth would be used 'for better uses' – and the Act for Bishoprics of 1539:[149]

> Forasmuch as it is not unknown the slothful and ungodly life which hath been used amongst all those sort which have borne the name of religious folk, and to the intent that henceforth many of them might be turned to better use as hereafter shall follow, whereby God's word might the better be set forth, children brought up in learning, clerks nourished in the Universities, old servants decayed to have livings, almshouses for poor folk to be sustained in, Readers of Greek, Hebrew, and Latin to have good stipend, daily alms to be administered, mending of highways, exhibition for ministers of the Church . . .

The Act (rushed through to complement the second Suppression Act) carefully avoided quantification, and Henry VIII did not himself carry out anything like the programme that its rhetoric, or his own notes of a scheme, appear to suggest, or that humanist and commonwealth reformers had hoped for.[150] Yet many of its suggestions came about in the following decades, whether by state or private action. Some of the larger monasteries were indeed not dissolved but were secularized; not only were the monastic cathedrals so translated, but six abbeys were made into cathedrals, and a few others became great collegiate churches. As had already been happening for two centuries, the smaller houses would clearly have been removed or at least combined in any reform, and their property used for other purposes, not necessarily ecclesiastical. Even so some retained their parochial functions.[151] Once dissolutions began to take place in earnest, the property of some monasteries was in effect resumed by lay patrons as escheats (even before 1536 in the case of Montjoy), in the manner envisaged in 1285 and 1529, as if they could be more usefully deployed than in praying for long-dead ancestors.[152] Professorships, Oxbridge colleges, and schools were indeed founded on the basis of monastic property.[153] Of course much monastic property passed into lay hands (some of it to become schools, colleges and almshouses), as the Crown sold it for cash, largely to pay for war in the 1540s. Yet even this redistribution had important effects: the more substantial and numerous gentry which emerged was thus, in enlarged benches of JPs, enabled to do more work for the Crown, setting the pattern of English local government for the

[149] 31 Henry VIII, c. 9; *Statutes of the Realm*, iii. 728.
[150] *LP*, xiv/2. 429–30; J. J. Scarisbrick, *Henry VIII* (London, 1968), pp. 511–26; Brigden, *London and the Reformation*, pp. 293, 318.
[151] Above, nn. 129–30.
[152] Blomefield, *Norfolk*, viii. 228–32. At least some of the property of twelve Norfolk monasteries went to patrons, and in other cases patrons may have been involved; I shall explore this in detail elsewhere.
[153] See n. 150; note that some property privately purchased was subsequently used for schools and colleges.

following three centuries.[154] In that as well as in its more specifically ecclesiastical features, the Dissolution was therefore following the grain of earlier developments more closely than the revisionist account of the Reformation allows for.

In broader historical terms, it is important to recognize that the laity were often important in executing ecclesiastical reform. Indeed, it was often undertaken to meet their needs – – not surprisingly given that the church was shaped by those needs in the first place. Monastic foundation was no exception, with religious houses being founded not only to satisfy the vocations of the committed and ascetic, but also the social and religious needs of noble founders and other members of local society. They were therefore inevitably exposed to changing needs and changing perceptions. But precisely because the laity had significant power over the church, reforms that did happen were not necessarily those which 'should' have happened; what was done was not necessarily what some regarded as what was needed. The redistribution of ecclesiastical property was nevertheless nothing new. While laymen (and clerics) were always making grants to churches, so did lands and churches move back in the other direction from time to time, whether through Carolingian rulers, Viking marauders and settlers, Norman barons and knights – by seizure and sub-infeudation – or later medieval monastic stewards and lessees. It was normal, on a long view, for property to circulate and re-circulate between churches and laymen. Part of the difficulty in later medieval England was perhaps that the common law provided such effective protection for all property that the more informal methods of circulation were less efficacious; this may have forced a more overt redistribution, legitimized by parliament.

In the *longue durée* of ecclesiastical history, it might equally be argued that monasteries had fulfilled their historic role. Having preserved the church in the early Middle Ages and initiated the process of revival in the eleventh and twelfth centuries, and thus helped create the characteristically secular

---

[154] A somewhat speculative statement, well beyond my brief; J. H. Gleason, *The Justices of the Peace in England, 1558 to 1640* (Oxford, 1969), esp. pp. 47–52, 96–122, and index *s.v.* monastic lands; MacCulloch, *Suffolk and the Tudors*, appx. 1; A. H. Smith, *County and Court: Government and Politics in Norfolk, 1558–1603* (Oxford, 1974), pp. 76–86, appx. 1; A. Fletcher, *Reform in the Provinces: The Government of Stuart England* (New Haven, 1986), pp. 3–4. This kind of argument was a feature of older writing on the Dissolution: if Cromwell had managed to endow the Crown, there would have been no taxation, as was allegedly promised; Edward Coke, *The Fourth Part of the Institutes of the Laws of England, concerning the Jurisdiction of Courts* (1644), p. 44; Fuller, *Church-History*, p. 338; Burnet, *History of the Reformation*, ed. Pocock, i. 430–31; Collier, *Ecclesiastical History*, pp. 161, 172; Froude, *History of England*, iii. 395–6; Gasquet, *Henry VIII and Monasteries*, ii. 440–49; Pollard, *Henry VIII*, p. 341, the latter taking the argument to its logical conclusion that if the Crown had been so endowed, the Stuarts would have been independent of Parliament, although not to the further (Whig) conclusion that there would then have had to be a bloody revolution against a despotic monarchy.

church of the later Middle Ages, they had handed on the baton of ministry and written themselves out of the story. Their belated attempts to make themselves useful were problematic because they conflicted with the monastic ideal of withdrawal, just as the comfortable practice of late medieval monasticism was out of step with the ascetic ideal. Of course one cannot ignore the role of radical evangelical views – Protestantism – in the Dissolution as it actually occurred. But even these would seem to fit the rhythms of the church's long history. Theologically, the role of the church has been to challenge society and make it uncomfortable, not to fit in with its needs and desires, at its behest. When the church fits too comfortably into the society it serves, as the recent revisionist, now orthodox, account of the late medieval church suggests, demands for reform are bound to emerge in some sections of ecclesiastical opinion. Indeed, this caught the church in another double-bind: in responding to lay needs and demands it 'secularized' itself, yet this made it vulnerable to reform precisely on those grounds. (Alternatively, it may equally be that secularization prolonged the monasteries' life precisely because it suited the laity). It is easy to fasten onto the mendacity of the dramatic – indeed over-dramatic – periods of the Act of 1536, and to ignore the fact that it was framed by laymen and clergy inspired by new religious ideals. Such men were as yet in a minority, as the long and complicated history of the subsequent Reformations would show. But with respect to the religious houses, they were able to draw enough support from other sections of opinion, and from the historical development of the monasteries, to effect their purpose quickly.

The Planning of Cistercian Monasteries in the Later Middle Ages: the Evidence from Fountains, Rievaulx, Sawley and Rushen

GLYN COPPACK

The problem with our knowledge of Cistercian planning is that almost all research has concentrated on the first fifty years of the order's existence, a time when monastic life was being returned to Benedictine purity and the architecture, size, and form of the community was being re-thought; and on the great surviving twelfth-century ruins typified in Yorkshire by Rievaulx, Fountains, Kirkstall and Byland. One could be forgiven for looking at these sites and thinking that Cistercian life and aspirations did not change much between 1150 and 1539. Certainly early buildings were retained, and indeed many of them are still there. Part of our problem is how ruins are read, another part is the fact that surviving ruins are only a fragment of what was built, and yet another part is how later medieval documentary sources relate to both surviving and lost buildings. Remarkably, the period with the best documentation has been the worst studied in terms of how buildings were used, almost certainly because the best documentation seems to relate to those sites which no longer survive above ground.[1]

Our interpretation of how Cistercian abbeys functioned still relies heavily on William St John Hope's analysis of Fountains Abbey developed in the 1890s[2] and largely disregards any of the evidence of suppression period surveys which described living organisms, albeit often in terms of the estate agent or dealer in scrap metals, that indicate something very different. We have, in fact, failed to understand that Cistercian buildings were capable of radical changes of use, even though we understand that historic buildings generally have only survived because they could be adapted to constantly changing needs. Why should Cistercian buildings be different?

There was also a plethora of Cistercian new-build from the late fifteenth century, highly significant in itself though little of it survives. Exceptions were Thomas Chard's work at Forde, where a new abbot's house was built to

---

[1] For a typical series of suppression period surveys see W. Brown, 'Descriptions of the Buildings of Twelve Small Yorkshire Priories at the Reformation', *Yorkshire Archaeological Journal* 9 (1886), pp. 197–215 and pp. 321–33.

[2] W. H. St John Hope, 'Fountains Abbey', *Yorkshire Archaeological Journal* 15 (1900), pp. 269–402.

the west of the cloister,[3] and David Juyner's south range at Cleeve, which was rebuilt in a style that was very un-Cistercian but appears to owe a lot to the planning of canons' houses.[4] Both were remarkable buildings, and to these we should add Leyshon Thomas's remodelling of the church at Neath,[5] and William Angel's rebuilding of the church at Sawtry,[6] both now lost to sight. What does this late renaissance tell us about Cistercian life? In this chapter, recent research on four sites, picked almost at random,[7] throws considerable light on how the planning of Cistercian monasteries began to change from the fourteenth century in terms that mark developing liturgy, the modification of communal life following the demise of the lay-brothers, and the development of the necessary economic infrastructure to support a changed community.

To begin at the beginning, early Cistercian planning was based on the requirement to house two separate communities within the same monastery. To take the case of Fountains, the house had roughly 120 choir monks and 400 lay-brothers when its buildings reached their maximum extent in the 1170s.[8] The east range housed the monks, with their own infirmary to the east and refectory to the west, the west range housed the lay-brothers, and again had its own infirmary. The church was effectively split in two by the rood screen, the lay-brothers' choir being in the nave, the monks' choir in the crossing. So separated were the two communities that they even had their own discrete water supplies. By the 1330s, however, the lay-brothers had ceased to be a significant part of the community, and yet their buildings were retained at their original scale. They must have been capable of re-use because otherwise there was no reason to maintain them and they are still there. Of course, the change is wider than the central buildings – the loss of the lay-brothers required the Cistercians to change their estate management centred on the outer court of the monastery, with the importation of lay servants and even women, and the modification or even demolition of service buildings once central to monastic life.

Starting with liturgy, the church at Fountains (Fig. 1) provides the classic

<hr/>

[3] For the most recent treatment of Forde Abbey see D. Robinson, 'Forde Abbey', in *The Cistercians in Britain*, ed. Robinson (London, 1998), pp. 109–10. See also the entry for Forde Abbey in *RCHME, Dorset 1* (London, 1952), pp. 240–46.
[4] R. Gilyard-Beer, *Cleeve Abbey* (London, 1990), pp. 32–7.
[5] D. Robinson, 'Neath Abbey', in *Cistercians in Britain*, ed. Robinson, pp. 149–50.
[6] G. Coppack, 'Sawtry Abbey', in *Cistercians in Britain*, ed. Robinson, p. 172; S. I. Ladds, 'Sawtry Abbey, Huntingdonshire', *Cambridge and Huntingdon Archaeological Society Transactions* 3 (1914), p. 372.
[7] The common factor is my own research, at the behest of English Heritage and Manx National Heritage, carried out to enable conservation and presentation of publicly maintained monuments. What is significant is that all four sites display consistent evidence of late medieval re-planning.
[8] The number of monks and lay-brothers at Fountains is assessed in G. Coppack, *Fountains Abbey* (London, 1993), pp. 30–31 where the method of calculation based on the dimensions of the dormitories is fully described.

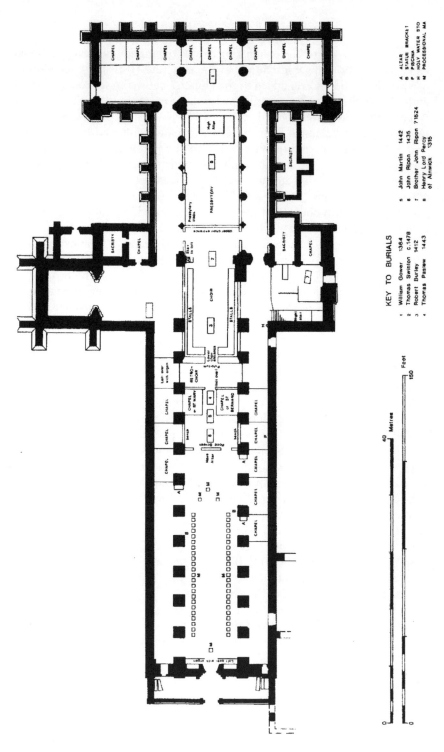

Fig. 1 The church at Fountains Abbey as it was organized at the suppression.

example of how a late Cistercian church was organized. However hard you look, there is no sign of alteration to the structure (with the exception of new windows and a tower added to the church), yet we know from historical sources that the church was replanned at least twice, once in the 1460s by Abbot John Greenwell[9] and between 1492 and c.1520 by Abbots John Darnton and Marmaduke Huby.[10] This is actually confirmed by excavation in the south transept and the fact that both Darnton and Huby signed their work with a rebus (and in Darnton's case with the dates 1492 and 1494). The removal of the lay-brothers' choir provided the excuse for using the nave for processions, and the aisles, originally mere passages, could be partitioned to form chapels, either as chantries or additional altar space for ordained monks to say mass. The plan can be reconstructed from the sockets cut into the masonry for screens, and in the south transept from excavation. This was a major undertaking: the nave and transepts were provided for the first time with tile floors, and a groat of Edward IV found in the bedding of the south transept floor indicates that this was done after 1457. Remarkably, the planning of the monks' choir and presbytery was little changed. What was changed, however, was the whole tenor of the church. Organs great and small appeared, as had happened at Meaux in 1396,[11] processional markers were laid in the floor of the nave, and from 1412 president burials were ranged along the axis of the church. The latest changes were even more structural. John Darnton re-windowed the gables of the church and the nave aisles and took down the vaults over the presbytery and provided new roofs of lower pitch. Marmaduke Huby commissioned new choir stalls, and both he and Darnton appear to have re-glazed large parts of the church. Fountains in the 1520s would have resembled Leyshon Thomas's church at Neath with 'crystal windows of every colour . . . a gold adorned choir, the nave, the gilded tabernacle work, the pinnacles . . . a vast and lofty roof'.[12] What it did not resemble was a Cistercian church of the twelfth and early thirteenth centuries. It even gained a monumental bell-tower, its string courses relieved with texts from the Cistercian breviary which conveniently contained the abbot's motto *Soli Deo honor et gloria* but that possibly tells us more about Marmaduke Huby (and possibly his contemporaries of Shap, Bolton, and Furness who were also building great bell-towers) than it does about the Cistercians in the late fifteenth century.

If the planning of the church had changed, so had the lifestyle of the monks. The great infirmary hall (Fig. 2) of the early thirteenth century was, by 1400, partitioned into a series of ten to twelve two-storey 'bed-sits' each

[9] J. R. Walbran, *Memorials of the Abbey of St Mary of Fountains I*, Surtees Society 42 (1862), p. 152. See also R. Gilyard-Beer and G. Coppack, 'Excavations at Fountains Abbey, North Yorkshire, 1979–80: The Early Development of the Monastery', *Archaeologia* 108 (1986), pp. 160–62.

[10] Ibid.

[11] P. Fergusson, *The Architecture of Solitude* (Princeton, 1984), p. 38.

[12] Robinson, 'Neath Abbey', pp. 149–52.

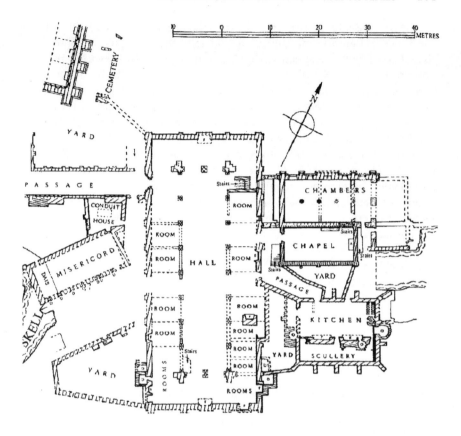

Fig. 2 The thirteenth-century infirmary hall at Fountains Abbey with evidence of partitioning into individual chambers with latrines (D) and hearths (F)

with a hearth and latrine. At Byland, the infirmary was demolished at this date and its materials used to build a similar series of 'bachelor apartments',[13] and similar arrangements can be seen at Kirkstall,[14] Waverley,[15] and Tintern.[16] While this appears to have begun as an increase of privacy for the sick, it is fairly obvious that as communities shrank, the senior members withdrew to the infirmary where they enjoyed greater privacy and comfort in their own cells. By 1500, a misericord had been added to the infirmary and any pretence that this was still the infirmary was lost. The dormitory

[13] S. Harrison, *Byland Abbey: North Yorkshire* (London, 1990), p. 15.

[14] W. H. St John Hope, 'Kirkstall Abbey', *Publications of the Thoresby Society* 16 (1907), pp. 38–40.

[15] For a reconsideration of Hope and Brakspear's excavation of the infirmary at Waverley see G. Coppack, *Abbeys and Priories* (London, 1990), pp. 77–8.

[16] D. Robinson, *Tintern Abbey* (Cardiff, 1995), pp. 64–6.

remained in use, and the night stair into the church was rebuilt in stone in the 1460s to demonstrate this. Unfortunately, the east range is too heavily ruined to tell what happened there, but if we turn to Rievaulx, the vast dormitory built for 200 monks was shortened to half its length and partitioned into cells, some with large windows and even window seats, providing similar accommodation to that seen in the infirmary at Fountains. The same can still be seen in a seventeenth-century context in the French abbeys of Royaumont and Noirlac.

Perhaps the clearest indicator is the development of a substantial abbot's house, as we have seen in Thomas Chard's work at Forde, and which was a remarkably common development from the fifteenth century. The abbots of Fountains developed a modest house attached to the end of the monks' latrines from the 1160s, and this remained remarkably modest until the late fifteenth century (Fig. 3). It was Marmaduke Huby (or just possibly John Darnton) who rebuilt it on a monumental scale, cannibalizing earlier buildings by appropriating their use. The section of the old monks' dormitory over the chapter house was converted to a chapel, accessed from a long gallery formed over the thirteenth-century passage to the infirmary, and a chamber was created within the east end of the now largely redundant monks' latrine. The abbot's household was expanding at the expense of the shrinking convent, something quite unthinkable to the early Cistercians. A single new building was erected, the 'nova camera versus ecclesiam' or 'churche chamber' where so many of Huby's charters and leases were witnessed, a permanent office for the abbot's secretariat. Effectively, both abbot and monks had withdrawn to the eastern part of the claustral nucleus, and it is perhaps significant that there is no evidence whatsoever for modifications to the south or west ranges after the early fourteenth century. We know from late leases that the warming house was used after c.1500 for the storage of cheese for instance.[17]

Just as significant as what was being built was what was being taken down in the later Middle Ages. The largest building in the precinct apart from central ranges was the abbey woolhouse,[18] a vast aisled warehouse with attached offices. Its primary use did not survive the restructuring of the abbey estates that followed the Scottish incursions after Bannockburn and the demise of the lay-brothers. First it was cannibalized to provide a fulling mill and perhaps a dye-house for the preparation of cloth, and later it was used by Greenwell as the location of the workshops of the glaziers, smiths, and bronze workers employed on his restoration of the church. Then redundant, it was simply demolished in the 1480s as surplus to requirements. Quite clearly, useless buildings were unlikely to survive as late as the suppression because they were not worth the expense of maintenance. Such a process

---

[17] D. H. Michelmore, 'The Fountains Abbey Lease Book', Yorkshire Archaeological Society, Record Series 140 (1981), p. xxvi.

[18] G. Coppack, 'The Excavation of an Outer Court Building, perhaps the Woolhouse, at Fountains Abbey, North Yorkshire', *Medieval Archaeology* 30 (1986), pp. 46–87.

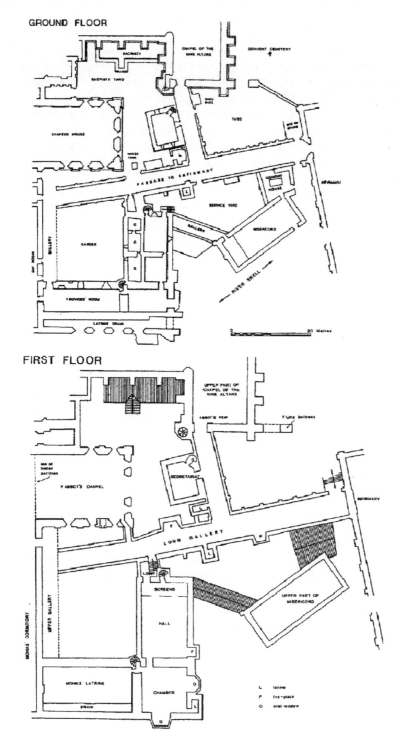

GROUND FLOOR

FIRST FLOOR

Fig. 3 The abbot's house at Fountains Abbey, largely built by Abbots
Darnton and Huby between 1490 and 1510.

might explain why the guest hall in the inner court was demolished but the nearby lay-brothers' infirmary was retained even though there were no longer any lay-brothers, almost certainly to replace it. Was the west range remodelled to provide extensive guest apartments?

What we can see happening at Fountains in the archaeological record was also happening at Rievaulx where it is well documented in suppression period surveys compiled for Thomas Manners, first earl of Rutland, in 1538–9 as a stage in his efforts to realize the value of his purchase.[19] Rutland's steward Ralf Baude had known Rievaulx as a working institution, and his descriptions of its buildings provide an exceptional insight into the planning of a late Cistercian monastery and the use of its spaces. As at Fountains, the church was remodelled, and we have not only the dedications of the altars that were set up, but details of the furnishings of their chapels and high altar. In Abbot Henry Burton's chantry, for instance, there was a retable with images of Our Lady, the Trinity, and St Margaret. We even have the location of the cope chest in the south aisle of the presbytery, and a bookcase, lacking its books, just inside the eastern processional door. The value of the Rievaulx surveys is that they paint a complete picture, and not always that which the ruins themselves seem to imply. The old lay-brothers' dormitory, for instance, was a granary associated with the bakehouse and brewhouse in the inner court immediately to the west, and the southern half of the east range had been converted to the abbey tannery. Service buildings (Fig. 4) which are no longer visible, lost below 1920s landscaping or the present village, provided for the convent smith and plumber, as well as the tanner, and there were three mills, a corn mill, a fulling mill, and the iron smithy. In all there were over forty buildings outside the church and claustral ranges; corrody houses in the outer court, chapels by the gate and in the monastic cemetery, an inner and outer gate house, guest accommodation, the swine house, the common stable, indeed every office necessary to the smooth running of a large institution. The same buildings can be traced at Fountains in the earthworks of the outer court, and indeed are common to all monastic houses. Religious life, like collegiate life, required sustenance, no less in the later Middle Ages than it did in the early years of the order, but historians and archaeologists have tended to overlook service provision even though over 80% of every monastery was non-religious in its focus. Rievaulx provides the clearest indication of how this was organized in the century before the suppressions.

As at Fountains, the most obvious change in the claustral nucleus took place on its eastern side, where the great mid-twelfth-century infirmary was

---

[19] These documents were first discussed in G. Coppack, 'Some Descriptions of Rievaulx Abbey in 1538–9: The Disposition of a Major Cistercian Precinct', *Journal of the British Archaeological Association* 139 (1986), pp. 100–33. Further research by Coppack, including the identification of the author and revision of some earlier conclusions is included in P. Fergusson and S. Harrison, *Rievaulx Abbey: Community, Architecture, Memory* (New Haven and London, 1999), pp. 175–86 and 226–37.

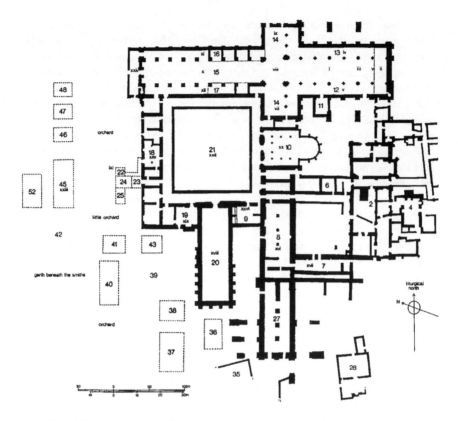

Fig. 4 The claustral nucleus at Rievaulx in its late medieval form from surviving ruins and a series of surveys made at the suppression in 1538–9.

converted to an abbot's house of remarkable scale and complexity. Ruination has left a complicated series of walls at ground-floor level which would be unintelligible without Ralf Baude's descriptions, for the bulk of the abbot's accommodation was at first-floor level and like its contemporary at Fountains simply has not survived. The hall had a great central fireplace; to the south were chambers for the abbot's household; to the north the abbot's great chamber above his parlour, and to the north of these three little wainscot chambers, one of which was a lobby to the chapel. To the west of the upper end of the hall was a long gallery extending up to the east range of the cloister. As at Fountains, there was a 'church chamber' that contained the abbot's secretariat, but at Rievaulx the abbot also had his own kitchen and a private dining room. The planning of these two abbot's houses at the turn of the sixteenth century confirm the rising status of Cistercian abbots at the expense of their convents. In both cases, the houses were built by abbots who were noted as capable administrators responsible for improved religious life and slowly expanding communities.

So far, we have been looking at two exceptional monasteries. Both Fountains and Rievaulx were large and wealthy houses with extensive estates. Their late medieval planning might not be typical if it was not confirmed by two of the poorer Cistercian monasteries, Sawley in Craven, and Rushen on the Isle of Man, probably the smallest medieval Cistercian abbey to be built. Sawley was a grand-daughter of Fountains established on a poor site and poorly endowed in 1147. It began in a grand enough style, but was slow to develop and reduced the scale of its buildings and its cloister as it developed up to about 1250.[20] If it had stopped there it would not have been so interesting, but it began a major reconstruction in the late fourteenth century which is quite remarkable. Sawley suffered badly from the Scots' incursions of the early fourteenth century, and had only fifteen monks and two lay-brothers in 1381, significantly John del Barkhowse and Robert del Brewhowse, probably lay servants rather than real lay-brothers.[21] The abbot had been living in the traditional location to the east of the dormitory in a small house of c.1200. After 1350, he moved his establishment into the west range now vacated by the lay-brothers, occupying the first floor. Although it has been destroyed completely, its plan can be reconstructed from the alterations necessitated at ground level to support the first-floor structures in a range that was not vaulted. The hall is marked by an oriel window that lit its upper end, and by the walls of its screens passage to the south. A stair from the convent kitchen led to the service rooms of the house below the screens, and the old outer parlour at the north end of the range was vaulted to carry the abbot's chapel. The intervening space must have been his chamber. In the late fifteenth century, a new kitchen was built to the west of the range, marking the abbot's effective separation from the rest of the community and the development of a household centred on the inner court, an almost exact parallel for Thomas Chard's development at Forde after 1500.

The building of a new abbot's house is not exceptional, though it does show that the Cistercians had begun the abandonment of the close association between president and community by the late fourteenth century. Sawley, though, was remarkably changed in the late fourteenth century, for its church (Fig. 5) was rebuilt in a curious but perhaps not atypical way. The greater part of the nave was demolished, and a new presbytery built. The stub of the nave was no more than a grand porch to a church which began with a transept at the centre of which was the

[20] G. Coppack, C. Hayfield and R. Williams, 'Sawley Abbey: The Architecture and Archaeology of a Smaller Cistercian Abbey', *Journal of the British Archaeological Association* (forthcoming).

[21] PRO, Clerical Subsidy 63/12. See also J. McNulty, 'Constitutions for the Reform of the Cistercian Order, 1334', *Transactions of the Lancashire and Cumberland Antiquarian Society*, 57 (1943), p. 165, n. 26. See also J. McNulty, 'Who was William Staynford, Abbot?', *Transactions of the Lancashire and Cheshire Historical Society* 54 (1940), p. 206, n. 4.

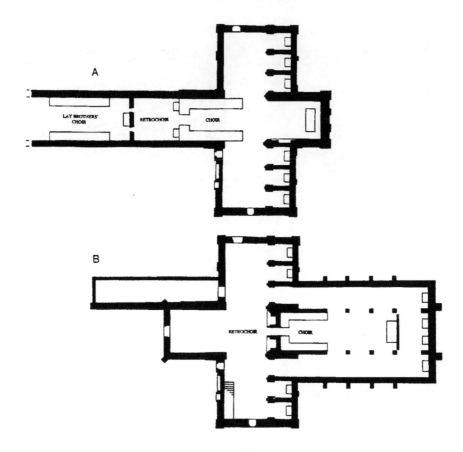

Fig. 5 The unaisled mid- to late-twelfth-century church at Sawley (A) was rebuilt in the late fourteenth century with a new aisled presbytery and no nave (B)

retrochoir. Clearly, with the demise of the lay-brothers the nave was no longer thought worth retaining for a small and fairly poor community, and all the effort was concentrated on a new aisled presbytery of five bays. The architectural detail that survives from this building suggests that it was a very grand structure, a fact that implies that poverty was not the motivation for the rebuilding, but that changing needs had led to the re-planning and that at Sawley we are seeing the plan that best served the Cistercians' needs in the late fourteenth century. Sadly, nobody has looked elsewhere for this kind of re-planning, but it may well explain the description of several churches, such as Garendon[22], being partly ruined at the suppression.

Rushen Abbey (Fig. 6) was a tiny monastery built by Olaf, King of Man, as

[22] For the most recent treatment of Garendon, see D. Robinson, 'Garendon Abbey', in *Cistercians in Britain*, ed. Robinson, pp. 119–20.

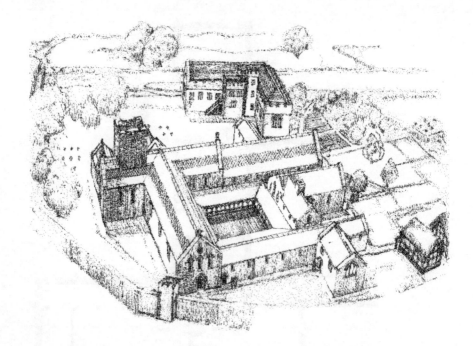

Fig. 6 A reconstruction of Rushen Abbey from the north west showing the abbot's house to the east of the cloister buildings and the late medieval bell-tower in the north transept (Brian Byron for Manx National Heritage).

a royal mausoleum from the mid-twelfth century, and but for its scale it is quite unexceptional. Like Sawley, it appears to have failed to develop as originally intended, but settled down to a fairly standard existence until the later Middle Ages. In the late fourteenth century, however, something remarkable happened. A new and substantial abbot's house was built to the east of the east range, with a north–south hall at first-floor level, and with a chamber block on three floors to its south, buildings which survive almost to full height though they have only recently been recognized and interpreted. Rushen was a daughter-house of Furness, and it perhaps comes as no surprise that its new abbot's house parallels a similar if somewhat grander development there.[23] The building is complicated by its post-suppression remodelling which includes a dovecote converted from a tower against the west wall of the hall, and only two medieval windows now survive, but it was a building of the finest quality, providing the abbot with accommodation on a

[23] J. C. Dickinson, *Furness Abbey: Cumbria* (London, 1987), pp. 10–11. Almost certainly the building traditionally interpreted as the infirmary at Furness (ibid., pp. 10–11) is the later medieval abbot's house.

scale that was remarkable compared with the compact cloister ranges occupied by the rest of the community.

Furness was probably the impetus for the other late medieval development at Rushen, the building of a bell-tower that occupied the greater part of the north transept of the diminutive church, an area previously given over to the necropolis of the Kings of Man. It effectively made the north transept inaccessible from the church and indicated that status had begun to modify liturgical needs.

What these four houses have demonstrated is that there is considerable evidence for the development of Cistercian planning in the later Middle Ages which is every bit as important as the developments of the first half of the twelfth century, but which has largely been ignored by scholars because it is difficult to reconstruct and because it requires the combined skills of historian, archaeologist, and architectural historian. These later buildings provided the framework of religious life for monks about whom we know far more than their twelfth-century predecessors, men who were very aware of their identity and 'religion', something their buildings were reshaped to reflect.

Dissolution

Departure from the Religious Life During the Royal Visitation of the Monasteries, 1535–1536

F. Donald Logan

Close on the heels of the declaration of the King's supremacy over the church came the appointment of Henry VIII's secretary, Thomas Cromwell, as the King's vicar general (or vicegerent) for a visitation of the English church. The letters patent of Cromwell's appointment bear the date 21 January [1535]. They commissioned him with the authority to visit throughout the realm 'each and every church, even metropolitan, cathedral and collegiate churches, as well as hospitals, monasteries both of men and of women, priories, preceptories, dignities, offices, houses and other ecclesiastical places'.[1] Envisioned as a visitation of the entire English church, the visitation, at least in its first stages, was confined almost exclusively to the religious houses of England and Wales. Also visited were the cathedral churches (e.g. Lichfield and York), collegiate churches (e.g. Beverley, Ripon) and the universities of Oxford and Cambridge; the houses of the friars were not included in the visitation.[2] This phase of the general visitation lasted seven months, from late July 1535 until 28 February 1536, and it is generally, if not accurately, called the Visitation of the Monasteries.[3] During the course of this visitation a number of religious departed the religious life. This chapter directs its attention to the general issues concerning departure from the religious life during this visitation. But first a prefatory word about dispensations.

When Pope Innocent III was asked in 1202 whether monks could be dispensed from their vows, he replied that not even the Roman Pontiff

---

I am grateful to Peter Cunich, Barbara Harvey and A. N. Shaw for reading drafts of this chapter and for offering useful suggestions.

[1] My translation from the Latin original PRO, C82/692: calendared in *LP*, viii. 75.1. For Cromwell's appointment see F. D. Logan, 'Thomas Cromwell and the Vicegerency in Spirituals: A Revisitation', *EHR* 103 (1988), pp. 658–67.

[2] For the visitation of the universities see F. D. Logan, 'The First Royal Visitation of the English Universities, 1535', *EHR* 106 (1991), pp. 861–88.

[3] The *locus classicus* on the visitation is Knowles, *Religious Orders*, iii. cap. 22. Other more recent discussions are G. W. O. Woodward, *The Dissolution of the Monasteries* (London, 1966), pp. 30–41, and J. Youings, *The Dissolution of the Monasteries* (London, 1971), pp. 37–41.

himself could so dispense, since the vows of poverty and chastity are essentially inherent to the religious life.[4] Others were to take a different view. Pope Innocent IV, writing as canonist and not as pope, held that for a good and serious reason the pope indeed could dispense, since implicit in every vow is the phrase 'unless it pleases God otherwise' ('nisi aliter deo placeat'), and who could know better what pleases God than the Roman Pontiff.[5] This became the common view of canonists. Although a few cases can be cited where reasons of state were involved, dispensations were virtually never granted, that is, until the mid-1390s. At that time the pope of the Roman Obedience, deprived, as he was, of substantial revenues because of the Schism, opened up what was almost a market in papal privileges, and among them was a dispensation for male religious. This dispensation, in effect, allowed a religious to live as a secular priest, provided he could obtain a benefice. Modern canonists would call this 'exclaustration', that is, a religious was still a religious technically but could live *extra claustrum*, no longer bound to poverty or to obedience to his religious superiors. Popes granted well over 800 such dispensations for English religious during the course of the long fifteenth century. In England the synonym 'capacity' was frequently used for this dispensation.[6] This type of dispensation pertains to the present subject because, when the monasteries were emptied of their inhabitants in the late 1530s, each religious was to be provided with a capacity, granted not by papal authority but by royal authority through the Faculty Office, set up at Lambeth Palace in 1534.[7]

To return to the Visitation of the Monasteries in 1535–6, we should ask what provisions were made for departure of religious from the religious life at this time. The injunctions drawn up for the visitation said nothing directly on this point, yet one injunction was to be the hinge on which policy was to be hung:

> No man be suffered to profess or to wear the habit of religion in the house 'ere he be 24 years of age completed.[8]

All that this injunction says is that no man under the age of twenty-four can make religious profession. On the face of it, it seems to be an injunction *ad*

---

[4] His response appears in the decretals of Gregory IX (*Liber extra*), bk. 3, tit. 35, c. 6 (*Corpus iuris canonici*, ed. E. L. Richter and E. Friedberg (2 vols., Leipzig, 1881), vol. 2, col. 600). For dispensation in general see J. Brys, *De dispensatione in iure canonico praesertim apud decretistas et decretalistas usque ad medium saeculum decimum quartum* (Bruges, 1925), especially, pp. 209–20.

[5] *Commentaria . . . super libros quinque decretalium* (Frankfurt, 1570), bk. 3, tit. 35, c. 6.

[6] For a fuller exposition of this matter see F. D. Logan, *Runaway Religious in Medieval England, c.1240–1540* (Cambridge, 1996), pp. 54–67.

[7] This process is fully described in *Faculty Office Registers, 1534–49*, ed. D. F. Chambers (Oxford, 1966), pp. xlii–lviii.

[8] *Concilia*, ed. Wilkins, iii. 791. Here and elsewhere in this chapter quotations from vernacular sources are silently modernized as to spelling and punctuation.

futurum. It made no mention of those religious already professed but under twenty-four and no mention of those who had professed when under this age but who were now older.[9] In its strictest reading, it applies merely to those under twenty-four who have not yet been professed. The visitors faced three questions: What to do about male professed religious who were under the age of twenty-four? What to do about female religious in the same situation? and what to do about religious, male and female, now over twenty-four who had professed while under this age? Confusion about these matters was not settled until nearly the end of the year.

In the first months of the visitation, the ambiguity of the injunctions led to a variety of interpretations by the visitors. John ApRice (or Price) was in favour of requiring all professed religious, even nuns, under the age of twenty-four to leave, whereas Thomas Legh allowed under-aged male religious – but not female – the choice to stay or leave and Richard Layton allowed the choice to male and apparently female religious. All seem to have expelled young religious, sometimes those under twenty years of age and sometimes those under twenty-two. By late October 1535 Cromwell had indicated the policy now to be followed: expel all under twenty and allow those between twenty and twenty-four of either sex the choice to stay or to leave.[10]

An undated petition, which may have predated Cromwell's new instructions, described the situation at the Poor Clare nunnery at London and underlined the human consequences of an unclear policy. Five nuns were forcibly expelled from their house: Jane Gowring, aged twenty-three and a half, Frances Somer, aged twenty-one, Mary Pilbeam, also aged twenty-one, and Barbara Lark, aged twenty, all professed, and Bridget Stravyn, aged fifteen, who was not yet professed. These nuns begged Cromwell to allow all of them to return to their house, the professed either as professed or to be professed again when they reached twenty-four. They also asked Cromwell what would happen to Margaret Fitzgared, a girl of twelve, who was deaf and dumb, and to Julian Heron, aged thirteen, who was an idiot fool. One of the visitors, perhaps John ApRice, had been intent on expelling all the

---

[9] The injunctions themselves give no reasons for using twenty-four as the age for profession. That age may have been used since it was the canonical age for ordination to the priesthood. Twenty-four was fixed by Pope Clement V (1305–14) as were the ages for other orders (twenty for the diaconate and eighteen for the subdiaconate). The text appears in the Clementine Constitutions, bk. 1, tit. 6, c. 3 (*Corpus iuris canonici*, vol. 2, col. 1140). In addition to the injunctions there was prepared an elaborate questionnaire of seventy-four questions with an additional twelve questions for nuns (*Concilia*, ed. Wilkins, iii. 786–91), but there is no reason to think that the visitors routinely used more than a few of these questions.

[10] The principal texts are *LP*, ix. 423, 622, 651, 661. The abbot of Winchcombe, writing to Cromwell, about 8 September 1535, wanted to know if 'he may admit any person so disposed to prove himself in the habit and religion till he be 24 years of age and then to be at his liberty to depart or to tarry in religion' (PRO, SP1/100, fol. 139v) (fol. 118v, new foliation); *LP*, ix. 1170). No response survives.

inhabitants of the London Poor Clares under the age of twenty-four, even poor unfortunates.[11] As late as 25 November the prior of Christ Church, Canterbury, was said to be holding six under-aged monks who wished to leave.[12] Cromwell must have thought that his new instructions had resolved the issues raised by these cases, which, indeed, they seemed to have, but another issue was still to be faced.

On 21 October Dr Legh asked Cromwell the question which was to cause a radical change: what should he do about those religious over the age of twenty-four who wished to leave their vows?[13] What should he do with religious like the half-dozen nuns at Denny Abbey near Cambridge, who 'kneeling on their knees, holding up their hands, desire to be delivered of such religion as they have ignorantly taken on'?[14] He had already reported that ten canons of Merton Priory in Surrey wished to leave.[15] At Swaffham Bulbeck, again near Cambridge, all the nuns would leave, 'if we would let them'.[16] On 5 November ApRice reported that at Bury St Edmunds eight monks under the age of twenty-four had left but five others over this age would leave, if they could.[17] Two weeks later Legh, still waiting for an answer, told Cromwell that two of the five monks at Horsham St Faith Priory in Norfolk want to leave, 'whom I have stayed until I know further your pleasure'.[18] Other visitors confronted the same problem. On 12 December Richard Layton reported that many of the brethren at Syon Abbey were 'right weary of their habit', but he did not dismiss them.[19] But by Christmas Legh had either overcome his scruples or had fresh instructions, for he reportedly allowed half the monks of Sawtrey Abbey in Huntingdon to depart. Several weeks later another visitor was nearby at Ramsey Abbey and took much abuse from two of the monks who wanted to leave and whom he refused to accommodate. They cited what had happened at Sawtrey only five miles away and the visitors relented.[20] Some time towards the end of 1535 there was a change in practice that now allowed any religious to be

11 PRO, SP1/99, fol. 233v (fol. 212v, new foliation); LP, ix. 1075. This house was probably visited in late September. All of these returned to their nunnery and are mentioned in the pension list of 3 April 1539 (LP, xiv/1. 680).

12 PRO, SP1/99, fol. 97v (fol. 85v, new foliation; LP, ix. 879). Richard Layton arrived at Canterbury on 23 October (LP, ix. 668–9); for a summary of the itinerary of the visitors see Knowles, Religious Orders, iii. 476–7, but see n. 2 infra concerning the need of revision.

13 PRO, SP1/98, fols. 47–8 (fols. 40–41, new foliation); LP, ix. 651.

14 PRO, SP1/98, fol. 84 (fol. 71, new foliation); LP, ix. 964.

15 PRO, SP1/97, fol. 59 (fol. 47, new foliation); LP, ix. 472.

16 PRO, SP1/98, fol. 110 (fol. 94, new foliation); LP, ix. 708.

17 Three Chapters of Letters Relating to the Suppression of the Monasteries, ed. T. Wright, Camden Society 26 (1843), pp. 85–6; also in G. H. Cook, Letters to Cromwell and others on the Suppression of the Monasteries (London, 1965), pp. 65–6; LP, ix. 772.

18 PRO, SP1/99, fol. 69 (fol. 60, new foliation); LP, ix. 849.

19 Three Chapters, ed. Wright, pp. 47–9; also in Cook, Letters, pp. 71–2; LP, ix. 954.

20 Three Chapters, ed. Wright, pp. 98–100; LP, x. 103. For the capacities given to the two monks see Faculty Office Registers, ed. Chambers, p. 45.

dispensed from the vows of religion. This was the practice followed by visitors for the northern visitation, which began in late December and was to last for two months. During the visitation of the north the monastery gates were now wide open for anyone of either sex and of any age to leave. What happened?

Before answering that question, a further word should be said about dispensations available to religious during the visitation and also a word about the *comperta*. Two types of dispensations were in use at this time. First, there were the traditional dispensations, granted since the 1390s by papal authority and now, since 1534, by royal authority through the Faculty Office at Lambeth Palace; these were recorded in a register that survives intact today, with not a single folio missing. Still, there was another way. We know of religious who were granted permission to leave and whose names are not in this register. How were they dispensed? The powers given by the King to Cromwell as vicar general were very broadly drawn and clearly gave him the power to dispense, a power he could delegate to the actual visitors.[21] The visitor at Ramsey Abbey told the two discontented monks that they could have 'licence to go from their cloister by the King's gracious authority or else have licence to repair to my lord of Canterbury to seek capacities': thus, dispensation either from Cromwell or from the archbishop (i.e. the Faculty Office).[22] The abbot of Hailes in Gloucestershire wrote to Cromwell that one of his monks 'had licence of you to depart and is gone'; this monk of Hailes does not appear in the Faculty Office register.[23] And at St Osyth's Abbey in Essex the visitor advised an unhappy canon to approach Cromwell to be dispensed.[24] Also there is the curious case of Richard Underwood (alias Lopham), a monk of Norwich Cathedral Priory, who was allowed by royal decree to live as a secular priest and who subsequently sought a capacity from the Faculty Office.[25] How many dispensations to leave were given by Cromwell and the visitors for which no reference survives one can only guess: perhaps a few score, perhaps a few hundred. We are on firmer ground when it comes to capacities granted by the Faculty Office. Although the visitation began in late July 1535, the first capacity was given on 20 October, then 10 during the month of November, 8 in December, 7 in January, 15 in February, 8 in March and 16 in April.

---

[21] 'Tibi . . . plenamque tenore presencium potestatis concedimus potestatem . . . dantes Thome Cromwell vicemgerenti, vicario generali et commissario nostro huiusmodi plenam et liberam tenore presencium potestatem et auctoritatem alium vel alios commissarium siue commissarios ad premissa vel eorum aliqua ordinandi, deputandi et constituendi . . . decernentes insuper plenam et indubitatam fidem et validitatem instrumentis, literis et rescriptis quouiscumque per te aut substitutum siue substitutos tuos' (PRO, C82/692). See Logan, 'Thomas Cromwell and the Vicegerency in Spirituals', pp. 661–2.

[22] See n. 21 above.

[23] PRO, SP1/101, fol. 203 (fol. 161, new foliation); *LP*, x. 192.

[24] BL, Cotton MS Cleopatra E IV, fol. 26; *LP*, ix. 1157.

[25] *Faculty Office Registers*, ed. Chambers, p. 63.

Although the visitation ended on 28 February, one should include the capacities for March and April, since it often took two months for a capacity to be processed. The total of capacities from the Faculty Office which may have been related to the Visitation of the Monasteries did not exceed sixty-five. This total does not include friars who received capacities at this time, since they were not affected by the visitation. There still remains a major source for us to consider: the *comperta*.

Two sets of *comperta* survive, one for Norwich diocese, which was visited in November, while some of the issues about departure from the religious life were still unsettled, and one for the north of England, visited in the two months from late December 1535 to late February 1536, when anyone was free to leave the religious life.[26] The recent work of A. N. Shaw has shown that the foliation for each *compendium compertorum* in the State Papers is erroneous and that the traditional itinerary of the visitors also needs revision.[27] The Norwich *compendium compertorum* is not as full as the northern *compendium*. Except in four cases it says nothing about super-stitions, which were regularly noted in the north. It lists the sexual sins of individual religious and little more, and comparatively little about religious wishing to leave. There are just three references to such: all the canons of Langley ask to leave; all the nuns of Thetford Priory save the prioress want to leave; and at West Dereham four of the canons reportedly told the visitor that all who wanted to marry should be allowed to do so. In fact, there is no evidence that any religious left from these houses at this time.

We can now return to the north and to the hanging question, how many actually left when they were free to do so? The north was visited fairly late in the visitation by the two senior visitors, Richard Layton and Thomas Legh, both northerners, both from Cumberland. Layton described his fellow northerners in an unflattering way:

> I am well and fast assured and dare boldly say that there can be no better way devised for the rude people of the north to beat his authority into their heads than that they may plainly see and evidently perceive how His Grace being Supreme Head intendith nothing rather than reformation and correction of

[26] The *comperta* for the north and East Anglia are PRO, SP1/102, fols. 91–114 (fols. 84–104, new foliation); they are calendared without names in *LP*, x. 364. Some fragments of other *comperta* exist, the longest being in John Bale, *The Pageant of Popes*, English translation (London, 1574), fols. E ii–iii. For the *comperta* see Knowles, *Religious Orders*, iii. 294–303, and more recently, A. N. Shaw, 'The *Compendium Compertorum* and Associated Correspondence of the Royal Visitation: A Comparison between the Norwich Diocese Visitation and the York Province and Lichfield Diocese Visitation, in the period November 1535 to February 1536' (unpublished MA Thesis, University of Warwick, 1998).

[27] 'The Northern Visitation 1535/6: Some New Observations', *Downside Review* 116 (1998), pp. 279–99, where he proves that there has been a mix-up in the folio arrangements of each compendium. The matter is further complicated by a set of stamped folio numbers latterly inserted by archivists, which are apparently meant to replace the traditional folio numbering.

religion, [a people] without doubt more superstitious than virtuous, long-time accustomed to frantic fantasies and ceremonies, much more that regarding than either God or their Prince, right far alienate from true religion.[28]

Layton and Legh, beginning their visitation in late December, followed an itinerary – sometimes singly, sometimes in tandem – that took them on a circuit from the diocese of Coventry and Lichfield all the way to the province of York. Their registrar kept a fuller record than was kept for the Norwich diocese visitation: sexual sins of individual religious (real or imaginary, recent or remote), superstitions such as pilgrimages and relics, the founder, the annual rent, current debts and the names of those seeking release from their vows.

How extensive is this *compendium*? It contains information concerning 122 ecclesiastical establishments, eleven of which were collegiate churches of secular priests. Of the remaining 111, only nine appear to be cells, although one can never be entirely certain about cells, and the rest, 102, were monasteries and priories of men or women. For the York province, that is, excluding Coventry and Lichfield, part of which had been visited earlier, reports on 80% of the houses appear in the *comperta*.[29] Not one large house, with the exception of the Cluniac Priory at Lenton (Nottinghamshire), is missing in the *comperta*, and those that are missing were almost all small houses, perhaps not worth a detour for the busy visitors.[30]

What response did the visitors get at these 111 houses when they gave the religious the choice to leave? In only twenty-five of these houses did any religious indicate a desire to leave. There were none seeking departure from such places as Durham Cathedral Priory, Furness, Whitby, Jervaulx, St Mary's Abbey (York), Whalley, Kirkstall, Holmcultram and scores of others. No pattern of the houses with members wishing to leave emerges: they were from every order and from large abbeys as well as small priories. Of the twenty-five houses from which departure was sought, in seven houses only one religious requested departure: there was a nun of Thicket Priory, a Cistercian from Rievaulx, another Cistercian, from Byland, an Augustinian canon from Repton Priory and another from Worksop Priory, a Gilbertine from Mattersey Priory and a Grandmontine from Grosmont. In addition to the nun of Thicket only two other nuns appear, both of Clementhorpe Priory in York. Two Carthusian monks, both of Mount Grace Priory, are listed. Four other houses should be singled out: the Cluniac Priory at Pontefract, where, out of possibly fifteen monks, five sought dismissal, the Cistercian abbeys at Rufford, where six asked to leave, and at Fountains, where also six petitioned dismissal – these will be mentioned again shortly –

---

[28]   BL, Cotton MS Cleopatra E IV, fol. 56v; *LP*, viii. 955.
[29]   It is just possible that some of the smaller houses listed in the *comperta* were not physically visited by the visitors, their religious being interviewed at another house. See Woodward, *Dissolution*, p. 33.
[30]   There were more than twenty monks at Lenton at this time: *MRH*, p. 100.

and, finally, the Augustinian priory at Thurgarton, where eight canons told the visitors they wished to be dismissed. When added up, the total number of religious from the north of England who are reported to have chosen to leave the religious life during the Visitation of the Monasteries is sixty-seven.[31] What percentage is this of the total number of religious in the houses listed in the *comperta*? It is always perilous to estimate the population of religious houses, yet A.N. Shaw provides a reasonable estimate of 1441 for these houses.[32] By this estimate, the sixty-seven who were said to desire to leave would amount to 4.6% of the total number of religious in the houses visited.[33] In nineteen cases it is possible to make some estimates about the ages of those petitioning departure by using ordination lists, where they are available, and by making assumptions about approximate ages for ordination to various orders.[34] Four of the nineteen may have been under the age of twenty-four, and five others under thirty. Only three were in their thirties, but six were in their forties and one was even in his fifties. Such a small sampling can scarcely permit conclusions, but it is suggestive of the range of ages of those seeking release from their vows. Another issue can be seen in the two Cluniac monks of Pontefract who were ordained subdeacons, deacons and priests on the same day, which suggests that they may have been friends who acted in consort. Something similar might have been at work at Fountains where three of the monks had received major orders at the same time twenty years before.

It must be emphasized that these were the religious whom the visitors reported as seeking to leave: 'petunt dimitti a religione, petunt dimitti a iugo religionis, petunt exonerari a religione, petunt exuere vestem religionis' and other similar expressions were used. Whatever the expression, these religious reportedly wished to leave at the time of the visitation, but one might wonder if they actually left. None of these sixty-seven appears at this time in the Faculty Office Register, which need not surprise us, since, as we know, there was another way to be dispensed.

It is now time to take a second look at the six monks of Fountains. The visitors reported, 'Petunt excutere iugum religionis'. They were William White, Robert Lythley, John Yonge, Thomas Diconson, John Hutton and Henry Selby. Monastic names are never easy, given the frequent use of aliases. Professor Cross suggests that William White is the same as William Donwell, who was still at Fountains in 1539, when he was pensioned, that

---

[31] Their names are listed in the appendix to this essay.

[32] Shaw, 'Compendium Compertorum', appx 7.

[33] Twenty-two of these religious had allegedly admitted to the visitors the commission of sexual sins.

[34] Ordination lists for Yorkshire houses are provided in C. Cross and N. Vickers, *Monks, Friars and Nuns in Sixteenth-Century Yorkshire*, Yorkshire Archaeological Society Record Series 150 (1995), passim. It can be assumed that the minimum ages (see n. 9 supra) were in most cases the actual ages of ordination, but some latitude must be allowed.

Robert Lythley is the same as Robert Brodebelt, also there at the end in 1539. Of the four others, John Yonge also was pensioned at the Dissolution as were Thomas Diconson and John Hutton.[35] There remains only Henry Selby, of whom there is no further trace and who was the only monk of Fountains who seems to have actually left at the visitation.[36] If this is true of Fountains, what of the others? The nun of Thicket, Maud Chapman, was still there when the priory was dissolved in 1539, at which time she received a small pension, which she was still receiving in 1583.[37] Of the six monks of Rufford Abbey, two were still there at the Dissolution and were dispensed with their colleagues.[38] The Premonstratensian canons Richard Hoglye and Richard Halifax were still at Welbeck in 1538, although the other canon mentioned in the *comperta* was not.[39] Similarly, at Garendon one of the three was still there at the Dissolution, and at Selby one of the four remained until the end.[40] At least as many as seventeen of the sixty-seven who reportedly petitioned dismissal did not leave at the time of the visitation. There seems to be no clear-cut pattern as to their ages. Seven of these seventeen are religious for whom we can infer their ages. John Hawkesworth (alias Marshall), a monk of Selby, was probably about eighteen; not only did he not leave at the time of the visitation but he was ordained an acolyte on 11 March 1536, about two months after he had reportedly asked to leave.[41] Robert Parker and Brian Braye of Holt Trinity Priory, York, may have been in their early twenties.[42] Two others may have been about twenty-six: Thomas Tanfeld of Rievaulx and Henry Durham of Pontefract, both of whom had been ordained priests two years before the visitation.[43] Three monks of Fountains would have been in their forties and were quite probably members of the same cohort of novices, since they were ordained deacons and priests at the same time in 1516 and 1517.[44] After the visitors left, these seventeen appear to have changed their minds.

How can we account for the disparity between the number of religious reportedly wishing to leave at the visitation and the number of those who actually left? Several suggestions present themselves. The report of the visitors could have been mistaken, as has been alleged about other parts of their *comperta*. Each religious was interviewed individually, and we do not know how the question was put to each monk. It could have been as simple as 'Do you want to leave?' Layton, well known for bullying the interviewees,

[35] These three were ordained together in 1517 (ibid., pp. 113–14).
[36] Ibid., pp. 115, 118, 120, 121, 123, 127, 128.
[37] Ibid., p. 541.
[38] *Faculty Office Registers*, ed. Chambers, p. 74.
[39] Ibid., p. 144.
[40] For Garendon see ibid., p. 85; at Selby, for Thomas Newburgh (alias Lightfote) see Cross and Vickers, *Monks, Friars and Nuns*, p. 39.
[41] Ibid., p. 33.
[42] He was ordained acolyte in 1532 (ibid., p. 61).
[43] Ibid., pp. 170, 209.
[44] Ibid., pp. 113–14.

may have intimidated some into giving what they thought was the answer Layton wanted.[45] Or there could have been a misunderstanding of the response, but, by and large, there is no reason to think that these entries are not accurate: the religious who are named probably did indicate to the visitors their desire to leave. Some may have reconsidered the matter and decided to renew their vocations. Another factor could well have been determinative for some: how were they going to support themselves in the world? Pensions were not on offer at this time, as they were to be later. Even those who chose to leave later when the smaller houses were dissolved received no pensions.[46] At most, a religious leaving at this time would receive a 'reward', similar to that given later to those leaving the smaller monasteries, perhaps 20s. to 30s., a once only payment, which would run out after a few months, and then what? One could hope for a benefice or failing that a chaplaincy or a curacy. At this point the security of the monastery may have taken on a new attraction. Considerations of this sort might have applied more generally to those who, when face to face with Layton or Legh, decided to answer 'no' to their question. Yet such speculations cannot take us far without hard evidence, which is lacking.

The conclusion must be that, when the chance to leave was given, when the monastic gates were thrown wide open, when anyone could leave without reproach or penalty, only about fifty religious from the north of England, less than four percent, actually left.

---

[45] Knowles, *Religious Orders*, iii. 288–9.
[46] At their dissolution the heads of the smaller houses had to leave and were provided with pensions, but the other religious of the smaller houses could either leave without pensions, receiving only a small 'reward', or transfer to another house.

Appendix

Religious Reportedly Petitioning to Leave During the Visitation of the Northern Monasteries

* indicates those who did not actually leave at that time

Augustinian Canons

Conishead Priory, Lancs.
  *Nicholas Willson[47]
  George Hardy
Guisborough Priory, NYorks.
  Richard Walker
  *Gilbert Haryson[48]
Repton Priory, Derbs.
  Nicholas Page
St Leonard's Hospital, York
  Richard Norton
  Richard Burton
Shelford Priory, Notts.
  Thomas Thurrington
  William Tratle
  Thomas Darby
Thurgarton Priory, Notts.
  Thomas Thurgarton
  Richard Lincoln
James Bullton
  Richard Newarke
  Thomas Woodborowe
  William Welby
  John Yorke
  Edward Elkstone
Worksop Priory, Notts.
  John Boo

Benedictine Monks

Holy Trinity Priory, York
  Robert Parker
  Brian Braye

[47] Willson stayed on until the Dissolution and was dispensed on 24 July 1536 (*Faculty Office Registers*, ed. Chambers, p. 67).
[48] Still there at the end in 1539 (Cross and Vickers, *Monks, Friars and Nuns*, p. 271).

St Werburgh Abbey, Chester
  William Vincent
  Ralph Poynton
  John Smyth
Selby Abbey, WYorks.
  William Seycroft
  *John Hawkesworth (probably alias Marshall)[49]
  *Thomas Newborough (alias Lightefote)[50]
  John Selby

Benedictine Nuns

Clementhorpe Priory, York
  Cecilia Warde
  Joanna Typping
Thicket Priory, EYorks.
  *Maud Chapman[51]

Carthusian Monks

Mount Grace Priory, NYorks.
  Thomas Barker
  Richard Davys

Cistercian Monks

Byland Abbey, NYorks.
  Thomas Moreton
Calder Abbey, Cumberland
  John Gisburn
  Richard Preston
Fountains Abbey, WYorks.
  *William White (probably alias Donwell)[52]
  *Robert Lythley (possibly alias Brodebelt)[53]
  *John Yonge[54]
  *Thomas Diconson[55]
  *John Hutton[56]
  Henry Selby
Garendon Abbey, Leics.
  Richard Barbour

[49] As Marshall, he was pensioned in 1539 (ibid., pp. 34, 39).
[50] As Lightefote, he received a pension at the Dissolution and dispensation (ibid., pp. 33, 39).
[51] She remained and was awarded a pension of 20s. in 1539 (ibid., pp. 540–41).
[52] Donwell was granted a pension in 1539 (ibid., pp. 115, 121).
[53] Brodebelt was pensioned in 1539 (ibid., pp. 115, 118).
[54] Pensioned in 1539 (ibid., pp. 115, 128).
[55] He too was pensioned in 1539 (ibid., pp. 115, 128).
[56] Granted a pension in 1539 (ibid., pp. 115, 123).

Richard Tomworth
*James Lughborough[57]
Rievaulx, NYorks
*William Tanfeld (probably alias Wordale)[58]
Rufford Abbey, Notts.
*Robert Watrall[59]
John Bull
Robert Fox
Henry Barbour
Richard Foster
*Edward Knaseborough[60]

Cluniac Monks

Pontefract Priory, WYorks.
John Bristall
William Pontefract
John Normyngton
*Henry Durham (probably alias Grene)[61]
Henry Hemley

Gilbertine Canons

Mattersey Priory, Notts.
William Cissons

Grandmontines

Grosmont Priory, NYorks.
William Knagges

Premonstratensian Canons

St Agathaís Abbey, Easby, NYorks.
Peter Ripeley
George Pulley
Shap Abbey, Westmorland
Thomas Evouwod

---

[57] He did not leave at this time: he was dispensed on 10 January 1537 (*Faculty Office Registers*, ed. Chambers, p. 85).

[58] Called William Tanfeld, he was dispensed on 10 November 1538 at the Dissolution (*Faculty Office Registers*, ed. Chambers, p. 156). He does not appear on the pension list under that name, but a William Wordale, almost certainly the same man, received a pension of five pounds (Cross and Vickers, *Monks, Friars and Nuns*, pp. 170, 185).

[59] He did not leave at this time and was dispensed on 20 September 1536 at the time of Rufford's dissolution (*Faculty Office Registers*, ed. Chambers, p. 74).

[60] Same as preceding.

[61] As Grene, he was pensioned at the Dissolution in 1539 (Cross and Vickers, *Monks, Friars and Nuns*, pp. 210, 213).

Thomas Castell
Thomas Gatefeld
Welbeck Abbey, Notts.
*Richard Halifax[62]
Anker Chesterfeld
*Richard Hogley[63]

---

[62] He was still at Welbeck at the surrender on 20 June 1538 (*VCH Notts.*, ii. 137).
[63] Same as preceding.

The Ex-Religious in Post-Dissolution Society: Symptoms of Post-Traumatic Stress Disorder?

PETER CUNICH

Cardinal Gasquet, the first modern scholar to attempt to gather together 'the mass of scattered material still unpublished and un-consulted' concerning the religious of sixteenth-century England, lamented that 'very little information can be gleaned about the interior and domestic life' of the inmates of religious houses.[1] Even though there are still serious gaps in the historical record, those who have followed in Gasquet's footsteps, from Geoffrey Baskerville at the beginning of the twentieth century, to the more recent scholars such as Claire Cross, Noreen Vickers, Joan Greatrex and Donald Logan, whose landmark volumes have appeared in the last five years, have blazed an impressive trail in the field of sixteenth-century monastic prosopography.[2] Despite all these advances, however, and the increasingly detailed biographies which we are now able to write, we are still left, as Donald Logan has reminded us, knowing 'precious little' of the inner lives of the monastic communities upon which we have focused our attention.[3]

In this chapter I would like to begin to explore an aspect of the inner life of the ex-religious that is largely hidden from us in the surviving historical record. I want to take up the theme of trauma and evaluate the evidence that we do have for the existence of traumatic states among the ex-religious both during and after the Dissolution. It is surprising how little attention has been paid to this aspect of the Dissolution in the past hundred years. When

I am grateful to the Hong Kong Research Grants Council for a grant (HKU7176/97H) that has enabled me to pursue some of the research upon which this chapter is based. I am also grateful to Fr Richard Copsey for his valuable comments on an earlier version.

[1] F. A. Gasquet, *Henry VIII and the English Monasteries* (2 vols., London, 1888–9), i. xv, xxiii.

[2] C. Cross and N. Vickers, *Monks, Friars and Nuns in Sixteenth Century Yorkshire*, Yorkshire Archaeological Society, Record Series 150 (1995); Greatrex, *BRECP*; F. D. Logan, *Runaway Religious in Medieval England, c.1240–1540* (Cambridge, 1996), esp. pp. 184–267.

[3] F. D. Logan, 'Ramsey Abbey: The Last Days and After', in *The Salt of Common Life: Individuality and Choice in the Medieval Town, Countryside and Church*, ed. E. Brezette DeWindt (Kalamazoo, 1995), pp. 513–14.

writing about the Dissolution most of us presume that the turbulent events of the 1530s must have had at least some traumatic impact on the psychological state of those who were expelled from their cloisters. This is quite natural in the post-Freudian world of the early twenty-first century, but you will search in vain for the words 'trauma' or 'psychological impact' in the index of any major reference work on the Dissolution. This is not to say that historians have totally neglected to consider the psychological impact of the Dissolution on the ex-religious. On the contrary, many monastic historians have alluded to the 'distress', 'hardship', 'despair', 'misery' or 'suffering' which the ex-religious experienced in the 1530s and 40s, but none of them have been able to pinpoint the psychological dimension of this state with any degree of precision. Most writers prefer simply to assess the material level of hardship experienced by the dispossessed religious. This was certainly one element in any post-Dissolution trauma-induced psychological problems, but probably not the most important consideration.

Cardinal Gasquet was the first serious historian of the Dissolution to refer to the 'deep distress and misery' experienced by many of the ex-religious, but his comments were clearly based upon the conclusion that most of the ex-religious were left without any financial means of supporting themselves after the Dissolution and therefore suffered primarily from material wants: 'Turned out of their houses, the monks and nuns, especially those to whom no pensions were assigned, must have endured great suffering and undergone many privations in their endeavours to gain a livelihood.'[4] He also noted that, 'On the other hand, some of the monks and nuns cast out into the world appear to have accommodated themselves to the circumstances of the times.'[5] This dichotomy in the response of individual ex-religious to the Dissolution had already been recognized sixty years earlier by the poet William Wordsworth who, in two of his Ecclesiastical Sonnets, contrasted the timid nun forced out into the world with those less-idealistic denizens of the cloister who were 'chained by vows' and could hardly wait to be free.[6] Wordsworth highlighted two extremes in the spectrum of responses made by ex-religious but was not interested in the majority whose circumstances put them in the grey area between these extremes.

Not all writers on the Dissolution have been as understanding as Gasquet and Wordsworth. Geoffrey Baskerville presented a rather less balanced view of the human dilemma facing the ex-religious, dismissing the idea that there may have been those who suffered either physical or psychological hardship with the observation that 'they made the best of a bad job'.[7] More recent studies have focused almost exclusively on the question of whether the

[4] Gasquet, *English Monasteries*, ii. 468–9.
[5] Ibid., p. 479.
[6] William Wordsworth, Ecclesiastical Sonnets XXII & XXIII in *The Poetical Works of William Wordsworth*, ed. E. de Selincourt and H. Darbishire (Oxford, 1946), pp. 372–3.
[7] G. Baskerville, *English Monks and the Suppression of the Monasteries* (London, 1940), pp. 270, 285–6.

pensions assigned to ex-religious by the Tudor state were adequate to sustain a minimum standard of living.[8] It is David Knowles, however, who has been the most influential historian of the last century in evaluating the plight of the ex-religious. He too concentrated primarily upon the provision of pensions and concluded that 'the Dissolution of the monasteries was accomplished with comparatively little personal hardship. It would not be easy to point to any revolution of the sixteenth century, or indeed to any comparable secularization of modern times, in which compensation on such a scale and with such security was offered.'[9] He does, however, note that another group of ex-religious existed, which he estimates to have included as many as one sixth of the total number, whose life after the Dissolution was characterized by despair. These were ' . . . the least fitted by physical, moral and mental disabilities to cope with the world's shocks. It was in this group, silent and unseen, that the social hardships of the Dissolution were most keenly felt.'[10] Ultimately, though, Knowles believed that the majority of ex-religious accepted the changes of the 1530s and adapted to the new order by fending for themselves as best they could.[11] There is no room here for psychological trauma. Coming from a man who had experienced much psychological injury in his own dealings with Downside and who continued to be emotionally wounded by those experiences for the rest of his life, this conclusion shows an extraordinary lack of insight and inability to empathize with the subjects of his life's work.[12]

What, then, is there to say about the psychological state of the ex-religious after the Dissolution? This is a notoriously difficult question to answer. The monks and nuns of the sixteenth century did not leave letters or diaries touching upon the problems they experienced in adjusting to life outside the cloister, nor did their contemporaries comment about the behaviour of ex-religious in post-Dissolution secular society. Is it possible, when there is so little direct evidence, for us to make any informed comments about the types and level of trauma experienced by the ex-religious? Indeed, is it appropriate for contemporary psycho-historical methodologies to be employed in attempting to understand the hidden workings of the sixteenth-century mind? This question is especially pertinent when the clinical condition which is used as a starting point for the evaluation of evidence in this essay is one which is as controversial and recently identified as Post-Traumatic Stress Disorder (PTSD). This chapter does not intend to prove that any substantial number of the ex-religious suffered from the same type of PTSD that has been identified by late

---

[8] See especially G. A. J. Hodgett, 'The Unpensioned Ex-Religious in Tudor England', *JEH* 13 (1962), pp. 195–202.

[9] Knowles, *Religious Orders*, iii. 413–14.

[10] Ibid., p. 413.

[11] Ibid., pp. 414–16.

[12] For Knowles's uncompromising attitude to Downside see A. Morey, *David Knowles: A Memoir* (London, 1979), pp. 80–98.

twentieth-century clinicians. Rather, an attempt will be made to apply some of the most recent clinical data on PTSD to suggest a set of symptoms that might indicate the presence of post-traumatic states among ex-religious after the Dissolution. Using these symptoms as a reference point, several tentative examples of trauma-related behaviour will be identified among the population of ex-religious in post-Dissolution society. Lower level and less debilitating types of trauma will also be considered. These examples will be discussed in an attempt to establish guidelines for further data collection by researchers investigating the later careers of the ex-religious.

PTSD tends to be thought of as a distinctly modern psychiatric affliction, and some critics dismiss the syndrome as an invention of the late twentieth century. There is, however, a solid body of historical evidence that indicates that PTSD has been around since ancient times. Moreover, psychiatrists have estimated that up to ten per cent of the population are affected by clinically diagnosable PTSD at some time in their lives. An even greater number exhibit some of the symptoms of the syndrome, and women are more likely to fall victim to it than men. It often occurs with or leads to other psychiatric illnesses such as clinical depression.[13] Of those who suffer from the disorder, approximately 30% recover completely, 40% continue to have mild persistent effects, and the condition of the remaining 30% of sufferers remains unchanged or gets worse with time.[14] The causes of PTSD are many, but the common denominator is the experience of an episode of major psychological trauma, especially trauma resulting from violent events such as war, rape, domestic violence, child abuse, natural disaster or torture. The types of trauma most likely to produce PTSD are those that involve a threat to life, or witnessing the violent death of others. The symptoms of PTSD fall into three categories and may arise as delayed or protracted responses to the initial trauma: intrusion, avoidance, and hyper-arousal. Intrusive symptoms are those that 'intrude' into the person's everyday life and are usually manifested in the persistent re-experiencing of the traumatic event in recollections, 'flashbacks', dreams, or the feeling that the event is being relived, and is usually accompanied by tears, fear or anger. Avoidance symptoms occur because the sufferer tends to avoid close emotional contact with family and friends due to an overwhelming feeling of emotional 'numbness' that makes intimate relationships difficult and diminishes the

[13] Some recent books on PTSD include: P. A. Saigh and J. D. Bremner, *Post-Traumatic Stress Disorder: A Comprehensive Text* (Boston, 1999); W. Yule, *Post-Traumatic Stress Disorders: Concepts and Therapy* (Chichester and New York, 1999); R. Yehuda, *Psychological Trauma* (Washington and London, 1998); S. Joseph, R. Williams and W. Yule, *Understanding Post-Traumatic Stress: A Psychosocial Perspective on PTSD and Treatment* (Chichester and New York, 1997); *Clinical Disorders and Stressful Life Events*, ed. T. W. Miller (Madison, 1997).

[14] L. Manson, 'Finding the Right Words', *The Independent* (1 July 1999), p. 3; S. Robinson, M. Rapaport-Bar-Sever and J. Rapaport, 'The Present State of People who Survived the Holocaust as Children', *Acta Psychiatrica Scandinavica* 89/4 (1994), pp. 242–5.

individual's interest in everyday life. The person with PTSD also avoids situations that bring painful reminders of the traumatic event, and will often feel guilty at having survived an event in which others were killed ('survivor syndrome'). Hyper-arousal is a biological alarm reaction through which the sufferer acts as if the trauma that caused the illness is an ever-present threat.[15] Those who suffer from chronic PTSD are likely to perceive higher levels of danger than healthy individuals when placed in new traumatic situations, and a prior experience of extreme stress does not 'innoculate' victims or make them more resilient in coping with other forms of stress.[16]

The Dissolution of the monasteries as a process was not necessarily violent, and only in a limited number of cases do we encounter death as a result of the Crown's attempts at suppression. It cannot therefore be directly compared with the great traumatic events of the twentieth century such as the trenches of the First World War, the Holocaust, or the dropping of the atomic bombs on Hiroshima and Negasaki. The brutality of the Tudor age was on a far smaller scale. Nevertheless, there are a number of instances in which particularly violent means were used to gain the submission of monastic communities in the 1530s. The brutal execution of nine Carthusian monks and the death from neglect and starvation in Newgate prison of nine others from the London Charterhouse is exactly the sort of violent treatment that produces PTSD in survivors. To these examples could be added the execution of four Observant Franciscan friars and the death in custody or prison of at least another twenty-eight between 1534 and 1537. These acts of persecution and torture against the most observant of the religious orders are by far the best documented from the period.[17] It is likely that many of those Carthusians and Observants who survived the storm would have suffered some degree of post-traumatic stress in the years which followed, especially those who had shared prison cells with their dead confrères and those who were forced to flee to the continent to avoid incarceration. Survivors from these two orders numbered approximately 270 men in 1540, a not inconsiderable group who, released into the secular world, must have experienced considerable difficulties in coming to terms with the suffering they had endured or witnessed.[18]

The only contemporary personal testimony which survives from these persecutions are the accounts of the Carthusian martyrdoms by Dom

---

[15] The symptoms are dealt with in detail in K. C. Peterson, M. F. Prout and R. A. Schwarz, *Post-Traumatic Stress Disorder: A Clinician's Guide* (New York and London, 1991), pp. 11–42.

[16] Z. Solomon and E. Prager, 'Elderly Israeli Holocaust Survivors During the Persian Gulf War: A Study of Psychological Distress', *American Journal of Psychiatry* 149/12 (1992), pp. 1707–10.

[17] Knowles, *Religious Orders*, iii. 206–11, 222–40.

[18] There were approximately 160 Carthusian monks from nine houses, and around 110 friars from the six houses.

Maurice Chauncy, written many years after the events they describe.[19] In his 'Short Narration' Chauncy admits to periods of deep despair in the 1550s, and it is almost certain that he suffered from 'survivor syndrome'.[20] He had been one of the ringleaders of the resistance at the London Charterhouse after the executions of 1535 but in 1537 made a false oath and avoided the fate of his confrères in Newgate prison. He clearly regretted not having held to his beliefs at this testing time and later wrote that 'I had not earned the right to drain that cup to the dregs with these holy fathers.'[21] Elsewhere he praises the constancy of the Carthusian martyrs as an example to all 'good and strong soldiers of Christ' who, 'faithful and staunch to the last', might 'win the crown of eternal life and that reward of faith and constancy which has been promised only to those who persevere and strive lawfully by God'.[22] Chauncy clearly felt that he had failed in this test of constancy and became increasingly bitter as he grew older and realized that he would never return to England. The last words of the 'Short Narration' have a ring of self-accusation about them: 'Here you may behold a brave struggle of holy martyrs, suffering but undefeated. You may gaze at our country, its pitiful plight, a picture of wavering and fickleness, of inconstancy and utter confusion.'[23] He had been one of those fickle men who lacked the constancy of a holy martyr and he relived that failure for the rest of his life. Chauncy's is the only first-hand account that survives from this period of persecution, but if a strong character like him fell victim to symptoms of PTSD we must assume that there were others who were similarly affected by their experiences at this time.

The second wave of violent persecution against the religious orders occurred in 1537 at the conclusion of the Pilgrimage of Grace and the northern rebellion. Many monks were involved in these risings, some as supporters of the rebels while others were compelled to join the rebellion or face the wrath of the commons. Anthony Shaw has estimated that of the 200 religious houses located in the seven counties affected by the insurrection at least sixty provided some positive contribution to the rising. Moreover, the number of religious who were executed or who died in prison, a figure which he puts at between thirty-one and fifty-two, represents as great a terror as the earlier persecution of the Observants and Carthu-

---

[19] The first account was written c.1547 while the fourth and final version ('The Short Narration') was published in 1570. See E. M. Thompson's introduction to M. Chauncy, *The Passion and Martyrdom of the Holy English Carthusian Fathers: The Short Narration* (London, 1935), pp. 28–32.

[20] Chauncy, *Short Narration*, p. 141; after the death of two brothers soon after his arrival in England in 1555 he admits to falling into 'the pit of despair' ('quin in desperationis foveam caderem').

[21] Ibid., pp. 37–8.

[22] Ibid., pp. 38–9.

[23] Ibid., pp. 32, 164–5.

sians.[24] We should therefore expect to find some symptoms of PTSD among the ex-religious in the northern counties, especially from those houses that lost members in the wave of violence in 1537. It should also be remembered that male ex-religious in the north were probably less successful in finding employment after the Dissolution, and the pensions assigned to the northern religious were generally much less generous than those granted to inmates of the wealthier houses in the southern half of the country.[25] The northern religious therefore lacked the same degree of material security that might otherwise have ameliorated the psychological impact of the Dissolution. Although no nuns were involved in the northern rising or its aftermath it is likely that they would have been just as horrified by the outcome as the male religious and, if Knowles is correct in his assessment that the nuns had a 'deeper sense of vocation' than the male religious, it would be reasonable to assume that they were even more affected.[26]

The violence of the early years of the Dissolution abated as the process gathered steam, but there were more executions to come. In 1538 the prior and eight monks of Lenton were indicted on charges of treason. Ultimately the prior and one or two of the monks were executed at Nottingham.[27] The abbot of Woburn was the next to suffer. He was already showing signs of 'survivor syndrome' at Passiontide 1538 when, in great physical pain from strangury (irritation of the bladder) and worn down by a conscience which 'grudged him daily for his failure', he reproached himself for failing to die with the earlier martyrs.[28] He and two of his monks were tried and executed in June 1538. In the last months of 1539 three of the most prestigious and largest Benedictine abbeys were brought to heel through the execution of their abbots and four other monks on charges of treason. The monks of Glastonbury, Reading and Colchester witnessed the same brutality of earlier executions and were continually reminded of these events by the dismembered and rotting bodies of their abbots and brothers that were displayed prominently as a warning to others. These last executions, together with the earlier deaths of religious at the gallows and in prison, brought the total number of violent deaths during the Dissolution to approximately 120, and the number of houses directly affected by these deaths to around 85.[29] This represents slightly more than one tenth of all the religious houses in England and Wales at the time and cannot be easily overlooked. It should also be noted that many more houses would have been indirectly affected by the

---

[24] A. N. Shaw, 'The Involvement of the Religious Orders in the Northern Risings of 1536/7: Compulsion or Desire?', *Downside Review* 117 (1999), pp. 104–5.

[25] Knowles, *Religious Orders*, iii. 410–11.

[26] Ibid., p. 413.

[27] *LP*, xiii/1, 787.

[28] Knowles, *Religious Orders*, iii. 374.

[29] Other religious executed during the 1530s included Richard Reynolds of Syon Abbey, Edward Bocking and John Dering of Canterbury Cathedral Priory, Elizabeth Barton of Canterbury St Sepulchre's Priory, and Adrian Fortescue of the Knights of St John.

executions, especially those in close proximity to the place of execution. In London alone, for example, there were more than twenty religious houses that observed at close quarters the persecution of the Carthusians.

While this small but nonetheless significant group of ex-religious are likely to have borne the greatest traumatic impact of the Dissolution, they were not the only ones who were at risk of permanent psychological damage at the end of the 1530s. The disabling impact of clinical PTSD was just one of a wide range of less serious but still intrusive psychological conditions with which many monks, nuns and friars had to deal. Probably the most pervasive psychological strain was characterized by the loss of identity that ex-religious would have felt when their houses were suppressed. Each religious in England shared a common sense of identity that varied considerably from one order to another, but elements of this identity that distinguished them from the secular clergy and the laity were held in common. Distinctive dress, a strict rule of life, the special observances of individual houses, and a sense of community centred around a particular set of buildings were some of the principal features of this monastic identity. This was an identity that many religious did not want to lose. We know, for instance, that many religious houses, especially the largest and wealthiest, held out against the Dissolution commissioners for as long as possible. Among the orders of monks nearly sixty per cent did not finally leave their cloisters until 1539.[30] It has also been estimated that the majority of English and Welsh monks had been professed for twenty years or more at the time of the Dissolution.[31] These monks had a sense of identity that was built upon their membership of a monastic family, and at the breakup of their religious communities we would expect to find some evidence of trauma. Not only were monastic families broken up, however, for the Dissolution also meant the wanton destruction of the physical locus of monastic life. Monastic churches were not only stripped of their lead and pulled down stone by stone, they also had their treasured shrines and sacred vessels confiscated and melted down for their gold, silver and precious stones. Relics were sacrilegiously scattered, monastic libraries were emptied and the precious books and manuscripts used for waste paper, monastic graveyards were left untended: all vestiges of the common life were removed. It has long been recognized that this iconoclasm and the physical devastation that it produced had a massive impact upon the antiquaries and historians who later wrote about the monasteries.[32] How much greater an impact, then,

---

[30] P. Cunich, 'Dissolution and De-Conversion: Institutional Change and Individual Response in the 1530s', *The Vocation of Service to God and Neighbour: Essays on the Interests, Involvements and Problems of Religious Communities and their Members in Medieval Society*, ed. J. Greatrex (Turnhout, 1998), pp. 33, 42; the percentage was much higher for the Benedictines (80%).

[31] Ibid., p. 33.

[32] M. Aston, 'English Ruins and English History: The Dissolution and the Sense of the Past', *Journal of the Warburg and Courtauld Institute* 36 (1973), pp. 231–55.

must it have had upon the monks and nuns who had lived and worked within those cloisters. This was certainly a lower level trauma but was no less real than the more serious PTSD.

There is a large body of evidence that suggests that many religious found it difficult or impossible to readjust to the loss of identity which expulsion from their cloisters entailed. This problem of readjustment manifested itself in a variety of ways, but for the purposes of assessing the traumatic impact of the Dissolution the most obvious symptom is that of 'avoidance'. Put simply, many religious could not accept the changes that had taken place even though by 1540 it was clear to everyone that there was no hope of a reintroduction of monasticism into England during the lifetime of Henry VIII. Indeed, the destruction of the monastic buildings and the progressive alienation of their lands during the 1540s reinforced this already self-evident fact. A surprisingly large number of ex-religious avoided facing the inevitable by attempting to continue with their community life. The most extraordinary example of this was the nuns and monks of Syon who initially split into seven groups and maintained a form of the conventual life in small household communities.[33] This was practised on a smaller scale by other groups of ex-religious. Elizabeth Shelley, abbess of Winchester St Mary's, gathered a number of her sisters around her at the 'sistern house' near to the old abbey and together they kept up some form of community life until at least 1547, while Morpheta Kingsmill, abbess of Wherwell, seems to have lived near, if not with, her sisters until her death in 1570.[34] Elizabeth Throckmorton and two of her nuns from Denny retired to the Throckmorton family home at Coughton where they maintained enclosure and followed the monastic horarium.[35] Another group of five nuns from Kirklees in Yorkshire lived with their prioress at Mirfield.[36] At Shaftesbury in Dorset there is no evidence of a reconstituted community, but two of the nuns, Margaret Mayo and Edith Magdalen, rented adjoining tenements that were adjacent to the monastic graveyard and there they stayed until the 1570s.[37] While there is no direct evidence to suggest why Mayo and Magdalen chose these particular tenements, it would seem that they wanted to be near their former home and their deceased sisters who lay buried in the monastic graveyard.[38] It is more difficult to find groups of male religious who continued

---

[33] For the story of this community see J. R. Fletcher, *The Story of the English Bridgettines of Syon Abbey* (Syon, 1933) and the Canon Fletcher manuscripts at the University of Exeter Library (Syon Abbey, FLE/12).

[34] D. K. Coldicott, *Hampshire Nunneries* (Chichester, 1989), pp. 143–4; Gasquet, *English Monasteries*, ii. 476–8.

[35] Knowles, *Religious Orders*, iii. 301, 412; VCH Cambs., ii. 302, VCH Warwicks., iii. 78, 85.

[36] Knowles, *Religious Orders*, iii. 412.

[37] Wiltshire and Swindon Record Office, 2057/S3, calendared in *Survey of the Lands of William, 1st Earl of Pembroke*, ed. C. R. Straton (Oxford, 1909), pp. 492, 516. Margaret Mayo(w) lived until about 1579–80 (PRO, LR6/13/12, m.6v).

[38] For the idea of the medieval English parish community consisting of both the living

to live as communities, but there is good evidence to suggest that William Browne, prior of Monk Bretton, gathered several of his brothers around him and together lived as a community until his death in 1557.[39] A small group of ex-Carthusians kept in close contact in London immediately after the suppression of their house and later fled to the Low Countries where they entered the Charterhouse at Bruges and made their second profession.[40]

In the vast majority of cases, community life ceased altogether at the Dissolution, but single members of communities still exhibited behaviour that might be interpreted as avoidance of this reality. Many ex-religious when making their wills made provision for the return of personal possessions to their former communities should they ever be re-founded. Elizabeth Shelley left a silver chalice for Winchester St Mary's,[41] John Hopton bequeathed half of his books to the Norwich Blackfriars,[42] Edward Heptonstall gave all of his books to Kirkstall,[43] the Carthusians Henry Man and Edmund Horde also left their books to their houses,[44] John Whitney left a chalice to Dieulacres,[45] George Richmond left a chalice and two vestments to Bolton,[46] and William Browne settled his house and close in Worsborough, his books, vestments and household utensils on any re-founded Monk Bretton community.[47] It also seems likely that the relics collected by ex-religious at the time of the Dissolution would have been returned to their communities in the event of re-foundation. Thomas Figg kept the foot of St Philip from Winchester Cathedral Priory with him until 1585, Thomas Madde of Jervaulx took and hid the severed head of one of his confrères executed after the northern rising in 1537, and John Fox kept the arm of John Houghton and other relics until their discovery by the authorities in the mid-1540s.[48] The nuns of Syon took into exile with them the stone post upon which the grisly remains of Richard Reynolds had been placed after his execution. In all these cases the religious involved were unable to come to terms with the reality of the Dissolution.

Other religious are known to have clung to the vestiges of their monastic profession. Agnes Badgecroft of Winchester St Mary's kept her profession

---

and the dead see E. Duffy, *The Stripping of the Altars: Traditional Religion in England, 1400–1580* (New Haven and London, 1992), pp. 327–37.

[39] M. C. Cross, 'The Reconstitution of Northern Monastic Communities in the Reign of Mary Tudor', *Northern History* 29 (1993), pp. 200–4 at 200.

[40] Chauncy, *Short Narration*, pp. 28–30.

[41] Gasquet, *English Monasteries*, ii. 478.

[42] PRO, PROB11/42b (PCC, 62 Chaynay).

[43] Cross and Vickers, *Monks, Friars and Nuns*, p. 146.

[44] Knowles, *Religious Orders*, iii. 413.

[45] Baskerville, *English Monks*, p. 253.

[46] Cross and Vickers, *Monks, Friars and Nuns*, p. 250.

[47] Ibid., p. 22.

[48] P. Bogan, 'Dom Thomas Figg and the Foot of St Philip', *Winchester Cathedral Record* 61 (1992), pp. 22–6; Baskerville, *English Monks*, p. 260; Gasquet, *English Monasteries*, ii. 488.

ring, psalter and monastic veils until her death in 1556.[49] Were these treasured simply as mementos of an important period in her early life or had they been used continually since the surrender of her convent in 1539? Another nun is known to have kept up appearances in this way. Isabel Whitehead of Arthington 'continued her state as she could' until 1587 when she was imprisoned in York Castle.[50] These are just two examples of the type of behaviour that could indicate some degree of post-traumatic stress, but they can just as reasonably be explained as perfectly normal human reactions to an unforeseen and disturbing event in an individual's life. Indeed, it is likely that the majority of ex-religious recovered very quickly from any trauma they experienced. Trauma is, after all, a normal part of life and most people manage to cope with it reasonably well. In the case of the ex-religious, no more than ten per cent had directly experienced any unusually violent treatment at the hands of the state. The rest had experienced trauma of a much less serious nature and the likelihood of chronic post-traumatic distress would therefore have been much lower. It must also be remembered that some ex-religious had more emotional and material support than others. Those who had been granted generous pensions had fewer financial worries and would have felt more secure. Monks who were immediately appointed to cathedral chapters and other ecclesiastical livings would have had little time to dwell on the tumult of the Dissolution. A new life as a member of the secular clergy and new opportunities for personal advancement would have softened the impact of the events of the late 1530s. It is likely, then, that the trauma of the Dissolution, although real and deeply felt by a large proportion of the ex-religious as it was occurring, was nevertheless a transient stage in an otherwise normal psychological life cycle.

For a portion of the ex-religious in England and Wales during the 1540s, however, the impact of the Dissolution was much more serious. Those who had witnessed executions of fellow religious, those who had lost their confrères through death in prison, and those who were expelled from their cloisters with inadequate or no financial support were most at risk. The situation was probably worse in some orders than others (and particularly the Carthusians and Observant Franciscans), and it is likely that there was much more hardship in the northern counties than elsewhere and among female ex-religious than among men. Age was probably also a factor, with the younger religious adjusting more quickly and more completely, although it is worth noting that modern studies have shown that children and young people are often damaged for life by their experiences of violence.[51] Unfortunately, there is very little evidence of the existence of post-traumatic states in the surviving records of post-Dissolution England.

---

[49] Gasquet, *English Monasteries*, ii. 477
[50] Ibid., pp. 488–9.
[51] Robinson, Rapaport-Bar-Sever and Rapaport, 'People Who Survived the Holocaust as Children', pp. 242–5.

Some tentative examples of trauma-induced behaviour have been cited in this chapter, but the picture is far from complete. Most of the evidence springs from circumstantial accounts of symptoms of 'avoidance'. Very little evidence of 'intrusion' and none of 'hyper-arousal' has been found. This is to be expected from an age when people did not generally write about their experiences and feelings and underlines the many difficulties involved in pursuing psycho-historical avenues of investigation in the late medieval and early modern periods.

Nevertheless, there is some scattered evidence to support the propositions made in this chapter and it seems likely that there is more evidence waiting to be unearthed. It is just a matter of knowing what to look for! It is also necessary for us to treat the ex-religious as individual human beings rather than just pieces in a larger jigsaw puzzle that must be squeezed into the accepted framework of Dissolution historiography. This requires a certain amount of empathy, but at the same time we must remember that the sixteenth-century man or woman was in many ways unlike us. Indeed, one of the major criticisms of psycho-history is that any attempt to impose twentieth-century psychology on the lives of men and women who knew nothing of Freud is an inherently unhistorical and invalid exercise. And yet we have all come across evidence of individuals during the Tudor period who exhibit at certain moments in their lives emotions which we can readily understand and appreciate. Take, for example, the tearful reconciliation of William Littleton, a former monk of Evesham, with the Benedictine missionary Augustine Bradshaw at Hindlip (Worcestershire) in 1603. We are told that upon seeing a brother Benedictine more than sixty years after the dissolution of his own house he was 'much mouved' and, when he actually met Bradshaw, Littleton 'fell upon his knees and with flouds of teares' beseeched to be reconciled.[52] That Littleton, who was in his mid-thirties at the dissolution of Evesham in 1540, would have been so emotional at this meeting after more than sixty years does not come as a surprise to the modern historian. What the incident does alert us to, however, is the likelihood that many other ex-religious suppressed deep emotions about the Dissolution for many years after the event. It will not do for us to dismiss such emotional and psychological turmoil with the lack of sympathy of a Baskerville or the view expressed by Knowles that those who suffered from trauma were simply those with 'physical, moral and mental disabilities'. A more balanced and humane evaluation of the Dissolution will reveal the great variety of experience among the ex-religious and not try to make sweeping and simplistic generalizations about the ex-monastic population as a whole.

---

[52] D. Lunn, *The English Benedictines 1540–1688: From Reformation to Revolution* (London, 1980), p. 27.

Index

Page numbers referring to illustrations are represented in italics.